D1543053

USES AND ABUSES OF POLITICAL POWER

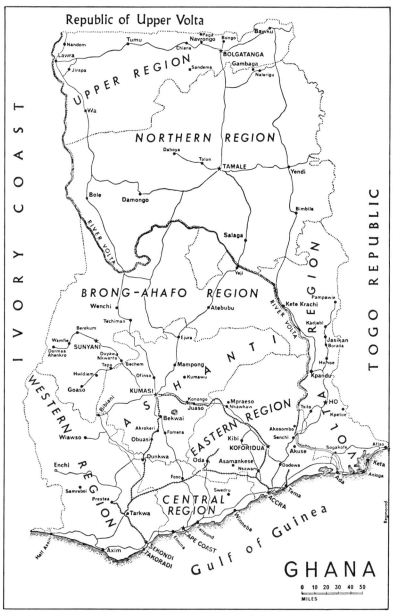

Reprinted by permission from Dennis Austin, *Politics in Ghana, 1946–1960*
(London: Oxford University Press, under the auspices of the Royal Institute
of International Affairs, 1964), facing page 1.

Maxwell Owusu

USES AND ABUSES
OF POLITICAL POWER
A Case Study of
Continuity and
Change in the
Politics of Ghana

The University of Chicago Press
Chicago and London

International Standard Book Number: 0-226-64240-2
Library of Congress Catalog Card Number: 73–121354

THE UNIVERSITY OF CHICAGO PRESS, CHICAGO 60637
THE UNIVERSITY OF CHICAGO PRESS, LTD., LONDON

© 1970 by The University of Chicago
All rights reserved
Published 1970
Printed in the United States of America

108457

To my parents

136880

Contents

Figures

Tables

Foreword

Ghana has been a central focus of African research for many years. Generations of scholars, political administrators, activists of all kinds, writers black and white have written extensively about Ghana and its people. For outsiders, the country has always exerted a pull. Its people have a remarkable vibrancy, call it a flair, which, extending throughout the population, is manifested in their daily lives and political institutions. No one who has lived or worked there remains quite the same, and many were deeply devoted to the country even when antagonized by events during the Nkrumah period. One result of all this concern is an important literature which, beginning early in the nineteenth century, is still read. Bowditch, Freeman, Ellis, Bosman, Ahuma, Mary Kingsley — all left important commentaries. The British tradition of historical scholarship, some of it monumental, began with Claridge's two massive volumes on the history of the country (published in 1915). David Kimble's excellent study covered the ground where Claridge terminated, to be followed by the fine contemporary historical work of Dennis Austin.

Classic anthropological work began in the twenties by Rattray, a political officer. His research resulted in a number of books on Ashanti life, politics, art, and custom which remain indispensible. Meyerowitz had what can best be described as a long (and at times influential) love affair with Ghana. The social anthropology continues to be exceptional, most particularly the work of Fortes on the Tallensi, Goody on the LoWilli and the LoDagaba (or Lobi), Tait among the Konkomba, and Brokensha in Larteh. Field did her work among the Ga, Jahoda and Foster concentrated on attitudes and education respectively, Wallerstein's study, Bretton's and perhaps my own although quite different in their approaches have been more concerned directly with politics although these latter five in particular have political implications, the first about racial attitudes, the second about political recruitment, and the third about pluralist associations. My own book, with which Mr. Owusu takes issue, deals with the formation of a national society by political means, and Bretton's is concerned with the demise of its founding figure.

Despite their number, however, few historians and anthropologists have put the various ingredients of their special studies into the kind of political frame which can effectively integrate them for analytical purposes. Perhaps the most important feature of Mr. Owusu's book is that it accomplishes just that. The material on the Agona and most particularly the description of the role of the asafo company in contemporary local politics is particularly valuable in view of the fact that no full study exists on the subject. This marriage or blending of the historical, the anthropological, and the contemporary political employed so successfully by Mr. Owusu is one of the most attractive aspects of the book.

Nor are the scholars the only ones who have come to Ghana to write about or participate in her history. George Padmore saw the Gold Coast as the first stage in the pan-African revolution and stayed on. Richard Wright exhorted Nkrumah to "militarize" African life but left. South African journalists, lawyers, doctors, English Aldermaston marchers, came to work and to write, both locally and for the foreign press because of Ghana's role in pan-African affairs. A fluctuating contingent, it had one thing in common, a fascination for the special quality of Ghanaian life which for very diverse reasons, some sentimental, some political, others as a result of work in the country attracted foreigners. Ghana was open, accessible. Color was not very relevant. It was, at the same time closed, elusive, and puzzling in important respects. Except for a very few observers, Ghana, for all its accessibility could be puzzling just when it seemed most familiar. It became a challenge to virtually all observers with more than a superficial interest in the country to go beyond the familiar to understand the more puzzling aspects of life.

Despite all this work, outsiders find it difficult to penetrate very deeply into the fabric and qualities of Ghanaian life. Fortunately there is a rich tradition of writing by Ghanaians themselves. Carl Christian Reindorf's history remains classic. J. B. Danquah's work on Akan law and custom and religion followed a tradition of political writing pioneered by John Mensah Sarbah (not to speak of the writings of Joseph Casely-Hayford and Joseph DeGraft Johnson). What was wrong in this tradition, important though it was, was a certain lack of professionality. It had, like the writers themselves, a derivative cast, combining the special qualities of the individual scholar himself with a rather Victorian flavor of English scholarship which was so seductive, especially along the coast, that it was sustained in the educational system long after it had disappeared at home. But whatever the faults, here was history, or law, or religion written from the inside. The contributions of Ghanaian scholarship added much of what was ignored or unseen by the outsiders.

Busia's book, *The Position of the Chief in the Modern Political System of Ashanti*, is perhaps the first Ghanaian analysis with a thoroughly professional flavor. Moreover, it combined contemporary social anthropology with that intimate knowledge which only belonging to a particular culture provides. He had the additional advantage of knowing the political administration from the inside, having served as a district officer before going to Oxford. A similar professional standard in historical studies is represented in the work of Adu Boahen. Until now, however, no equivalent in political studies has appeared in which the intimate knowledge which no outsider can provide is blended with professional control. It is that gap which the present work by Maxwell Owusu bridges. Not only is this the best "inside" political analysis, but it also takes the field of African political studies a great deal further, not only as a contribution to understanding Ghana politics, but also as a particular theory of economic motivation. I would like to make several comments on both these points.

Those of my generation of scholars who were concerned primarily with political matters dealt on the whole with the problem of transition from a limited political arena, confined by and large to main urban centers, and to the politicalization of society by means of nationalist movements. In turn, these were viewed as breaking down more local ethnic structures surviving from the pre-contact period and which, sustaining themselves in varying degrees during colonial rule, continued to provide an alternative to national life. In addition, we saw the same force of nationalism taking shape, both organizationally and normatively, under our noses as it were, by means of activities designed to generate participation in alternatives and utilization of the political framework as it existed during the colonial period, while at the same time discrediting it, so as to kindle a concern with a future which, to say the least, was not part of the colonial plan. The work of Coleman and Sklar (a bit later) on Nigeria, Rosberg on Kenya, Zolberg on the Ivory Coast, Morgenthau on French West Africa, Leys on Northern Rhodesia, Foltz on Mali, shared this same concern. The result was a tendency to look at politics as a particular combination of forces which produced nationalism and from a societal point of view. As these forces gathered in strength and coalesced, we interested ourselves in the effects upon the political structure of the country involved and in the people themselves.

Such a national focus, and the concern with ramified political organizations, valid though it is, tends to obscure somewhat what actually happened in the villages where life might appear to change more than it did, and where the combinations of old and new were infinitely more complex than at the center. The center pulled together the forces of change, and nationalism was its expression. The local areas were more stubborn and resistant to innovation. The turning point came with Bienen's analysis of Tanzania which explicitly concerned itself with the analysis of what went on more locally and exhorted Africanists to look below the surface of nationalism. Peter Lloyd's work on Nigeria is even more deeply devoted to that tradition. The present generation of scholars continues to probe more and more deeply into specific aspects of political culture as in Lucy Behrman's work on the Muslim Brotherhoods in Senegal, or Ojo's work on Yoruba culture.

Owusu's analysis represents this new concern extremely well. He is able, moreover, to supply the necessary detail enabling the reader to see how politics "really works" at a local level, in Swedru. One of the best things about this work is that it is done with a sense for theory in general, with Swedru treated as the microcosm for a reality which the macrocosm obscures. The change in focus adds a quite new dimension of understanding and represents precisely the way cumulative scholarship ought to proceed.

Turning now to the theory proposed by Owusu, we find it a familiar one; essentially that of economic self-interest. A position dear to the heart of economists of the neoclassical school, it has a kind of realism about it. Clearly there is a high correlation between people's behavior and their interests, and a similar correlation between their interests and how they make their money. Behind this point of view is a political position, namely that politics as a moral force is merely an embellishment of the reality served up as an ideological concoction. For every part rhetoric, one adds several parts manipulation and tactics. In this respect the theory is not too different from that offered by colonial administrators during British rule who saw Ghanaian nationalism essentially as a system of corruption, payoffs, and self-interest. That, of course, is where Mr. Owusu and I are farthest apart in our views. As a result, we differ about the significance of the concept of charisma and the evidence for it. Partly that is a result of the difference in focus; local area as distinct from national, small commercial town as distinct from larger centers. Partly, too, it is hard, almost twenty years later, to recapture the flavor of those days.

But there are other aspects of our differing views which bear further reflection. One is on the character of authority itself, the blending of those elements which at one time give exceptional latitude to an individual leader and at another hedge him in with restrictions. In my view, Mr. Owusu dismisses the charismatic aspect too quickly. It was not a matter of personality but rather a phenomenon of central politics the momentum for which derived from increasing participation in legislative bodies. These, as they became more representative, provided a basis for overwhelming power. Power and charisma were mutually reinforcing, enabling Nkrumah, by means of the local government reforms of 1951, to attack the local areas where political life remained separated from the new national politics. In my own field work in 1952 and 1953, the name of Nkrumah in local areas did not evoke as much uniform support as it did fear.

Nevertheless, fear alone does not explain fully why the people voted for Kkrumah. True, in a study of the CPP from the standpoint of local politics, it was a matter of survival, gains and losses, control over trading licenses, land, and so forth, which formed the practical side of political life. Here I think Mr. Owusu is exactly right in his analysis. Moreover, at a national level, charisma once dead is hard to recall. Even in its apogee, few of Nkrumah's most ardent supporters were without misgivings, and it is the misgivings which they will remember today when asked about their former roles. It is an awkward business to question an ex-CPP "fanatic," to use a Ghanaian expression of the day, how committed he really was because it was not (and this is my point) an entirely rational business.

But even if Mr. Owusu is correct in his analysis, it remains to be explained precisely why it was that the United Gold Coast Convention and those who had the economic advantages to dispense and the education and skills on which to capitalize failed both in organization and payoff. What prevented Grant and Danquah from

making the most out of the political situation in the Gold Coast after
the war? Clearly they held all the cards. Not explained in the study
of Swedru is why the CPP came to power in the first place; nor the
circumstances of Nkrumah's success. This is why in my own work,
I tried to treat the matter not as a facet of Nkrumah's "personality"
or even his leadership per se, but rather as a special role which generated authority, allegiance, support, against other and presumably
more powerfully entrenched ones (at least at the start).

Whether Mr. Owusu is right in this regard or I, the question remains a perplexing one. Perhaps there is a sense in which both of
us are right. I have tried to make a distinction between consummatory values or the concern with ultimate (and essentially nonem-
pirical) ends, and instrumental ones. Mr. Owusu rejects the
consummatory aspects, particularly as embodied in the charismatic
period of Nkrumah, in order to rely more on the instrumental.
I would argue that it was precisely the capacity to combine them
which accounts for Nkrumah's significance. His ability to do so, for
example, was apparent in the manner in which he used the left and
right wings of the party. The former was to keep its "eye" on the
"next stage" and be less concerned with what went on in Swedru
(or for that matter, any other local area other than Kumasi) than
with the future. The attention of the left was focused, for example,
on the trades union movement, the Young Pioneers, the Ideological
Institute. It was the "right wing" and the constituency party which
was involved locally. Indeed, in describing the CPP, I commented
on the pragmatism of the party, and the right wing in particular, by
far the largest part, which catered to those who saw in nationalist
politics "opportunities for personal advancement, reward, and prestige positions." [1] The CPP depended on the constituency parties
and yet began to destroy them in favor of the left.

Perhaps the problem raised by Mr. Owusu lies in a fundamental
ambiguity which remains disguised in all commitments to leaders
and causes until these connect with some ill-defined set of grievances, or awakened by hortatory injunctions arouse possibilities
which even though dimly seen are suddenly and urgently felt. Then
those who shout the loudest and who feel commitment most in-
tensely will be motivated to do things not otherwise open to them.
But even under the most extreme circumstances, the mixture of mo-

1. See D. E. Apter, *The Gold Coast in Transition* (Princeton: Princeton
University Press, 1955), p. 210.

tives, the rationalizations for a given line of behavior, and the shifting quality of these for any individual through time do not simply succeed one another in a kind of progression. They also exist simultaneously so that the same person who can be made to feel part of a larger cause can, on occasion, piously help himself to part of the exchequer on the grounds that a true believer is more worth rewarding than a nonbeliever. A great deal of this went on and is one reason why after the quality of earnestness and conviction and the anger which went with these during the high moments of Ghana nationalism had disappeared, all that was left was the imbalance of accounts. But was there no more to Ghana nationalism during the Nkrumah period than that? I think there was.

Whatever future scholars will have to say about these matters, however, it is precisely this kind of debate which is necessary to draw attention to the next level of work which needs to be done. I wish Mr. Owusu had paid more attention to my attempt to equate the functions of chieftaincy with the functions of charisma. There are some real problems in that. And precisely because Mr. Owusu has combined professional knowledge of an anthropological kind with political analysis, he could have challenged the theory as well as the substance of the argument. But that is perhaps a parochial interest of my own. Mr. Owusu's work reflects a mixture of genuinely intellectual concerns as a Ghanaian deeply interested in his own society and the more abstract and impartial professional role. He is both participant and external observer, precisely the combination of skills which, exceedingly rare, is necessary to take African studies to its next stage. When Okumu in Kenya, Rweyamu and Mushi in Tanzania, and others like them in the Congo, Senegal and elsewhere following (perhaps in the footsteps of a Mazrui or an Owusu) produce their political studies, then the Africanization of African studies will also result in a vast increase in the professional level of work. Such a change is coming very fast with important implications for the training of Africanists, especially the outsiders. For example, it is no longer sufficient for Americans, with a smattering of ignorance in African studies and a postdoctoral gloss in political science, to expect to accomplish something new and different in the usual period of field work. To dig deeper without committing the sin of parochialism, that is, to keep an eye on the general in the particular, also becomes harder and harder to do. In this respect

Mr. Owusu's study serves us well. He uses intensive study of Swedru and the particularities of that place to illustrate the character of an historical experience for the country as a whole while describing a theory of how political change occurs in the real context of names, people, events, transactions. The texture is there. The people are alive.

One last point. The study ends with the downfall of Nkrumah. Since then, the country has gone through substantial changes. The military government which after the coup consolidated its power by eliminating the CPP has given way to a democratic parliamentary system under Dr. Busia. The long-frustrated political ambitions of the opposition under the Nkrumah days have at last come to fruition. The present leaders of Ghana are on the whole more unpretentious in their political goals especially in pan-African affairs. They are very much concerned with political instrumentalism. In this they may be close to the views of economic self-interest held by Mr. Owusu. Perhaps it is left to an outsider to speculate on the emergence of a residual "consummatory vacuum" left by the downfall of Nkrumah and the CPP. To a new generation will Nkrumah appear romantic and be regarded in a more favorable light than at present? Or will Nkrumah's Ghana seem comic, pretentious, and hollow, its slogans absurd, its "philosophy" mumbo jumbo? That is one of the concerns not included in Mr. Owusu's study, the answers to which, I am sure, would interest us both.

DAVID E. APTER

Acknowledgments

My greatest debts are to men, universities, and books, in that order. Professors Lloyd A. Fallers and Raymond T. Smith of the University of Chicago advised me in the preparation of an earlier version of this study as a doctoral dissertation. Professor Lucy Mair, of the London School of Economics and Political Science; Professor T. B. Bottomore, formerly of the London School of Economics and Political Science; and Professor Edward Tiriyakian, formerly of Harvard University, have been my teachers, guides, and friends, both directly and indirectly, in this undertaking. Professor David Apter, of the University of California, Berkeley, read the first draft of the manuscript. His extended scholarly association with Ghana made his critical comments particularly valuable. If there is any merit in what I have attained, they are much responsible for it, but the weaknesses of this study are my own.

My years of association with the Committee for the Comparative Study of New Nations at the University of Chicago and the eminent scholars connected with it — especially Professors Edward Shils, Philip Foster, Leonard Binder, and Robert Levine — gave me new insight into the complexity of the problems of the developing nations of Africa and Asia. I profited greatly from the seminar on Max Weber in the autumn of 1966, given by Professor David Easton of the Political Science Department, University of Chicago.

There are many other people to whom I am very much indebted. They include Omanhene (Nana Nyarko Eku IX of Nyakrom; Joseph A. Essel, stool clerk of Nyakrom; J. O. Arthur, Opanin Kofi Donkoh, Opanin Kofi Osei Tutu, all elders of Nyakrom; Gyasehene Kofi Amponsah II of Agona-Swedru; Abusuapanyin Kofi Biri (J. B. Ansah) of Agona-Swedru; my research assistant, Isaac Kwaw Wallace, also of Agona-Swedru; Nana Kum of Dwinhu; Kojo Essilfie of Yaabamu; H. T. Mafo, clerk of council, SUC; and S. K. Osafo,

Yaw Ampadu, S. Y. Annobil, E. K. Mensah, F. B. Osei, and Zerikin
Zongo Malam Darfi, all of Agona-Swedru.

Finally, I thank the Committee on African Studies, the University
of Chicago, for sponsoring my field work, which made this study
possible.

USES AND ABUSES OF POLITICAL POWER

Introduction

A modern society is not just a complex of modern institutions. It is a mode of integration of the whole society. It is a mode of relationship between the centre and the periphery of the society. . . . It involves a greater participation by masses in the values of the society, a more active role in the making of society-wide decision.[1]

This is primarily a study of national integration: of social, economic, but more especially political, unification in Ghana as seen through the particular development of the people of Swedru in the Agona area of south-central Ghana. The study covers the period of the contact with Europe, from about the end of the seventeenth century to the time of the military coup d'état in Ghana on 24 February 1966. It is the story of continuity and change in the political life of the local inhabitants — both indigenous and foreign — of the town of Swedru and, in a sense, of Ghana as well. The research concentrates on how traditional political institutions, symbolized by the rule of the chief and his elder-councillors, have adapted or failed to adapt to the changing environment of Eurocolonial domination, decolonization, and of one-party state and society under the Convention People's Party (CPP). I analyze the changing political structure and political process in Swedru in terms of the way they affect or are affected by the functioning of similar processes at the regional and national levels. The basic question of the whole nature of politics is raised and discussed in a way which I think offers better understanding of political development in Ghana and, perhaps, in other parts of black Africa.

The fundamental thesis of this study is that political relations are considered extensions or primary dimensions of economic relations. That is, the set of relations concerning the mobilization of resources, of production and exchange, of distribution and allocation of scarce values, primarily defines, establishes, or influences power relationships and patterns of authoritative domination and subordination. Economic relations also greatly influence legitimate control of public policy-decisions and support for these decisions. Possession

1. Edward Shils in Clifford Geertz, editor, *Old Societies and New States* (New York: Free Press, 1963), p. 21.

3

and control of wealth or economic resources is, no doubt, an important ingredient of power, actual or potential, but wealth and, to some extent, power may be sought for their own sake, as ends in themselves, if by this we mean their social recognition symbolized by according high social status and status-respect to wealthy men. Wealth, in fact, to many Africans is power itself.

We have here a dynamic conception of power by which power becomes an instrument, a means to more wealth and higher social esteem. A different way of stating this is by saying that though in the traditional political system of the Agona (or of other tribes of Ghana) political power and authority were largely conferred ascriptively by membership generally of kinship and descent groups or categories, the chief had also to achieve, so to speak, his power and authority over his people by his ability to maintain and expand the economic resources — lands, the efficacy of rituals relating to ancestor worship, and so on — he controlled.[2] Political relations, then, had primary reality in terms of scarce resources — land, property, and the important ritual resource of prayer to the ancestors. The very religion, utilitarian and materialistic in emphasis, justified the primacy of economic action or relationships. Fortes and Evans-Pritchard make the same point when they argue that "the material interests that actuate individuals or groups in an African society operate in the frame of a body of interconnected moral and legal norms the order and stability of which is maintained by the political organization."[3]

This brings us to yet another important consideration. Tra-

2. The Akan concept of land tenure was related directly, particularly in the seventeenth and eighteenth centuries, to their definition of power relations. During those periods the chiefs exercised tight control over land and its products. The chief's consent was required before farmers could clear a plot of land for agriculture. All farmers were by custom obliged to cultivate, communally, the chief's land before they could work on their own, and part of the income from the sale of farm produce from individual farms was compulsorily paid to the chief as farm rent. Land was the major source of wealth, and political power derived largely from the control of wealth and scarce resources. The stratification system of society, to a great extent, closely followed wealth differences. The chiefs occupied the top of the ladder of privilege; next to them in a descending order were wealthy traders and heritors of property; then freeborn commoners with limited resources, and finally the slaves. The last two categories generally depended on the customary largesse of the chiefs and wealthy men for their livelihood. (See Kwamina B. Dickson, *A Historical Geography of Ghana* [Cambridge: At the University Press, 1969], especially pp. 76 ff.)

3. M. Fortes and E. E. Evans-Pritchard, eds., *African Political Systems* (London: Oxford University Press, 1940), pp. 20–21.

ditionalists — upholders of tradition — are not necessarily against change; they resist change only when it destroys the economic and coercive basis of traditional power and privilege. (Tradition, in this sense, means social arrangements, including their political and symbolic aspects, that are thought of as, or believed to be, right at any one period, because these arrangements are associated with the past, immediate or remote, and therefore worth maintaining or passing on to posterity.) Thus, tradition or custom as a complex set of expressive symbols, beliefs, norms, values, justifications, and validations is strategically reinterpreted, redefined, and manipulated in situations of social change, as groups and individuals compete for political and economic advantages.

The view of politics presented here differs significantly from that of Dr. Lloyd Fallers, who holds that "more typically [in Africa], production and exchange have been undertaken as an adjunct — a means — to the organization of power, the field in which, it appears, the African genius has really concentrated its efforts."[4] Contrary to Fallers, I will argue that power is rather a means, an important one but by no means the only one, to the organization and accumulation of wealth. In fact, one may argue that both wealth and power are related means to the supreme social value — high status, social recognition, and social dignity.

SELECTION OF RESEARCH SITE

The urban town of Agona-Swedru (pop. 20,546, 1960 Government Census), which I selected as a base for my study of political structure and process in the context of national integration — that is, unification of "center and periphery" — is particularly appropriate.[5] For one thing, the town played a crucial role in the political evolution of Ghana; for another, I know the town, its region, and its people rather well. Located in the Central Region (sometimes included in the Western Region), one of nine administrative regions into which Ghana is divided (see frontispiece map), Swedru has an area of seventeen square miles (Ghana is ninety-two thousand

4. L. Fallers, "Social Stratification and Economic Processes in Africa," in Reinhard Bendix and Seymour M. Lipset, editors, *Class, Status and Power* (New York: Free Press, 1966), p. 142.
5. In fact, it is hard to find a prototypical Ghanaian town which portrays better a combination of indigenous, accommodationist, and alien elements in a predominantly commercial setting.

square miles in area), and a population density of 1,209 persons per square mile (1960 census), one of the highest in the country.

The outlines of the history and early growth of Swedru can now be said to be clear, but the details of its early development and, in fact, the circumstances of the founding of Agona State still need more intensive and painstaking research over a period of years.[6] The disentanglement of the knotty and confused history of the Agona state would require a comparative study of the history of each of the ten chiefdoms of which the Agona traditional state is made up, and of Gomoa Assin — a study which would demand the joint effort of historians, anthropologists (social and cultural), and possibly archeologists.

The original inhabitants of the Agona area, and of much of Southern Ghana, are believed to have been the Guan.[7] The Agona seem to have displaced the Guan in waves of successive migrations from Tekyiman as early as the middle of the seventeenth century.[8]

The traditional chiefdom of Agona-Swedru, headed by the *adontenhene* of Agona, was (and still is) organized around the principle of matrilineage (*abusua*) common among the Akan peoples of Ghana, of whom the Ashanti are undoubtedly the prototype and the best known. Agona clans were exogamous, and inheritance and succession passed through the female line: from brother to brother, then to eldest sister's son, then next eldest sister's son, then to sisters, and finally to sister's daughters, in that order. In practice, there were a number of exceptions. The political structure of the Agona seems to have been fairly centralized and appears to have been similar, with few exceptions which we shall have occasion to note, to that of other Akan states, with centralized authority, a structure which was modelled after the traditional military organization.[9]

The growth of Swedru from a village of largely clan- or descent-based wards of subsistence farmers and hunters to a heterogeneous,

6. This would be true of much of the history of various peoples of Sub-Saharan Africa.

7. J. D. Fage, *Ghana: A Historical Interpretation* (Madison: University of Wisconsin Press, 1966).

8. Ellis notes that, though the Agona are now considered a distinct group, they are linguistically Fante, who were once subjected by the Gomoa (after the Sasabor war of the 1690s, as I shall argue), and part of the Agona lands was at one time occupied by the neighboring Efutu of the Winneba area. J. B. Christensen, *Double Descent among the Fanti* (New Haven: HRAF, 1954).

9. K. A. Busia, *The Position of the Chief in the Modern Political System of Ashanti* (London: Oxford University Press, 1951).

modern urban center has been phenomenal yet typical. The town has, especially after the Second World War, become an important administrative, educational, and commercial center, not only for Agona but for the Central Region as a whole. The town is polyethnic. Apart from the Agona proper, who constitute 19.8 percent of the local population, there are the Fante (40.5 percent); the Ashanti (2.1 percent); the Kwahu (4.1 percent); and many others, including the Lebanese, Syrians, and Europeans (1960 census).[10] Commerce and transport are the two dominant occupations in Swedru. In fact, the basic character of the town derives from these relatively modern occupations.

Retail trade in secondary products is effectively controlled by migrants, particularly the Kwahu, the Indians, the Levantines, some Fante, and, of course, Europeans. The Agona are still mostly engaged in primary production, producing both for subsistence and for the ever-growing market. Thus the cosmopolitanism of Swedru — such as it is — developed, it is clear, not out of the sophistication of the rural traditions of the leading elements of the local Agona population but, rather, somewhat like Geertz's Modjokuto, out of the intrusion of already highly cosmopolitan groups — European, Levantine, and African peoples with entrepreneurial skill (the Kwahu, Fante, and Yoruba) into the local scene.[11] Indeed, Swedru is the most cosmopolitan town within a forty-mile radius.

The socioeconomic and political unification of Swedru, as an integral part of the region of which it is the center and of the nation, seems to be based on the following factors: (1) Economic interdependence through an extensive, nation-wide network of production, exchange, buying, and selling related to functionally specialized activities, and through a complex system of internal and external credit and indebtedness. (2) Social integration based on membership of crosscutting ethnically heterogeneous local, regional, and national voluntary organizations or associations — for example, football clubs, churches, religious sects, and political parties; and on patterns of obligatory joking relationships among different ethnic groups on the basis of the relevant ethnic stereotypes available to the local populations, a joking exchange of abuse which is both

10. The Fante and the Kwahu are perhaps the two most important African groups.
11. See Clifford Geertz, *Peddlers and Princes* (Chicago: University of Chicago Press, 1963).

cause and consequence of the fact that all the diverse groups are aware of their mutual interdependence and realize that they need one another, and of the fact that there has developed over the years a strong identification of all migrant groups to Swedru, with Swedru.[12] (3) Political unification founded on administrative, legal, and territorial unity. A national civil service, a national police force (and an army), a national school system, a national judiciary, a centralized local government, and, until the military coup, a national political party or parties and their leaders, and a national legislature — all helped to bring the periphery very near to the center and vice versa.

THE METHODS USED IN THE STUDY

I spent approximately twelve months in the field. To this research period should be added an extended stay in Swedru for more than eight successive years (1950–58) that literally made me not only *Swedruni* but Agona. I am Ghanaian. I speak Agona fluently and with hardly any trace of my "foreign" background. I also have almost equal facility in the major languages — Twi, Fante, and Ga — of Southern Ghana and Ashanti. The importance of linguistic acquisition as a principal key to any worthwhile, certainly reliable, and even objective research in any society cannot be overemphasized.

I had an additional, perhaps unique, advantage. When I returned to Ghana after nearly eight years' sojourn in England and America, people from all walks of life including, of course, my relatives and friends spent about two hectic weeks reviewing, in infinite detail and with some exaggeration, all the events and incidents, particularly economic and political developments, which had taken place while I was overseas. These culturally expected, even obligatory and intensive, "homecoming" seminars proved invaluable and provided some of my primary data on politics and economics.

Other methods used in the course of the research included the usual anthropological ones: the collection of biographies or personal

12. This sense of local identification, certainly found in some other West African towns, is usually expressed by the claim, "We are Swedrufo" — "citizens" of Swedru — heard from all ethnic groups. In many social situations this sense of Swedru-ness overrides that of ethnic and primordial attachments.

histories of selected individuals and families, especially those who
obviously knew much about the political, social, and economic history of the town in relation to its surroundings – among these were
elders of the town, chiefs, early migrants, ex-party officers and leaders, exmembers of Parliament, the clerk of the Swedru Urban Council, excouncillors, and popular local influentials; interviews with
individuals; participant observation of various social activities (a
method more effective when a trained native is studying natives!);
the collection of genealogies; analysis and use of published and un-
published documents pertaining to the town, the traditional state,
the region, and the nation – historical papers, oral history, local
government records, colonial reports, records of local court cases,
local council minutes, reports of committees and commissions of inquiry; parliamentary debates; minutes of party meetings and
conferences.[13]

An attempt to use a self-administered questionnaire on a random
sample of eight hundred based on electoral registers to collect statistical data on past political behavior, particularly voting behavior
in local and national elections, and to determine, among other
things, party affiliation unfortunately proved unsuccessful. The failure was due to a misunderstanding with the local police (the Special Branch) about questions raised concerning party membership.
As a result, the police had to recall all the distributed questionnaires, many of which had been completed. Eventually only about
one hundred of the questionnaires were returned to me. It is anybody's guess what happened to the rest. The background to this
confusion, which caused my detention at the Swedru and later at the
Cape Coast police stations for questioning, was that, after the military coup of February 1966 (I arrived in Ghana in October 1966),
the National Liberation Council (NLC) had issued a number of decrees, two of which – NLC Decree 3 and NLC Decree 92 – I could
have infringed.

NLC Decree 3 bans all political activities and parties and makes
it an offense to summon or attend meetings of a political organiza-

13. The time I spent in the field was divided as follows: about three months
in the Government Archives in Accra, Cape Coast, and Winneba; and nine
months in Swedru, punctuated by occasional return trips to Winneba, Accra,
Cape Coast, Nyakrom, and Nsaba whenever necessary. The latter two towns
have been alternatively and simultaneously the seat of paramount chiefs in
Agona.

tion or of a political nature or to use slogans and labels of political organizations, and so forth. NLC Decree 92, on the other hand, makes it an offense to reproduce or publish statements, rumors, or reports likely to cause fear and alarm among the public, to disturb public peace, or to cause disaffection against the NLC or among the public, members of the armed force, or the police.[14] On the basis of the kind of questions the police asked, it was clear that they thought I might be a hired agent of the deposed president, Kwame Nkrumah, and was possibly "indulging in politics." I was even accused of causing fear among the public. The political atmosphere in Ghana remained uncertain and tense at the time and the police could, perhaps, be forgiven for their action.

Finally, I must mention that I spent numerous hours in casual but directed conversation with many local people of diverse backgrounds on virtually any topic, on street corners, in bars, in shops, at the local market (where the market women became very interested in my continual presence in a place traditionally taboo to men), and on pavements in front of stores where people generally gathered at midday and in the late afternoon to play or watch others play draughts and where burning questions of the day, from the independence of women to the corruption of public officials, were discussed from many angles in good humor. My involvement here proved very rewarding indeed.

THE OBJECTIVES OF THE STUDY

This study has a double purpose: one relates to the reexamination of some of the general theories of political change in Africa and to the explanations based on them; the other has to do with the consequences of the research for policy formulation. I hope that the work will provide a case study of interest and value to social scientists, particularly those interested in the political aspect of social life and in problems of nation-building in Africa.

It is perhaps needless to point out that a single case study cannot, with all good intentions and care in this world, provide answers to most of the general questions associated with modernization. Such questions can be answered only through the collection, study, and analysis of data drawn either from many different societies undergoing change or from different regions of the same society. Such

14. *Ghanaian Times*, 15 April 1967.

comparative studies have just begun.[15] But a case study can certainly accomplish at least two things: it can test some of the hypotheses generated in the course of previous studies in the same society or of studies elsewhere [16] and can itself stimulate new hypotheses.[17]

Thus I have found Apter's and Wallerstein's "charismatic leadership" hypothesis wanting or misleading, and Zolberg's claim that "an examination of political parties, the best studied feature of the African scene, reveals such a wide gap between the organizational model from which the leaders derived their inspiration and their capacity to implement such schemes that the very use by observers of the word 'party' to characterize such structures involves a dangerous 'reification' " [18] mystifying and confused. To pretend that the CPP did not exist as a party between 1949 and 1966 because *presumably* there was a wide gap between its organizational model and the ability of party leaders to "implement such schemes" is to misunderstand what a political party is, what a model is, and what the CPP succeeded in implementing. After all, a model is just that; it is precisely not action but a framework for action, a guide to action, which may be changed in response to changes in party aims and circumstances. The CPP constitution was in fact changed in 1962. It must also be remembered that a certain gap between a model and action based on the model is inevitable. I am still not sure of what a real political party is.[19]

Commenting on the structure of party decision-making (after the

15. M. Kilson, *Political Change in a West African State: A Study of the Modernisation Process in Sierra Leone* (Cambridge: Harvard University Press, 1966); D. W. Brokensha, *Social Change at Larteh, Ghana* (London: Oxford University Press, 1966).

16. A. R. Zolberg, *Creating Political Order: The Party-States of West Africa* (Chicago: Rand Mcally, 1966).

17. Examples of this (and there are many) would be the testing of Apter's and Zolberg's hypotheses on the nature of political institutions and political change in Tropical Africa, especially in Ghana. David Apter, *The Politics of Modernization* (Chicago: The University of Chicago Press, 1965); "Nkrumah, Charisma, and the Coup," *Daedalus*, vol. 97, no. 3 (1968). A. R. Zolberg, *Creating Political Order*; "The Structure of Political Conflict in the New States of Tropical Africa," *American Political Science Review* 62, no. 1 (March 1968): 70–87.

18. Zolberg, "Structure of Political Conflict," p. 72.

19. In its application to the CPP, Zolberg's generalization based on limited and unsystematic data from second-hand sources is unwarranted, on the basis of the evidence, and dangerous to the development of comparative politics.

1962 Party Constitutional Revision) characterized by "Democratic Centralism," *The Dawn*, the organ of the CPP overseas branches, culling from the *Evening News*, a Ghanaian daily newspaper, writes:

Very often when the expression "The Party (CPP) is Supreme" is used, the impression is formed that some individual Party members or Party functionary is supreme or has supreme powers by virtue of the position he occupies in the Party set-up.

This view is incorrect. The supremacy of the Party derives essentially from the principle of Democratic Centralism. For example, the Central Committee of the Party, the highest organ of the Party, may consider a certain course of action necessary having regard to the general trend of inner Party thought and feeling on a specific subject or organizational problem.

To test the mass line on the particular issue, the Committee refers the proposals to various echelons beginning right at the units for a decision. The rank and file of the Party village, town, municipal and city branches hold general meetings and thoroughly discuss the matter from all angles and arrive at a decision either unanimously or through the majority vote.

The branches then pass their decisions on to the District level. The District Executive Committee may either convene an emergency District Party Conference which is itself composed of two delegates from each branch, if they are in doubt.

Almost inevitably the decision of the District Party Organization coincided with the collective decision of the branches and so the matter goes forward to the Regional Steering Committee until it reaches the Central Committee through the National Executive.

The proposal, which was referred to the entire membership of the Party, has now travelled back to the highest body. The Central Committee now puts the collective decision into suitable form and releases it as a Party decision or policy.[20]

The above is a clear statement of the model of party decision-making of the CPP between 1962 and 1966. But, as I hope to show on the basis of my material from Swedru, there were certain important departures from the model, many of which reflected situational demands, environmental exigencies, and the personality of regional commissioners and district commissioners. In the final analysis, I think, a political party is judged not by its highly articulate formal organization, though this is important, but by the quality and enthusiasm of the membership and the degree to which the members are willing, in the national interest, to work so that they may carry out programs and fulfill the objectives of party through party

20. *The Dawn*, vol. 1, no. 20 (Wednesday, 17 February 1965).

activity — through regular attendance at party meetings, service on party committees, assistance given at local and general elections, and the like.[21]

Now let us return to the aims of this study. The study may make a distinct contribution to the comparative study of political systems, particularly to the largely neglected area of micro- or grass-roots politics, by providing much-needed descriptive material and by suggesting new ranges of variation of which comparative analysis must make use. The second objective of the study is its relevance for policy decision. By systematically exploring the primary basis of political action, my intention is to draw attention to some of the basic causes of political instability and general economic stagnation in the hope that the correct diagnosis of a national disease must precede prescription and cure.

Finally, I hope that the study will induce serious-minded Africans to look critically at themselves and their societies, which are undergoing rapid and sometimes confused transformation, so that they may be in a position to forge a better and more realistic weapon to fight the enormous problems facing us — problems which, it must not be forgotten, may be related to our whole historical development and cultural focus.

21. Writing on political behavior of the electorate of Newcastle-under-Lyme, F. Bealey, J. Blondel, and W. P. McCann note in *Constituency Politics: A Study of Newcastle-under-Lyme* (New York: The Free Press, 1965), p. 273, that "local activity is *a minority* occupation even among party members in Newcastle reflecting the low level of interest in local political affairs. . . . Only about 3 out of every 100 of the electorate are members of political parties, and of the total number of the party rolls, only a minority are consistently *active*. Putting an X on a ballot paper at stated intervals still remains the one political activity which involves an overwhelming majority of the English electorate." With reference to party organizational models, the three authors found wide gaps between the organizational models of the Conservative and Liberal parties of England and the implementation of the model in the early and middle 1950s. They found, for example, that the Conservative party had a low level of organization in the wards of Newcastle, in some of which there was no organized group in existence. The Liberal party had no ward organization at all.

1

THE AGONA PEOPLE
AND POLITICS
The Historical Background

Commenting on the state of the writing of African history, Basil Davidson notes that "African history now yields a picture of long, continuous and broadly definable movement from one phase of socio-political relationships to another" and that the picture "is valid for every large region of the Continent." [1] This picture of continuous sociopolitical relationships is even clearer when one considers a very small subregion in Africa, the Akan forest areas of West Africa.

One significant feature of the rise, expansion, and collapse of the Akan states has been the close relationship of the sociopolitical pattern with the opening of new trade routes between the hinterland and the markets of the coastal areas. In fact, the interaction between politics and economics is so close that they are both cause and effect of each other. It is no accident that the Akwamu, Denkyera, Ashanti, and even the Agona states all arose in the wake of Portuguese and other European trade and commerce in the sixteenth, seventeenth, and eighteenth centuries. The major ingredient in state formation was therefore trade and commerce. Centralization of political power was in part necessitated by the desire of indigenous rulers to forge a more effective means of monopolizing the control of access to the flourishing trade in men and merchandise on the coast. The sociopolitical continuity seems to have been based primarily on socioeconomic continuity. The state system under kings or powerful chiefs, made it possible, at any rate before effective European colonization, to secure and organize servile labor and, in largely pre-cash economy, to exploit considerably the tribute system, with a correspondingly greater economic surplus for kings who might even at this early stage be described as political entre-

1. Basil Davidson, *Can We Write African History?*, Occasional Paper no. 1, African Studies Center (Los Angeles: University of California at Los Angeles, 1965), pp. 6–9.

preneurs. In the Akan areas, the gold trade, as Davidson argues, began to be organized and extended by new methods about 1400 [2]; so was the trade in ivory, spices, and slaves in the sixteenth and seventeenth centuries. The Agona were organized particularly for the trade in men.

For analytical and existential or empirical reasons, I distinguish three broad periods: the traditional precolonial, the Eurocolonial, and the postcolonial, which may be thought of, at least for the Akan areas, as relatively unbroken periods marked throughout by increasing attempts by chiefs and other rulers to extend their spheres of power by setting up centralized political systems in order to monopolize the control of economic resources, and by an increasing scale of sociopolitical relationships caused to some extent by increasing commercialization or "economization" of society. The most crucial links uniting peoples of the various tribes became increasingly economic as barter and sporadic trading and exchange were gradually superseded by more stable and more generally diffused trade based on money, which led to the institutionalization of the cash-nexus. The introduction of a cash crop, cocoa, and the commercial activities with which it was associated was to have long-range effect on society and polity. Each of the socioeconomic changes appears to have generated ideas about the organization of the state which differed very little from period to period. Whether we are dealing with the era of tribal kings or of colonial governors, the style has been the use of the state apparatus, including the means of violence, to control the economy. Economic control was in turn used to further the concentration of political power as a means to the organization and maintenance of wealth, high social status, privilege, and prestige. The very ideas which affected political relationships, and maintained these relationships (the relationships between leaders and the led), were often — not exclusively, of course — economic in origin. In the Akan states, it seems that legitimate domination was crucially based, in the last analysis — considerations of kinship [3] notwithstanding — on the economic effectiveness of the rulers, on their ability to maintain and expand the conditions for the material well-being or prosperity of their subjects. The desire for

2. Ibid., p. 14.
3. Kinship provided a powerful idiom in terms of which economic and political relations were organized and articulated.

economic betterment appears to be at the very root of the organization of power.[4]

The basic determinant of political action is seen here as economic in origin. In this sense, the persistence of a viable and prosperous economy, especially the economic well-being of individuals, groups, and communities, becomes a necessary precondition for the ultimate survival of any political arrangements. The Agona chief, no less than his brother in Ashanti, had to pray for the material well-being of his subjects. The very religion of the Akan, as we have seen, was utilitarian in nature. Religion functioned here as a mechanism of political and economic control.

THE ORIGINS OF THE AGONA STATE:
MEYEROWITZ AND THE AGONA

Agona is one of the Akan native states of the Winneba District and lies in the north, while Gomoa, formerly one state, now consists of two independent states, Gomoa Assin and Gomoa Adjumako, which lie neighborly to the south of the district, forming direct boundaries with Agona lands (see figures 1 and 2).[5]

Certainly, one of the first attempts (in fact, the only one known to me, short of occasional references to the Agona in various contexts) at the systematic account of the origins of the Agona state is that provided by E. Meyerowitz.[6]

Vansina, reviewing her original effort, points out that the "monograph on the Akan by Mrs. E. Meyerowitz is one of the best works devoted to the past history of pre-literate peoples." Vansina goes on to refer to von Fuehrer-Haimendorf, who has equally extolled Mey-

---

4. W. W. Rostow, *British Economy of the Nineteenth Century: Essays* (Oxford: Clarendon Press, 1949), pp. 140–42. Discussing the interrelationship between economics and politics in nineteenth century England, Rostow theorizes in a way which may be relevant here. He suggests that certain long-run movements in an economic system — in the Akan case, cash-crop farming, monetization, commercialization of society, the desire for accumulation of wealth, etc. — set the framework within which social life and its concepts evolve, pursuing, on the whole, a sluggish life of their own. He goes on to say that these long-run economic movements "have their main influence on *politics*, having worked through the social structure, where they have been generalized, associated with non-economic aspirations and crystallized into ideas and particular, often structural political objectives" (my italics).

5. The Agona number about forty-nine thousand (1960 census). Twenty-eight percent of their number were migrants to other areas of Ghana.

6. E. Meyerowitz, *Akan Traditions of Origin* (London: Faber, 1952), pp. 79–80.

erowitz's monograph as a shining example of "the results which can be obtained by studying oral traditions with a combination of scrupulous care and rich imagination."[7]

Vansina is not wholly happy, however, about the way in which Meyerowitz treats oral traditions, the latter's most serious defect being that she does not exercise "much critical judgment in her handling of her sources," and Vansina gives two examples of this lack of critical judgment. As I hope to demonstrate presently, Meyerowitz's treatment of the Agona is even more notorious for her conspicuous neglect of extant respectable recorded sources, which leads her to mistaken, but avoidable conclusions.[8]

The contention of A. B. Ellis that the Agona were once subjected by the Fante and that part of their lands was at one time occupied by the Efutu of Winneba area, and the implications of this are never examined by her.[9] I will soon show that any account of the Agona that omits Agona-Gomoa-Fante relations is bound to be fallacious or misleading.[10] Again I think the major weakness of Meyerowitz's account derives from the fact that she did not speak to the elders of Nsaba (until 1931 Nsaba was the seat of the *omanhene* of Agona),[11] who gave me a completely different version of the establishment of the Agona state.

There is reason to believe that the elders whom Meyerowitz interviewed through an interpreter — another stumbling-block — deliberately withheld certain information from her. For example, the defeat of the Agona by the Gomoa-Fante in the seventeenth

7. J. Vansina, *Oral Tradition: A Study in Historical Methodology*, translated by H. M. Wright (Chicago: Aldine Publishing Company, 1965), pp. 15–17.

8. On her own admission, information on the Agona was given in 1945 by "the Elders of the Agona State at Nyankurom [Nyakrom]." It is obvious that Meyerowitz did not consult such standard works as Reindorf's *History of the Gold Coast and Asante* and she does not seem to have made serious use of the works she did consult. For example, Bosman's *A New and Accurate Description of the Coast of Guinea*, which she cites in her bibliography, contains references to the Agona which, if she had pursued them, would have produced different results.

9. A. B. Ellis, *The Tshi-Speaking People of the Gold Coast of West Africa* (London: Chapman and Hall, 1887), and *A History of the Gold Coast of West Africa* (London: Chapman and Hall, 1893).

10. There is no doubt at all that I interviewed in 1967 the same elders of Nyakrom who were Meyerowitz's informants, but the results of the two efforts are quite different.

11. There are now two paramount chiefs in Agona recognized by the National Liberation Council, with their seats in Nyakrom and Nsaba respectively.

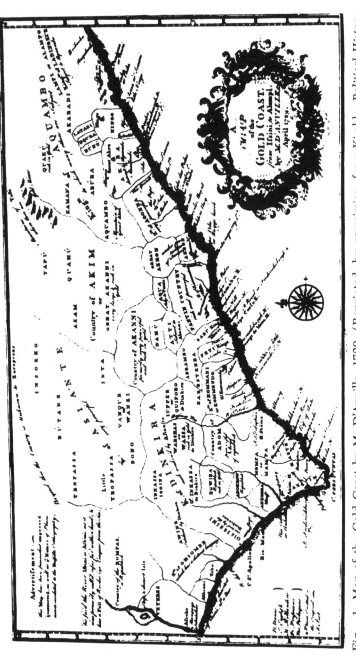

Fig. 1. Map of the Gold Coast by M. D'Anville, 1729. (Reprinted, by permission, from Kimble, *Political History of Ghana* [Oxford: Clarendon Press, 1963], facing p. 1.)

century, a watershed in the political history of the Agona, is never mentioned even in passing.

The elders surely wanted to forget a defeat which, as we shall see, made Nyakrom lose her paramount position in Agona to Nsaba for nearly two centuries.[12] Meyerowitz, perhaps faced with a deliberate distortion of Agona oral traditions, was forced to use her imagination to put the date of the establishment of the Agona state at 1750, thus dismissing into historical oblivion nearly a century of Agona political development. The range of her imaginary excursion was limited, however, by the fact that the European maps she consulted were made in the eighteenth century and on them "Agwana," "Aguna," or "Agonna" appears. But we also know now that a Dutch map refers to the "Agwanna Kingdom" in 1670.[13] A. B. Ellis mentions that on 28 May 1662, "the King of Aguna, instigated by the Dutch, had plundered their [English] factory at Winnebah."[14]

Meyerowitz's story is simply this: The Guan, whom she relates, perhaps wrongly, to the Ilagua (plural Laguantan), a place in the Sahara, were the earliest inhabitants of the area now occupied by the Agona,[15] who, according to her, were conquered by the Akwamu in the seventeenth century. After the fall of Akwamu in 1734, the Guan were again conquered by Mbooko people from Ahafo and originally from Tekyiman.[16]

Meyerowitz goes on to say that the Mbooko were taken prisoner by Osei Tutu, the founder of the Ashanti state, in the Dormaa-Ashanti war, and were given to Okomfo Anokye, the creator of the Golden Stool myth, to people Agona, his newly founded village and

12. When I confronted the omanhene and elders of Nyakrom, having already discussed Agona political history with one or two elders from Nsaba, with the facts of the Gomoa war, they had to recount to me what they remembered of the war. The chief told me, "You are our son, and we want you to write a true account of our history, once and for all."

13. *Ghana Notes and Queries*, the Bulletin of the Historical Society of Ghana (Accra), no. 9 (November 1966).

14. Ellis, *History of the Gold Coast*, p. 55. In an interview with the Agona elders at Nyakrom, they told me with some pride that their ancestors used to plunder the factories at Winneba and Apam.

15. Vansina, *Oral Tradition*, p. 16. W. W. Claridge, in *A History of the Gold Coast and Ashanti* (London: John Murray, 1915), 1:145, also holds that the Agona "are descended from some of the survivors of the original inhabitants of the coast line prior to the date of the great Fante invasion."

16. It is worth noting that most Akan peoples claim to have originated from Tekyiman. It is possible that if the Guan suffered another defeat, this time at the hands of the Mbooko people, it could have been earlier.

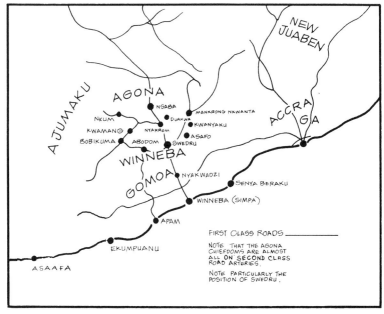

Fig. 2. Ghana Road Network, 1960. (Adapted from Survey of Ghana, Africa 1:250,000, Accra Sheet, 1960.)

personal residence.[17] After some time, the Mbooko fled with other Agona inhabitants and founded Kuntanase, where they were discovered and attacked by the Ashanti under Opoku Ware. They fled south and found political asylum with the Esikumahene of the Breman state. Their leader, according to Meyerowitz, was "Nyanku Atu" (Nyarko Eku), who finally built their town, "Nyankurum near Esikuma."

The Agona soon quarreled with the Breman people and, in the ensuing battles, "conquered the Breman State and some other towns in this region — Kwaman, Asenka, Bobokuma [Bobikuma] Abodom, Swedru, Asafo, Koniako [Kwanyako], Duakwa, Nsaban [Nsaba], Odabeng [Odobeng] Brakwa, Akuntanase [Kuntanase], Ochiso and Okyi, and founded the present Agona State (1750)."[18] In the list of towns or villages mentioned above, we do not hear of Nkum, which in fact was a major market town, burned down by Nyarko Eku on his march to Agona. Contrary to Meyerowitz's claims, it is clear from the accounts that Kwaman, Duakwa, and the others, were not really conquered by Nyarko Eku. What seems to have happened was that these various villages, some of which now form the ten divisions or chiefdoms of the Agona state, submitted to the superior force of Nyarko Eku after the destruction of Nkum. Nyarko Eku is supposed to have come down to Agona — with Nyakrom elders' characteristic exaggeration — followed by "half the 'Ashanti' nation"! However invalid the theory of mass immigration of "Ashanti" under Nyarko Eku, there is no doubt, as subsequent events were to show, that Nyarko and his followers were better organized and had better weapons than the people they met.

It is true that Nyarko Eku's journey to Agona took him through Okumaning near Kade, Breman-Esikuma, where he defeated the people but quickly moved on to Nkum. At Nkum, Nyarko found out that the river there would not provide sufficient drinking water for his large following, and so when his scouts discovered the Akora

17. It is highly probable that Nyarko Eku and his followers, joined by other refugees, might have fled southeastward in the course of a pre–Osei Tutu, Ashanti war with Denkyera during the last half of the seventeenth century and could not have been the same group of slaves given to Okomfo Anokye to people his village — Agona. It appears that Okomfo Anokye was already Agonahene long before the decisive Osei Tutu war with Dormaa. (See C. C. Reindorf, *The History of the Gold Coast and Asante* [Accra: Ghana Universities Press, 1966], chap. 4.
18. Meyerowitz, *Akan Traditions*, pp. 79–80.

River a few miles away, he decided to build his village near the
river at *Odumto* ("at the root of the Odum tree"). This village was
later named Nyakrom after the first omanhene, Nyarko Eku. The
chief of Nkum at this time was Ofori, Kwaa Gyaako, also of Ashanti
origin.[19]

Reindorf agrees with Ellis and Bosman that at the end of the seventeenth century there were already in existence eleven powerful
native states on the coast of the Gold Coast in addition to the states
of the forest area.[20] The Agona state was one of them. Akwamu was
also one. In fact, this directly contradicts Meyerowitz's chronology.
Meyerowitz has argued, as we have just noted, that the Agona state
came into being in 1750 — that is, in the middle of the eighteenth
century. That she is wrong is given additional support, for Dapper's
extract on the Akan forest states, written in 1670, notes that "the
Territory of Sanquah touches Fantin [Fante] on the south, Ahim
[Akim] in the north and Agwana [Agona] in the east. The people of
Sanquah buy a great deal of fish from Rauchen Ecke which . . . [?]
they carry inland. The territory mainly comes under the *Kingdom
of Agwana*" (my italics).[21] Although very little is said here of the
organization of the various states — the extent, for instance, of the
centralization of political power — the economic relationships of the
Akan states were clearly emphasized.

It is obvious from the European records of the Gold Coast that,
from about 1688 on, the rise of the Akwamu and Denkyera states
led to a series of wars of aggression and conquest aimed at capturing and monopolizing the European trade. That these wars promoted further the growth of larger political units to insure adequate
defense, offense, and effective monopolization of trade, is beyond
doubt. In 1688, according to Kumah, the Denkyera appeared on the
coast ready to go to the help of the people of Agona faced with an
invasion from Akwamu.[22] Akwamu itself was, it seems, originally a

19. Nkum is five miles from Nyakrom and between 1957 and 1966 had a
joint Urban Council.
20. C. C. Reindorf, *The History of the Gold Coast and Asante* (Browne and
Nolin, Dublin: Richview Press, 1966); Ellis, *Tshi-Speaking People*, and *History
of the Gold Coast*.
21. "The Akan Forest States," a provisional translation of an extract from
O. Dapper, *Beschreibung von Afrika* (German edition, Amsterdam, 1670), in
Ghana Notes and Queries, The Bulletin of the Historical Society of Ghana
(Accra), no. 9 (November 1966), p. 15.
22. See J. K. Kumah, "The Rise and Fall of the Kingdom of Denkyira,"
Ghana Notes and Queries, no. 9 (November 1966), p. 35. It needs pointing out

minor state in the hinterland of Agona west of Accra and east of Winneba, but, as Fage indicates, by the 1650s its center of gravity had shifted eastward to the north of Accra. Akwamu captured Accra between 1677 and 1681, and its king and many of his subjects fled to Little Popo. Akwamu then proceeded to conquer Agona, in 1688 according to Fage, but in 1689 according to Basil Davidson.[23] Perhaps in this connection Meyerowitz was confusing the Agona and the Guan, whom she believed to have been conquered in this period by the Akwamu.

It must be emphasized again that in this period of Akan history all the states, great and small, had an active policy, judged by the frequency of intertribal wars of conquest and imperial aggrandizement, a lust for booty, and a strong desire of rulers and subjects to monopolize the trade in men and commodities. This policy of political entrepreneurship was later to account partly for the European involvement and intervention, again in the interest of trade and commerce, in indigenous politics and the resultant introduction of colonial rule.

Reindorf recounts repeatedly that, in the seventeenth and eighteenth centuries, slave trading was carried on extensively by the Akwamu, the Gomoa, and their neighbors the Agona, with Akra (the Ga?) as brokers. Incessant fighting, man-stealing, and plunder among the Agona, Gomoa, and Akwamu covered the main part of their political histories.

It is not clear from the historical records on what basis formal alliances, if any, were made between states. These various states probably did come to some understanding about the slave trade and about the method of waging competition for slaves. All the same, alliances must have meant very little, because states which were on friendly terms today would be seen engaged in a fierce battle tomorrow. For the most part of the seventeenth century, Gomoa and Agona were friendly with Akra. Yet in 1680, Akwamu, growing en-

that before the emergence of Ashanti, the most powerful of the Akan states was Akwamu. As J. D. Fage correctly shows in *Ghana: A Historical Interpretation* (Madison: University of Wisconsin Press, 1966), the Ashanti state was in many ways a repetition on a somewhat larger and more successful scale of the earlier Akwamu model. See R. S. Rattray, *Ashanti Law and Constitution* (Oxford: The Clarendon Press, 1929), and Busia, *Position of the Chief*, for a discussion of the organization of the Ashanti state.

23. Basil Davidson, with F. K. Buah and J. F. A. Ajayi, *The Growth of African Civilisation, 1000–1800* (London: Longmans, Green and Co., 1965).

vious of the wealth of Akra, fought Akra with mercenaries from
Gomoa and Agona. When the Akwamu refused to pay the fee
promised the mercenaries, the Agona, according to Reindorf, made
up the difference by kidnapping the Akwamu and selling them.
There is no doubt that Agona-Akwamu relationships deteriorated
after these incidents and were finally, in 1688–89, to lead to the conquest of Agona by Akwamu. Fage argues that Agona was apparently captured to prevent the Akim from securing an independent
outlet to the sea.[24]

It is interesting to note that in 1730–32 the Akim finally crushed
the Akwamu. The disintegration of the Akwamu Kingdom into its
component parts — including, among others, the Akim Abuakwa,
Akwapim, Ga, and Adangbe states — was immediate. It is clear from
the foregoing that the Akan kingdoms of this period (except perhaps the Ashanti with their golden stool myth) lacked any overarching political ideology to sustain or maintain them in times of
crises. They were hardly highly centralized except perhaps in times
of war, when sheer survival and the chances of booty and the accumulation of wealth made it imperative for component groups to
stick together. Communication between the center of the state and
the periphery — the outlying political units — must have been weak,
infrequent, and in times of peace — barring the annual tribute from
subject groups — uncertain.

The Agona State from the Seventeenth to the Nineteenth Century

The period of Agona history between 1690 and 1900 is the period of
Gomoa-Agona relations and of European colonialism. The last quarter of the seventeenth century in particular provides us with the
background to some of the almost insoluble political problems
which are endemic in the structure and organization of the Agona
state today. In 1928 and again in 1931, as we shall have occasion to
discuss, the consequences of the Goma-Agona war were still being
hotly debated in the state councils of the Central Region of the
Gold Coast. Let us take a look at the great war between Agona
and her Fante neighbors, the Sasabor war of 1693.

24. Fage, *Ghana*, pp. 52–53.

The Causes of the Sasabor War

In a very important sense, the Sasabor war was Nyarko Eku's personal battle. For the history of the Agona people, like the history of the Ashanti at the same period, was the history of its first king and founder of their respective states. Nyarko Eku founded the Agona state; Osei Tutu, the Ashanti state. Brown, writing on the Agona under the heading "Sasabor War," proclaims in the initial paragraphs, "The famous King Nyaku-Eku of Agona, like the renowned Osei Tutu of Asianti [Ashanti] was born as a result of a propitiatory sacrifice to Eku, the national god of the Agonafu, after which he was named, for his mother called Tutuwa was well nigh becoming barren when he was born." [25] No one knows exactly when Nyarko Eku (or Nyarko Kweku, as he was familiarly known) became the king of the Agona. What is known is that before Nyarko Eku, the Agona state as it is presently organized on the basis of ten divisions, or chiefdoms, and *adikuro* — that is, villages with headchiefs — did not exist. And even with him, it was not until after the Sasabor war that the state became more and better organized. Even so, today there is much uncertainty in Agona about where the seat of the paramount chief should be and about the relative seniority of the component divisions.

In this connection I find the evidence of Kofi Agyekum, the principal spokesman for the Nsaba *oman*, before the Bewes Commission very interesting and suggestive despite the fact that it is mostly discounted and dismissed, especially by the supporters of the Nyakrom claim.[26]

In the Bewes Report of 1931, to which frequent references will be made in the course of my presentation, Kofi Agyekum, speaking for Nsaba Oman, contends that Boaba Asiedu was the first chief of Nsaba. At this time there was no omanhene of Agona, which is the same as saying that there was no Agona State. Nobody knows when Boaba Asiedu ruled over Nsaba; however, Nyarko Eku had not

25. E. J. P. Brown, *Gold Coast and Asianti Reader* (Cape Coast: 1921), 1:143–48.
26. See Bewes Report, 1931, S.N.A. Papers, Ghana National Archives. The Commission was set up in 1931 under G. P. Bewes to inquire into the Nsaba-Nyakrom dispute. It must be pointed out that, because of the division in Agona, it is extremely difficult, if not impossible, to get a true and accurate picture of Agona history. The claims of Nyakrom are bound to be dismissed as easily as those of Nsaba, for obvious politico-economic and prestige reasons.

come to Agona. At this time, Agona consisted of isolated villages
without a paramount chief claiming allegiance of all the villages. We
could infer that the villages were ruled by headmen or chiefs
who were most likely the founders, or the descendants of the founders, of the villages. The point which I find particularly interesting
is the assertion by Agyekum (Bewes Report) that when the Ashanti
were about to fight the Agona (we may conveniently take this to
mean the arrival of Nyarko Eku and his group in the middle of the
seventeenth century), Boaba Asiedu "gathered the Agona people
together, gave them guns and stones [ammunition] and other things
for war; after this war he was made the Omanhene."

It is possible, and in fact it seems to have been the case, that
Boaba Asiedu had tried to unify the scattered and semi-autonomous
Agona in an effort to resist the invasion by Nyarko Eku and his
Ashanti conquerors. When Nkum was destroyed, it looks as if the
Agona, instead of going to war against Nyarko Eku, submitted to
him. Whereupon all, or most of, the ten villages — Nsaba, Swedru,
Kwanyako, Asafo, Duakwa, Abodom, Bobikuma, Kwaman, Nkum,
and Nyakrom — came under Nyarko and their headmen were made
the *safohene* or *dekohene* (captains) to Nyarko Eku.

What this means is that the state was organized on a military
basis and, except for attacks on Agona, when these headmen fought
under Nyarko Eku, and except for the annual tribute to Nyarko
Eku, the villages were in the main autonomous. It was not until
after the Sasabor war, however, that the state structure became
somewhat crystallized. Before this war, Nsaba, which lay within the
important trade route between Winneba and Kumasi, was responsible for supplying the king, at the time of the annual festival, with
a bathing sponge. The name *Nsaba* (*sa-boroe*) means literally "a
place where sponge is beaten."

The immediate causes of the Sasabor war were the nefarious
practices carried on by the Agona, on the orders of Nyarko Eku, of
plundering Fante villages, man-stealing, and waylaying Gomoa
traders and travelers, taking their goods, and beheading them.
These human heads, considered trophies, were shown to Nyarko's
infant sons with the message, according to Reindorf, "these are thy
toys, grow up and play with them." [27] The Gomoa Assin, angered
by these continual depredations and Agona atrocities, decided to

27. Reindorf, *History of the Gold Coast*, p. 63.

wage war against the Agona. The Gomoa Assin were supported by Fante forces not only from Assin but from Adjumako, Abora, Kurentsi, Ekumfi, Enyan and Nkusukum, and hence the name Sasabor — that is *san, san Borbor* Fante — involving literally all Fante states.

Kusa Adu of Gomoa was the commander of the allied Fante forces. After a fierce battle, the Agona were defeated and Nyarko Eku, the king of the Agona, fled, taking refuge with an Akwamu friend. It should be remembered that Nyarko had in the past executed the son of the Akwamu king for having committed adultery with one of his wives. Here, in vengeance, Nyarko was murdered in cold blood — it is said that he was cut to pieces when having a bath (Alfred Hitchcock's *Psycho* come alive) and that his dismembered body was taken to the Akwamu king. Oduro Tibo of Assin, hearing this, sent his men to Akwamu to demand the body. Akwamu refused to hand over the body to Tibo, so Kusa Adu and Tibo, with their forces, attacked and defeated Akwamu, and the body of Nyarko was taken. One story has it that the various parts of Nyarko's body were distributed among the Fante chiefs.

On their way home from the Akwamu battle, the Gomoa were again attacked by the Agona, whom they once more defeated with heavy losses. Many captives, mostly women, including Agona *adehye*, were taken by the Fante. The children of many of these captured women were therefore reared in Fante states. The Agona were obliged to negotiate for peace. Reindorf indicates that "a meeting was held at which the Agona were severely reprimanded and Yaw Minta, an *utter foreigner*, was placed *on the stool* of Agona" (my italics).[28] Reindorf's statement is indeed misleading, and confuses the facts.

First, it is grossly misleading to describe Yaw Minta as an "utter foreigner." It is true that Yaw Minta had come from Akim Abuakwa State to Osonase and thence to Nsaba, where he had been living for years. He may not even have taken part in the Sasabor war. It goes without saying, however, that the principle of clanship is one of the most integrative forces in Akan societies, the bonds of clanship which make the idea "foreigner" lose much of its meaning.

Thus Yaw Minta was given authority by Ahunaku, the king of Gomoa, through Kusa Adu, the former's war hero, to rule over

28. Ibid.

Agona — "to look after Agona" — on the principal ground that Ahunaku and Minta were both members of the same Asona matrilineal
clan.[29]

It is not the case, as Reindorf would have us believe, that
Minta was "placed on the stool of Agona." There was no such stool
at Nsaba. The stool of Nyarko Eku was not taken, according to my
Nyakrom informants, in the Sasabor war. What was given to Minta
as a symbol of authority by Ahunaku was a sword, which in Agona
and Akan tradition is always junior or subordinate to the stool. As
Kofi Mensah, the oman linguist in Agona State, put it when cross-
examined by the Bewes Commission (1931), "Agona people considered it a disgrace to have a sword without a stool and [so] they
made one secretly [for Minta]." The attachment of the Akan to the
stool, the symbol of life itself, is proverbial. Brown is equally wrong
in asserting that Nyarko Eku's stool and territory were given over
by Borbor Fante to Yaw Minta.[30] Nyarko Eku's stool was safely hidden in the course of the Sasabor war and was never taken by the
Fante and therefore could never have been given to Yaw Minta.[31]

In return for being given power to rule over Agona State from
Nsaba instead of from the old seat, Nyakrom, Yaw Minta had to
render annual homage by offering tribute in kind, to wit, firewood,
plantains, yams, sponges, oil, eggs, mortar and pestle, snails, and
sheep to Assin at the annual festival of Ahunaku. This practice went
on, according to my informants, the elders of Nyakrom, from about
1693, when Nyarko was shamefully defeated and Minta was given
authority over Agona, till 1874, when slavery was abolished. Let us

29. It should be mentioned that M. Fortes in "Kinship and Marriage among
the Ashanti," in *African Systems of Kinship and Marriage*, edited by A. P.
Radcliffe-Brown and D. Forde (London: Oxford University Press, 1950);
Busia, *Position of the Chief*; R. S. Rattray in *Ashanti* (Oxford: The Clarendon
Press, 1923); and many others have noted and discussed the importance of clan
membership as a unifying factor in the political system of the Akan. Fortes, for
instance, points out (p. 260) that "chiefs who belong to the same clan call
one another 'brother' and this is not a mere title of courtesy. . . . These ties
are thought of as holding between chiefdoms [one may add states] — the
stools . . . and they often in the past formed the basis of concerted political
action."

30. Brown, *Gold Coast and Asianti Reader*, p. 148.

31. In his evidence before the Bewes Commission, Osekyere III, gyasehene
of Gomoa Assin, indicates that in the course of the war Nyarko Eku's sister
Anobea and other members of the royal family sought asylum at Akim Manso,
from where Anobea was later taken and married to one Osan of Assin. It is
highly probable that Nyarko's stool was hidden at Akim Manso.

listen to the story in the words once again of Kofi Mensah, the Agona state linguist before the Bewes Commission:

Q. What is the authority in the Agona State, a State sword or a stool?
A. A sword.
Q. Where is the sword given by Kusa Adu?
A. It is still at Nsaba.
Q. If Agona was serving Nsaba, then the authority came from Assin?
A. When the English Government came, liberty was established everywhere.
Q. Explain this. What is the main cause [why] you stopped serving Assin?
A. English Government abolished slavery.

We should note here that the ordinance for the abolition of slavery was passed in 1874. In 1899 the Agona state was finally declared independent of Gomoa by the colonial government, when all pretentions to the paramountcy over Agona by Kojo Nkum, king of the Gomoa state at the time, ceased to be recognized.[32]

With the freeing of the Agona from the Gomoa yoke in 1874–99, the paramountcy should have reverted to the original, ante bellum seat – that is, Nyakrom. This did not happen until some unfortunate events forced Agona chiefs to withdraw their allegiance from the Nsaba stool in 1931.

The present stool at Nsaba is stated by the Agona oman to have come into existence when, as we saw earlier, the Agona oman thought it proper to add a stool to Yaw Mintah's sword. At Nyakrom, there is also the ancient paramount stool of Nyarko Eku which the oman of Agona presumably served from about 1660 or earlier, till the Sasabor war of 1693. It is very important to remember these two facts – the existence of two paramount stools in Agona – for they are pivots around which the political conflicts in Agona today

32. In the S.N.A. minutes of 1899, the following notes appear: "King Kudjo Inkoom Assin Gomoah – 25th September, 1899, claiming to be King Paramount of the district of Aguna. . . . His Excellency in a letter to the King 12th October, 1899, refuses to recognize the claim, he warned that any action to assert rights over the country of Agona will be sternly repressed. . . ." Again, "In a letter to His Excellency . . . the King of Gomoah said . . . that . . . [in] ancient times kings and chiefs have [had] their own way to manage their court matters and other purposes, but now as the world has so opened [modernized] . . . anything we do, we have to learn [follow] the British Government, for fear, that we may not put ourselves in trouble." Here we get an insight into one of the bases of colonial authority – the fear of physical coercion or superior force.

revolve. The Bewes Commission of 1931 (whose report shall be examined in some detail later on), on the basis of the evidence before
it, recommended that, since the majority of the Agona wished to go
back to serve Nyakrom instead of Nsaba and since there is nothing
in customary law which prevented such a transfer, the paramount
authority given to Nsaba (and symbolized by a stool) by the Agona
oman could be withdrawn.[33] Nsaba then automatically becomes subordinate to the stool of Nyakrom instead of vice versa. Nsaba was
never to accept a subordinate position in the state. The story of this
intransigent stance taken by Nsaba is described in the next section
and in the following chapters.

The Paramountcy, Personal Rule, and the Agona Chiefdoms

So far, in sketching out some of the major issues in Agona political
development, I have concentrated on the personal rule of Nyarko
Eku, whose "despotism and tyrannous rule," and plundering of European forts at Simpa (Winneba) and Apam, had antagonized not
only his own subjects, but his Fante and Efutu neighbors and had
eventually led to the Sasabor war in the last decade of the seventeenth century. But Nyarko was not to be the first or the last Agona
king or chief to have been highhanded and, in a sense, tyrannous.
The descendants of, or successors to, Yaw Minta behaved no better.
As a matter of fact, it was the gradual but persistent misrule of the
paramount chiefs of Nsaba, accompanied by deterioration of interchiefdom relations, particularly between Nsaba and Nyakrom, with
each claiming the hegemony of the Agona state, and between
Nsaba and Nkum, Abodom, Swedru, Kwanyako, Asafo, Bobikuma,
Kwaman, and Duakwa, that finally led to the withdrawal of allegiance by Nkum and the others from the Nsaba stool in 1931.

It is significant to note that the Nsaba-Nyakrom struggle for tribal
leadership, the conflict "of the sword and the stool," produced division in Agona as one might expect. A few stood by Nsaba, while
many of the others supported Nyakrom, on a basis ranging from
personal interests and ambitions, clanship or lineage ties, and bribery, to threats and physical coercion. At times any one chiefdom,

33. In fact, the Nyakrom case is similar to that of the paramount authority of
Gomoa, which was given to Kusa Adu also during the Sasabor war on the decision of the oman but was later taken away from him by the oman and transferred back to the stool occupied by Ahunaku, then ohene of Budu Atta.

say Swedru, might be internally divided, as was in fact the case, half or nearly half of its people siding with Nsaba, the other half or so supporting Nyakrom, depending on the issues of the day, and how they perceived which side would best further their politico-economic interests.

These divisive patterns were to persist and provide much grist for the political mill of latter-day political parties which played on and exploited to the full traditional political conflicts and personal and group interests to feather their own political, if personal, nests. Both the CPP and the National Liberation Movement (NLM) were to use kinship and local conflicts in the service of nationalism and even national unity, while at the same time pursuing sectional and personal economic interests.

The Period of Regional-Tribal Integration

We have already alluded to the defeat of the Akra in 1702 by Akwamu, a defeat which had as one of its purposes the denial of any access of the Akim to the coast. In the 1730s the Akim, under the leadership of Firempong, sought the help of the Gomoa, the "overlords" of the Agona at this time, and encamped at Nyakrom, the ancient Agona capital. The Akim-Gomoa alliance proved effective and Akwamu was crushed. This was the period of the beginning of the rise of the Ashanti nation under Osei Tutu and Opoku Ware, a rise to power which was to force the Fante states to come together to forge a united front to counter Ashanti aggression. The Ashanti wars, which ended with the capture of Yaa Asantewa, the "Jeanne d'Arc of Ashanti," in 1900, were to bring a new kind of political and economic integration first by regionalizing political-territorial groups.

For a whole century — 1800–1900 — the growth of Ashanti power threatened everybody in the Gold Coast, particularly the coastal Fante. The Ashanti (Colonial Reports) molested traders, failed to keep open the roads to the coast, disrupted trade, and endangered the peace of the land. It is important to stress again one crucial feature of political relations among the Akan. None of the kingdoms of Akwamu, Denkyera, Ashanti, in that order, attempted any permanent occupation of the lands under their rule as a result of conquest, nor did the kings establish in the conquered states any effective administration beyond exacting annual tributes in kind and in men, women, and children, or being ready to fight in the wars of the conqueror states.[34] The most kings were prepared to do was to march against any tributary state which defaulted in the annual tribute or rebelled against their sovereignty, both of which meant the same thing — the loss of revenue and power. It is clear that political rulers were interested in power because of the control it gave them over wealth and other material resources — including, of course, services — in the nineteenth century, over trade and commerce, and the coveted royalties.

In the day-to-day administration of any state or even the components of the state, the state enjoyed unparalleled autonomy. We have already seen how the defeat of the Agona by Gomoa in 1693 led to only one significant change in the management of the affairs in Agona — that is, the establishment of tributary relations between the two states and the transfer of the Agona capital from Nyakrom to Nsaba under the leadership of Yaw Minta, an Akim man of the Asona clan. This arrangement, of course, made "foreign rule" relatively tolerable.

From about 1806 onward, under the constant threat of Ashanti invasion, the coastal tribes, mainly the Fante and including the Agona, who were still under the Gomoa-Fante, looked to the British for protection, protection to enable them to engage freely in their very rewarding material pursuits. The British, incidentally, also saw their main opportunity for gain in preventing the disruption of trade that would result from an Ashanti invasion. The Agona claim they were engaged, along with the Fante, in a series of battles or wars against the Ashanti, namely, Nsamakow, 1824; Dodowa, 1826; Akantamasu, 1854; Bobikuma, 1863–64; and the 1873–74 war. It is clear, however, from the accounts that their performances left much to be desired.[35] In the Ashanti battle of 1873–74, fought over the exchange of forts between the British and Dutch and involving the Elmina "castle," the chief of Nyakrom, Yamfo Eyisa, was taken captive by the Ashanti. This capture led to the famous Eyisanku oath of the Agona.

In 1826, when Osei Yaw marched against the coastal tribes, we

34. In fact, until Europeans began to prospect for minerals and to work mines and cocoa was introduced as a cash crop, lands did not have much economic value beyond providing for subsistence livelihood for the population and rent for the chiefs.

35. See Reindorf, *History of the Gold Coast*; Claridge, *History of the Gold Coast.*

learn that that Kwamena Asomaning, chief of Nsaba and king of the Agona, and his captains prepared themselves against the Ashanti.[36] The Agona later joined the other coastal tribes — Ga, Akuapem, Fante, Assin, and Denkyera — who combined to form the left wing, under Kwadwo Tibo, of the grand allied troops of the south. But the Agona were to let the side down, for, as Reindorf puts it, Kwamena Asomaning, "who could easily have captured the King of Asante [Ashanti] was coward enough to permit him to escape, saying 'One should not allow himself to be overrun by an army of Asantes [Ashanti].'"[37] The Agona king fled with his men, taking shelter under the shade of a huge tree whence he saw the capture of the wives and other relatives of the Ashanti king. Writing on the Agona in 1824, Collier, MacCarthy, et al., said that "personal courage is certainly not a striking feature in their character."[38] Again, in 1863, the Agona were routed at Bobikuma (S.N.A. Papers, 1928). This produced the great oath of Yaw Duodu I, their king, who lost his life — "Yaw Duodu Kwasida."[39]

At this juncture, we may summarize in a statement or two the main issues in the history of the Akan people. First, we note that leadership in these societies was highly personalized. In all the wars briefly discussed here, the purpose is to get the chief-captain who immediately controlled the tribal forces under him. Thus when, in 1826, the king of Agona fled the field, his army collapsed with him. This throws another light on military formation and logistics. Where various tribes combined in an allied army under one supreme commander against other allied tribes or states, each of the component tribes fought under and obeyed commands directly from its own tribal captain or king and not from the supreme leader of the combined forces.

The political organization of the kingdom was not highly centralized, despite increasing efforts at centralization for purposes of

36. Reindorf, *History of the Gold Coast*, pp. 200–202.
37. Ibid.
38. Sir G. R. Collier, Sir C. MacCarthy, et al. *Agoona Country in West African Sketches: Compiled from the Reports of Sir. G. R. Collier, Sir MacCarthy and Other Official Sources* (London: L. B. Seeley and Son, 1824). Mimeographed at the Institute for African Studies, University of Ghana, Legon, June 1963.
39. Akan oaths refer to dramatic incidents in the history of the people, in this case the Agona, and often to a calamitous military defeat, allusion to which is a serious offense because it makes the ancestors angry and threatens the well-being of all the people. It was an important sanction wielded by the chief.

trade and economic control. The component units, especially those in the outlying areas, enjoyed relative freedom from central control. It looks as if allegiance was based primarily on a combination of fear of superior force and opportunistic self-interest. Allegiance was consequently fickle. No wonder chiefs spent at least some of their time marching against "rebellious" states. Thus, we find Kusa Adu, now Dade Adu, who had given to Yaw Minta after the Gomoa war authority to "look after Agona," marching against the latter, his subject, in the middle of the eighteenth century, when he refused to render the annual tribute and continued the nefarious occupation of man-stealing and plundering of the Fante and Ga states.[40]

Again, we note the operation of three principles or criteria on which tribal leadership was recruited in Agona, namely, kinship, clanship, and appointment. Thus, Yaw Minta, like Kusa Adu, partly achieved his position and partly got it by ascription-membership of the Asona matri-clan. Finally, we see the capacity of the various states to come together on a regional basis — that is, combine for action to protect themselves and their material interests. This ability to submerge past hostilities and forget past atrocities in the interest of material well-being is perhaps the strongest and also the most reliable link in Akan political development. Past conflict is never a hindrance to progressive political-economic integration.

THE EUROCOLONIAL PERIOD IN AGONA HISTORY

The period between the 1660s and 1900 was dominated by the relationship between Agona and her neighbors, expressed in fierce intertribal wars which were really wars fought over the control of trade and commerce and economic resources and generated by the contact with Europe. The first quarter of the twentieth century, however, the period of effective colonial rule in the Gold Coast, signalized decades of relative external or intertribal peace during the Pax Britannica, and great interchiefdom or intrastate disputes and conflicts, again over the control of economic resources. The later period was marked by extensive socioeconomic changes, especially because of the introduction in 1879 of cocoa as a cash crop. Thereafter, lands ceased to be a free economic factor; they now had economic value, a price. Little wonder then that in Agona, as elsewhere in the Gold Coast, the disputes were mainly over land, over

40. Reindorf, *History of the Gold Coast*, p. 92.

hegemony of the state, over chieftaincy, which meant over land and its resources. The disputes were over the control of local taxes or rates, of court fines and fees; in fact, over the very survival of the state, as the state itself became drawn into more extensive and sometimes new networks of political, administrative, social, and economic relations.

In considering this later period, we are in fact looking *mutatis mutandis* at the changing political and economic organization of the Agona. We have already alluded to the evolution of the Agona state from relatively independent and isolated groups of villages, based mainly on matrilineal descent and under lineage-elder headmen, to something approaching a full-fledged state in the last half of the seventeenth century. Let us now examine in some detail the main features of the Agona state.

THE AGONA POLITICAL SYSTEM

Perhaps we should begin with Claridge's account, which, on the basis of the evidence carefully collected by me in the field, cannot be seriously maintained, though it is not so farfetched as it sounds; it is even possible.[41] I describe it here now because of the implied emphasis on the matrilineal principle and its plausibility as mythical justification for matrilineal inheritance and succession. In fact, there is a similar legend in Ashanti which made the first rulers women until some unavoidable problems in war time related to menstruation forced the women to hand over their political authority to their brothers.

According to Claridge, the Agona, from about 1694 to 1699, were ruled by a queen, "which had been their custom from time immemorial." The queen, perhaps like the *mujaji* in Lovedu, Transvaal, was not allowed to marry, but sought male slaves whenever she pleased as paramours. Her eldest daughter, who succeeded to the stool, was given a similar privilege as soon as she attained a marriageable age. These slave-paramours were resold whenever their mistresses grew tired of them. They lost their heads if they were caught intriguing with other women. Naturally, all the female children were kept, and any males born to the queen or to the heiress-apparent were sold into slavery. A reference to the chiefly succession in Nyakrom from about 1660 to the present is enough to dis-

41. Claridge, *History of the Gold Coast*, p. 145.

miss on empirical grounds the claims of Claridge (see figure 3 for list of chiefs).

The description of the Agona political system by Collier, Mac-Carthy, et al., is more relevant and realistic and merits a lengthy quotation.[42] Describing the "Agoona Country," the authors had this to say of the political organization:

The government and political institutions and laws of Agoona [Agona] resemble in a great degree those of the Fantees [Fante]. . . . Sometimes the . . . chiefs of petty districts are hereditary; in others elective [elected by the people]. These chiefs occasionally assume despotic power, but in general they do not retain it long, due to revolts and expulsions.
The chiefs are aided in the administration of the laws by a kind of judicial senate, the members of which, called *Pynims* [*mpanyin*] (as among the Fantees) are chosen by the people from among the elders of the district, and it is their office to hear and decide causes and pronounce the sentence of the law.

They go on to point out that the elders "have a share in all fines and forfeitures. The pynims are the only depositories of the laws. They have frequent meetings at which laws are rehearsed to enable them to transmit them." They again indicate that crimes were punishable by a fine or slavery. Murder, the penalty for which was death (though the penalty was commutable by the payment of seven slaves), was of rare occurrence. The mechanism of the ordeal by poison was available to the Agona. The "ordeal called doom [*odum?*] consisted in administering to the accused the bark of a poisonous tree. If the accused retained it on his stomach, he was pronounced guilty; if otherwise, innocent." Refusal to submit to the ordeal was tantamount to admission of guilt.

We learn from the authors also that the elders, "pynims," were both judge and jury and are supposed to have been very accessible to bribes, with the result that no person "who was liberal of his gifts was likely to be found guilty." The authors cleverly and realistically link religion and politics. First they show that religion

consists almost entirely in the superstitious dread of suffering from some malign influence; and in the faith they repose in the fetishes or charms which are furnished by their fetishmen or priest for the purpose of averting the dreadful evil. The people in general do not seem to engage in any kind of worship [except ancestor worship] — on certain days they abstain from their ordinary employments in accordance with custom. . . . the

42. Collier, MacCarthy, et al., *Agoona Country*, pp. 58–63.

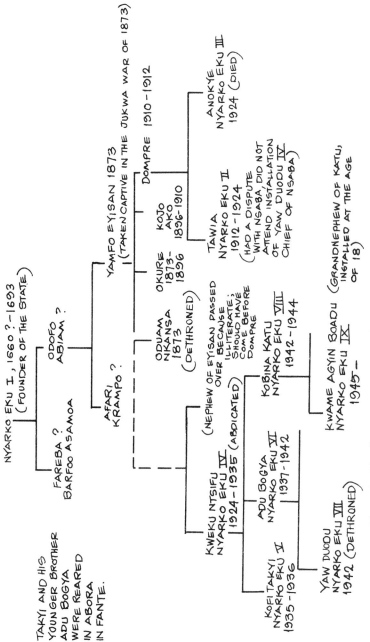

Fig. 3. Chiefly Succession in Nyakrom. Succession was from brother to brother and in the absence of brothers to nephew (sister's son).

Fetishmen engage in certain forms of worship and religious ceremonies.
They constitute an order of priests. [They are] supposed to hold communion with the demon or Fetish and to obtain from him the knowledge
which is requisite for the exercise of their profession which is to solve
the doubts and perplexities of their followers, and to furnish them with
the means to avert evil either actual or possible. Presents were made to
Fetish by votaries and *Fetishmen connect themselves with persons in
power and are often serviceable in strengthening the government and
enforcing obedience to laws,* since priests were very influential and respected even when government [chiefs?] has fallen into disrepute. [*Italics
mine.*][43]

I quote the authors at some length because they provide us with
one of the few, and one of the better, accounts of the social, political, economic, and religious systems of the Agona in the nineteenth
century. Their description is particularly useful today when, as I
discovered in my field work, most of the priestly rituals have fallen
into desuetude and been forgotten. Although the authors had much
insight into the operation of the political system, a few of their contentions were either mistaken or misleading. I propose to clarify
some of these.

The political organization of the Agona, like that of the other
Akan peoples, is primarily the organization into ranks of stools,
swords, and people directly related by descent who occupy these
stools and wield the swords. The stool first and the sword second
have always remained through history — precolonial, colonial, and
postcolonial — the symbol of indigenous authority and the source of
religious sanctions and economic and material well-being of the
people, the source of the good life. Whatever the occasion, in success or defeat in war, in the acceptance or rejection of individual
chiefs, as we have seen, the stool is the most stable element, the one
socially, politically and morally integrative factor in Akan, and
hence in Agona life.

As Adu puts it, "chiefs come and go, but the stool lives on." Yet
the occupant of the stool is the "head of a great big family of which
his subjects are members. He is their ruler and their judge, their
counsellor and their moral guide, a tower of strength in time of
trouble and their captain in time of war. He is all-powerful (Otum-

43. There is no doubt that chiefs, aided by fetish priests, did manipulate religious and social taboos to maintain or further their economic and political ambitions or interests.

fuo), a conquerer (Osagyefuo), courageous (Katakyie), a benefactor (Daasebre), a kind master (Odeefuo), and wise (Nana)." [44]

The chief, in a word, had administrative, judicial, religious, politico-military and economic functions, functions which were all
oriented toward the primary goal of achieving peace and prosperity
and the material well-being of the people — that is, politics justifies itself in terms of economics, the good life — the promotion of economic
prosperity and abundance. This point should be stressed because
one assumption I maintain throughout this analysis is the remarkable continuity in the political orientation of Ghanaians. In the 1960s,
Ghanaians were still judging their political structure and process
through the glasses of economic satisfaction. This is one of the main
reasons why only very well endowed stools — for example, Akim
Abuakwa and Kumasi — can still command and maintain to a remarkable degree the allegiance of their subjects in a rapidly changing socioeconomic environment. These rich stools, able to dispense
patronage, are more likely to become centers of conservative traditional opposition to the new forces and their upholders. Tradition is
not necessarily against change; it resists change only when change
is used to destroy the economic base of traditional power, privilege,
and high prestige. Tradition operated to insure the economic and
social preeminence of chiefs and elders.

THE POLITICO-MILITARY ORGANIZATION

The organization of stools and swords in Agona is nothing but a
military formation based on the logistics of war developed by the
people. Political organization in Agona is ipso facto military organization. The Agona state, like the Ashanti, Fante, Akim, and other
Akan states, has the following military division: [45]

1. *Adonten* ("the carrier of the foot of the Omanhene") — main
   body
2. *Nifa* — right wing
3. *Benkum* — left wing
4. *Kyidom* — rear guard reinforcement
5. *Gyase* — bodyguard of the omanhene.

The Agona further divide adonten into two, and this may be a

44. A. L. Adu, *The Role of Chiefs in the Akan Social Structure: An Essay*
(Accra: Government Printing Department, 1949), p. 18.
45. See Busia, *Position of the Chief*; Rattary, *Ashanti*.

slight departure from the general Akan model: the senior (*adonten panyin*), and the junior (*adonten kuma*). The same goes for kyidom: *kyidom panyin* and *kyidom kuma*. Over each of the above five divisions is placed an ohene (chief), namely, *adontenhene, nifahene, benkumhene,* and so forth. Other ranks found in Agona are *mankrado,* the keeper of the padlock of the state and the chief supporter of the stool of the omanhene; *tufuhene,* head of all the fighting men, or the *asafomma* of a state or division (the division is a chiefdom); *odikuro,* the headman of a village; and finally *supi,* the principal captain of each town company — the *asafo.*[46]

It is necessary at this point to emphasize that the politico-military structure at the state level must not be confused with the slightly different organization at the lower division, town or village, levels. Each of the ten component divisions of the Agona state has a somewhat different politico-military structure. This is partly due to the differences in the origins, size, and growth of the towns and villages.[47] What is said about the internal organization of the divisions or wings goes for the asafo system, which, again, should not be confused with the military basis of the chiefdoms.

THE AGONA ASAFO ORGANIZATION

Before the Pax Britannica, the safety of Agona divisions — that is, individual towns and villages — largely depended on the efficiency of its military organization. We have already observed how, in fact, all the Agona *ahenfo* were initially (and to a limited extent still are) the *asafohenfo* of the omanhene, in the remote past of Nyarko Eku I (and in the immediate present of Nyarko Eku IX) and in war time had to take their proper places, as such. The companies (asafo) — that is, the military organization of the towns — acquired a very prominent position in the body politic. A discussion of the political system of one of these towns or divisions (Swedru) in the next chapter will clarify this contention. In any case, even in recent times, Nkrumah in his *Guide to Party Action*[48] suggested seriously

46. In Agona there are at present two Adikuro — Mankrong and Otenkorang.
47. Here an intensive comparative study of the ten divisions making up the Agona state may be particularly fruitful, not only in demonstrating the range of variation but also in providing new information about the early political history of the Agona people.
48. Kwame Nkrumah, *Guide to Party Action* (Accra: Government Printing Department, 1962).

that "the Asafu companies . . . should be properly uniformed and perform their traditional role in a modern manner," an example of a conscious adaptation of institutions to changing functions.[49]

The asafo or company system, like the abusua (or *ebusua*) or clan system, is found among all the Akan groups in Ghana. It is, it seems, more fully developed in the Central Region, especially among the Fante. There is no town or village in Agona without it. Despite the fact that one hears in Agona many and various names referring to asafo groups, in point of fact there are really two main companies in each Agona division — *dontsin*, a senior group, and *twafo*, a junior group, although they have different names in the different towns, as shown in table 1. The asafomma of the smaller towns or villages form part of the company or companies of which-ever of the towns they serve.

TABLE 1 THE AGONA ASAFO COMPANIES

Town or Division	Dontsin	Twafo
Nyakrom	Adanse	Kyirem
Nsaba	Dontsin	Twafo
Swedru	Apegya	Nkrantwia
Abodom	Nkrantwia	Kyirem
Asafo	Amferefo	Kyirem
Kwanyako	Nkrantwia	Kyirem
Bobikuma	Nkrantwia	Kyirem
Duakwa	Nkrantwia	Adanse
Kwaman	Nkrantwia	Amferefo
Nkum	Nkrantwia	Amferefo

NOTE: The S.N.A. note of 1929 from the assistant D.C., Swedru, mentions other names, including Akomfodi, Apisimaka, Kyirem, and Minsuro for Nsaba; Akomfodi and Dontsin for Nyakrom; Nkumansa and Dontsin for Kwanyako; Amferefo for Bobikuma; Dontsin for Duakwa; and Kyirem for Nkum.

Before going on to matters of organization, we may pause for a moment to consider in general terms the company system. Every Agona (and for that matter every Akan) belongs to some asafo on the father's side (patrilineally) as he or she belongs to an abusua on the mother's side (matrilineally). This fact has led anthropologists to argue whether or not the Akan, in this case the Agona, Fante, or Ashanti, is truly unilineal or double-unilineal in their descent pat-

49. C. E. Black, *The Dynamics of Modernization: A Study in Comparative History* (New York: Harper and Row, 1967), p. 8. In Swedru, for instance, asafo drums are now beaten on the soccer field to cheer on the locally based Agona Fankobaa football team in the national league competition.

terns.[50] Whatever their eventual conclusion, the information available to me, coupled with my own observation, seems to suggest that
matrilineal ties are definitely stronger than patrilineal ones in most
social situations. One literally gets bored with frequent references
by the Agona to the abusua, *mena* (mother), and *mbaamu* (the
women's section of the traditional household).[51] The importance of
uterine descent derives from the fact that it defines and controls
vital property and political relations.

The asafo as a social institution is made up of both men and
women — the children of one man, in the same way that the abusua
is composed of men and women, this time children of one woman.
But as a politico-military institution for offensive and defensive purposes, it consists mainly of all males capable of bearing arms. In
Swedru, however, it was the function of a priestess, the descendant
of the clan sister of the founder of the town, who performed the ritual which insured success of the company in time of war. The senior company is *apegya*, whose war god, *bosom a wode tu sa* — that
is, the god under whose aegis wars were fought — is Okyin Kwesi,
in the "custody" of the Tufuhene. In time of war, the junior
company — *nkrantwia* — stayed behind at home and was under the
ritual protection of the *akomfode* priestess.

Each asafo has its own officers and distinctive emblems and flags,
which in Swedru in recent times are paraded only during the annual *Akwambo* festival or on the death of an important member.[52]
Although in time of war or crisis the Agona asafomma would march
in two bodies — dontsin and twafo — the internal organization of
each of these companies was in accordance with the towns —
divisions or chiefdoms — composing it.

Each town has a *tufuhene* whose function is the provision and
control of ammunition of war but who has no disciplinary powers
over the companies.[53] The tufuhene has a stool, occupies a promi-

50. Fortes, *"Kinship and Marriage"*; Christensen, *Double Descent among
the Fanti.*
51. *Wona wu a na wo abusua asa* ("if your mother dies, you have no lineage kin left") is often heard.
52. The Akwambo festival, celebrated in late August, commemorates the
beating of the path and the establishment of the posuban — the military
outpost — by the first asafo who accompanied the founder of the town or division.
53. In Swedru, the tufuhene, Nana Yeboa, is the head of all able to bear
arms — that is, the two asafo groups.

nent position in town, and is in charge of the *posuban* (post of the asafo company). His office is hereditary "to a specified patrilineage"; but the asafomma of Swedru have a decisive voice in his election and deposition. In Swedru, as we have observed, he has in his custody the asafo *bosom* ("god"), Okyin Kwesi, who is carried in a brass basin and paraded at Akwambo festivals.

Next in rank to the tufuhene is the asafo supi, whose functions are mainly disciplinary. One young Agona man summarized his duty thus: "He is just like the policeman." He is seconded by a *safohene* whose duties appear to be the same except that he takes his orders from the supi.[54] The tufuhene has important functions relating to the enthronement and dethronement of the adontenhene. For instance, he swears the oath of allegiance to the new chief on behalf of the people. In more recent times, in Swedru, any "foreigner" — that is, non-Agona — who demonstrates by his individual contributions to local development that he has a strong sense of civic duty is made a supi by the adontenhene with the consent of the tufuhene, honoris causa. Thus Bandeley, a Fante-Yoruba and a former hotelier in Swedru, later appointed traditional member in the new local council, and R. A. Chahal, a Lebanese trader, in 1967 a member of the Town Development Committee, were both honored in the 1950s with supi status. The consequences of this act for social and political integration in the town cannot be overemphasized. This act reinforced the existing tendency among "aliens" to identify with Swedru. It made the foreigner feel more at home and made both himself and others consider him an integral part of the town.

The symbols of office of both the supi and the *asafohene* are similar — a captain's whip and a dagger — longer in the case of the senior, shorter in the case of the junior officer. Both offices are hereditary, but here again the asafomma have the deciding voice in their election and deposition. In Swedru, there is one supi and one asafohene for each of the four traditional wards of the town, so that the town and wards — quarters (*bron*) — retain their identity within the companies. The Agona say *agua biara abaa da ho*, meaning "every stool has asafohene," symbolized by the "whip."

In control of the whole Agona company organization was an officer called *Obatan* ("mother"), who had no stool and was chosen

54. It should be noted that in some Fante towns the supi is the chief captain and he keeps the ammunition. The asafohene is the junior captain.

from a family in Swedru by an electoral body composed of the various supi and asafohene. This body may also depose him at the request of the companies. He was the general commander in time of war, provided ammunition, and presided at any company meeting. This office corresponds to that of tufuhene in other Akan states — for example, Oguaa — but the Agona are definite in stating that the title attached to the office is "Obatan." Other important officers of the Agona asafo included the *asafompanyin* (elders), *frankaatufo* (flagbearers), *akyiremma* (drummers), and *abrafo* (executioners). The military organization was certainly very complex.

It has been necessary to dwell a little longer on the asafo system for three reasons: (1) It points to the fact that before the Pax, most political decisions must have been decisions about offense and defense; political relations were also military relations. (2) A large proportion of the state "budget" must have been devoted to the provision of arms and ammunition to wage "economic" wars and to control trade and commerce in men and goods — imported consumer items and military supplies. (3) Political rights of commoners were exercised through the asafo.

THE RANKING OF AGONA CHIEFDOMS

We cannot leave the discussion of the political organization of the Agona state without at least a summary statement about the relative ranks of the individual towns or chiefdoms constituting it. I approach this subject with some trepidation. For one thing, there is so much confusion today about what division occupies what rank. Do we have one paramount chief or two *amanhene* in Agona? If one, what is the rank of Nsaba? Nsaba, which lost the paramountcy to Nyakrom in 1931 and regained it in 1958, when both Nyakrom and Nsaba were recognized by the central government as amanhene, and lost it again in 1966, felt (before it was again recognized by the NLC in 1968) that its claim was as good as any. For another, there is dispute over how the various towns originated and grew. The fact that some of the towns are wont to exaggerate their role and status in the Sasabor war adds to the general confusion.

In a memorandum relating to the Agona state, written in the 1910s, Francis Crowther, then secretary for native affairs, observed that the Agona oman comprises ten stools — Nsaba, Nyakrom,

Swedru, Abodom, Asafo, Duakwa, Kwanyako, Nkum, Kwaman, Bobikuma. He ranked the stools as shown in table 2.

He went on to state, wrongly, that the state constitution varies from the normal Twi-speaking (Akan) type in that there appears to be no stool of an odikuro. As I have said, there are two adikuro villages in Agona — namely, Otenkorang and Mankrong. He noted the smallness of the Agona state and suggested that its size accounted for the fact that to each stool are attached the privileges and duties of some office of state. It is not the size but the emphasis on military functions that accounts for that fact. He indicated, and this needs some attention, that "the relative degrees of seniority between the stools of Nyakrom and Abodom, of Kwanyaku and Nkum and of Kwaman and Bobikuma are apparently little more than ceremonial for the occupants of all the stools approach the Omanhene direct."

TABLE 2 THE RANKING OF AGONA CHIEFDOMS, 1910s

Town or Division	Status or Rank
Nsaba	Paramount
Nyakrom	Adonten
Abodom	Adonten
Swedru	Nifa
	Gyase
Asafo	Benkum
Kwanyako	Kyidom
Nkum	Kyidom
Kwaman	Tuafo
Bobikuma	Tuafo
Duakwa	Banmu (keeper of the royal cemetery)

Crowther remarks that only the omanhene is entitled to the use of a palanquin and an unlimited number of drums and horns. No subordinate chief may be borne in a palanquin. The adontenhene is entitled to two drums and two horns, and the other subordinate chiefs to one drum and one horn each. Yet Kokrodu I, the sixth chief of Swedru, who ruled probably during the last quarter of the nineteenth century, was given the following stool property:[55]

One state sword
Two horns

55. See Agona State Council Proceedings (1932), Botchey versus Domye.

One set complete Bomba drums . . .
One set of Native drums (Mpintin)
Two hammocks [palanquins?]
Two state umbrellas [etc.]

THE INTERNAL ORGANIZATION
OF THE CHIEFDOM

The Agona village, town, or chiefdom, like that of other Akan divisions, is divided into a number of quarters (bron).[56] These quarters are the original settlements of the founders. Each quarter is under a lineage or clan head whose position is hereditary in the maternal line and who possesses a family stool and comes directly under the chief of the town. In Swedru, the early *abron* are Anaafu, headed by the *tufuhene*; Owani, headed by the *mankrado*; Kubease, headed by the *gyasehene*; and Ankyease, headed by the town chief, *Swedruhene*. These and other lineage elders of the quarters — *mpanyinfo* — with other persons who may not hold a hereditary office, but are selected for their personal ability and wisdom and known as *apamfo*, form a council of advisers to the chief and members of the chiefly tribunal — that is, *begua*. Here again, we find the interplay of achievement (appointive or elective) and ascriptive (kinship) principles.[57]

The young men — *mmerante* ("commoners") — have representatives selected territorially — that is, one for each quarter — known as *mmeranteasafohene*. His office is obviously not hereditary and he is not a member of the chiefly council or tribunal. He, however, bears the *asafokyene* ("long drum") and beats the *odawuru* ("gong-gong"), by which the young men and others in the town are summoned for public services or communal labor. The ohene has his *dawurubofo*, whose duty it is to inform the public, by beating the gong-gong, about decisions taken by the council or tribunal. He, with his linguist, represents the people at various elections. The ceremonies of his own appointment show that his office is military in its inception.

CLANSHIP AND CHIEFTAINCY

We have already referred to the clan system as a unifying factor in the political organization and as an expression of the cultural unity

56. Busia, *Position of the Chief*.
57. For a similar discussion, see Rattray, *Ashanti Law and Constitution*.

of the Akan people. As Fortes correctly puts it, "The fact that there are only seven or eight clans and that one or more high-ranking chiefships are vested in each of them strengthens this effect." [58] The Agona are divided into eight exogamous clans.[59] The paramountcy has been variously vested in the Asona and Oyoko clans. The principal clans to some Agona are certainly Asona or Dwumina, Oyoko, Abrade, and Nyego. In Swedru, chiefship is vested in the Asona clan. The paramountcy was, until its transfer from Nsaba to Nyakrom, also vested in the Asona clan.

Inheritance and succession descend in the female line — that is, from brother to brother of the same mother and then to the sister's sons, preference being guided by seniority, suitability, and merit. This rule applies to all stools, whether that of a paramount chief, subchief, or the lineage head. It is not my intention here to go into land tenure in Agona except to point out that each stool holds its land independently of the paramount or of any other stool. [60]

This relative economic independence of the chiefdoms partly accounts for the relative political independence and even instability, due to the economic weakness of the center, of the component Agona divisions and their near-equality of ranks in the state. In fact any attempt on the part of the omanhene to centralize political power by controlling the economic resources is usually resisted by the component chiefdoms. This economic and political laissez faire is a major motif of Agona and even Akan political and economic relationships.[61]

The Chief and His Tribunal

Despite the relative political and economic autonomy of the various divisions, the omanhene had the principal tribunal in the state, the

58. Fortes, "Kinship and Marriage," p. 260.
59. See Christensen, *Double Descent among the Fanti*, for a detailed discussion.
60. The *Duakwahene* remarked in 1929 (Provincial Council of Chiefs, Central Province, Inquiry into Land Rent Dispute. . . .) that the lands of Nkum and Duakwa were in the past all stool lands. This was not the case in other Agona chiefdoms, where most of the lands belonged to families. For example, in the time of Kokrodu I (1921 Agona State Council Minutes), the Swedru stool had ten small parcels of scattered lands.
61. It should be mentioned in passing that the rules for land tenure in Agona are the same as those described for other Akan societies. J. B. Danquah, *The Gold Coast Akan* (London: 1945); P. C. W. Dennis, "A Note on Land Revenue and Local Government in Ghana," *Journal of African Administration* 9, no. 2 (April 1956): 85–92.

great oath *Yaw Duodu Kwasida* in the case of Nsaba, and *Eyisanku* in the case of Nyakrom being attached to his stool. But each sub-chief or chiefdom had a tribunal and cases constituted under his oath — that is, the oath attached to the stool of the subordinate chief were heard in the lesser tribunals, with the omanhene's tribunal as the appellate court. Public opinion, strong enough to be considered, according to Crowther, "an unwritten law," however, seems to have dictated that all "big cases" should immediately be taken to the omanhene's tribunal. Of course, what constituted a "big case" was something which was differently defined by the oman-hene and the other subchiefs, as is shown in particular by the disputes in the 1920s between the omanhene and his subordinate chiefs over the competence of the lesser tribunals to try certain cases. Here the main issue was the control of fees and fines deriving from adjudication. This revenue war was to lead to a deterioration of interchiefdom relations and finally to the withdrawal of allegiance by the subordinate chiefs from the paramount stool of Nsaba in 1931.

The omanhene does not exercise any direct authority over the subjects of the subordinate stools, nor does he participate in the choice of persons for election to the subordinate stools although, once elected, the latter demonstrate their submission to him by swearing an oath on the sword of state (*afona*) to serve him day and night. A similar oath is taken by the people — that is, their representatives — to the subordinate chief. The paramount chief, at the time of his election and installation, swears to serve his subjects and subchiefs by night and day and to answer to their call in times of need, and the subordinate chiefs and elders representing the people, in turn, take the same oath in a like manner.

Finally, a paramount chief communicates with the subjects of subordinate chiefs about tribal, political, or other matters only through the medium of the subordinate chief, with each chief represented by his linguist. The same procedure holds for intersubchief communication, up and down the ranks. So far, what I hope I have succeeded in doing is to present here the political evolution in broad outline in Agona — that is, at the most inclusive level of state operation. In the next chapter, I narrow down my perspective and focus on the political structure and process of one of the most important of the Agona chiefdoms — Agona Swedru.

2

THE POLITICAL EVOLUTION OF THE AGONA
The Case of Swedru

"This is my own land; I shall not move to any other place. I have become a fixed rock [*Fankobaa*]. I shall not move to any other place in preference to this humble land on which I reside." This saying is attributed to Nyarko Eku, the founder and the first omanhene of the Agona state. Nyarko's statement, like many of its kind, is pregnant with the dynamics of Agona history and is significant in its implication, at any rate, for two related reasons: it reveals the story of a long and tedious pattern of migration southward, a continuous struggle of peoples against man and nature to find a "sleeping" place, a better place to hunt, farm, trade, even to conquer a little, in order to hold on to a potentially precarious existence. It also tells a tale of economic scarcity. It is generally believed that in the past, at least, for the Akan areas of the Gold Coast, land for subsistence agriculture has been plentiful, and hence the custom of extending to strangers the privilege of clearing land for farming in return for a mere token payment.[1]

This proverbial claim needs to be modified. It is clear from Nyarko's dictum above that one major cause of migration in the past was to seek *better* land elsewhere. Nyarko Eku and his followers found it in Nyakrom. What is more, the words point to the close relationship between the economy (land and its resources) and political authority, a point of particular interest to me.[2] The nature of this relationship will be explored in the course of this chapter and the next. It must be said at once that what is true of Nyarko Eku I is even truer for Kwatutu, the founder of the chiefdom of Swedru.

1. Christensen, *Double Descent among the Fanti*, p. 11.
2. In this connection, the germinal and brilliant, if overdrawn in places, treatment by Audrey I. Richards in *Hunger and Work in a Savage Tribe* (Cleveland and New York: World Publishing, Meridian Books, 1964). pp. 140–61, and her conclusion that "the political power of the chief himself is derived very largely from the functions he performs in the economic sphere" are noteworthy.

The Agona traditional state, as we have seen (see chapter 1), is
made up of ten chiefdoms, or divisions or towns, and two adikuro
or villages. Each of the towns or villages, needless to say, has its
unique history of settlement. They were all founded at different times, if within the same broad historical period; by different,
though on occasion related, peoples; and grew at different rates.
What binds them together today, or did so in the past, has been
their common allegiance to a paramount stool, and a common language, other considerations apart. It goes without saying that in the
reconstruction of the formation of any particular Agona, or for that
matter Akan, town or village, one is handicapped by lack of much
reliable evidence.[3] What trustworthy evidence there is suggests that
the earliest inhabitants of Swedru were migrants from Tekyiman.
All the Fante claim to have migrated from Tekyiman in northwestern Ashanti about the thirteenth century; but unlike the founders of
Nyakrom, who were of the Oyoko clan, they were members of the
Asona clan. The leader of this branch of the Asona clan was Kwatutu.

Kwatutu and his group first settled at Akrodo in Fante, where
they were hit by famine and were forced to move en bloc, joining
with the Fante near Mankesim.[4] From the Mankesim area Kwatutu
and his followers, along with other unrelated groups, moved south,
because of overcrowding and the scarcity of food, to the coastal
areas near Winneba to look for a "sleeping" place.[5] Kwatutu,
finding the coast rather cold (and most probably lacking the skill to
exploit the resources in the sea) migrated farther inland to Abasa,
Osamkrom, Ekwamkrom, and Jukwa, now Gomoa areas, where he
hoped to fare a little better on subsistence agriculture.

During this period, the latter part of the seventeenth century,
there was a flourishing market at Eguabiriso, within the southern
boundary of the modern Swedru, roughly near where the Labour
Office and the Rest House are located. Eguabiriso, to which Kwatutu was to migrate a little later, like many West African markets,
was significantly not only a place for economic exchange — buying

3. Busia, *Position of the Chief.*
4. At this time, about the late seventeenth century according to my informant, a lineal descendant of Kwatutu, Mankesim, was the "head [capital] of the
Fante."
5. The Winneba (Simpa) vicinity was then peopled by a group of heterogeneous tribes — hence the name "Efutu" meaning literally, "the mixed [tribally]
group."

and selling – but also a center for adjudication and settlement of intertribal and other types of disputes. As we shall see, it was at Eguabiriso that his followers made a stool for him, made him their chief. The discovery of a virgin and resource-laden forest and the perennial supply of fresh water of the Akora River, with its possibility of river fish, less than a mile away (see figure 4), induced Kwatutu and his people, by this time including some Fante and Efutu as a result undoubtedly of intermarriage, to build a farm near the present Ankyease. Later some of Kwatutu's lineal relatives made their farm at the nearby Kubease. These were initially not permanent settlements, for Kwatutu and his group – lineal and affinal – still lived near Eguabiriso. In time, other people – this time of the lineages of the Abradzi and Twidan clans – cleared the virgin forest for farms near those of Kwatutu and his mainly Asona followers.

The Abradzi people farmed to the south of Kubease, in Anaafu, and the Twidan members occupied Owani. The general area on which these farm villages – Ankyease, Kubease, Anaafu, and Owani – stood was teeming with plantains (probably wild), the fingers of which "were as long and big as a man's arm." The owners of these farms were wont to take bunches of the plantains to the nearby market and home settlement, Eguabiriso, for sale on market days. But no individual, it is alleged, could carry more than one bunch or headload of plantain at a time on account of its tremendous weight. Soon the area of Ankyease, Kubease, Anaafu, and Owani became known as the place from which one could bear only one bunch (soa, "carry"; dur, "bunch"; and hence, Soa-dur, later Swedru) of plantain. These four farms were later to become the original settlements of Swedru town, the autochthonous abron (wards) of the town.[6]

Thus, one branch of Kwatutu's group of Asona was known as Ankyeasefo – "people under the akyea tree" (a tree like the cashew nut); the other branch, as Kubeasefo – "people under the kube

6. It should be noted that each of these abron was essentially (after the desertion of Eguabiriso) a small settlement inhabited mainly, but by no means exclusively, by the members, both male and female, of the lineages or clans concerned. The members of the lineage had their dwelling houses close together, grouped around the house of the lineage head. With successive migration of other lineages of various clans, such as, Nyego and Oyoko (see Danquah's list of clans in Christensen, *Double Descent among the Fanti*) into the Swedru area, first the bron and later the lineage itself came to be distinguished either by geography or by flora or fauna said to have been found near the first settlement of the ancestors of the lineage.

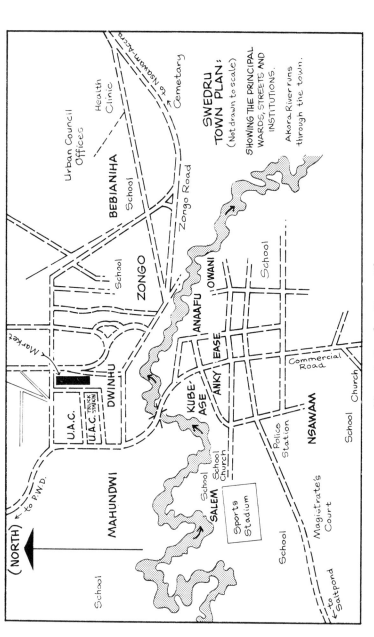

Fig. 4. Swedru Town Plan

(coconut) tree." The Abradzi people became identified by geography, *Anaafu-fo* — "people to the south"; and the Twidan by *Owani*, a word, in fact a shibboleth, meant to identify the original inhabitants as wanderers (who finally found permanent settlement). In the old days the greeting was met by the only appropriate response, *Ye atra ase*, meaning "We have settled down." The four abron, now organized under a new name, Swedru, were headed by Kwatutu, the most senior man of the Asona clan.

With the founding of the Agona state by Nyarko Eku I, which we have tentatively dated back to the early 1660s, the various village leaders of Agona became dekohene or captains of the omanhene at the level of state organization. It is fair to say that it was probably not until after the Sasabor war (see chapter 1) that the relative positions, however unstable, of the villages and towns were established.

In fact, according to my informants, it was only after the Sasabor war of 1693, fought between the Agona and the Gomoa, with its attendant dispersal and migration of people, that Kwatutu, now a tired old man, decided finally to retire to his relatively new farm-village in Swedru. Kwatutu, it is believed, was greatly disturbed by the Gomoa war, and it is even alleged that he and his followers refused to take part in the war.[7]

In the new politico-military structure of the state, the chief of Swedru (Kwatutu and later his descendants) became Nifahene (chief of the right wing) and later adontenhene (leader of the main body) and the one "carrying the foot of the oman," of the omanhene. The head chief or leader of the Kubease bron, a clan brother, was given the title of gyasehene; the subchief of Owani became the mankrado ("keeper of the lock and key of the oman"); and the leader of Anaafu became the tufuhene (see Chapter I for discussion of these offices). All these offices, except the last named, which is partly elective, are vested in specific lineages and inherited matrilineally.

It should be remembered that, as people moved into the now

7. Nsaba also claims it never supported the war. In a sense this should not be surprising. The units of the state evinced much political autonomy. Political centralization was weak. Again, to the leaders of Swedru and Nsaba, both of the Asona clan, perhaps the war was Oyoko clan war — Nyarko Eku was Oyoko; in any case, the highhanded and "tyrannous" behavior of Nyarko Eku troubled most people outside Nyakrom. Little wonder, then, that when Yaw Minta, an Asona man, was given the "paramount" chiefship of Agona, Swedru was given a prominent position in the state structure.

slowly growing settements, each bron became more and more heterogeneous in tribal and clan terms as the bron area became more
and more extended in territorial terms. It was thus not unusual to
find, say in Ankyease, the Nyego, Twidan, and members of the original Asona clan all represented there. Again, with the segmentary
lineage structure, each segment was defined in relation to other segments of a similar order by reference to common and differentiating
ancestresses.[8] This facilitated accretion to and differentiation within
lineages. In Swedru this has meant, in the case of the chiefly lineage, or lineages, that as different branches of the Asona clan arrived a little later from other places — Akwamu and Fante Abaase —
they became attached to the localized, now growing, lineage of
Kwatutu, the lineage of the first settlers; and, in fact, almost merged
socially and jurally with the latter. As my informants put it, "In the
olden days they [the other branches of the Asona abusua] all did
things together; they observed funeral taboos, rules of exogamy,
and, most important, shared funeral expenses of deceased members."
    The important thing to note about Akan clans is that the maximal
lineage — usually with a depth of eight or more generations from
the living adult members — found in any town or community is
thought of as the local branch of a widespread matrilineal clan. Yet
the members are carefully distinguished by *yafunu* — or *yem*, as the
Agona would have it — the uterine descendants of an ancestress,
about three or four generations antecedent to its living adult members, and within which category the mother's brother is the key
jural figure.[9] The maximal lineage of the Asona clan in Swedru will
therefore be considered the widest local extension of the uterine
segment and the kinship terms used in the matrilineal household
are applied to all the members of the maximal lineage. The kinship
terms are the same as in Ashanti except that *sewa*, the female member of one's father's lineage, that is, one's father's sister, is in
Swedru, among the Agona, *agyabaa* ("female father").[10] The term
abusua is applied both to the clan and to the lineage.
    The belief, still strong, is that all the lineages of a clan are the
matrilineal descendants of a single remote ancestress who, in myth

    8. Fortes, "Kinship and Marriage."
    9. Consult particularly Fortes, "Kinship and Marriage"; Rattray, *Ashanti;*
and Busia, *Position of the Chief,* for a fuller discussion of the lineage system,
which applies here.
    10. Fortes, "Kinship and Marriage."

of origin, emerged miraculously from the ground or sea. It is, no doubt, difficult to demonstrate *actual* genealogical connections of related local lineages of the same clan. Nevertheless, they all observe the same rules of exogamy and, if no suitable candidate for a lineage office can be found locally, the elders may accept a clansman from elsewhere. We have already noted the application at the state level of a variant of this rule when, after the Gomoa war, Yaw Minta was given the chiefship of the Agona state by Ahunaku on the grounds of clanship. At the local level — that is, in Swedru — the application of the principle just cited produced some of the fiercely fought out conflicts around the succession to chiefship in the late 1920s and early 1930s, as we shall soon see. Clanship, it is necessary to stress, does not automatically confer rights to property and office in a different lineage from one's own.

Brief references have already been made to the three different but localized chiefly lineages of the Asona clan: the lineage of Kwatutu, or his descendants — today the stool family of Kwame Ata or Kweku Agyei; the stool family of Domye; and that of Dankwa. Many, many years ago the senior members of the three lineages or "families" assembled to nominate the chief of Swedru. After all, they "shared funeral expenses" and so on. It is not clear from the accounts whether chiefship in Swedru rotated among these three families. What seems to have happened is that it was only when the most senior of these lineages — that of Kwatutu — had no suitable and fit candidate that the next senior group, Domye's lineage, was considered for a chief. This fact only goes to demonstrate one other crucial feature of clanship among the Agona or Akan. This practice seems to differ from that of the Ashanti, by which, as Fortes points out, "There is no hierarchy of jural status or religious authority corresponding to the hierarchy of segments. The corporate unit recognized for political, legal, and ritual purposes is generally the most inclusive lineage of a particular clan in the community." [11] Although Kweku Agyei's and Domye's lineages are of the same clan, the fact that they are of different local lineages is particularly crucial. Although to the outsider members insist on the identification with one another of all lineage kin, degrees of matrilineal connection and origin are closely and carefully observed in intralineage and intraclan relations, especially in matters of inheritance and succession.

11. Fortes, "Kinship and Marriage," pp. 255–56.

KWATUTU AND THE SWEDRU
ASAFO COMPANIES

Kwatutu's lineage, to the old Agona, is the most important *abusua* in Swedru.[12] Kwatutu's lineage or, better still, Kwatutu himself, is famous for a number of reasons. First, he founded the chiefdom of Swedru. Second, he created a redoubtable asafo company which protected the settlement in the difficult days of inter- and intratribal wars, and built the posuban, the military outpost, that marks the exact spot where Kwatutu and his followers defeated their enemy.[13]

The posuban is also associated in Swedru with the great *akwambo*, ("clearing of the path") by the asafo, to the new settlement.[14] The posuban is under the guardianship of the tufuhene of Swedru. We cannot leave the discussion of the posuban without recounting an incident I was involved in while in the field.

When General Kotoka, a member of the National Liberation Council of Ghana, was killed in an abortive counter-coup by some young military officers in April 1967, the Swedru asafo (in fact, the various asafo groups throughout Ghana) plunged into a period of mourning, marked first by attendance at a wake, near the posuban, and a night of drinking, drumming, and singing, and followed in the morning by more drumming and drinking and a parade of the asafo throughout the town. According to one young man, the asafo was "commemorating the death of their own hero-captain," a "hero-chief" who had saved them from general economic disaster.

12. To most Agona under forty — including, surprizingly, one head of the royal lineage — this may not be the case; and in fact their knowledge of the past chiefs of Swedru does not go beyond Kojo Nyarko, who was succeeded in 1932 by Kobina Botwe.
13. The posuban performs a quasi-religious role for the patri-asafomma. The posuban, which in Swedru is situated at Ankyease, is considered an *obosom* ("god"). The posuban is a simple structure consisting, perhaps, of the original akyea-tree surrounded by a split-bamboo fence (*ban*). Outside this fence are rocks and some broken black clay pots on which sacrifices were made before a battle or war. The posuban is still the mustering place of the asafo. See Christensen, *Double Descent among the Fanti*, 16:112–26, for a detailed account of the posuban among the Fante.
14. Akwambo is now an annual festival in August of the Agona asafomma. In Swedru the festival, which starts, significantly, from Eguabiriso with a procession of the asafo companies, clad in dry plantain leaves, amidst drumming, dancing, singing of war songs, and firing of musketry (Dane guns) and ends at the posuban, commemorates the first effort by Kwatutu, the chief-captain, and his warriors to build Swedru. Akwambo was not observed in 1966 and 1967 for lack of funds for drinks and gunpowder.

I was at Ankyease in the morning to observe and participate with them. The asafo had already assembled near the posuban and were drumming hard when I arrived there. Everybody was under the influence of the potent local gin, *akpeteshie* or "VC10." Two of the asafomma asked me to take a picture of them. I agreed and suggested that they stand by the posuban. I wanted a picture of members of the asafo and their historic landmark. One young man protested, saying that they had no right to take the picture by the posuban. This led to a very interesting argument, which went something like this:

MR. A.: What do you mean by we can't take the picture by the posuban? Are you the owner of the posuban?
MR. B.: I am not the owner, and you are not the owner.
MR. C.: (*asking B*): Who do you think looks after the posuban? It is the tufuhene.
MR. B.: I know it is the tufuhene.
MR. A.: The posuban belongs to all of us.
MR. C.: Mr. B. is very officious and ridiculous. His brother is being put up as a candidate for the vacant stool of the ohene of Swedru [the Swedruhene had died when I was in the field]. He feels his brother will be elected. He must be joking indeed. The oman and the asafo wouldn't have him. Should his brother become chief of Swedru, there will be no peace here."

Whereupon one of the senior members of the asafo intervened and begged them to stop quarreling, for "you are all one people." I finally managed to take the picture somewhere in nearby Kubease.

There is a strong sense of clan and lineage as opposed to tribal identity among the Agona of Swedru, and certainly the Agona of the other divisions.[15] The bandsmen of the nationally famous Swedru Brass Band, founded by Teacher Amakyi's father, were until recently mostly Asona people and proud of the fact. Again, while in the field, I watched a national soccer league match played in Swedru between the Agona Fankobaa XI (the Agona team based in Swedru) and the Kumasi Great Ashanti XI. One of the spectators, an Agona man next to me, was so pleased with the performance of one of the players that he remarked aloud, "He is *Osonani*," a member of the Asona clan. Another Agona man who overheard the remark asked if the brilliant player was a member of lineage X

15. This is because it is the lineage and the chiefdom and not the tribe that are property owning and controlling and within which power is vested.

of the clan. "No," said the first man, "he belongs to lineage Y of the clan [his own lineage]." I would like to draw attention here to the various ways in which clan and lineage members are distinguished and united in social, political, and other contexts.

In concluding this section, special mention must be made of the economic achievements of Kwatutu, without which, according to one old and shrewd observer of the local scene, "there could be no chiefship and no Swedru." Kwatutu's name and rule are associated with economic abundance. It is claimed that he led his people to plenty. "In the olden days, thanks to our *nananom* ["chiefs"], there was plenty to eat. There was so much food that *cassava* [now a popular food crop] was considered fit only for pigs," remarked one informant.

KWATUTU AND CHIEFLY SUCCESSION
IN SWEDRU

Nobody knows exactly when Kwatutu died. He must have died, it appears, sometime shortly after the Sasabor war and he was buried near Eguabiriso, where he had settled before moving to Swedru. Since then, all the deceased chiefs of Swedru have been buried at Eguabiriso, now the royal mausoleum, and, significantly, the site of the few archeological researches done in the area.

Kwatutu was succeeded by his nephew Ayisa (see figure 5). It does not seem that Kwatutu had any brothers, at least not any who were suitable to succeed him. Ayisa was followed by his younger brother, Gyan Kwadwo. Gyan Kwadwo was succeeded in turn by his nephew, Kwateng, who was succeeded by Kobina Kuma, the great uncle of the late chief, Kobina Botwe, who ruled from 1932 to 1967 and "went to the village" — a euphemism for the death of a chief — in the latter year. Kobina Kuma was the direct descendant of one of the five women, children of Ayiaba, who founded the Swedru dynasty. Ayiaba is believed to have had sixteen children, most of whom died in infancy.

The rule of Kobina Kuma was to mark the beginning of a fierce interlineage and intraclan conflict over chiefship which continues to this day. In very simple terms, the three lineages, or "families," of the Asona clan, who in the past gave unanimous assent and acclaim to the individuals nominated for the chiefship, now stand with claws at each other's necks, each lineage trying hard and going to

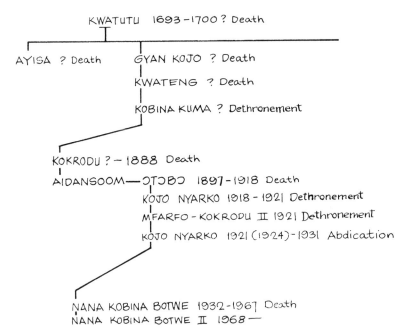

KWATUTU 1693-1700? Death

AYISA ? Death   GYAN KOJO ? Death

                       KWATENG ? Death

                       KOBINA KUMA ? Dethronement

KOKRODU ?—1888 Death

AIDANSOOM—ƆTƆBƆ 1897-1918 Death

          KOJO NYARKO 1918-1921 Dethronement

          MFARFO-KOKRODU II 1921 Dethronement

          KOJO NYARKO 1921(1924)-1931 Abdication

NANA KOBINA BOTWE 1932-1967 Death
NANA KOBINA BOTWE II 1968—

Fig. 5. The Chiefs of Swedru

almost any length to arrogate to itself and itself only the right to provide a candidate for the chiefship of Swedru, but in fact the supreme right of Kwatutu's dynasty is incontrovertible. The trouble began the day Kobina Adu, the brother of Akua Tia (see figure 6), brought the latter to Swedru from Cape Coast — where her mother, Amisa Kuma, had been living as the wife of the chief of Oguaa, Aggrey Boropo.[16]

Kobina Kuma, it is said, ignored all customary rules of clan exogamy and familial incest and, at the very first opportunity, seduced Akua Tia and "married" her. This was about the middle of the nineteenth century. Kuma was accordingly and naturally accused of the "sin" of having sexual congress with a "sister," a real *odehye* — that is, a person of free matrilineal descent. He was therefore dethroned forthwith. Kobina Kuma's father was Kwatu, not to be confused with Kwatutu, the first chief of Swedru. Kwatu's elder brother was Mbronna. Mbronna's son was Kokrodu or Kwokrodoo. Kobina Kuma and Kokrodu were therefore classificatory brothers.

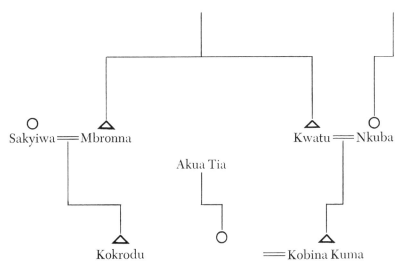

When Kobina Kuma was dethroned he fled to Senya-Beraku. Akua Tia, believing that her husband had been killed or murdered, reported the matter to the district commissioner resident at Winneba,

16. We have to remember that Amisa Kuma was the sister of Nkuba. They were both daughters of Ayiaba, whose mother was Kyirema, the sister of Kwatutu, the founder of Swedru.

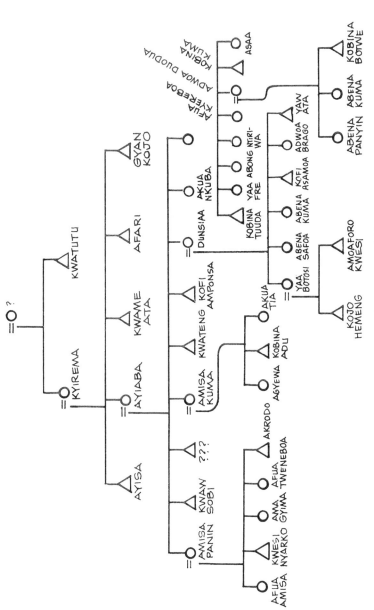

Fig. 6. The Chiefly Lineage of Kwatutu

accusing Ankyeasefo of the alleged murder of her husband, the exchief of Swedru. Almost all the elders of Ankyease were duly arrested on the orders of the district commissioner (D.C.).[17]

The arrest of the elders — one of many such arrests in the state, it
merits stressing — reflected the new colonial administrative and judicial structure with its associated loss of some power by the chiefs.
Before judgment was pronounced, however, Kobina Kuma reap-
peared. The elders were therefore found not guilty and freed. At this
time, Kwame Ata was the *abusuapanyin* (lineage head) of the dynasty founded by Kwatutu. Nana Kwame Ata afterwards gave the
stool to Kokrodu on the grounds that Kokrodu and Kobina Kuma
were classificatory brothers and were of the same Asona clan
though of different lineages, and, more important, that Kokrodu's
mother was a member of the Asona royal lineage of Fante Abaase.
Lastly, Kwame Ata's lineage had no suitable candidate at the time.
The fact that, according to my principal informant, the stool was
given to Kokrodu to "look after until such time that Kwame Ata's
family had a fit and suitable candidate" should be particularly
noted. For this was later to be the bone of contention between the
lineages of Kwame Ata, represented by Kobina Botwe, and Domye
in 1932. The cause of the conflict has the flavor of the Nsaba-Nyakrom dispute which was discussed at some length in the first chapter.

The Chiefs and the Beginnings of Eurocolonial Rule

Kokrodu ruled until he died in January 1888, at the age of seventy-
five. His reign is remembered particularly for the fact that in 1887
Swedru Ahenfie, the royal palace, caught fire and burned down.
He wrote to the district commissioner at Winneba for help and
the latter kindly contributed five pounds toward a new palace.
The Swedru Ahenfie still stands where Kokrodu's rebuilt palace
stood nearly eighty years ago. The present ahenfie was put up by
Kojo Nyarko. It may be helpful to cite the minutes (S.N.A. Papers)
concerning the death of Kokrodu and the succession to the stool of

17. It must be pointed out that, in keeping with the rationalization of British
colonial administrative and judicial control, district commissioners' courts, replacing the civil commandants, had been set up in the Gold Coast colony in
1876 on the suggestion of Commander Strahan, then governor of Cape Coast,
and D. C.'s were stationed at Cape Coast, Winneba, and other coastal towns in
1878.

Aidansoom, his nephew. These minutes may provide us with some insight into the nature of emergent colonial rule in the late nineteenth century and how it affected the status of chiefs.

October 8, 1888.
Subject: Cobinah Aidansoom
Enstoolation of as successor to Kwakrodoo of Swadur reported.

D.C. Winnebah:
    Is the chief recommended a fit and proper person as a successor to Quaw Crodoe [Kokrodu] and one in whom the government [Colonial] can place confidence?
                                    [Signed] 10.10.88
                                            Agona Swadur
                                            8th October '88.
To His Majesty
The Governor,

Sir,
    We wrote you last in remembering [reminding] you [about] the death of late Chief Kwakrodoo of Swadur to which you directed the D.C. of Winnebah to write to us that you have received it.
    We have now put a suceeder [successor] into the throne [on the stool] by name Cobinah Aidansoom, and have changed his name to the same Kwakrodoo and therefore we have to let you know.
                    Your most obedient and humble Servants,
                        We are,

                        Coffie Amponsah
                        Yaw Moayaw   X their
                        Coffie Yamkur   mark

With colonial rule, the chiefs, in pre-European days all-powerful, were now "the obedient and humble servants" of the governor, whose assent and confirmation were necessary for valid installation. Lest it be misconstrued, this did not necessarily mean that the governor or the D.C. interfered with or influenced election of chiefs in any way. We shall have occasion to discuss the nature of the relationship between the chief and the D.C. Suffice it to say here that it was not colonial rule as such which led to loss of power by individual chiefs — in fact, a few chiefs consolidated their power through the indirect rule. Rather, it was changes in the economy — the introduction of money, the cash crop, and education which helped increase one's economic opportunities — that wrested power and influence from the traditional leaders.
    Kobina Aidansoom, the seventh chief of Swedru, died and was

succeeded by his brother Otobo (Attu Bo, S.N.A. Papers), who ruled during the reign of King Kofi Chintor (Twinto) of Nsaba, in 1897. It is worth noting that in that year "King Kofi Chintor of Agoona" was forcibly dethroned and deprived of his property by the people of Nsaba. The dethronement was instigated by Kofi Sakyi, subchief of Nsaba, "chief next to myself [omanhene]." The king appealed, it should be noted, to the D.C. in Winneba on the grounds that the dethronement was most illegal since the Agona oman-in-council was not consulted. King Ghartey of Winneba, then a prominent member of the Fante Confederation, and the D.C. came down to Swedru to look into the matter. Swedru at this time was gradually emerging as an important town and gaining official recognition as the center of Agona, at first, mainly by virtue of its geographical location. Later on, in the twentieth century, an assistant D.C. was to be stationed in Swedru.

On 4 May 1897, the D.C. was able to report that, though the deposition of Kofi Chinto by the people of Nsaba was clearly illegal — that is, contrary to customary practice — initially because of the failure to consult the council of Agona chiefs made up of all the divisional chiefs, it appeared to him to have been legalized, the chiefs "having as the result of bribery, popular feeling or some other influence" given in to the wish of the Nsaba people. "Kofi Chintoh now appears resigned to his fate and content to retire quietly on the condition of the restoration of his private property alleged to have been taken from him" (S.N.A. Papers).

The circumstances surrounding Chintoh's dethronement (for "drunkenness and misconduct," whatever this meant precisely) are worthy of our consideration. The Eurocolonial era in West Africa has been characterized as the great period of innovation and social change. The Europeans brought with them into Africa not only a new racial category but also new ideas and new tools, new ways of looking at things, and new sources of power — not necessarily in all cases better ways of doing things. This was the period of Dane guns and gunpowder, the intensification of intertribal wars, slavery and slave trade, money, cash crop, Christianity, education, and colonial rule and pacification. The economy, society, and polity of various regions were cracking under the new intrusion.

We have seen that a D.C., the symbol of the new colonial authority, had been stationed in the Swedru area in 1878. The Methodist

Church – popularly known as "Wesley" – had opened a mission
and an "experimental" school in Swedru in the 1880s. In 1896, the
Presbyterian Church founded a mission and acquired land in 1897
for a permanent church near Kubease at Salem (see figure 4).[18] The
mission was headed by the Reverend J. Sitzler, then stationed at
Nsaba, and he acquired the plot on behalf of the Reverend Theo-
dore Cehler, the West Indian missionary, and Kojo Bani, a convert
and an Agona from Swedru.

THE EARLY CHURCH AND LOCAL POLITICS

Although the Christian missions did have some initial and largely
predictable difficulties concerning evangelical work – the hand
bell which the Methodist mission rang on Sundays to summon
people to the sermon and literacy classes was, for example, stolen
and thrown into the bush by some local Swedru people on the
grounds that it was making too much noise! – it is known that the
chiefs tolerated their activities and a few even were converted to
Christianity. Some of their subjects also received and accepted the
words of the Bible. In a letter to the governor from the D.C. in 1897,
reference is made to the fact that "the Christian community at Nsabang [Nsaba] is acting in defiance of native custom" (S.N.A. Papers).
It was this community that, it was alleged, instigated and supported
the dethronement of the drunken and disorderly King Kofi Chintoh
so that his grandson, a boy of fifteen and more amenable to the
Christian point of view, might be enthroned.

Yaw Duodu, for that was the name of the grandson, was described
as a "Basel [Presbyterian] Mission scholar." In other words, he was
not only Christian, but literate, a perfect model of the new generation of "modern" Africans. The D.C., of course, in the interest of
"peace and good government," warned the Basel missionary, the
Reverend J. Sitzler, to refrain absolutely from participation in
political matters and from allowing the members of his "Christian
community" to act contrary to native custom. The D.C. was not
against Christianity and its propagation, but rather he was con-

18. In 1896, J. E. Casely-Hayford became the first Gold Coast African to be
admitted to the English bar. In the following year he helped found the famous
Aborigines' Rights Protection Society, which marked "the beginning of local, on-
the-scene nationalism in Africa." Victor C. Ferkiss, *Africa's Search for
Identity* (New York: Braziller, 1966), pp. 81–82. See also G. Padmore, *The
Gold Coast Revolution* (London: Dennis Dobson, 1953).

cerned that "unless this interference stopped there would be serious
trouble in Agona before long." After all, the D.C. was being paid to
establish and maintain peace and order in his district. Yaw Duodu
succeeded Kofi Chintoh, but the "Basel Mission scholar" was not to
last, for he proved himself neither Christian, scholarly, nor respectable. The D.C., in the minutes of 10 July 1899, noted that
the king was a young man who commanded little respect and
wielded little authority in his kingdom. This was demonstrated by
the fact that the people of Bobikuma and Kwanyako, two of the
ten chiefdoms of Agona, refused to appear before him when summoned to his court. Yaw Duodu was finally dethroned in 1899 on
the grounds of "seducing the wives and daughters of his subjects."
It should be remembered that it was in 1899 when Agona was finally
declared independent of Gomoa.

KOJO NYARKO AND CHIEFTAINCY IN SWEDRU

It may be remarked that in 1900 Swedru was still very little developed. Much of it was virgin forest and the exchange economy
was largely based on the preparation of palm kernel and palm oil.
One of my informants, an elder of the local Presbyterian Church,
who was born in 1888, vividly recaptured the period thus: "Swedru was very small, most of the town was bush.[19] The town proper
stretched from Sam's Junction to the old Methodist Church near
the present Methodist Book Depot, about four hundred yards
away.[20] Palm-oil lamps were used for lighting. At 4:00 P.M., if sent
there, I was afraid to go to Salem, the home of the Basel Mission.
There was no bridge on the Akora River, which runs through the
heart of Swedru. A canoe belonging to the gyasehene resident at
Kubease was used to cross the river. The fare was threepence or sixpence a crossing, depending on one's luggage. The palm-nut business was as popular at the time as cocoa is today. There was plenty
of food; three bunches of plantain were sold for threepence." It
was not until after 1912 that the growth of modern Swedru really
began. The story of this spectacular growth and its bearing on local

19. Collier, MacCarthy, et al., *Agoona Country*, estimated the population of
the whole of Agona as "not more than 10,000 souls, of whom 7,000 were
women and children."
20. Sam's house at this junction was the first two-story building in Swedru.
It was later remodelled (or restored?) and bought by E. K. Bensah, and was in
the late 1940s and 1950s the Regional Headquarters of the CPP.

and national politics will be examined later. It is significant to mention that though Nana Otobo, the chief of Swedru, and his elders tolerated the missionaries, unlike Yaw Duodu of Nsaba, they did not themselves become members of the Church.

When Otobo died, about 1918, Kojo Nyarko, his nephew, was made chief of Swedru. The years 1900 to 1931, in fact, may be described as the worst period in Agona political history and perhaps the beginning of the best in her economic history. Dethronements and the attendant disturbances became more frequent. During this period, the colonial government was in conflict with the people, the people with their chiefs. Old wounds were reopened as the Gomoa, despite the 1899 ruling by the governor, did everything to remind the Agona of their past subjection to them. The atrocious behavior, mainly economic, of the amanhene of Nsaba finally led in 1931 to the withdrawal of allegiance by a majority of the chiefdoms or divisions in the state from Nsaba to Nyakrom. The chiefly lineages in Swedru fought and quarreled, each denying the other the right to provide a candidate for the stool. And the D.C. had to deal with all these "urgent matters which disturbed peace, order and good government."

Kojo Nyarko's rule in these circumstances could hardly last. In 1921, three years after his enthronement, he was dethroned for "salaciousness." Mfarfo, the nephew of Kojo Nyarko, succeeded him as Kokrodu II. The latter in turn was found "intolerable" and dethroned the same year. The charges against Kokrodu II are worth recounting here, since they most emphatically reflect the changing socioeconomic and political environment.

1. That the Ohene has credited from several stores certain things which he refused to pay on demand.

2. That when a person sues his debtor in his tribunal and if the money is paid by the debtor, he misappropriates it rather than give it to the owner.

3. That he makes use of the quarterly road dues paid by the Government.

4. That he has pledged almost the whole stool properties, which from time immemorial has never been heard of during the reigns of the past Ahenfo.

5. Recently he caused trouble as a result of which search warrant was issued against him from the Supreme Court in Winneba and the stool room was searched by policemen and this [we consider] sacrilegious according to native custom, [and] we asked him to slaughter a sheep to

purify for the disgrace brought upon the stool but he refused [refusal was considered detrimental to the well-being of the subjects].
   6. He refused to answer the call of our Omanhene of Nsaba.
   7. He is difficult to deal with, very unsympathetic, and has his own way in everything. [S.N.A. Papers.]

In view of the foregoing complaints, the oman considered it advisable to give him the chance to explain his conduct at a meeting of the elders of Swedru, held at the ohene's premises. At the meeting it was unanimously decided that he should be dethroned forthwith.

Kojo Nyarko, his uncle, was recalled. But his confirmation, despite the relative popular reaction in his favor and his acceptance by the omanhene and the commissioners for the district, was withheld by the fact that Sir John Ridgins had ruled in a previous case (S.N.A., no. 312/07) that no exchief should be reelected within five years of his dethronement. The ruling was waived, however, when it was realized that Kwamin Bassayin, the exchief of Upper Wassaw, was reelected within five years of his dethronement. This precedent was drawn to the attention of the governor. Kojo Nyarko's enthronement was therefore confirmed in 1924. He remained on the stool until about the middle of 1931, when the asafomma formally preferred twenty-one charges against him. He abdicated in the same year. Most of the charges concerned misappropriation of stool funds and property. In 1921 he had been dethroned primarily for "committing adultery with his brother's wives," which is "against equity and good conscience"; for having sexual intercourse with female prisoners awaiting trial at his tribunal as "a means of favouring them in their cases"; for sleeping with widows, an act which constituted "filth and contempt against the stool of Agona Swedru"; and, finally, for changing the officiating day for the celebration of Okyin Kwesi (the god of war) in connection with the stool from Sunday — when from time immemorial the celebration had been held — to Wednesday, without the knowledge and unanimous consent of the "stool councillors, chiefs, and sub-chiefs" of Swedru. The sacrilegious behavior of the chief was believed to affect the material and physical well-being of his subjects.

From the accounts, it may be said in passing, it appears that the descendants of Sakyiwa (see diagram, page 60), who have been ruling since Kokrodu II, have fared a little worse than the descendants of Amisah. When Kojo Nyarko abdicated, the three stool families of Kwame Ata or Kweku Agyei, Domye, and Dankwa met to nominate a candidate. It was decided at the meeting that Amisah's descendants, the most senior and the real chiefly lineage, should come back to the stool since they now could provide a fit and suitable candidate. Kobina Botwe, then working in the mines of Tarkwa and Aboso, was the suggested candidate.[21]

The two families of Sakyiwa and Domye refused to accept Kobina Botwe, claiming that his predecessors had never been chiefs of Swedru. In fact, some went so far as to say that he was really a Gomoa Fante and not a true Agona. But there is a tolerable limit to the gross distortion of history, of any history. Three other meetings were held by the three chiefly lineages at various times but no agreement was reached at any of these. At this time the Nyakrom and Nsaba dispute over the hegemony of the Agona state was on, so the Swedru interlineage dispute was shelved for settlement until after the resolution of the one at the paramount level. Both disputes will be reviewed here, for they throw much light on some of the almost insoluble political problems endemic in the Agona state, the kind of issues that any clever political party or politician could exploit to much advantage.

THE STRUGGLE FOR TRADITIONAL
LEADERSHIP IN SWEDRU

The dynastic struggle was essentially between Kobina Botwe, the chief-elect, representing his stool family, the family of Kwame Ata; and Kojo Domye, representing his family and the candidature of Mfarfo. Before the Agona State Council in April 1932 were, therefore, Kobina Botwe, the plaintiff, and Domye, the defendant. The evidence of the former, before the state council, is particularly in-

21. Christensen, *Double Descent among the Fanti,* 16:11, wrongly refers to "the ex-omanhen of Agona Swedru, a man who had been reared as a Fanti in Abura state until his call to accept that position. . . ." Christensen is mistaken on two counts. First, Swedru has never had an omanhene. Although one chief of Nyakrom, Takyi, had been reared at Abura (his female relatives had been captured in the Sasabor war, and so his mother was born in Fante and married a Fante), when he ruled, the paramount seat of Agona was Nsaba. Nana Kobina Botwe, whom Christensen presumably had in mind, went to live for a time at Gomoa Adam when the mother remarried a man from that town. This did not necessarily follow from matrilineal inheritance of positions as chiefs, and patrilocal residence as the norm for males, as Christensen would have it. (Of the 221 Agona households surveyed by my assistant between April and July 1967, 106 were matri- or uxorilocal; 81 were patri- or virilocal). One cannot simply derive what is from what ought to be.

teresting and is worthy of quoting at some length. In an impressive opening, Kobina Botwe declared,

I am a sawyer. I live at Swedru. About ten months ago, ex-chief Kojo Nyarku [Nyarko] was then Ohene of Swedru; in consequence of certain charges preferred against him, he abdicated the stool. When the Oman of Swedru asked the stool family to elect a new candidate, Kojo Domye, the then *acting* Head of the stool family, elected [nominated] one Nfarfu [Mfarfo] as [for] Ohene, and Yaw Bedidi as adiakyiri [assistant]. The Oman and Town Company [asafo] objected to the former and said he has [had] once been on the stool but owing to his misbehaviour he was destooled. The Oman of Swedru together with the Town Company, seeing that I, the Plaintiff, having got good character and [being] entitled to the stool, I . . . was unanimously elected as Ohene of Swedru . . . which election was objected to by the Defendant and his family and as a result the dispute was before [taken to for settlement] the assistant D.C. (resident in Swedru) who put question as to why the two stool families should not make one [agree] to elect a candidate on the stool. When the D.C. was made to understand that I had been elected, the Defendant rose and said, "Kobina Botchey [Botwe] is not known as a member of the family and he is not entitled to the stool."

I put question to the defendant as to whether he had never heard Kobina Kuma late Ohene of Swedru was my uncle and his reply was negative. The Defendant further said he never knew Kobina Kuma had been on the stool, but only Kokrodu I and that I was not entitled to the Swedru stool. I claim . . . the stool of Swedru because it [is] my ancestral property which is known to everyone in the town of Swedru. The owners of the stool of Swedru were Ayisa, Gyan Kojo [Kwadwo], and Kwantsin [Kwateng] my great-grand uncle. Gyan Kojo succeeded Ayisa after his death, Kwantsin succeeded Gyan Kojo, and Kwabena [Kobina] Kuma succeeded Kwantsin. Kobina Kuma was my uncle. One Kokrodu I was half-brother to my late uncle Kobina Kumah and when Kobina [Kumah] was destooled for misconduct, Kwame Atta [Ata], the then head of the stool family, and his sister Akua Nkumah [Nkuba] suggested that as there was no grown up person in my family Kokrodu I, half-brother of my late uncle Kobina Kumah, should be given the stool of Swedru as *caretaker* until such a time a proper person could be elected and installed as Ohene of Swedru. On the death of Kwame Atta, [whose] successor is Kwaku Agyei [Egyei], they said Kokrodu I was made Ohene of Swedru owing to his carefulness.

After the death of Kokrodu I, Adonsum [Aidansoom], his nephew, succeeded him. One Tobooh [Otobo] also succeeded Adensum and the ex-chief Kojo Nyarko also succeeded Tobooh. When Kojo Nyarko was deposed, Kokrodu II was installed. Kojo Nyarko was reinstated as Ohene of Swedru when Kokrodu II was destooled. During which time I had been away at Tarkwa [as a migrant laborer]. The stool of Swedru being my ancestral property and [as] the defendant has objected to my election, I now sue the defendant claiming the stool of Swedru and also cease [stop] the defendant to [from] act[ing] as the Head of the stool family.[22]

Before the case was finally adjudged, Kwame Afram, the head supi of Agona state, added that another candidate, Kobina Kurant-sin, was provided by Domye, but "owing to his [Kobina Kurant-sin's] circumcision was objected to by the Oman of Swedru," in accordance with Akan custom. The State Council gave judgment in favor of the plaintiff and "orders that the proposed election and installation of the plaintiff as Ohene of Swedru to be continued and . . . the defendant should cease to act as the head of the stool family of Swedru and Kweku Agyei, whose predecessors have been exercising such power, should assume the position." Botwe's election was thus recognized. On the day of his installation, however, he was shot at (the gun misfired) by Nyarko's supporters. The great local oath, Botwe Benada (Botwe's Tuesday), came into being.

It is perhaps hardly surprising to observe that in the Nsaba-Nya-krom dispute, which I will consider presently, Botwe's group sided with Nyakrom against Nsaba — that is, they were all for the withdrawal of allegiance from the stool of Nsaba. Nyarko, or Domye's group, were supporters of Nsaba. Why did Swedru — at any rate, the chief-elect and his family — support Nyakrom, especially when it was obvious that paramount power was passing into Oyoko clan hands? There are many reasons, but I think the most important was to make sure, seeing that most of the divisions in any case backed Nyakrom, that the senior rank of Swedru as adontenhene was maintained. Adonten was the most senior rank below that of omanhene.

22. The plaintiff stressed later on, when cross-examined by Council, that: (1) Kokrodu I was merely asked to look after the stool of Swedru; (2) that Kokrodu I was from the same clan, Asona, and was half-brother to his late uncle, Kobina Kuma; (3) 'after Kokrodu was given the stool "my family paid funeral donations [nsaawa] jointly and severally with him"; (4) that Kokrodu I did not pay any money for the stool; (5) that the stool family lands and property were entrusted to Kokrodu [The following stool property was given to Kokrodu I: 1 state sword; 2 horns; complete Bomba drums (1 set); 12 state brooms; 2 golden swords; 1 golden linguist stick; 1 golden headband; 1 golden broom with horse hairs; set of native drums (Mpintin); 2 hammocks; 2 state umbrellas; 1 silver linguist stick; Wraba, Adumasa, Sankowa, Ayesuasi, Akuam-krom, Odumaffua, Duato (near Ndelbehi), Ota-piriow (near Asafo), Anaafo Street (Swedru), Swedru Ahenfie lands, including Oman land under the supervision of the stool of Swedru.] when he became Ohene; and (6) that Kwatutu brought the stool of Swedru from Eguabirisu after the great war which took place between Agona and Gomoa.

THE DISPUTE BETWEEN NYAKROM AND NSABA:
SOME IMPORTANT ASPECTS

The Nsaba-Nyakrom dispute goes back, as we have seen, to the Go-moa-Agona war in the seventeenth century. That atrocious war automatically wrested from Nyakrom its supreme position of hegemony in Agona, and power passed to Nsaba. Yet until about the turn of the century, 1900, the real power and authority wielded by Nsaba over the rest of Agona was minimal. The king of Gomoa was the "overlord" of Agona when Nsaba became at best a senior asafohene to Ahunaku and acted as a medium through which tribute, mainly in kind, would flow from Agona to Gomoa.[23] Examination of the grievances will shed some light on the political issues of the day.

Since about 1912, with the rule of Dompre, the chiefs of Nyakrom have refused to serve Nsaba. It should be pointed out that the period between 1910 and 1931 was one of dramatic socioeconomic change in Agona and elsewhere in the Gold Coast and Ashanti. The troublesome Ashanti had been finally defeated in 1900 and brought under firm British control. The introduction of cocoa in 1879, at first on an experiment and later on a commercial scale, meant the clearing of many virgin forests for cocoa farming. Roads were needed to facilitate transportation of the produce to such coastal ports as Winneba and Cape Coast for shipment overseas. This was also a period of great in-migration to slowly developing towns as peace-time conditions, plus the great attractions of wealth in urbanizing areas, induced many people to venture beyond their tribal boundaries. We have already noted that the Swedruhene himself spent a long time as a young man in Tarkwa and Aboso as a semiskilled migrant worker.

Not that tribes were completely isolated before the Pax Britannica. We know that kinship rules made it possible to incorporate stranger lineages of the same clan into the local lineages. Marriage and affinity, clan exogamy, slavery, slave trade, and ordinary trading in goods and services were all features of the past, but during the first half of the twentieth century the scale and pace definitely in-

23. Thus, in the 1852–53 Poll Tax Income and Expenditure statement, we see "Goomooh [Gomoa] and Ahgonna [Agona] grouped together as having collected 5,312 heads and 33-¾ string of cowries." D. Kimble, A Political History of Ghana: 1850–1928 (London: Oxford University Press, 1963).

creased. Settlement of aliens in new territories meant the reexamination of rights over land; land litigations became more rampant as lands began to have higher and higher economic value. Chains of stores, carrying all kinds of imported European goods and owned or managed at first by Europeans, then by Levantines and Africans, became a familiar feature of the growing towns of the coast and in the hinterland. New consumer items, commanding new prestige, appeared everywhere on the market and, with Christianity and the school fairly well established, new status groups began to emerge all over the country, but initially along the coast in particular. The colonial situation also introduced a new dimension of politics.

Thus it is not surprising to learn that Nyakrom "seceded" because of certain rights over land which the omanhene of Nsaba refused to honor. Writing in the 1910s, Crowther presented in an official report (S.N.A. Papers) the relative ranks of the chiefs of Agona thus:

Gyase:	Soadro (Kobiase)
Adonten:	Nyakrom and Abodom
Nifa:	Soadro
Benkum:	Asafo
Nkyidom:	Kwanyako and Nkum
Tuafo:	Kwamang and Bobikuma
Banmu:	Duakwa

Agona law and custom have it that the benkumhene is the senior divisional chief in the absence of substantive holders of the offices of adontenhene and nifahene. The hierarchy is therefore:

Omanhene:	Paramount
Adontenhene:	First Division
Nifahene:	Second Division
Benkumhene:	Third Division

Because of the dispute between Nyakrom and Nsaba, we observe the omanhene quite unconstitutionally, it is believed, taking the following measures. In a letter to the secretary for native affairs (S.N.A.), dated 13 March 1922, the omanhene upgrades Swedru to the rank of adonten, so that the chief of Swedru becomes adontenhene. From Crowther's list of an earlier date, it is obvious that Nyakrom is adonten and Swedru only second-in-command, that is, nifa.

The new list supplied by the omanhene in 1922 to the D.C. in Winneba of the various positions held by the chiefs of Agona is:

Agona Swedru:	Adontenhene
Agona Asafo:	Nifahene
Agona Abodom:	Benkumhene
Agona Bobikuma:	Tuafohene
Agona Kwanyaku:	Nkyidomhene
Agona Duakwa:	Banmuhene
Agona Nyakrom:	Adontenhene
Agona Nkum:	Nkyidomhene
Agona Kwaman:	Tuafohene
Agona Nsaba:	Omanhene

The changes, as may be noted from the above list, affected Nyakrom, Swedru, Asafo, and Abodom. The assistant D.C., obviously confused, interviewed the chief of Swedru on 22 May 1922 about it, but the latter naturally upheld the position that "both Swedru and Nyakrom are officially Adontenhene" to the omanhene of Nsaba and that "they occupied this position *before* the dispute between Nyakrom and Nsaba!" In any case, the ohene of Nyakrom refused to recognize the omanhene as his head chief and consequently did not regard himself as one of the adontenhene. Although the D.C. upheld the case of Nyakrom as constitutional (in accordance with native custom) in a letter to the commissioner of the Central Province, this, it should be emphasized, did not alter the nature of the political and economic conflict between Nsaba and Nyakrom, nor did it affect the "new" status of Swedru and the other chiefdoms.

In time, the behavior of the amanhene of Nsaba became more and more intolerable, unbearable, and erratic, and led to much political unrest in the state. The amanhene's cup of misrule was full. By 1931, each of the divisions of Agona, at any rate many of the inhabitants of each division, had had enough grievances, mostly economic, as we shall see, against Omanhene Yaw Duodu VII of Nsaba for a majority of them to decide to withdraw their allegiance from the stool he occupied.

It has already been mentioned that one of the immediate conditions that forced Nyakrom to stop serving Nsaba was a land dispute in which Nsaba had allegedly neglected the financial interests of Nyakrom, causing the latter to waste a lot of money. Already *money*, or whatever it commands, had entered the field as a major and powerful competitor to traditional status as a primary source of prestige, even power and influence. The man who possessed more money and education (in some cases both factors were mutually supportive) was becoming the dominant type in the social and political arena. The Ashanti proverb, "Money is sharper than the sword," attained more relevance and meaning. In every town and village the term *osikani*, ("the rich or wealthy man") came to symbolize prestige, potential power, and influence.[24] The mere possession of wealth and money, however, does not confer the desired end — that is, high social status and prestige. What does confer high social status and prestige is the generous consumption of wealth in the form of patronage and liberal gifts to followers and friends. Since money must be conspicuously spent or distributed in order to maintain one's status, the difficult problem in Ghana is how to acquire wealth and hold on to it.

RENT AND POLITICS IN AGONA

At this point, we may devote a few pages to an inquiry into the land rent dispute between some Gomoa cocoa farmers on Agona lands and the chief of Duakwa in 1928–29. It may help us to appreciate better the complex interaction between the changing economy and political leadership in Agona — and in the Gold Coast, for that matter. The rent dispute to some extent illustrates vividly the various ways in which traditional leaders attempted to cope with, or maintain, their power and influence, which were becoming increasingly threatened by new groups. In fact, the chiefs had to achieve the new osikani status in order to be respected and to wield any sociopolitical influence at all. They had to become entrepreneurs or *rentiers* and compete in the economic field with their subjects, who in most instances were better prepared than the chiefs. The findings of the Committee of the Provincial Council of Chiefs, Central Region, provide material for the present discussion.

The opening statement of the committee is certainly noteworthy: "This inquiry does not present any difficult problems for solution, except that it gathers to itself in an extensive scope commercial interests of far reaching importance." This is followed by a brief historical background to the dispute. That the amanhene and ahene should realize the extreme importance of commercial interests, which

---

24. Social scientists still have paid very little attention to the new osikani status and role, a role whose correct analysis might open new ways of understanding the socio-political behavior of the Agona and many others like them.

are mainly related to new economic roles, is equally significant. Commenting on the fact that the proceedings had taken so long, the members had no apologies, for "the Committee has had to take into special consideration the commercial interests of the District, which depend *solely*, at present, upon the progress of the cocoa industry." As a matter of fact, in the first half of the twentieth century, cocoa, commerce, and communication went together and grew together. With the extension of communication, in the broadest sense of the term, there emerged a new form of socioeconomic and therefore political integration based primarily on economic interests or values.

The various ways in which the cocoa industry, western education, Christianity, and colonial rule interacted and affected both jointly and severally traditional political roles have been adequately and realistically covered by Busia and others and need not be repeated here.[25] One point, however, is important. In Agona the most conservative (in terms of the stress on traditional patterns of social differentiation and leadership) chiefdoms have been precisely those with much land and wealth, in most cases derived from cocoa, and therefore able to maintain their chiefs in style — for example, Duakwa, Nyakrom, and Nsaba to some extent, as compared with Swedru and Asafo.

But colonial rule, with the introduction of English law and justice has also ushered in new means of controlling the chief and has added new dimensions to the relationship between chiefs and their subjects. The chief may now sue his subjects for claims and damages and in turn be sued by them. In precolonial days, the subjects' only weapon against their chief was dethronement. Now subjects may disgrace or even punish their tribal leaders in the courts with relative impunity — with the effect of reducing the de facto influence of a chief in a community. Thus the Gomoa farmers, faced with rents they considered exorbitant exacted by the chief of Duakwa, took court action against him.

The Gomoa farmers had at first complained against the increase in their rents to their own paramount chiefs, the amanhene of Gomoa. In a letter to the ohene of Nsaba, the Gomoa chiefs had asked for better and more lenient treatment for their subjects residing in Agona. They had even argued in their letter that, but for the British, Agona would still be under Gomoa. This latter argument

25. See Busia, *Position of the Chief.*

was felt by the chiefs of Duakwa and Nsaba as a grave insult. The Gomoa messengers who carried the letter to the Agona chiefs were treated discourteously by the paramount chief of Nsaba on account of its insulting tone. The messengers were compelled to slaughter two sheep and Kofi Ayam, linguist of the omanhene of Adjumako, was forced to put his mouth into the blood of the sheep. According to the omanhene of Agona, had it not been for "the power of the Government," the messengers "would have been beheaded as in the olden times." Both paramount chiefs of Gomoa and Agona did admit the limitations imposed on their freedom of action by colonial rule.

After a protracted deliberation, the committee finally made the following recommendations, which were accepted in each case: (1) that the omanhene of Agona shall pacify the amanhene of Gomoa with three *preguans*, or a sum of twenty-five pounds, and twelve bottles of whisky, and (2) that the Gomoa amanhene also shall undertake to slaughter one sheep to pacify the dignity of the remains of the departed amanhene of Agona "whose resting place was thus disrespectfully referred to." The committee further ruled out the increases in rent, the cause of the dispute, but urged the Gomoa farmers to pay the arrears of the rents at the rates theretofore paid to the Agona landowners.

It hardly needs mentioning that the Gomoa farmers' rent dispute was a cause célèbre primarily because of the vested financial interests involved. In fact, we may not close discussion of the rent case without noting one or two interesting features. To begin with, it is important to indicate that the Gomoa farmers had started migrating to Agona in the 1910s to farm because of the suitability of Agona soil for cocoa. Second, plots in some cases were purchased outright by the migrant farmers, a few of these plots included stool or family lands. When stool or family land was thus alienated, at the death of the seller his successor might demand to repurchase the land or take the land away from the buyer on the grounds that the seller had no right to sell. This was a dishonest but important source of wealth to the original landowners, but such action almost always led to long, drawn-out, and costly litigation in the courts. Even plots which were acquired under the *abusa* system, a three-part division whereby two-thirds of the produce of the plot went to the farmer and one-third to the landowner, were not spared litigation.

Thus battles over land, whose yield now commanded high commercial price, were waged on all fronts: between chief and subjects, between chief and chief, and between chiefs supporting some subjects against other chiefs and subjects, and so on. This takes us directly to the grievances, including disputes over land, which led to the transfer of Agona paramountcy from Nsaba to Nyakrom in 1931.

THE ECONOMIC BASIS OF POLITICS IN AGONA

Nsaba had already lost allegedly about three hundred pounds in the Gomoa farmers' dispute over land rents. But the worst was still to come. In 1931, things came to a head. In that year the chiefs — excluding Nsaba, of course — of Agona all agreed to withdraw their allegience from the stool of Yaw Duodu VII. From thence, Nyakrom was to be given back its ancient, pre–Gomoa war, paramount status. The reasons for this extreme action were various. The immediate and necessary cause was the fact that Yaw Duodu was believed to have consulted with an Ashanti Mohammedan for "medicine" to kill some of the elders of Agona, a sociopolitical reason. But the major sufficient ones were mostly economic. An analysis of the Bewes Report of 1931 yields three broad categories of grievances: economic, social, and political. These grievances reflect glaringly not only the new opportunities existing in the environment but also the changing socioeconomic and political roles. As Lucy Mair describes it, in the new situation "people have to weigh the loss of esteem in some quarters against the material or other advantages to be sought in new relationships," as they enter large-scale society with the expansion of the existing field of choice by the creation of new situations offering new economic opportunities.[26]

The principal political grievance, which itself had economic roots, was the general insecurity in the state since the transfer of paramountcy to Nsaba. The crucial index was the frequency of dethronements — eight in number, and one abdication. Even frequent deaths, four in all of paramount chiefs, were considered a factor. Yamfu Asuaku III put it in these words, "When paramountcy was given to Nsaba . . . [there was] no peace at all in the state. . . . There was *prosperity* when paramountcy was at Nyakrom." Kwasi Kwakum, Kyidomhene of Kwanyako, had this to say, "I am the first [to go to Nyakrom]. The Omanhene does not agree

26. Lucy Mair, *New Nations* (London: Weidenfeld and Nicolson, 1963), pp. 8–9.

with Kwanyako. There was a dispute in Kwanyako at one time and the Omanhene went to settle it. He abused the people in Kwanyako that 'they are strangers and slaves to Nyarko Kweku of Nyakrom.' When he said this the whole of Kwanyako decided to go to the original head. . . . Omanhene offered £40, 4 sheep, 1 case of gin as apology, we accepted pacification." One subchief's grievance was that his tribunal, his source of revenue, had been closed down by the omanhene and the latter was mulcting the subchief's people heavily at the omanhene's own tribunal.

Kwaku Mfarfo of Bobikuma complained bitterly that the omanhene once advised Bobikuma to "make a market" (hold a meeting?), to which the D.C. had objected. The dispute which ensued nearly resulted in a fight among the people of Bobikuma, and "Bobikuma lost two hundred pounds which the omanhene took from us." Again the people realized that they were owing allegiance to strangers — descendants of Yaw Minta — who were maltreating them. The *banmuhene* of Duakwa had this to say: "When Yaw Minta came to Agona, he met my ancestors. We gave him land. The dethronements in Nsaba are too frequent. As Banmuhene [the one responsible for the burial of the omanhene] I am tired of burying deceased persons."

The economic grievances, whatever the idiom in which they were expressed and justified, were even more telling, and particularly reflected the changing environment. The *banmuhene* was very much to the point when he lamented, "Nsaba's rulers for the past eleven years have been having intention[s] towards Duakwa — taking Duakwa's lands." Kofi Mensah, chief linguist of Nyakrom, harped on a similar chord. Nyakrom stopped serving Nsaba because "over a land dispute Nsaba did not regard Nyakrom [take her interest into account] at all and caused them [Nyakrom people] to waste money." The *kyidomhene* of Kwanyako was angry and displeased with Nsaba because "Omanhene Duodu VII ordered that we should not *sell* our cocoa to any European firm, while Nsaba [people] were selling their cocoa freely." Kyidomhene II of Nkum, with a flair for precision, complained that "7 years 3 months and 9 days ago I had [shared] a boundary with the chief of Akroso. The [latter] chief took the whole of my land. I brought the case before the Omanhene. Omanhene obtained bribe of £200 from Akroso and decided against me. My tribunal was closed down. I was having too many cases [note that chiefs kept the fines] so he [the omanhene] took

some of my cases to Nsaba. Nsaba employed touts to get cases at
Nkum for him." Kwaman and Asafo tribunals were also closed
down. That these tribunals should become a major source of
income — and means to maintain chiefly authority — in an era of
land and other litigations about money cannot be overemphasized.[27]

The point was made when I interviewed the fifty-eight-year-old
gyasehene of Agona, now, thanks to his cocoa farm, living in a modern concrete and very spacious house at Mahundwi (his traditional
seat was Kubease), that chieftaincy, for him, was synonymous with
four elements: (1) the oath — an important means of social control
in the hands of the chief, and source of income; (2) settlement of
disputes and adjudication — the means of maintaining order in society, and a source of wealth (court fines, etc.); (3) lands — an object of religious devotion (the ancestors concerned with our well-
being are associated with them) and source initially of subsistence
and now of wealth and income; and, finally, (4) *Mma ne Nananom*,
that is, children and grandchildren — the guardians of stool property and the providers of services. In a general sense the category
includes all the subjects of a state or chiefdom. It requires hardly
any demonstration that all the factors, whether ritual or mystical,
were, both independently and in combination, very important
sources of wealth, revenue, or money without which, as we shall
soon see, chieftaincy anywhere in Ghana becomes hollow and easily
swept away by new economic and political forces.

27. The grievances reflect attempts by the Omanhene to monopolize control
over economic resources to ensure centralized political control in Agona. Chiefly
tribunals were generally agencies of extortion.

3 POLITICAL PARTICIPATION AND NATIONAL INTEGRATION IN SWEDRU
The Social and Economic Background

In the preceding pages passing references have been made to some of the social and economic changes occurring in Agona in particular and the Gold Coast (Ghana) in general. We have noted the new economic roles which monetization and the introduction of cocoa as a cash crop have occasioned. Also, we have noted the extension in the scale of social relations beyond parochial kin and tribal boundaries as demonstrated by increasing migration – particularly by the Gomoa farmers, who came to Agona after 1910 – into areas other than their place of birth for primarily economic reasons.

The migration was made possible not only because of the existence of peaceful conditions, but also because of the increasing homogenization of British administrative and judicial institutions in the colonial situation. Education and Christianity had been brought into Agona in the latter part of the nineteenth century. An important new class of men, in a number of cases economically self-sufficient, a new community of "Christian scholars" started to emerge in Nsaba, Swedru, and especially Kwanyako. That these new men stood for ideas that were, on occasion, contrary to some of the most cherished views about political institutions centering on the role of the chief (traditional leadership) was amply shown by the alleged refusal of the Nsaba "Christian community" to act in accordance with native custom in the reign of Yaw Duodu II, omanhene of Agona. What happened is not exactly clear. They may have refused to participate in rituals associated with ancestor worship. The immediate effect of this attitude was the diminution, however minimal and gradual at first, of the authority and influence of the chief.[1] The economic changes were to prove even more antagonistic to the pre-European indigenous political institutions. To give but one example, the chief had to find a way to communicate with and control

1. See Busia, *Position of the Chief*, pp. 102–38, for a realistic and pertinent discussion.

81

migrants who had no political status in the traditional system based on kinship and land grants and who did still owe allegiance to the chiefs of their home towns. In the past, strangers had asked for and been granted lands by the local chief. The fact that most of these migrants were now economically independent of the chief made political control by the chief difficult.

The opening of new economic roles, new economic opportunities, meant the growth of new status groups, or incipient classes, whose prestige and influence were based on extra-kin factors, and increasingly on their position in the market situation. It also marked a slow shift away from particularistic — lineage and family — to individual claims of ownership of land, from Henry Maine's "status to contract," as the case of the Gomoa farmers on Agona lands has illustrated.

THE ROAD TO THE URBANIZATION OF SWEDRU

We have seen that Swedru, like the other Agona chiefdoms, began, about two and a half centuries ago, as a cluster of farm settlements, hardly a town. The inhabitants, mainly Agona (of one or two related tribes), were subsistence farmers who were also engaged for the most part in the slave and palm-oil trades, which cocoa was subsequently to replace.[2] Today a majority of the Agona are still subsistence farmers and hunters. No doubt, the growth of Swedru into a dynamic urban center provides an interesting commentary on Eurocolonial rule and the rapid economic and social transformation in the country.

The two decades between 1900 and 1920 may be considered as representing the first period of modern economic expansion, which was related to, indeed brought about by, the rapid growth of transportation facilities, such as roads and railroads, in the Gold Coast.[3] Before 1905, the most important developments were two: the exten-

2. In 1824, Collier, MacCarthy, et al., *Agoona Country*, described the chief vegetable products of the Swedru area as "maize (two crops in a year), millet, yams, cassada [cassava], sweet potatoes, plantains, cotton, rice, sugar cane, ochrae [okra], oranges, pineapple." The domestic animals included "sheep, goats, hogs, dogs, cats, common fowl, etc."
3. The nationally integrative importance of the growing network of roads cannot be overemphasized. As P. R. Gould convincingly argues in *Transportation in Ghana* (Evanston: Northwestern University Press, 1960), p. 22 ff., officially maintained roads strengthened the traditional north-south alignment of commodity movement by linking areas of export agricultural production to the coastal outlets.

sion of the Accra road north to the area of expanding cocoa production at Osino and Apedwa, and the improvement in the road surface to Nsawam; and the construction of two new roads north from the roadstead coastal ports of Winneba and Apam to the palm-oil centers of Swedru and Abodom, two of the chiefdoms of the Agona state. In fact, it is claimed that the Swedru-Winneba, Accra-Osino roads were the first motorable roads.[4]

Between 1905 and 1915, considerable road development took place in the Gold Coast colony and improvements on existing roads were carried out to make them fit for motor transport. Motor transport was growing at a rapid pace at this time, and it is significant for the subsequent growth of Swedru that, according to Gould, the first scheduled trucking services went into effect between Winneba and Swedru in 1912.[5]

The decades following World War I, 1920–40, saw the initiation of a "second transport revolution" in the Gold Coast with the introduction of large numbers of motor vehicles, particularly the Ford truck. This obviously increased the number of workers in the service sector of the economy as more and more drivers were needed to operate the trucks, and mechanics and fitters were needed to maintain and repair them. Tarred roads, able to bear heavy traffic, were built. Road extensions, tarmac improvements, and bridge construction in the Central Region made it possible for the ports of Cape Coast, Saltpond, and Winneba, to capture much of the cocoa traffic, the consequences of which for Swedru will be discussed in a moment.[6]

The importance of road construction was clearly indicated in the Gold Coast Report on Ashanti, 1920: "To a population of gregarious

4. Ibid., p. 38. It should be mentioned in passing that road construction and maintenance was the responsibility of two government departments. The main trade roads — e.g., Swedru-Winneba — came under the PWD (Public Works Department), while the so-called bush roads came under the D.C.'s, who paid the local villages 10 shillings per mile on a quarterly basis to keep them clear. We have already noted how some of the chiefs of Swedru misappropriated the money from this source.

5. The central province in which Swedru lay had, by 1916, 130 miles of PWD roads and 504 miles of roads locally maintained, a majority of them cocoa roads focusing on the seaports of Cape Coast, Saltpond, and Winneba.

6. In 1922, the Akora River, which meanders through Swedru, overflowed its banks and swept away the first iron and wooden bridge over the river, built in 1912. But it was not until 1929 that a more permanent set of iron and concrete bridges was constructed over the river.

habits . . . a motor road is a great boon, for it brings and keeps
them in close touch with a larger world. Villages situated a mile or
two from the main roads will have feeder roads leading to them, or
if natural objects should prevail, the village will be transplanted
from its own site and set astride the motor road." This observation
is equally valid for the Central Region and, indeed, the importance
of Swedru derives from its nodality as a center of important road
networks (see figures 7 and 8). Better communication led to economic prosperity, which in turn produced demand for changes in
the political and administrative system.

That cocoa, communication, and commerce went together cannot
be gainsaid. In fact, the chief cocoa areas were also those with the
best service of roads and railways. In Swedru the first European
firms or stores were opened soon after the completion of the first
motorable road in 1912. The growth of trading firms was at first
slow, but by 1930 Swedru had emerged as a commercial center.[7]
The ten years between 1920 and 1930 may be considered the high
tide of commercial activities generated by the growth of the profitable cocoa industry.[8] Swedru had certainly entered the mainstream
of the money economy and international trade.

THE EMERGENCE OF NEW ECONOMIC ROLES,
1910–1950

The new employment opportunities opened up by the introduction of the motor vehicle in Swedru and other places have been
mentioned. Many people — especially Fante, with elementary school
education, ex–Standard V and ex–Standard VII pupils — were required to fill a host of skilled, semi-skilled, and unskilled positions,
from messengers and porters to ledger clerks, in the trading compa-

7. Among the European firms or trading companies which arose to take advantage of the growing prosperity, thanks to cocoa, of the Swedru area, were
(1) F. and A. Swanzy; (2) Millers; (3) H. B. W. Russell; (4) Anglo-Guinea;
(5) Commonwealth Trust Company; (6) John Walkdon; (7) Association; (8)
G. F. Overbeck; (9) Henry Warner; (10) SCOA; (11) CFAO; (12) Basel
Mission Factory; (13) UTC; (14) GBO; (15) Woerman; (16) John Holt;
(17) W. Bartholomew; (18) SAT; (19) UAC; and (20) A. G. Leventis. The
names of these stores need documentation since few of them now remain in
operation.

8. In 1909, cocoa represented about 30.8 percent of the export of the Gold
Coast; in 1928, it formed over four-fifths of the total export, about 82.39 per-
cent. D. T. Adams, *An Elementary Geography of the Gold Coast* (London:
University of London Press, 1949), p. 89.

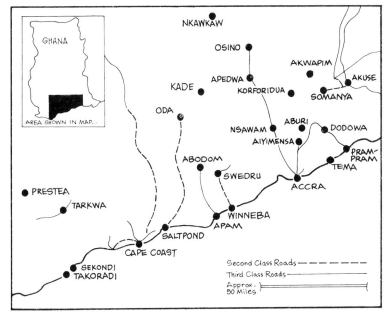

Fig. 7. Ghana Road Network, 1910 (adapted from P. R. Gould, *Transportation in Ghana* [Evanston: Northwestern University Press, 1960], p. 39.

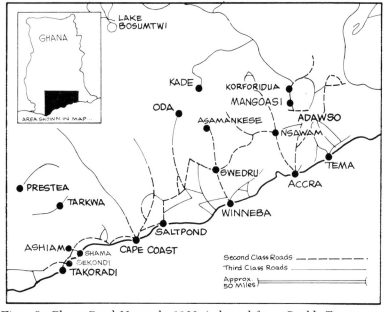

Fig. 8. Ghana Road Network, 1922 (adapted from Gould, *Transportation in Ghana*, p. 41).

nies.[9] Some who completed elementary school became pupil teachers. This last category of people was to become in the 1950s one of the most important groups politically.

An examination of the occupations of men and women in the Gold Coast presented in the 1921 census gives us an idea of the nature of the changes going on in the society and economy. Occupations of men in thirty-two towns included the following:

Farmers	21,272	Blacksmiths	825
Clerks	12,273	Goldsmiths	802
Fishermen/boatmen	9,502	Motor drivers	536
Carriers/laborers	8,870	Teachers	458
Traders	5,555	Fitters/mechanics	347
Domestic servants	3,243	Printers	120
Carpenters	2,159	Ministers of religion	66
Tailors	1,204	Lawyers	50
Bricklayers/masons	1,024	Doctors	7

Of the 47,131 women listed as employed in the 1921 census, 11,957 were "farmers," 11,613 were trade-hawkers, 16,666 were engaged in the preparation and sale of food, 80 were teachers, 20 were civil servants, 1,678 were dressmakers, and 1,641 were described as "labourers." In some instances it was difficult to determine which occupation was primary.

The cocoa industry itself, needless to say, created enormous opportunities for farmer-landlords, farm laborers who were mostly migrants, middlemen or cocoa brokers, and various categories of clerks. Naturally, the chiefs who controlled or owned large acreages of land benefited tremendously from land alienation and, to some extent, from the growth of cocoa farming. Some of the traditional chief cocoa-farmer landlords — the chief of Duakwa in Agona state, the asantehene, the omanhene of Akim Abuakuwa, to name but a few — became very rich and thereby undoubtedly increased their power and influence. In fact, the richer the chief the greater the likelihood that he would be the center of traditional political conservatism. In 1928 the worsening of the farmers' terms of trade — as reflected in the low price they received for their cocoa and the high price they paid for imported goods — led directly to the formation, at the instance of some chiefs and with their support, of a Gold

9. A number of the African UAC (incidentally, one of the largest firms in the country) managers of today started as messengers in the 1930s.

Coast Colony and Ashanti Cocoa Federation, which organized in
pre–trade union days a widespread, popular, and very successful
holdup of cocoa during the 1930–31 season.[10] There was no doubt
at all that the degree of power and authority wielded by any chief
varied *ceteris paribus*, directly with the degree of his economic success and the amount of resources he controlled.

But the chiefs had no monopoly of the wide range of economic
opportunities, the very bases of upward social mobility, available to
commoners, some of whom became richer, more influential, and
even more powerful than the chiefs. The chiefs were in any case
powerless to improve the lot of the tremendous influx, for example,
in Swedru, of population in the 1940s and 1950s, most of which, as
we have indicated, owed them no direct allegiance. For these migrants, the chiefs were useless because they could not, in most
cases, perform their traditional economic function, for instance, the
granting of farm lands.[11]

ECONOMIC INTERESTS AND POLITICAL PARTICIPATION

That the primary basis for the legitimation of the authority of the
chief, in fact of any political leader, is, in the final analysis, economic cannot be denied.[12] And in the Gold Coast economic protests
have been at the very root of almost all political change, traditional
and modern.[13] As far back as the early eighteenth century, and even
earlier, the peoples of the Gold Coast had exploited new economic
advantages and had on many occasions combined to protest eco-

10. The fall in the price of cocoa was partly the result of a pooling agreement, at the time of the Great Depression, between all the major European
merchants concerned in the purchase of cocoa in West Africa. The old men of
Swedru refer to the period of the "Pool" as the worst in the economic and
political history of the area, for a series of economic abuses by chiefs led to
frequent dethronements, succession disputes, and the withdrawal of allegiance
from the paramount stool of Nsaba.

11. Even if the chiefs prayed to their ancestors for the material well-being of
their subjects, as they undoubtedly did, the prayers were becoming increasingly
meaningless to many.

12. Leadership effectiveness (judged by the leader's ability to maintain, expand and allocate resources to his followers) was closely and almost inextric-
ably linked with the legitimacy of his authority.

13. I have argued elsewhere that the intertribal wars and many major political conflicts of the past, with their attendant shifts in political allegiances, were
nearly all wars or conflicts about or over the control of economic resources —
coastal trade, for instance.

nomic grievances from whatever source.[14] These various protests (often couched in the idiom of kinship or tradition), including the cocoa holdups, whether organized by commoner-workers or by chiefs, in my thinking demonstrate two things: (1) the priority or primacy of economic interests (as opposed to, say, religious-spiritual interests common in Asia), as shown by increasing preoccupation with economic grievances; and (2) that a key to an understanding of the political development in Swedru and in the Gold Coast generally lies in the multiple ways in which people have perceived and demonstrated their economic interests — which may, it must be noted, include the satisfaction of sheer biocultural subsistence needs.[15]

This has produced a dominant pattern or style of politics whose leit-motiv is the "economization" of political relations.[16] Much of the "nationalism" of the 1940s and 1950s was in a crucial sense, and again not entirely, economic nationalism. In fact, it is in this respect that I tend to agree with Padmore's claim that the Aborigines' Rights Protection Society and the Fante Confederation, made up of Fante chiefs and their educated lawyer subjects, of the latter part of the nineteenth century were the forerunners of modern Gold Coast nationalism.

It should be stressed at once, lest it be misconstrued, that the present endeavor, which I hold makes for better and more realistic understanding of politics in the Gold Coast and British West Africa, is not an affirmation of economic determinism, not a statement that economic values alone determine human action.[17] What I am saying here is that, precolonial, colonial, and postcolonial societies of Ghana, while not considering economic processes as ends in them-

14. The first reported workers' strike occurred in 1736, when the Anomabu workers employed in the construction of the Anomabu castle struck over low wages.

15. I am not arguing that Ghanaians are *always* concerned *entirely* with the pursuit of economic self-interest.

16. In the struggle for economic and political control interest groups (class, status and local) deploy a host of symbols and ideologies, traditional and modern, as organizational weapons.

17. As a matter of fact, the theory of social stratification of K. Davis and E. W. Moore in "Some Principles of Stratification," *American Sociologial Review*, 10, no. 2 (1945): pp. 242–49, that isolated material advantages and associated prestige as more or less the sole motivational factors in human behavior in industrial societies has been criticized on this very point by M. Tumin, "Some Principles of Stratification: A Critical Analysis," *American Sociological Review*, 18:672–73.

selves, gave very definite postive value to them and thus made economic values, in fact, *seem* at times to be ends rather than means to
other ends. What have no doubt been desirable intermediate values
include political power and authority, which have continued to
offer access to wealth and greater consumption of economic goods,
the basis of high social status and prestige.[18] Yet authority needs
wealth, money, backing for its survival, even for its recognition. In
West African cultures, this is expressed by the emphasis placed on
the organization of production and exchange as a central concern.[19]

The theory of interplay between economic interests and political
process flows from the consideration that trade and commerce have
been important ingredients in the organization of power. The assessment of the role of chiefs in the past, in intertribal wars and so
on, points to this conclusion. Even Akan religion makes economic
pursuit by the chief a primary point of departure. Central to the religious function of the chief is praying to his ancestors for life and
prosperity of the community in an utilitarian, matter-of-fact way.[20]
Again, the demonstration of a chief's authority in the past was, interestingly, effected by a conspicuous display, at strategic periods,
such as annual festivals, of accumulated wealth and equally conspicuous redistribution of part of the wealth or resources in keeping
with the cultural demand that a powerful chief must also be a rich
and generous one.[21] The interaction of politics and economics is
clear. In more recent times economic power is *potentially* political
power, and, equally, the latter has a tendency to enhance one's economic power. The present position is summarized by Fallers thus:
"In their recent economic contacts with the outside world Africans

18. It is no accident that any economically successful man — whatever his
occupation — in Ghana is referred to as "Nana" or "Chief."
19. The Federation of British Industries report (1955) hit the nail on the
head when it said, discussing trade and representation in Nigeria and the Gold
Coast, "One begins to feel that everyone . . . man, woman, child is a trader
and that for most commodities there are long chains of intermediaries between
the original producers and the ultimate consumer. . . . Trade as a sideline is
indeed a vital element . . . in the economy. . . ." The report went on to indicate that "the traders themselves, at all levels, are not companies or firms
but *individuals* or at most families; and it is interesting to note what a large
part women play in these transactions."
20. Maxwell Owusu, "Tallensi and Ashanti Responses to Change: A Comparative Study of How Two West African Societies Have Reacted to Socio-Cul-
tural Change" (Master's thesis, University of Chicago, 1966).
21. The chief must be both *Otumfo* ("all powerful") and *Osagyefo* ("conqueror"); *Odeefo* ("kind master") and *Daasebre* ("benefactor").

have on the whole responded in this essentially *utilitarian* way" (my italics).[22] One of the primary uses of money in Ghanaian society is its consumption and distribution to acquire high social status and prestige. It is also variously expressed by the people I talked to in the field: "Wowo sika a na woye ohene," said one middle-aged man, meaning, "He who has money is a chief." "Ohia ni te se aboa," that is, "A poor man is like a beast," said another. Even modern education confers high status and power principally because it opens up vast economic or material advantages.

This should not be surprising, given the material emphasis in the cultures of the tribes of the Gold Coast with the added fact that when the first Europeans, the famous "merchant adventurers," came it was not primarily in the social, the political, or the cultural spheres, at least for a long time, but in the *economic* that the tribes of the Gold Coast felt the impact of Europe. The Portuguese, the Dutch, the Danes, the British — all came initially to trade in a variety of commodities, bringing to our shores and hinterland the goods of a technologically advanced society. It is significant that nearly four centuries of commercial dealings preceded British colonial political control. The application of the indirect rule principle made this control somewhat incomplete. Little wonder that economic relations, and motivations of more or less materialistic sort, became dominant (in a sense this was consistent with traditional value-orientation) in the cultures of the Gold Coast as social change continued at a rapid pace.[23]

When British rule was finally firmly established, it is not unreasonable to argue that, the fear of physical force apart, the colonial situation was largely acceptable because it fostered that peaceful environment which was so essential for orderly trade and commerce and the accumulation of wealth and power, the opportunities for which were now present and could be seized by anyone enterprising enough.[24]

22. Fallers, "Social Stratification," p. 142.
23. Thus, when the slave trade was abolished in 1807, it is claimed that the African suppliers, who included chiefs, protested against the abolition of a trade — as the Committee to the Lords of the Treasury Report quoted by Kimble, *Political History of Ghana*, p. 2, has it — "[the slave trade was] not inconsistent with their prejudices, their laws, or their notions of morality and religion and by which alone they have been hitherto accustomed to acquire wealth, and to purchase all the foreign luxuries and conveniences of life."
24. After all, what the British wanted, according to Fitzgerald, in ibid., p. 9, was "a race of *native* capitalists in West Africa . . . and we will do our best

It is fair, I suppose, to say that while the colonial government, European traders, and even the Basel Mission encouraged capitalism among the peoples of the Gold Coast, very little attempt, if any at all, was made to prepare the people for civic responsibility founded on democratic or any overarching political values, the political side of the economic equation. This point should be particularly stressed, especially when political instabilities characterize the new states of Africa. Whatever politics was present was largely associated with economic grievances related to questions of status, class competition, and upward mobility (or the prevention of downward social mobility) – hence the dominance of "grievance politics," the politics of economic scarcity.

As R. L. Sklar in a recent article concludes, and I tend to share this conclusion, despite the existence of status ambiguity in some situations, "In Africa today, the new ruling classes are based on power, wealth and opportunity for personal achievement. The criteria of inclusion are high-status occupation, high income, control of wealth producing enterprises, and superior education." [25] Superior education itself leads to wealth and wealth is a means to the organization of power, which in turn may lead to more wealth and to higher social status and prestige. The rich man in Swedru today is potentially influential in a community and is actually influential if he spends money freely on people and may in fact make important decisions for his community. He undoubtedly settles minor interpersonal disputes and may be the leader of communal labor. A very distressed old man lamented the situation thus, "If you have no money, no one listens to you these days." Yet he felt that life itself is the highest value – "ehia wo a nwu."

THE URBANIZATION OF SWEDRU: COCOA KINGS,
COMMUNICATION, AND CAPTAINS OF COMMERCE

In the 1960 Ghana census, Swedru emerges, on the basis of the demographic variable of population size, as one of the fifteen urban

---

to help in the creation." *In Eighteen Years on the Gold Coast* (London, 1853), 2:36, Cruickshank expressed surprise at "the peculiar partiality of the natives of the Gold Coast . . . for pedling. . . . One is at a loss to conceive where there is any room for buyers among such a nation of pedlers"; a comment quite reminiscent of Napoleon Bonaparte's view of England – "a nation of shopkeepers" – in the eighteenth century.

25. R. L. Sklar, "Political Science and National Integration: A Radical Approach," *Journal of Modern African Studies* 5, no. 1 (1967): 7.

POLITICAL PARTICIPATION AND NATIONAL INTEGRATION

centers of Ghana. With a population of 20,546 occupying an area of seventeen square miles, the density of 1,209 persons per square mile is one of the highest in Africa. In a sense, this is hardly surprising, for over half of the over 67,000,000 inhabitants of West Africa are concentrated mainly in the southern, more economically productive, areas of Nigeria, Ghana, Liberia, and Sierra Leone.[26] Urbanization involves, however, more than changing structure and composition of the population. It represents changes in the structure of society, as demonstrated by (1.) highly complex and distinctive forms of social differentiation, (2) a high degree of functional specialization and functional inter-dependence, (3) the possibility of industrialization, (4) an increase in the shape and spatial location, and (5) changing norms and values related in some way to the changing structure of relations. Thus, according to Scott Greer, urbanization may be conceptualized as a form of social organization representing a transformation in the total organization of society.[27] An urban society becomes a particular way of organizing people and a distinctive way of life.

Swedru is a nonindustrial, partly agricultural, and mostly commercial town. It provides an instance of *urbs in rure*, the "urban island in a sea of rurality." This point should be noted for, as I hope to show, it has interesting political implications. Before proceeding to a discussion of the specifically urban characteristics and their effects on political process and political participation, let us first outline briefly how Swedru achieved urbanism or became urbanized.

In their reports, Collier, MacCarthy, et al., estimate, as we noted, the population of the "Agoona Country" in 1824 to have been ten thousand, made up of three thousand men and seven thousand women and children.[28] Allowing for gross errors and fanciful guesses in their estimate, it could still be said, on the basis of inferences from what the elders say about the villages in the nineteenth century, that Swedru's share of the total could not have been more than five hundred for the combined four original wards of the village. Swedru, therefore, was nothing but a small-scale, largely ho-

26. Norton Ginsburg, *Atlas of Economic Development* (Chicago: University of Chicago Press, 1961); UNESCO, *Social Implications of Industrialization and Urbanization in Africa South of the Sahara* (Paris, 1956).
27. Scott Greer, *The Emerging City* (New York: Free Press, 1962), pp. 11–50.
28. Collier, McCarthy, et al., *Agoona Country*, pp. 55–64.

mogeneous, descent-based agricultural society familiar to classical anthropologists as the "folk type."

By 1924 that picture had changed a great deal. This change was due mainly to cocoa, which gradually but surely was replacing palm oil as a major export crop. Cocoa depots or stations having sheds, some with a holding capacity of about three thousand tons, were opened in Swedru by European firms,[29] especially after the First World War, to enable them to purchase through a long chain of African intermediaries or brokers the cocoa produced mainly in the surrounding farms in such towns and villages as Duakwa, Nsaba, Odobeng, Otenkorang. In some cases these firms also established a number of stores in which various "made in Europe" or "Empire made" consumer luxury and other prestige items were sold. In the 1920s the first Kwahu traders began to trickle into Swedru, initially as peddlers and later as store owners — petty traders. The Levantines were to follow in the late 1930s and the 1940s. The Kwahu were to become in the 1950s, as we shall see, one of the most powerful economic groups in Swedru.

The establishment of commercial firms and the in-migration of cash-crop farmers, not to mention the introduction of motor vehicles and the associated improvement in road transport, led to two significant changes in Swedru which were to form the bases of further societal transformations, namely, an increase in the size and composition of the population, and an increase in the complexity of functional specialization. The growth of communication, road expansion, and development of the cocoa industry resulted, for example, directly in the intensification of commercial activities, mainly by "foreigners."

Yet Swedru, just fifteen road miles from coastal Winneba and in complementary relation to it, was overshadowed in importance by the latter, which was in 1929 the "third shipping port in the country," the district administrative center, the district headquarters of the European firms, and a major resort and residence for Europeans. Winneba was the outlet for the cocoa and palm oil produced in Agona, Gomoa, and Akim Kotoku.[30] Swedru, however, stood out

29. E. g., Swanzy, Lyons, Cadbury and Fry, and the UAC, which flanked both sides of Swedru's main road, appropriately named Commercial Road.
30. The 1921 census has the following population figures for these towns: Winneba, 6,980; Nyakrom, 6,257; Swedru, 2,582; Nsaba, 2,343. The last three towns are all in Agona and centers of the booming cocoa industry. In 1931, the population of Swedru was approximately 3,867. Swedru was thus still essen-

as one place in the area whose growth, though modest at first, was the result primarily of in-migration of "aliens" and not of natural increase of the indigenous population. Again, it was the only Agona town with resident Europeans and a resident assistant district commissioner. The significance of the presence of Europeans, perceived by local people as carriers of modernity, cannot be overemphasized.

Geographic location has been crucial to the urban growth of Swedru. Swedru enjoyed the good site as the node of the network of the main roads in the Southern Gold Coast (Ghana). It lies on the Sekondi-Takoradi to Accra motor road, and crosses the Winneba to the Nsaba, Oda, and Nyakrom motor roads. There is little doubt that the road network is one of the principal factors influencing life in the area. The inhabitants, both indigenous and migrant, agree that the opening in 1958 of the Accra-Takoradi "coastal road" and the Achiase-Kotoku railway has had adverse effect on the otherwise continuous growth of Swedru.

The 1960 Ghana census defined towns as those human settlements with at least 5,000 inhabitants.[31] Nevertheless, on the basis of this minimal definition of urban status, Swedru begins to emerge as a "true" town only after World War II, when the 1948 census figure for its population was about 11,000. The figure included 10,913 Africans and 44 non-Africans, mainly Europeans, Indians, and Levantines.[32] The presence of "white men" (aborofo) needs comment. It is popularly claimed that in a welcome address to the first European businessmen who came to Swedru to work, the Agona omanhene at the time said, "I beseech you to build up Swedru, the way you built up Accra." It is interesting that part of the social definition of the urbanization of Swedru consisted in the relatively permanent residence of Europeans. The Europeans, despite their racial background, were seen as an integral part of the society and were accepted by the Africans, chief and subject alike, basically because of their functional contribution to the socioeconomic development of

tially a small rural town, despite its great growth potential, in a way very little different from Nyakrom, (pop. 6,442), larger in population terms, or from Kwanyako, both of which in 1931 duplicated some of the commercial firms found in Swedru.

31. The difficulties associated with single variable categorizations are obvious — e.g., crucial socioeconomic characteristics are ignored.

32. The Europeans were British, French, Greek and Swiss managers of the European firms: UAC (British), SCOA (French), PZ (Greek), and UTC and SAT (Swiss).

the town. Thus in 1953–54, the Swedru Urban Council (about which more will be said in our discussion of the development of modern politics) resolved to approach the district manager of the United Africa Company (UAC) to recommend to the general manager in Accra the council's humble request to the UAC to build a community center in Swedru "as a mark of the cordial and loyal friendship existing between the Council and the U.A.C." (Council Minutes). The Europeans were also a positive reference group whose living standard was highly admired and imitated, and who were envied in some quarters for ostensibly doing no work — "just signing of names" for big pay. Let us at this point turn to a consideration of some of the characteristics of the 1948 census.

THE 1948 CENSUS: SWEDRU

The African population was 10,913, of whom 5,694 were male and 5,219 were female. There were 3,306 men and 2,859 women of age sixteen and over. There were also 4,748 people of both sexes who were fifteen years old or under. The figures for education are hardly impressive. There was a total of 1,085 people with some formal education. Of these, 553 had had Standard VII or higher, and the other 532 had had between Standard III and Standard VI educations.

The level of demographic stability in Swedru may be gleaned, to some extent, from an inspection not only of where residents were born but also of how long they have been residents. Of the 10,913 African population, 4,204 were born in Swedru; 5,016 were born in the colony of the Gold Coast; 387 were born in Ashanti; 464 in the Northern Territories; 223 in British Togoland; 366 in a British colony (Nigeria); 253 were born in foreign colonies. The total number of nonlocal, "alien"-born residents in Swedru was 6,709, making the migrant population exceed the local-born by 2,505. Although not all "aliens" are necessarily "foreign" and not all Swedru-born are necessarily Agona, I think the picture is clear. Again, of the whole population, 2,013 had been residents of Swedru for less than one year; 3,422 had been residents of Swedru for between one and five years; and 5,478 had been there for five years or more. The picture points to a pattern of relative demographic stability of the population.

The occupational structure is equally interesting. The number of people in modern economic roles indicates the slow shift away from a pre-Eurocolonial economic base (subsistence farming), the shift being one index of increasing urbanization. In 1948, 2,883 people were listed as occupied, and 502 were listed as unemployed. Of the employed, 199 were in road transport; 416 were engaged in commerce and related jobs; 255 were wage laborers; and 719 were in primary production. Eight hundred seventy-one, therefore, were employed in modern occupations, and 719 were still in the traditional sector. This should be particularly noted, for in 1948 only about 10 percent of the population had any level of formal education at all. The political and administrative consequences of this fact should not be overlooked. The year 1948 marked the beginning of the emergence of an incipient modern political party in the Gold Coast. It is against this demographic background that the initial and subsequent performance of the Convention Peoples Party, the United Gold Coast Convention, and others should be assessed.

Although in 1948 there were still fewer people engaged in the modern sector of the economy in Swedru, the town could lay claim to being *urbs in rure*. Swedru was described even in 1948 as the Agona-Nkran, the Accra of Agona State, but the characterization emerges lucidly in 1960. In any case, it was the commercial center par excellence of the area and was to become in the 1950s an important political center as well. But the greatest real urban growth occurred between 1950 and 1960, a period described by the inhabitants as the most prosperous of all times. Despite the tremendous socioeconomic development of the period, Swedru still experienced some significant loss of population, which I presume was directly related to the undulating pattern of commercial societies that depend heavily on overseas imports for economic vitality and viability.

The population of Swedru almost doubled in the decade 1950–60. In 1960 the population was over 20,000, and was growing at an annual rate of 4.4 percent, compared with the pre–1948 annual average increase of 1.6 percent. Here again, the growth was primarily due to in-migration of "foreigners" attracted there by the economic boom which had resulted from the good cocoa price paid to local cocoa farmers. It is of interest to note that, from about 1929 to 1939, the cocoa price in local terms averaged 7s. 6d. per sixty-pound load. By 1960, the price per load of cocoa was to average £3 (sterling), the controlled price of the Ghana Cocoa Marketing Board. The very generous advances, in some cases over £1,000, paid by the Cocoa

Purchasing Company between 1952 and 1956 to farmers generated much spending power in Swedru. This was the era of the great Kwahu migrant "captains of commerce" — Yaw Booh, Kwame Boateng, Kwame Addo, Kodjo Fordwoo, to mention a few of the most famous; of the Lebanese-Syrians — Ahdab and Zraik, Byrouthy, Norris Court, Chahal and Dakiz, who controlled the retail trade in automobiles and dealt in motor spare parts; and of the big transport owners — Tabicca, Hammond, owner of the "Bye-Bye Transport" Fleet. As one shrewd observer put it, "Cocoa made kings out of commoners."

Swedru grew toward greater urbanization, as reflected by the occupational structure. We noted in the 1948 census that there were in Swedru nearly as many people in agriculture as there were in the tertiary sector. In 1960, though the population had grown tremendously, only 20.0 percent of the men and 21.6 percent of the women were engaged in agriculture (63.0 percent of all employed males in Ghana were in primary production).

The following selected distribution of occupations may give us an idea of the high degree of functional specialization. In 1960, 7,923 people, 4,571 men and 3,352 women, had employment. Of these, 375 were in the professional, technical and related occupations. There were 82 men and 1 woman occupying nongovernment administrative, executive, and managerial positions, with an additional 23 men in government administrative, executive, and managerial positions. Three hundred thirty men and 1 woman were classified as drivers (in road transport), and 2,405, 568 men and 1,837 women, as sales workers. In the retail trade, which consisted mainly of petty traders, there were 2,086, 362 men and 1,724 women. Craftsmen, production process workers, and laborers, such as tailors, goldsmiths, and carpenters numbered 2,484, 1,925 men and 5 women. The shape of the town itself changed. New wards were added to the four original abron.[33] Yet the rise almost everywhere in town of huge one-, two-, and three-story concrete houses, owned mainly by migrants — Kwahu, Lebanese-Syrian, and Fante — was even more diagnostic of the transformation. Each of the wards of Swedru now became associated with at least one modern institution or home, namely:

33. Zerikin Zongo, founded by a Wangara migrant from Upper Volta, Malam Salifu Darfi (*Zongo* or "resting place" means "stranger" quarter) attracted a motley group of people including Hausa, Kotokoli, Fulani, Mosi, Zambrama, Yoruba, whose crumbling and congested tenements and compounds are a familiar sight.

Name of Ward	*Associated Institution*
A Asisim	Methodist School
B Nsawam	Magistrate's Court
C Owani	Post Office
D Ankyease	Police Station (Ahenfie)
E Anaafu (Desuenyim)	Swiss African Trading Company
F Salem (including Kubease)	Presbyterian Church
G Akorakyi (Transflumen)	Ghana College
H Mahundwi	Health Department
I Nsusuoso	Mr. Lartey's House
J Dwinhu	Zion School
K Zongo	Mr. Dixon's House
L Bebianiha	Urban Council Offices

It is significant to mention that it is possible in 1970, despite the ethnic heterogeneity of the town, to describe a number of these wards (also electoral wards) as having a preponderance or core group of either Agona, Pepe, or Fante voters. A few are distinguishable by religion rather than by ethnic origin.

1960: ETHNIC OR TRIBAL COMPOSITION OF SWEDRU
Total population: 20,550
Not classified by tribe: 70
All tribes: 20,480

AKAN. TOTAL: 14,920

1. NZEMA. Total: 220
   Nzema: 140
   Ahanta: 80
2. TWI-FANTE (FANTE). Total: 12,380
   Fante: 8,320
   Agona: 4,060
3. TWI-FANTE (TWI). Total: 2,340
   Wasa: 10
   Denkyera: 20
   Asen (Assin): 40
   Akyem (Akim): 460
      Bosome: 10
      Kotoku: 10
      Akyem, without other specification: 440
   Akuapem (Akwapim): 410

Akwamu: 40
Kwawu (Kwahu): 850
Asante (Ashanti): 440
Boron, including Banda: 30
Akan, not elsewhere specified: 40
4. GA-ADANGBE. Total: 470
Ga: 340
Adangbe: 100
  Ada: 20
  Shai: 20
  Krobo: 60
Ga-Adangbe, without other specification: 30
5. EWE. Total: 1,520
Ewe: 1,520
Fon: 0
6. GUAN. Total: 640
Efutu: 300
Awutu: 120
Kyerepon (Cherepong): 10
Larte (Larteh): 20
Anum-Boso: 60
Guan, not elsewhere specified: 130
7. CENTRAL TOGO TRIBES (e.g., Buem, Ava-
time). Not represented.
8. YORUBA. Total: 690 (Nigeria)
Yoruba: 690
Atakpame: 0
9. IBO. Total: 30 (Nigeria)
Ibo: 30
10. GURMA. Total: 140
Pila-pila: 60
Kyamba (Tchamba): 60
Gurma, not elsewhere specified: 20
11. TEM (KOTOKOLI). Total: 660
Tem: 660
12. MOLE-DAGBANI. Total: 210
Nanumba: 0
Dagomba: 100
Walba (Wala): 30

Dagaba (Dagarte): 10
Builsa (Kangyaga): 20
Frafra: 20
Talensi: 10
Mosi: 20
13. GRUSI. Total: 130
Mo: 10
Vagala: 10
Sisala: 10
Grusi, without other specification: 100
14. SONGHAI. Total: 120
Songhai: 10
Zabrama: 110
15. MANDE. Total: 260 (Sierra Leone)
Busanga: 30
Wangara: 230
16. HAUSA. Total: 360 (Nigeria)
Hausa: 360
17. FULANI. Total: 40 (Nigeria)
Fulani: 40
18. KRU. Total: 70 (Liberia)
Kru: 70
19. OTHER TRIBES. Total: 200
Mostly originating from Ghana: 10
Mostly originating from Nigeria: 130
Mostly originating from other African countries: 60
20. NOT CLASSIFIED BY TRIBE: 70
Including Europeans, Indians, Lebanese, and Syrians.

The above figures are adapted from the 1960 Ghana census. Tribes 8 and 9 are popularly called *Alatafo*, meaning "people associated with pepper," because the first Yoruba women migrants were sellers of pepper. Tribes 10 through 17 are popularly referred to as *Pepefo*. The origin of the word is not known to me.

It is necessary to make a few observations about the ethnic or tribal composition of the population. The Akan constitute the major category. This, of course, is in keeping with the national distribution. There are six principal individual tribes or subgroups of the Akan in Swedru. These are the Fante; the Agona, "owners" of Swedru; the Kwahu; the Asante (Ashanti); the Akuapem; and other Twi groups. Apart from these, there are other important groups — the Ewe, Yoruba, Guan, Tem (Kotokoli), and Ga-Adangbe. It is noteworthy that the Fante alone constitute 40.5 percent and the Agona 19.8 percent of the population, this despite the fact that the latter are the original settlers of Swedru. This distribution naturally must have interesting consequences for political participation and national integration.

The Kwahu, controllers of petty trade, make up 4.1 percent of the population; the Asante (Ashanti), 2.1 percent; the Akuapem, 2.0 percent; and other Twi groups, 4.2 percent. Despite their relative numerical inferiority, they form a powerful economic category as landlords, financiers, and the like. The Kotokoli, mainly cocoa farm laborers, constitute 3.2 percent; Ga-Adangbe, 2.3 percent; and all other tribes, 7.8 percent. The homogeneity index, it must be indicated, for the major tribes equals 54.2 percent, and the index for individual tribes equals 21.7 percent.[34] (We may note that for the 1960 census purposes only individual or major tribes representing at least 2.0 percent of the total population of the local authority [local government area] are shown separately. The remainder of the individual tribes are grouped under "other" of the same major tribe.) The homogeneity indices are very interesting and point to the fact that, despite ethnic heterogeneity as determined by place of origin, Swedru is relatively homogeneous, since more than half of the population belong to the same cultural or linguistic group.

Under these circumstances, plus the fact, as we shall see, that people in Swedru belong to nontribal cross-cutting voluntary associations and occupations, a fairly high degree of social integration must be expected.

34. For the 1960 census, the index expresses the ratio between the existing homogeneity and the maximum possible homogeneity. The formula is:

$$\frac{(\text{No. of people in the major tribe [language group] A})^2 + (\text{No. in group B})^2 + \ldots}{(\text{Total population in a given area})^2}$$

The index is 1.00 (100 percent) when the entire population in the area belongs to one and the same major or individual tribe.

ETHNICITY, INCOME, AND RESIDENCE PATTERNS

It must be confessed at once that only a tentative and highly impressionistic account may be given here of the relationships between ethnic background, income, and residence in Swedru. The conclusions, nevertheless, are suggestive. In Swedru, as in much of Africa, people are often not separated from each other because they have higher incomes, or better education, or even because they come from different tribes. Rich people in all occupations are expected to, and on the whole do, assist the less fortunate members of their families and lineages by letting them live in their houses, by educating their children, and by caring for them generally. Rich and poor still mix and must do so freely with each other. The following account will illustrate the point.

When I was in the field, I rented an "apartment" in a modern two-story complex owned by a wealthy Kwahu trader. The building, House no. I208, is in an area referred to locally as *Asikafo amma ntem* (the area developed by wealthy recent migrants). The economic and ethnic backgrounds of the residents are interesting and, in fact, are quite typical. During November 1966 and until September 1967, the complex was occupied by the following persons: (1) myself, then a predoctoral research student who in local terms was a "been-to" (a person who has been to England, Europe, or America and therefore must be an upper income person); (2) a British-trained Ashanti lawyer, his family, and an Hausa servant; (3) a taxi-driver, an illiterate nephew of the landlord, his illiterate wife, and children who went to school and who did not pay rent; (4) a Fante clerical officer with the Swedru Omnibus Transport Corporation (SOTC); (5) an Akim court registrar and his Agona wife and children; (6) three female Agona untrained primary school teachers; (7) the daughter of the late chief of Swedru and her Fante husband, both working with SOTC; (8) an illiterate Ewe market woman, her husband, who was an educated Ewe general police officer, and their children; (9) a young Akuapem storekeeper and his wife, and his wife's sister and brother.

It is true that the Agona form the core group of the original settlements of Ankyease, Anaafu, Owani, and Kubease; the Gomoa Fante, of the Bebianiha ward; and the Pepefo almost all live in the Zongos. Yet each of the twelve wards is to some extent heterogeneous ethnically and economically. A few high-income group members — European business managers, African business managers, and high administrative officers — may be partially segregated residentially and may occupy the bungalows or rest houses A/B just within the Swedru town boundary on the Swedru-Winneba road (even here, it is occupation that is salient). But this is still somewhat atypical. The Lebanese-Syrians, Indians particularly, live on the floors above their stores or shops along the main road, the Commercial Road, but Africans live in the adjacent apartments. As a matter of fact, the Levantines and Indians and a few of the Europeans are immediately surrounded by Africans. The Kwahu also generally live in their stores along the Commercial Road.

There is no statistical information available, even in crude form, about the relative wealth of each of the wards, but judging from personal experience and observation, and judging by the number, quality, and size of houses, dwellings, and buildings, and by general sanitation, the poorest sections are the Zongos, Ankyease, Kubease, Owani, and Anaafu (it should be said that there are a few rich men recognized as such in each of them). But, unlike the Kumasi case described by Austin and Tordoff, Swedru does not have the extremes of wards ranging from the wealthy and professional-class district of Mbrom to the squalid alleyways and crowded compounds in Adum and Ashanti New Town.[35] The wards of Swedru for the most part fall between the two extremes.

ETHNICITY AND OCCUPATION

Various studies have shown that members of a particular tribe or ethnic group are sometimes suited to, good at, or accept readily certain occupations or jobs. Thus the Lugbara in Uganda, considered physically strong, are mostly engaged in heavy-labor work; the Kikuyu in Nairobi, Kenya, are in the main traders.[36] In Swedru, according to popular stereotypes, the Kwahu are skillful petty traders and do nothing but trade; the Agona young men are painters and bricklayers; the Kru are conservancy boys, removers of night soil (any

35. See D. Austin and W. Tordoff, *Voting in an African Town*, University of London Institute of Commonwealth Studies. Reprint Series no. 8, from Political Studies 8, no. 2 (June 1960): 133.
36. N. Oram, *Towns in Africa* (London: Oxford University Press, the New African Library, 1965).

conservancy boy, whatever his tribe, is *kruni*); the Hausa are butchers; the Calabar women from Nigeria are prostitutes, in fact, any local prostitute is now *Calabar-ni*; the Mosi or Dagarte (Pepefo) are night watchmen. The Anum-Boso group control the drug retail business; the Lebanese-Syrians, motor spare-parts and automobile sales; the Indians, fancy goods and imported jewelry. Although this picture, and others like it, is generally true, it is wrong to assume that members of various tribes may not be found in the "wrong" line of business. There are Hausa tailors and Kwahu school teachers.

To demonstrate this, a limited survey of the staff of seven elementary schools and of the staff of the Electricity Corporation (established in 1949), both of Swedru, was carried out in the "summer" of 1967. The schools and the Electricity Corporation are the two most important employers in the public sector in Swedru — in fact, in the country. The social composition of their staffs is in itself interesting. A total of 135 and 111 persons, representing nearly all the employees of the Electricity Corporation and the schools respectively, were interviewed and were very cooperative. It is important to state that recruitment to these institutions is fairly open and is based primarily on achievement — education, impersonal examinations, and performance at interviews are the crucial criteria — and not on one's ethnic background. This is in keeping with modern bureaucratic norms. If the popular view that the Ewe and the Ga "control" the civil service is true, this situation should be the result not only of the number of available vacancies over time, but of geography as well, as my limited conclusions indicate. There are many Ga in the civil service or in the army because they live near centers of recruitment. They are more informed of available vacancies, and they do not have to travel long distances to look for jobs. It seems Ghanaians, on the whole, would rather stay at home than travel for jobs if they can help it.[37]

My analysis of the staffs of seven schools and one corporation suggests that the ethnic distribution reflects more of geography — Swedru is surrounded by the Fante, the Efutu, the Awutu, the Akim, and the Ga, and Accra is only fifty miles away — and of pat-

37. M. Peil, "Aspirations and Social Structure: A West African Example," *Africa* 38, no. 1 (January 1968): 74, notes that in Ghana "most school leavers in this area [central and western regions] apparently prefer unemployment to migration." She found nearly three quarters of the boys in the national sample still at home seven months after leaving school.

terns of in-migration and occupational mobility through transfers than specific ethnic preference for particular jobs. Tables 3 and 4 show certain distributions and clusters that need little comment. First, the figures point to a fact already noted, that is, the ethnic heterogeneity of the population of Swedru. Second, the school system and the Electricity Corporation are both national institutions in two related senses. To begin with, the personnel are recruited on universalistic criteria which cut across ethnic lines, and their employment is theoretically subject to transfers to any place in the country, irrespective of an employee's private wishes and ethnic background. In addition, the post-acceptance training (for the Electricity Corporation) or preteaching training (for the schools) is in most cases obtained outside the candidate's home area or place of birth. The personnel therefore constitute an important factor in the process of national integration. The staffs consist of nonlocalized circulating or mobile elites who are subject to spatial transfers

TABLE 3 ELECTRICITY CORPORATION PERSONNEL,
APRIL 1967

Tribe	Number	Place of Initial Employment and Transfer
Ga	15	67% Central Region; 27% Eastern Region; 6% Western Region
Ewe	9	34% Northern Region; 66% Central Region
Fante	42	89% Central Region; 2% Western Region; 5% Ashanti; 2% Northern Region; 2% Eastern Region
Agona	18	95% Central Region; 5% Northern Region
Efutu	15	80% Central Region; 14% Eastern Region; 6% Volta Region
Akuapem	8	94% Central Region; 6% Northern Region
Nzema	2	100% Western Region
Kwahu	2	100% Central Region
Nigerian	2	50% Central Region; 50% other
Liberian	1	100% Central Region
Krobo	1	100% Central Region
*Mosi	6	100% Central Region
*Hausa	2	100% Central Region
*Kotokoli	4	100% Central Region
*Wangara	4	100% Central Region
Total	131	

NOTE: The personnel considered here are mainly skilled and semiskilled: technicians, clerks, engineers, and accountants, all with post–primary school training. Tribal affiliation is not specified for the Nigerian and Liberian tribes.

*Unskilled wage laborers.

throughout Ghana. They are the links between the rural, or less developed areas, and the urban, or more developed, regions. Each of
the institutions has a head office in the national capital, Accra.

TABLE 4 SOCIAL COMPOSITION OF THE SEVEN
ELEMENTARY SCHOOLS, APRIL 1967

Tribe	Number	Place of Initial Employment and Transfer
Akuapem	10	80% Eastern Region; 10% Central Region; 10% Volta Region
Fante	48	67% Central Region; 16% Eastern Region; 7% Ashanti; 7% Western Region; 3% Northern Region
Agona	17	77% Central Region; 17% Eastern Region; 6% Ashanti
Ewe	3	67% Eastern Region; 33% Central Region
Efutu	5	60% Central Region; 20% Volta Region; 20% Northern Region
Awutu	2	50% Central Region; 50% Eastern Region
Ahanta	2	50% Western Region; 50% Central Region
Nzema	1	100% Ashanti
Nigerian	2	50% Central Region; 50% Eastern Region
Ga	1	100% Central Region
Krobo	3	67% Eastern Region; 33% Volta Region
Akim	6	50% Central Region; 50% Eastern Region
Anum-Boso	5	80% Eastern Region; 20% Central Region
Kwahu	4	60% Eastern Region; 40% Central Region
Ashanti	2	50% Ashanti; 50% Eastern Region
Total	111	

NOTE: Both trained and untrained persons are teachers in these schools. Tribal
affiliation is not specified for the Nigerian tribes.

One area of research related to urbanization concerns the relationships between ethnicity, tribal origin, and migration. From tables 3 and 4, the inference seems to be that, wherever people have a
choice, migration tends to be short and most probably within the
region of the migrant's place of birth. Thus, there is a high concentration of Akuapem who had been recruited initially in, or transferred initially from, the Eastern Region; of Agona and Efutu, in or
from the Central Region; and of Nzema or Ahanta, in or from the
Western Region. That is, whenever there are in any two regions job
opportunities offering a similar range of rewards, people will more
than likely accept offers near where they were born. This fact
should make us re-examine carefully the claim so often made that
one of the principal reasons for migration in Africa is the desire to
get away from burdensome kinship obligations. In Ghana, it is clear

that migrants return home quite regularly for festivals, for funerals, or just to visit the relatives and friends there. All the thirty adult Kwahu petty traders (all had been living in Swedru for over five years) I interviewed claimed they went home at least once a month and stayed there for an average of three days on each visit. My familiarity with the situation even supports the fact that some of these Kwahu went home almost every weekend, traveling a distance of 220 miles round trip. The Efutu, wherever they are, journey to Winneba for the nationally famous "Deer Hunt" Festival, on which occasion, as the chief of Winneba put it during the 1967 festival, "many of our young men come home to get married." The Ga go home for the annual *Homowo*; the Akuapem, for the annual *Odwira* celebrations. Distance does not seem to be positively correlated with the degree of avoidance of kinship obligations.

In fact, this frequent shuttling between place of birth and place of in-migration does produce some degree of instability in urban societies which affects the functioning of voluntary and other associations, a majority of whose members are migrants. In a discussion with me, the resident Fante minister of the Swedru Methodist Church regretted the fact that church attendance was directly related to the periodic movement to and from Swedru of Fante and other migrants who made up the bulk of the membership. The Akuapem Presbyterian catechist and the Dutch Roman Catholic priest made similar complaints.

ETHNICITY AND RELIGION:
THE CHURCHES AND SECTS

Many writers on West African societies have discussed and in a number of cases analyzed the large number of tribal and ethnic,[38] occupational,[39] and religious voluntary associations, some modern and others traditional. They have described political parties, dancing clubs, mutual aid societies, and progressive unions in these societies.[40] Wallerstein, for instance, has considered the strategic role of voluntary associations in the emergence of modern Ghana and

38. K. Little, "The Organization of Voluntary Associations in West Africa," *Civilisation* 9, no. 3 (1959): 283–300.

39. P. C. Lloyd, "Craft Organization in Yoruba Towns," *Africa* 23, no. 1 (1953): 30–44.

40. See T. Hodgkin, *African Political Parties* (London: Penguin, 1961), for a discussion of political parties.

the Ivory Coast.[41] These associations, especially the ethnic unions, according to Wallerstein (borrowing a leaf, of course, from Durkheim) mediated changes in values, socialized urban migrants, and established links which cut across kinship groupings.[42] Lloyd, in discussing Yoruba towns, argues that Christian churches and political parties go beyond traditional tribal boundaries and, as I hope to show, are sources of national integration.[43] He further notes that these religious and political voluntary organizations provide an important basis of opportunity for young people to achieve a recognized status distinct from the traditional rankings based on age.

Again, membership in religious institutions, which cuts across occupational and tribal lines, and membership in voluntary associations within the church, such as youth guilds, contribute to the integration of urban life by bringing together literate and illiterate members and by reducing the social isolation of town life. It should, perhaps, be mentioned in this connection that these functions performed by church groups are more or less duplicated by nonreligious associations (functional equivalents). A first visitor to Swedru is bound to be surprised at the growing number of religious associations which are always competing for members. But what is happening in Swedru is quite consistent with a national trend — the proliferation of churches, sects, and cults throughout Ghana. Most of these, particularly the separatist churches and sects, are very recent indeed and in Swedru many date back only to 1960. Without going into what motivates individuals or groups to found churches or into the general reasons for them (some believe the separatist churches were established in response to the general social-psychological stress associated with the CPP government), it is obvious that they serve a variety of needs ranging from hardly definable spiritual and emotional ego-involvement to purely materialistic, financial needs.

The "financial" here does not refer to a "Protestant ethic, spirit of capitalism" type of analysis. What I mean is that clearheaded people primarily interested in making money establish churches the

41. I. Wallerstein, "Ethnicity and National Integration in West Africa," *Cahiers d'Etudes Africaines* 3 (October 1960): 129–39.

42. E. Durkheim, *The Division of Labour in Society*, translated by G. Simpson (Glencoe: Free Press, 1947).

43. P. C. Lloyd, "The Yoruba Town Today," *Sociological Review* 7, no. 1 (1959): 45–63.

way others set up businesses. Ostensibly, the sects and separatist churches are there to show votaries the true way to the "everlasting Kingdom" and salvation. The votaries believe they fulfill these functions. Really, however, as a few skeptics admit, they are a major source of income and power for the founders. A thirty-year-old Fante member of the Garden of Eden Church confided to me that he himself was thinking of spending some time in one of the religious schools in America and returning to his village to found his own church because "it is one of the quickest and surest ways these days of making good money."

During 1966–67, there were congregations of various sizes of the following religious groups in Swedru: Presbyterian (Basel); Methodist (Wesley); Roman Catholic; A.M.E. Zion; Salvation Army; Anglican (English Church mission); Musma Disco Christo; Baptist; African Faith Tabernacle (Nkansa); Christ Apostolic; Ghana Apostolic; Church of Pentecost; Twelve Apostles (Awoyo); Cherubim and Seraphim (Aladura); Church of the Lord; Calvary; The Lord Is There Temple; Seventh-Day Adventist; Faith (Kyiri Bentoa); Jehovah's Witnesses. There were also congregations known by the names of the founder or leader, such as Aunty Mary of Yaabamu and Mame Annan. There were two Muslim groups, the Fante Nkramo, with their mosque at Mangoase, and the Islam at Zongo. In addition to these, the traditional shrines (*abosom*) and the more recent Tigare cult claimed votaries. The impression, however, is that the new sects and separatist churches are gradually displacing some of the traditional shrines.

In a recent account of the Presbyterian Church, Noel Smith argues strongly that the proliferation of churches and sects points to the still unsolved problem of integrating the church into the African society.[44] On the basis of my limited work, I would argue rather that African societies have shown tremendous capacity to accommodate these alien institutions. The various shapes the Christian churches have assumed in the African environment may very well indicate the adaptation of the institutions to changing functions.

As a matter of fact, many Africans today, whatever their personal views about the churches, see them as part of their society, an integral part of an ongoing tradition. The churches function in an envi-

44. Rev. J. N. Smith, *The History of the Presbyterian Church in Ghana, 1821–1960* (Accra: Ghana University Press, 1967).

ronment quite different from that of their society of origin, and it is purposeless to suggest, as Noel Smith does, that education could integrate the churches into African society. Commentators on the voluntary associations of West Africa are wont to argue that associations such as labor unions, churches, and political parties promote in various ways adjustment to urban living and build new commitments to replace old tribal bonds.

Although this conclusion may be valid generally, the functional consequences for urban society should not be assumed. There are indeed many ways, manifest and latent, in which the churches of Swedru and elsewhere contribute toward the process of local and national integration, that is, the creation of fairly durable structural and emotional bonds of unity across the town and nation. All the established churches, including now the Roman Catholic Church, are members of the Ghana Christian Council with its headquarters in Accra, the national secretary of which was, in 1967, a Methodist minister.

The Protestant ministers all receive their training in the same institution, Trinity College — formerly in Kumasi, now in Accra — which in the past served only Methodist ministers. The Christian Home Week, during which joint interdenominational services are held and special prayers said for the sick, is observed at the same time in June by all the churches throughout Ghana. During this week, the emphasis, as reflected in sermons, is on solidarity, bonds of unity of the Christian community. On 25 June 1967, for example, a joint special memorial service for the late General Kotoka, a member of the NLC, was held by all Christians in the new and modern Methodist Church in Swedru. The school system has also helped break down the mutual isolation of the churches. Although as a rule parents would wish their children to attend schools managed by their denomination, in recent years the demand for classroom space has far outstripped the supply of these places, with the result that parents have sent their children to whatever institutions have places for them.

One should certainly mention here the very popular voluntary organizations, membership in which is open to Christians of all denominations. These include the Catholic Mbuakuw, Christ's Little Band, Minstrel Choir, Honest Society, and the Hope Society. The Hope Society has branches throughout Ghana, and the regional headquarters is at Cape Coast. According to an informant, at a general conference of the society held at Cape Coast in 1966 over twenty-nine branches from all over Ghana were represented. The executive officers of the Swedru Hope Society in June 1967 were: Mr. Baiden (Anglican Church), a Fante; Mr. Awia (Methodist Church catechist), a Fante, chairman; and Mr. Ntsifu (Presbyterian Church), an Agona, secretary. The members, mostly women, also belong to the occupational associations, such as the Breadsellers Union and the Association of Market Women, of the town.

The Hope and other societies like it exist essentially to give mutual aid. Although they may on occasion arbitrate or settle disputes between members, the main function pertains to death and funerals. They assist by giving financial contributions and holding sing-song wakes in order to give a culturally defined decent burial for a deceased member or much-needed financial help to a deceased member's immediate relatives. In fact, some of the women in town admitted joining churches "so that we may have good burial, an honorable interment in the denominational cemetery." The importance of funerals in the socioeconomic life of the peoples of Ghana has been well described by Brokensha and need not be repeated here. All these societies are polyethnic and accept everybody provided they are Christians, that is, members of any of the local churches.

Funerals apart, the societies also function to cater for the general welfare of members and their families. Since a majority of the members are also mothers, the societies provide a forum for the dissemination of new ideas about health, child and baby care, and good citizenship. Thus in April 1967, the groups were specially invited to the Swedru town hall along with the local branch of the Ghana Red Cross Society to participate in the National Health Day.

CHURCH MEMBERSHIP AND PARTICIPATION

For any voluntary association, various means are used to distinguish members from nonmembers. These may include requirements to pay dues; carry a membership card; regularly attend meetings, ceremonies, services, and celebrations of the society or association; wear specially designed clothes; and so on. What is usually difficult is to distinguish committed from nominal members, the members who always adhere to the rules and aims of the association, and those who are members because membership is socially significant in some situations. These latter will immediately disassociate themselves from the society or association in cases of socially defined difficulties and demands. The committed-nominal distinction is in most cases, but by no means all, related to the active-nonactive or occasional member distinction. The fact that in 1960 72.3 percent of the population of Swedru claimed to be Christian and only 14.5 percent described themselves as votaries of traditional African religions, and yet that 93.8 percent of all the marriages were contracted in the customary, non-Christian form is interesting in this connection. In fact, only 2.0 percent were married by church or court ordinance. A majority of Christians were obviously not participating fully in their churches, to the extent that Christian marriage had little value to them. I hold that the distinction is very important to an understanding of the rise and sudden fall of voluntary associations in Ghana. An association having a majority of nominal or symbolic members or participants is more unstable, other things being equal, than one with committed members.

Voluntary associations, we have noted, help meet certain cultural needs. But these needs or functions, it must be stressed, may be served in a number of functionally equivalent or alternative ways. Again the needs and the values associated with them are ranked, some being *socially* more important than others. Thus, although religious societies may provide the socially recognized means of upward mobility, the achievement of recognized status and of wealth and power, for individual self-expression, and may serve as training grounds for the assumption of urban roles, these needs may be equally and perhaps more efficiently met through membership in political parties and football clubs. And despite the fact that, as a Christian, one is expected to attend service regularly on Sundays and to marry monogamously, one may in practice value attendance at funerals more and have a number of wives.

Let us now look at the social characteristics and membership participation of the two oldest churches in Swedru, the Methodist and the Presbyterian, both established during the last quarter of the nineteenth century. In June 1967, after about seventy years in continuous existence, the Presbyterian Church could boast of only 115 (hardly regular) communicants. Of these about 64 percent and 36 percent were adult women and men, respectively. Yet nearly all the Twi-speaking tribes in Swedru, such as the Kwahu and the Aku-

apem, claim to be Presbyterian. The figure of communicants does
not include schoolchildren. The Methodist Church, slightly older,
fared slightly better. There were 450 communicants (some of whom
were more or less permanently away!) and, here again, nearly two-
thirds were women. Again, at the nominal level, a majority of Fante
claimed they were members of the Methodist Church, because the
Methodist Church is popularly associated with Fante-speaking people in the area. What is immediately obvious is the sex distribution,
the high proportion of women members. All the ministers and the
heads of all the churches and sects agreed that in every case women
were in the majority. The equally dominant role of women in trade
and politics in West Africa, particularly in Ghana, has been the subject of much discussion.

It should be pointed out, however, that size of membership, however defined, has no direct relation to church participation through,
say, regular church attendance or attendance at communion. Except at annual festivals — Harvest Thanksgiving in November–
December, Christmas, New Year, Easter, and Good Friday —
church attendance for all religious groups is very poor indeed. On
ordinary Sundays, during a tour of churches one is struck by the
rows and rows of empty pews. The Reverend I. C. Ewoodzie of the
Methodist Church explained the situation thus: "Sometimes there
are about fifty women and only ten men at a service; since most of
our members are strangers [migrants] the attendance *cannot* be satisfactory, for they may have to travel on Sundays, when they don't
have to go to work, to their home towns for funerals or to attend to
other family matters." The catechist of the Presbyterian Church,
himself headmaster of the local Presbyterian Primary School, expressed a similar worry when he said, "The members are mostly
strangers; progress is directly related to their comings and goings.
The natives of Swedru [the Agona] should take more interest [in the
church]."

On the other hand, the priest of the Roman Catholic Church, a
Dutchman, put it bluntly that, though church attendance left much
to be desired, "Strangers are definitely better." "The Agona," he
went on, "are lazy people [a view shared, incidentally, by many
strangers]. They are active only for burials and drinks." He noted
with contempt that in the Catholic Church choir only two were
Agona, most of them were Ewe and Fante. Since the migrants have

a high percentage of educated members and also, perhaps, a greater need for adjustment to the new urban environment and for eliminating social isolation, their slightly better participation in common interest associations should not be surprising. The Smythes, for example, have demonstrated for Nigeria the high positive correlation between education, particularly level of education, and membership in political parties, civil groups, churches, and so on.[45]

This section was begun by a reference to the proliferation in recent times of separatist and syncretistic churches and other forms of religious groups. Some see the emergence and growth of these "churches under charismatic African leadership" as a characteristic cultural response to the alien church in the same way that not a few of the apologists for the one-party system in Africa saw its growth as an African response to colonialism and Western imperialism. However this may be, despite the rapid growth of the number of separatist or syncretistic churches — what are known locally as *sumsumsore* ("spiritual churches") in Swedru — they are all facing or have faced acute problems of their very survival, problems of dedicated and regular participation beyond the nominal or symbolic. In fact, the problem of participation extends to nearly all voluntary associations in town. There is a need for what one man described as "responsible involvement" in these associations.

My studies of voluntary associations in Swedru left me in no doubt that, for each of the associations, there was a core group of persons — about six or seven, but even at times only three — who were responsibly involved, dedicated to organizational survival and the achievement of organizational goals. To this group, the organization was more than merely a means to certain desired goals, the association was an end in itself. This small group — at once organizers, activists and mobilizers, and executive officers, the real decision-makers — included in absolutely all cases the foundation members. In the case of the political parties, particularly the CPP, the recruitment function seems to have been minor, since the main concern of the core group, the "cadre," was to insure the survival of the organization through all effective and reliable means open to them (such as rallies and conferences), that is, the raising of the level and size of symbolic participation and support for organizational ob-

45. H. H. Smythe and M. M. Smythe, *The New Nigerian Elite* (Stanford, California: Stanford University Press, 1960).

jectives and decisions. It was also expected that organizational action could thus have legitimacy.

The extent to which the core group succeeded in raising the level of symbolic participation was directly related to the various needs of individuals at any one time and the popularity of the organization, which was to a very large extent dependent on "what one gets out of it" in utilitarian and socially symbolic terms. From this point of view, participation in organizational action was instrumental. This instrumental form of participation may account for the meteoric rise and the sudden collapse of voluntary associations, not the least of which was the CPP, in Swedru and in Ghana generally.

4 EUROCOLONIALISM, ECONOMIC NATIONALISM, AND THE EMERGENCE OF POLITICAL PARTIES

In the previous chapters, I have tried to sketch out some of the principal and more lasting consequences of European contact with the Africans of the Gold Coast. There I emphasized that the contact situation immediately set in motion a series of social and economic changes which were expressed, in the main, through new wants and ways of doing things, new tastes and interests, and new values and cultural alternatives associated with a technologically superior culture.

It is this set of changes, this new socioeconomic environment and the economic protests flowing from it, that provided the setting for the economic-grievance nationalism which was later to lead to the formation of groups seeking to gain control of national-territorial political decision-making in order to cure the economic ills, and then to the political independence of Ghana in 1957. The politics of the Gold Coast and Ghana is in an important sense the politics of privilege, whose true end is wealth and its consumption, the politics of the various reactions to and strategies for dealing with what the people perceive as harsh economic needs. Although one of the ingredients of the political process, anywhere, is undoubtedly power and its possession, in West Africa — and perhaps in most of the developing areas of the world — the control of economic resources which the possession of power confers is an even more important dimension of politics. This should not be surprising.

After all, one of the most important and obvious features common to the new states of Africa and also of Asia is their economic poverty. Poverty, which embraces the need for sheer subsistence and, beyond this, the need for material possessions to meet both traditional and newly acquired status demands, is a major defining criterion of the developing nations. The primary goal of most of these new states is, therefore, economic prosperity or development. This makes the struggle for power for the sake of power not only meaningless but dangerous. From the point of view of a majority of the people in these countries, politics has no right to autonomous existence. Politics must produce economic rewards for everybody (at least for socially powerful groups); it must somehow be concerned with the accumulation and distribution of wealth, of economic resources to significant groups of people — this is its major raison d'être. In periods of general economic well-being, politics becomes superfluous, and one's political participation mostly symbolic-expressive. In a sense, in the poor states of Africa, politics and economics are inseparable.[1]

It has been pointed out that the Gold Coast chief, the embodiment of the traditional political system, justified his leadership in the economic realm primarily. The creation of new and relatively open social and economic roles associated with monetization and urbanization, as we have noted in the case of Swedru, has made the position and authority of the chief increasingly difficult to justify and maintain. The emergence of new groups of educated and Christian men who are mostly dependent on nontraditional sources of income or material reward — the new elite, in the sense of a positive reference group for a majority of the people — has created problems for the chief. In fact, the new men have on occasion displaced the chief and in any case have from time to time exerted strong political influence on rural chiefs in particular.

The Gomoa farmers' dispute, to which reference has already been made, provides an illustration of the role of the new elite (the new influential in the changing society) and of the diminution of the authority of the chief. In the course of the inquiry into the land rent dispute in 1928–29 between Gomoa cocoa farmers on Agona lands and the chief of Agona Duakwa, the paramount chief of Gomoa — who thought that the complaints by his Gomoa farmer-subjects were becoming too frequent and numerous and that his people undoubtedly had been unduly ill-treated in Agona — significantly, approached the late Dr. Kwegyir Aggrey, the famous Fante Gold

1. In the words of T. Parsons, "When a social system has only a simply defined goal, the provision of facilities, or the 'adaptive' function, is simply an undifferentiated aspect of the process of goal attainment." *Economy and Society* (New York: Free Press, 1957), p. 18. The adaptive function (the distribution of income or economic resources) is here necessarily linked closely to the goal attainment function (the political dimension) since adaptation is concerned with the problem of controlling the environment for the purpose of "attaining goal states."

Coast educationist, who lived and died in the United States of America, to see what he could do for them in the matter. Aggrey agreed to take up the issue on his return from leave in Europe, "but unfortunately the poor Doctor never returned" (he died).

For want of a better term, I expressed the new socioeconomic system in terms of competitive status-class system or complex.[2] The problem in West Africa is that traditional status systems have not been completely, and perhaps never will be, displaced by the new class structure based primarily on modern economic roles.[3] Clearly, in Ghana as in West Africa, both status and class still compete for position in the foreground, but it is fair to say, despite the recency of the emergence of class, that with increasing education, urbanization, and industrialization, class may in time end up as the *dominant* feature of the social stratification. In fact, political conflicts are to some extent class conflicts. Among the classes or incipient classes may be mentioned small- and large-scale cocoa-farm owners and cocoa-farmer *rentiers*, land- and immovable property-owners, the old colonial civil service bureaucrats, lawyers and doctors, minor clerks and teachers, wealthy chiefs, the new party bureaucrats and functionaries, the elite of education and university scholars, market women, traders, and merchants, and taxi drivers. These are salient but very crude categorizations.

The fact, however, that the literate high income and illiterate, unskilled, and low income classes do combine from time to time for a common purpose — defense of what they perceive as their strong communal economic interests — and that ethnic loyalties and pri-

2. One gets the impression — in the absence of any systematic and more refined analysis of social stratification in Ghana or in West Africa beyond, of course, broad categorization of socioeconomic groups on the basis of combined indices of occupation, education, income, and traditional status — that there is a tendency toward more and more class stratification. See especially M. Kilson, "Nationalism and Social Classes in British West Africa," *Journal of Politics* 20, no. 1 (May 1958): 368–87; and T. Hodgkin, *Nationalism in Colonial Africa* (London: Frederick Muller, 1956), pp. 86–87, for a discussion of social classes in West Africa.

3. Max Weber comments on the transitional problem thus: "When the bases of the acquisition and distribution of goods are relatively stable, stratification by status is favoured. Every technological and economic transformation threatens stratification by status and pushes the class situation in the foreground." He goes on to suggest that " 'property' and 'lack of property' are . . . the basic categories of all class situations." Max Weber, *From Max Weber*, H. H. Gerth and C. W. Mills, translators and editors (London: Routledge and Kegan Paul, 1948), pp. 180–95.

mordial ties may still be strong in some social situations, should suggest caution. As I have intimated earlier, one or two factors, among others, which link all Ghanaians together and which foster bonds of integration are the pursuit of economic interests and of a real community of economic life and cohesion. The wage-earning system has been democratized over time to involve both rural and urban populations; this has helped trans-social integration through unrestricted intrastate, in-out migration. We have seen that Swedru is largely an urban migrant and commercial society. We have discussed its growth as typical of the mutuality of influence between the development of cocoa, the main industry of Ghana, and commerce and communication. Cocoa and commerce assisted in the construction and extension of a complex network of roads, rails, and ports, the first of these especially running throughout the length and breadth of the country. Movement of people and goods along these communication arteries also influenced the expansion of trade and commerce and made people economically interdependent for survival or at least for the satisfaction of their growing material needs.

BRITISH COLONIAL RULE, THE CHIEF, AND ECONOMIC
NATIONALISM: A CONSIDERATION OF
THEIR INTERACTION

In what may be considered a classic statement, Georges Balandier characterized colonial rule in Africa as a system whose outstanding features are the state of dependency and the centrality of the market economy.[4] These two features, it may be added, go together. The state of dependency, in the Gold Coast situation, was defined by the dependence of the chief, the embodiment of precolonial traditional political authority, and his subjects on the district commissioner (at any rate, at the local level), the symbol of the new authority structure, of colonial rule. Although the British flag followed commerce and trade in the Gold Coast, as elsewhere, the important thing to note is that the colonial system was essentially an economic (and not a political) system of primary producers of cocoa and other raw materials, and of consumers of much-demanded imported European utilitarian and luxury goods on the one hand and the European manufacturer-overlords on the other. In an important sense,

4. Georges Balandier, *Sociologie des Brazzavilles Noires* (Paris: Colin, 1955), p. 178.

the colonizers' one most far-reaching "contribution" was the creation of a politico-administrative atmosphere, peace and order, for a
mutual economic exploitation in which the colonized were unequal
partners.

What began as a dependency relationship soon became a relationship of economic interdependence, an interdependence whose
dynamic aspects consisted of calculated movements of the partners,
each trying to secure a position, however temporary, from which to
take advantage of the other. Both the colonizer and the colonized
developed a vested interest, the nature of which changed over time,
in the colonial situation. European contact, a commercial contact at
that, and British colonial rule reinforced each other in the provision
of new opportunities for the colonized and the creation of new material wants in them. No wonder much of the politics of the Gold
Coast and Ghana has been the politics of finding, controlling, or
increasing the *means* for the satisfaction of these cravings. The
politics here has therefore been pragmatic (both radical and conservative) and utilitarian, even opportunistic.

The chief, for example, cooperated with the D.C. (the photo-
graphs taken with D.C.'s and governors on various occasions and
still hanging proudly on the walls of the living rooms of paramount
chiefs illustrate this) and resisted him; he worked hand in hand
with the educated class and resisted or rejected them; he even hob-
nobbed with the rowdy and restless urban wage-earners and resisted them in turn. This undulating pattern of cooperation and resistance was dictated both by the exigencies of the situation and, to
a large extent, by what may have been a shrewd calculation by the
chief about how best to hold on to the plums of office. A wealthy
chief is a respected and an influential chief; he is a powerful chief.
Unfortunately, everybody else wanted the plums if not the office.
Has the colonialist succeeded in producing, as Fitzgerald suggested
in the nineteenth century, a "native capitalist" in the Gold Coast in
the economic and not political sense of the term?

Summarizing the political history of the Gold Coast from 1850 to
1928, Kimble put it in words quite consistent with my own position.

In the story which follows, many of the themes will recur: perhaps the
most significant is the role of the chiefs. They appear initially as the
natural representatives of the people in the Poll Tax Assembly of 1852;
but soon they proceed to challenge British authority, either individually
as did King Aggrey of Cape Coast, or collectively, as in the short-lived

Fanti Confederation and the prolonged Ashanti resistance to British arms.
The chiefs next emerge in alliance with educated politicians in the
A.R.P.S. [Aborigines' Rights Protection Society] only to resist the claim
of the intelligentsia to leadership on a national scale in the National
Congress of British West Africa; and finally we see them turning to the
Colonial Government for support in their defence of the traditional
system.[5]

Reference has already been made to the reliance of the coastal
chiefs on the British for protection against Ashanti raids and for the
protection of their highly favorable trading position. Kimble continued, "The story of nationalist agitation is . . . organically connected; each protest grew out of the success – or, more often, the
failure of the last. The *economic* and *social changes* . . . provide
the backdrop for the political drama" (my italics).[6]

Thus, in 1852, two years after the establishment of the first Legislative Council in the Gold Coast, we see Commander Hill calling a
meeting of the governor (of the Cape Coast castle) and his Council, made up of the chiefs and headmen of the native states under
British protection, and constituting the body as "a Legislative Assembly with full powers to enact such laws as it shall deem fit for
the better government of those countries [native states]." In this Assembly, it is significant to note, the chiefs agreed to the poll tax of
one shilling per head of population, toward the cost of administration and protection, in return for which the chiefs were to be paid
annual stipends.[7] At this period the Agona, as we have seen, were
under the Gomoa, and in fact the chiefs of Gomoa and Agona together were able to realise "5,312 heads and 33 3/4 strings of
cowries" – that is, about £730 10s. 0d. in tax money. Yet in the following year the chiefs were to join their subjects, if not lead them,
to overthrow the poll tax which was at this time considered unfair,
most probably because the chiefs were dissatisfied with the amount
of stipend which accrued to them.

In the 1840s the chiefs had surrendered to British administration
and justice in return for British protection. In the 1860s they saw
their interests endangered again by the exchange of forts between

5. Kimble, *Political History of Ghana*, p. 167.
6. Ibid.
7. It is interesting to observe that the seventy signatories, headed by Aggrey,
chief of Cape Coast, included "chiefs and cabboceers from the following
towns and villages: Abbarsen and Eyen, Abrah, Adjumacoon, Agah, Aggonah
[Agona] . . . etc."

the British and the Dutch, who were considered the allies of the Ashanti. The immediate pragmatic answer was the Fante Confederation, considered the first nationalist movement among the chiefs and the people of the colony and formed to be both a military alliance against the Ashanti and a union of coastal states for mutual economic and social development independent of Dutch control.

THE CHIEFS BOTH RESISTING AND COOPERATING WITH COLONIAL AUTHORITIES

This ambivalent attitude of cooperation and resistance toward British colonial authority by the chiefs, the mass of the people, and even the emergent educated class was to be one of the major features of the state of dependency throughout the colonial era. The system of dependency was a source of both gratification and frustration: gratification when British presence was used by the chiefs to legitimize their own selfish, occasionally state-wide, claims; frustration when British authority became a hindrance to their acquisitive actions, as when the chief of Gomoa, the overlord of Agona, in 1899 was forced to renounce his claims over Agona. It was also characteristic of the colonial government to play one status group, or class or social category, against the other, according to "divide and rule" tactics. Whenever the chiefs were thrown into the protective and paternalistic arms of the colonial masters, described on such occasions as "good friends," it almost invariably meant the rejection of the claims and demands of their lawyers and other educated subjects.

Whenever people talk about British colonialism in Africa, they usually mean indirect rule, or "dual mandate." Although systematic indirect rule — called "the giving of administrative responsibility to traditional rulers," by Lucy Mair, and considered by some the foster child of Lord Lugard in the Gold Coast — was to wait till the time of Governor Guggisberg for its legislation and popularization in 1926–27, it may be argued that the first attempt to institute native authority or indirect rule dates back to the Legislative Assembly of the governor and chiefs in 1852.[8] Lord Grey, secretary for colonies at the time, saw it as a "rude Negro Parliament" which, according to him, "has converted a number of barbarous tribes, possessing nothing which serves the name of government, into a nation,

8. Mair, *New Nations*, p. 100.

with a regularly organised authority and institutions simple and un-pretending, but suited to the actual state of society, and containing within themselves all that is necessary for their future development, so that they may meet the *growing wants* of an *advancing civiliza-tion*" (my italics). This comment, though false in some respects — the Ashanti, Agona, and Fante tribes had "regularly organised au-thority and institutions" before the British came — is interesting in that it draws attention to the economic nature of the Anglo–Gold Coast tie, the establishment of an administrative environment for meeting the "growing wants" of the peoples of the Gold Coast. Three broad periods stand out as watersheds in Anglo-Agona rela-tions. It is to these periods that the old Agona endowed with long memories refer in their discussion of the evolution in modern times of Agona political institutions. The periods were initiated by (1) the presence of a local D.C. in the Agona district (in 1878); (2) the emancipation from Gomoa (in 1899); and (3) the systematization of indirect rule (in 1927). These years marked the effective exten-sion of British administration and justice in Agona and elsewhere in the Gold Coast.

The Abolition of the Slave Trade and the Gradual Crystallization of British Colonial Administrative Structure

In 1874, Captain G. C. Strahan summoned the important chiefs in the Gold Coast, including those of Gomoa-Agona, Cape Coast, Win-neba, to Cape Coast and informed them that it was the desire of Queen Victoria of England to do away with the slave traffic, in re-turn for the still much-needed protection against the Ashanti, to which some agreed. I say *some* because when, in December of the same year, two ordinances, one abolishing slave dealing and the other emancipating existing slaves throughout the colony, were passed, a number of the chiefs protested strongly. The Agona were certainly and naturally ambivalent toward the stipulation of the or-dinances.

The 1874 ordinances dealt a great blow to the major source of wealth and income of the Agona, which remained trade in slaves. The chiefs especially stood to lose by the ordinances. Nevertheless, we also saw that in 1693 Agona, after losing the Sasabor war with Gomoa, came under the rule of Gomoa and was tributary to it. In the course of and after the war, many Agona peoples including *ade-hye* became slaves in various parts of Fante-Abora, Cape Coast, Ekumfi, and Assin. Thereafter, tributes in the form of such products as palm oil, snails, sponge, yams and eggs flowed annually from Agona to Gomoa. The 1874 ordinances dealt another blow to this slave-tributary relationship, much to the annoyance of the chief of Gomoa. From 1874 the Agona to some extent stopped serving Gomoa, and the descendants of the Agona slaves in Fante returned home.

In 1878, for the first time, a D.C. was stationed at Winneba, about fifteen miles from Agona Swedru. To the people of the area, the presence of the D.C. (the first D.C.'s were generally young and hardly experienced constabulary officers) was the first real physical reminder of the new and changing order, and in 1899, as a result of the local reports of the D.C. to the governor, Agona was declared politically independent of Gomoa. The D.C. replaced the chief as the most important judge and administrator, and in this connection something must be said about the administrative structure of the Gold Coast.

The Structure of Administration in the Gold Coast: 1916 and After

Briefly, the constitutional progress of the Gold Coast, particularly in 1916 and after, had been the gradual transformation of the criteria of membership of the Legislative Assembly and later the Executive Council from the appointive, nominated principle and official majority to the fully elective and representative principle and unofficial majority. My concern here is not with tracing this development (which has been done so well by Hodgkin, Austin, Price, Jennings, and many others) in any detail. My task is a modest one. I hope to demonstrate the relationships between the chief and the D.C., between the chief and the local councils, and between the chief and the emerging political parties, within the framework of a changing administrative structure.

For administrative convenience the Gold Coast had been divided into three provinces — the Colony (Eastern), Central, and Western. In 1916, Sir Hugh Clifford, then governor, appointed a paramount chief to represent each of these provinces. In 1926–27, the constitutional reforms of Governor Guggisberg made the chiefs, both paramount and divisional, salaried Native Authorities of the British Government, subject to the official discipline and control of the D.C.'s. The legal expression of the change was the passage of the Native Authorities Ordinance and the establishment of the Provincial Council of Chiefs and the Joint Provincial Council, which gave the chiefs the right to nominate themselves to the Legislative Council of the Colony. The chiefs were permitted under the new ordinance twice the number of members granted to the educated, Europeanized Africans in the towns. This had the effect of pitting the chiefs against the intelligentsia, who felt that they had a better claim to more representation and its rewards than had the traditional rulers. The Legislative Council of 1927 had thirty members including the governor, who was president of the Council. Fifteen of these were official and fourteen were unofficial members. Of the latter, six were paramount chiefs selected by the Joint Provincial Council — three from the Colony province, two from the Central, and one from the Western province. There were five Europeans representing foreign banking, shipping, mercantile, and mining interests. The ratepayers of Accra, Cape Coast, and Sekondi-Takoradi elected a representative each. Thus, as Padmore put it, "The urbanised communities, the most politically advanced sections of the country, were not even as well represented on the Legislative Council as the foreign capitalists not to speak of the Native Authorities symbolised by Gazetted Chiefs." [9] What Padmore did not realize is that, at this period at any rate, the Legislative Assembly could be fairly described as the executive committee of foreign financial and business interests and of their local partners. However politically advanced the urbanized populations were, and however vocal, they could not have been considered the representatives of the broad mass of the population, most of whom felt that their interests, mainly economic, were being taken care of by the chiefs. Again not every urban dweller, it could be argued, was really urbanized. Cape Coast still had a majority of illiterate fishermen who could hardly be considered politically advanced.

All the same, Padmore was quick to point out, and with this I completely agree, that there was considerable economic distress and social discontent among all sections of the African population throughout succeeding periods, during and after the 1929 Depres-

9. Padmore, *Gold Coast Revolution*, p. 91.

sion and after the Second World War, especially among civil servants who wanted "European appointments [positions]" and the laboring classes and farmers, and this was to lead to a number of serious economic protests and political change. At this point, let us turn to the colonial structure and look at some of the processes that illustrate the structure as it operated. In the Crown Colony system (see figure 9), the secretary of state, a minister usually of cabinet rank, was responsible to the British Parliament for the administration of all the colonial territories. He advised the king or queen of England on the appointment of governors, theoretically the personal representatives of His or Her Majesty. The governor was responsible to the secretary of state for the good government of his territory — in this case, the Gold Coast — in accordance with the British government's general policy.

He formulated and executed policy and was responsible for the appointment, discipline, and dismissal of public servants, including judges. He was the president of both the Executive and the Legislative councils and had overall control over the legislative and executive policy. The governor was expected to seek the advice of the Executive Council when formulating policy but he was not bound by it. The governor thus, at least in theory, appears to have wielded absolute power — subject, of course, to the wishes of the secretary of state for the colonies. It is interesting to note that, after 1960, Nkrumah, the president of Ghana, seems to have wielded powers similar to those held by the colonial governor. I hope to enlarge upon this point later on in the analysis.

The Executive Council was made up normally of the heads of the most important departments of government, such as Justice, Finance, and Military. The Legislative Council, as we have just noted, consisted of both official and nonofficial, nominated and elected members. It had power to legislate for the colony, though legislation was subject to the governor's assent, which could be withheld at his discretion. It should be obvious from the account that the colony was essentially an administrative, relatively modern, bureaucratic structure and an economic empire whose head was the Crown, represented by the colonial secretary in London.[10] At the local level, the governor administered the territory through a num-

10. See J. H. Price, *Political Institutions of West Africa* (London: Hutchinson Educational, 1967), pp. 1–18, for a fuller account.

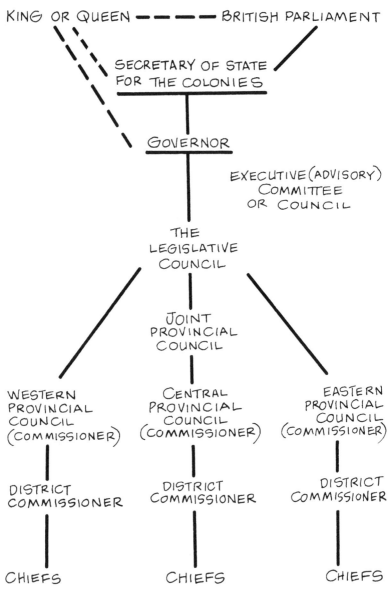

Fig. 9. The Crown Colony: Gold Coast Structure

ber of provincial and district commissioners and their intermediaries, the chiefs. Sir Alan Burns, governor of the Gold Coast in the early 1940s, commenting on the governor's power of recognition of chiefs vested in him, had this to say:

Under the new law [of 1927] the election of the chiefs is left to the people as it always has been, and always must be, for so long as the chiefs remain responsible for priestly as well as civil functions. But the chief is not necessarily the Native Authority *recognised* by the Governor, although as a rule the Governor willingly recognises the chief and his state council as the Native Authority. When the people themselves cannot agree as to the election of a chief, or where the chief and his council prove incompetent to perform the functions of Native Authority, *the Governor has power, under the law, to appoint other persons as the Native Authority.*" [my italics.] [11]

The provision in the last sentence has led to confused debates, mostly theoretical, about the nature and extent of the power wielded by the governor. In the Central Region, in any case, the so-called absolute and autocratic power in relation to the chiefs and people was hardly ever, if at all, exercised by the governor.

COLONIAL RULE, AUTOCRACY, AND THE ONE-PARTY STATE: A RECONSIDERATION OF THEIR RELATIONSHIP

From the earlier statements about the reserve powers of the governor, it is clear that the governor controlled some of the major policy decisions for the Colony. Thus it has been argued by a number of eminent scholars — Ferkiss, Harvey, and others — that colonialism predisposed British Africa to centralized and undemocratic rule.[12] The latter-day one-party state, such as Ghana before the 24 February 1966 coup d'etat, and Tanzania, was seen as a necessary carryover from colonial rule by the governor and the colonial officials' tendency toward theoretically absolute control of decisions. There is no doubt that some important colonial patterns of government have survived colonialism: the existence of a bureaucratic civil service; the emphasis on the belief that politics can only be a means to power and, more particularly, the emphasis on the material rewards of power, on instrumental values; and the absence of any form of

11. Sir Alan Burns, *Colonial Civil Servant* (London: George Allen and Unwin, 1949), p. 204.
12. See Ferkiss, *Africa's Search for Identity*; and W. B. Harvey, *Law and Social Change in Ghana* (Princeton: Princeton University Press, 1966).

political education or ideological orientation transcending merely economic well-being. But it would be wrong to deduce the reasons for the emergence of one-party rule from the so-called colonial autocracy. It is equally misleading to claim that the one-party state is the result, directly or indirectly, of traditional forms of popular consensus over political decision-making.

It is true that under the Native Administration Ordinance of 1927 the governor was given authority to grant legislative, executive, and judicial powers to the chiefs and to withdraw these powers if the chiefs became persona non grata with the D.C.'s. Some observers have pointed out that, under the new system, the chiefs were given autocratic powers and became "real puppets of the British Officials." One cannot seriously rule out the possibility of this in a few instances. There are, however, numerous examples or cases from the local level which show, or at least suggest, that the chiefs and people, far from being the unwilling agents of the D.C., effectively participated in decisions affecting their state, by voicing consent or dissent and by consulting with the local officials. The chiefs on occasion refused, with relative impunity, to accept the ruling of the D.C. The D.C. could not overrule the majority decision of the people of a state.

The D.C., the local agent of the governor, depended on the chiefs for advice on major issues affecting their states, and a chief could and did criticize the D.C. without being declared persona non grata. The Agona chiefs' habit of addressing the D.C. or even the governor as their "good friend" was no accident, nor was it merely a symbolic gesture. The popular notion that colonial rule was necessarily autocratic everywhere needs a careful reexamination. Nothing illustrates better the nature of the relationship between the D.C. and the chief than the address delivered by the omanhene of Mankesim on the occasion of the opening of the inquiry in 1931 into the political dispute between Nsaba and Nyakrom.[13]

13. This was an intrastate dispute, as we have seen, over the seat of the paramount chief of Agona — that is, over hegemony of the Agona state — involving the withdrawal of allegiance from the stool of Nsaba and transfer of allegiance to that of Nyakrom. On the advice of the D.C. at Winneba and the assistant D. C. at Agona Swedru, the commissioner of Central Province referred the matter to the Provincial Council of Chiefs, Central Province. Cases between subchiefs of Agona were usually referred to the Agona State Council if there was one in existence, whereas disputes involving paramount chiefs were taken up by the Provincial Council of Chiefs, the highest chiefly tribunal of the Province.

The omanhene of Mankesim, as chairman, took great pains to point out that they were meeting (he and his "brother" Amanhene of Akim Bosome and Assin Attandaso) to settle the dispute on the orders of the government. They had gathered, he said, to help and to give an impartial hearing and go into the matter officially before the D.C., Mr. Bewes. The committee of Amanhene had met to help the D.C., who, being a Britisher, was not from their country and could therefore not sit with the Provincial Council of Chiefs. The paramount chief of Mankesim reiterated that "the D.C. cannot alter our custom." He emphasized that "we are here to help the D.C. We are to define to him our native custom as to what our forefathers did in the administration of their country [states]. If any question comes before us, that he wants our advice we will give it." There were plenty of questions about which the D.C. wanted and did ask for advice.

The intransigence of the people of Nsaba at the inquiry demonstrates how powerless the D.C. could be in certain situations. The regent of Nsaba protested vehemently against the D.C. and the members of the commission of inquiry throughout the period of the commission's deliberations, on the grounds that the D.C. was biased and was against the Nsaba people, and threatened that Nsaba would not appear at the commission or feel bound by its decision and recommendations. Before discussing the nature of the protest, an example of how the colonial structure worked in practice, let me sketch out briefly the background to the protest.

Between 1920 and 1931, as a result of what the majority of the people of the ten chiefdoms of the Agona state saw as misrule by the paramount chiefs of Nsaba — misrule characterized by a series of frequent dethronements — they considered it necessary to withdraw allegiance from the stool (the symbol of chiefly authority) of Nsaba, which after all was not the "ancient" paramount stool of the Agona but that of Yaw Minta, the chief, who had been more or less imposed on Agona by the Gomoa when Agona lost the Sasabor war. The opportunity presented itself in 1931 when the paramount chief of Agona at Nsaba, Yaw Duodu VII, offended the whole Agona state by, according to the allegation, "sending messengers to Kumasi for medicine from one Mohammedan man to kill his elders." The asafo companies of Agona took the initiative and approached the benkumhene of Abodom, head of the left wing and the third senior chief in Agona, and asked him to put their complaints, including those against the wicked intentions of the paramount chief on his subjects and elders, before the omanhene.

The benkumhene invited the omanhene to Swedru in order to go into the case. But when the chiefs and asafomma of Agona met at Swedru, the omanhene did not come himself but sent his elders, linguists, and personal friends with one hundred pounds in cash, ten sheep, and two cases of gin to pacify his subjects, and he asked for forgiveness. This gesture on the part of the omanhene constituted an admission of guilt, a fact which strengthened the hands of the complainants. The latter, of course, accepted the pacification but never forgave the omanhene. They therefore declared him dethroned on the grounds of his own admission of guilt — signified, as we have observed, by the pacification.

Soon after, a letter signed (or marked) by the chiefs and asafomma assembled was sent to the assistant D.C. in Swedru, notifying him of their decision. The assistant D.C. invited the complainants and the Nsaba oman and omanhene, the defendants, for a hearing. The omanhene refused to attend the hearing, but the representatives of the oman of Nsaba were present. The linguist of Nsaba, representing the omanhene, drew the attention of the D.C. to the fact that the procedure adopted by the chiefs and asafomma was "unconstitutional" and contrary to native custom. Hence, the linguist remarked, Yaw Duodu VII was still the paramount head of Agona. In fact, according to the representatives of Nsaba Oman, only the Oman of Nsaba had the right to dethrone the paramount chief.

After hearing both sides, the D.C. adjourned the meeting, but asked all the parties to the dispute to attend another meeting in a day or two, this time at Bobikuma. At the Bobikuma hearing, Yaw Duodu was again absent. The plaintiffs reiterated their decision to dethrone the chief and the grounds for doing so. The D.C., however, felt that the procedure for the dethronement was somehow incomplete. He said that they should meet Yaw Duodu VII personally and discuss the issue, instead of sending messengers to inform him of his dethronement by them. Thereupon, the complainants, suspecting the D.C. of partiality, decided on another course of action. The ohene of Abodom suggested that the omanhene be dethroned by force, if necessary. All the subchiefs agreed to the suggestion.

Meanwhile, the D.C. had received information about the military preparation of the asafo companies and their plans to march to

Nsaba on a given Friday and effect the dethronement by coercion. The D.C. anticipated their move by traveling, along with the assistant superintendent of police of Swedru and a few constables, ahead of the asafo companies on that Friday. The D.C. and his group waited for the "foot" soldiers just outside the town of Nsaba. When the asafomma got there, the D.C., who obviously had been expecting them, merely asked them to return at once to their respective towns and assured them that he himself would collect the keys to the Nsaba ahenfie (palace) — another object of their march — for them. The decision of the D.C. was clearly dictated by the concern for the maintenance of peace and order in his district. The asafomma obliged. Not long after this, the D.C. called the parties to the dispute to another meeting in Swedru. Again the omanhene refused to attend, but the Nsaba oman did come. The D.C. informed the chiefs and people there assembled of the letter he had received from the oman of Nsaba, to the effect that without the consent of Nsaba any dethronement was most irregular and that when an omanhene was "constitutionally" dethroned the keys to the ahenfie were kept by the *dabihene* of Nsaba. The plaintiff replied that when an omanhene was dethroned by the whole state, as was the case then, the gyasehene of Swedru and not the dabihene looked after the ahenfie.

The D.C. then asked Kwaku Bah, the head of the Nsaba stool family, to bring the keys to him at a later date so that he could hand them over to the gyasehene of Swedru. The D.C. promised to take any action necessary to restore order in Agona. The meeting broke up, amidst general dissatisfaction. The benkumhene, by now the obvious leader of the complainants, who were a majority of the Agona chiefdoms, called almost immediately a meeting of the chiefs and asafomma of Agona at which he proposed that, with the consent of the other chiefs and subchiefs, they would march again to Nsaba to collect the keys themselves. The D.C. was seen as being too weak, an officer hardly capable of enforcing his own decision. They agreed that Abodom, Kwaman, Nkum, and Bobikuma should take the road from Abodom to Nsaba, and that Swedru, Asafo, and Kwanyako should take the Swedru road to Nsaba.

The party which took the Abodom road actually reached Nsaba, went to the ahenfie, and forcibly demanded the keys from the stool family; but again the D.C. was there to restrain them from any action which might lead to a breach of the peace. The Swedru party, on the other hand, was arrested by the Swedru police before it could get to Nsaba. Its members were returned to Swedru and fined a total of £156 12s. 6d. for behavior likely to lead to breach of the peace. When the D.C. returned to Swedru, representatives of the Agona oman protested to him about the brutality of the police, the court fine, and the shameful and rough treatment meted out by the people of Nsaba to the elders who had tried to collect the keys. Another meeting of the Nsaba oman and the other chiefdoms was convened at Swedru, at which the D.C. once more promised to send a messenger to Nsaba to collect the keys. The Nsaba oman agreed to the suggestion of the D.C. The Agona oman had their doubts. To make sure that the ahenfie was in the firm hands of the gyasehene of Swedru, the latter was advised to proceed immediately to Nsaba with his sleeping mat and spend the night at the ahenfie, that is, to occupy the ahenfie.

When the gyasehene arrived at Nsaba he was assaulted, as one might have expected, and was told that there were no keys for him. The people of Nsaba threatened that if the gyasehene spent the night in the ahenfie they would kill him. He returned, humiliated, and reported what had transpired to the Agona oman. The Agona oman were definitely angry. There was clearly a deadlock and the D.C. was obviously helpless in the matter. Although the D.C. could, with the assistance of the police, arrest anyone who was a potential danger to peace and order, he must have been aware that decisions enforceable only by the use of coercive sanctions were in the long run self-defeating. To break the political deadlock, the Agona oman as a last resort decided that they would not serve the Nsaba stool any longer since, after all, "they know their history." Their ancient paramount stool is that of Nyarko Eku I of Nyakrom.

Messengers were therefore dispatched to Kwaku Bah, the head of the Nsaba stool family, to say that they were transferring their allegiance to the ancient stool at Nyakrom. The decision was taken and acted upon by the Agona oman before the D.C. was notified. After swearing the oath of allegiance to the stool of Nyarko Eku, the D.C. was informed of the measure by letter. Nsaba naturally protested vehemently. The D.C. communicated with his immediate supervisor, the provincial commissioner of the Central Province, to inform the governor of the decision of the Agona oman. In accordance with instructions issued by the governor, the D.C. (Lieutenant G. P. H. Bewes) and a committee of paramount chiefs representing the

Provincial Council of Chiefs, Central Province, were asked to consider the matter and make recommendations to the governor. The committee met from 16 October 1931 (daily except on 21 October) until 27 October 1931. It decided in favor of the Agona oman, and the omanhene of Nyakrom was duly gazetted in 1931. Nsaba refused to be bound by the 1931 decision and in 1967, thirty-six years later, Nsaba petitioned the National Liberation Council against the 1931 ruling.[14]

Let us now turn briefly to the nature of the Nsaba protest. First, we have observed that Omanhene Yaw Duodu VII refused categorically to make personal appearances at any of the meetings of the oman called by the assistant D.C. in Swedru. The behavior of his representatives, of the head of the Nsaba stool family as regent, and of the elders of the Nsaba oman was equally intransigent.[15]

14. In April 1968 the NLC recognized the paramountcy of Nsaba.

15. In a protest note to the D.C., the omanhene made the following complaints:

1. When the ohene of Nyakrom was installed as omanhene of Agona at Nyakrom amidst drums and firing of guns, though Nsaba strongly objected to this to the D.C. at Winneba and the assistant D.C. resident in Swedru, no action was taken. But when Nsaba had a similar installation, the D.C. issued orders to the police and summons were taken against the Nsaba oman for beating drums and firing guns.

2. When the Nkum supporters of Nsaba (note that in the Nyakrom-Nsaba dispute Swedru was divided in her support, part was for Nyakrom and the other part for Nsaba, and there was minority support for Nsaba from Nkum and Abodom) joined in the installation ceremony of the omanhene at Nsaba, the chief of Nkum complained to the assistant D.C. and the said supporters of Nsaba were arrested and later discharged. The regent (the head of the stool family) at Nsaba accused the D.C. of not acting fairly in the interest of justice.

3. The D.C.'s are against Nsaba, hence the people of Nsaba strongly protest and object to Lieutenant Bewes as fit to enquire into the matter.

4. At a previous meeting of the Provincial Council of Chiefs at Oda, though the Nsaba-Nyakrom dispute was discussed, no settlement was reached and Nsaba lost money in the process. Nsaba again objected to the three amanhene taking part in the enquiry; and

5. During the recent Gomoa farmers' dispute, Nsaba lost about £300.

The D.C.'s answer to the above charges is equally significant and tells much about aspects of the relationship between the D.C. and the chiefs of Agona. The D.C. pointed out that:

1. The regent of Nsaba defied the assistant D.C.'s instructions. The futility of electing omanhene of Agona without the cooperation of all the chiefs entitled to, as approved by the Agona State Council and published in the Gazette of 1929, has been frequently pointed out to him (the Regent).

2. Permit from the police to fire arms and beat drums (note that before the Pax, drum beating and the firing of arms were associated with wars) was

Thus, even under colonial rule, chiefs and subjects, within limits consistent with the maintenance of law and order or peace, could articulate their grievances and protest against the decision of the D.C., without being necessarily suppressed by the so-called colonial autocracy. It should be indicated immediately, lest it be misconstrued, that this restatement or interpretation attempted here does not constitute an apology for colonialism.[16] Another case, this time from Swedru and on another level, will illustrate the relationship between the colonial government and the chief.

In the previous chapters we discussed the dispute between the stool family of Kobina Botwe and that of Domye, the rival claimants to the stool of Swedru. In this particular case, the D.C. referred the dispute to the Agona State Council for settlement instead of to the next higher level body, the Provincial Council of Chiefs. The Swedru case is an example of an intrachiefdom conflict, not an interchiefdom one involving two chiefs as had been the case in the Nyakrom-Nsaba leadership conflict within the same state. A letter from Nyarko Kwaku (Eku), the omanhene of Agona, to the assistant D.C. in Swedru tells us a bit about how the system worked on the ground. This letter deserves quoting in part.

My good friend.
Swedru Stool Dispute
According to section 8 of the Native Authority Ordinance I have the honour to report through you for the information of H.E. the Governor that the Swedru stool dispute which existed since last year has now been finally determined [settled] by the State Council of Agona and the name of the person whose election was approved by the State Council is Kobina Botchey [Botwe]. . . .
3. I am to add that the opposite people the supporters of [Kojo Nyarko] in Swedru have determined [decided] to cause a riot when the ceremonies as to installation of the said Kobina Botchey take place; and to avoid all these I strongly ask that about one dozen escort police may be provided by the Government to prevent any riot which may take place.

refused Nsaba because the election and installation at Nsaba were contrary to native custom.
    3. The Nkum supporters were arrested and fined, not discharged, because of their insulting behaviour towards the chief and not because they took part in ceremonies at Nsaba.
    16. My purpose has been to demonstrate the complexity of the reaction of the colonized to the colonizer, and to point out the weakness of a "tribal" ideology in situations where group, individual or local economic and political interests are at stake.

4. Kindly let me know when the police escorts will be ready so that I
may inform you of the exact date of the event.

> I am
> Your good friend
> Nyarko Kwaku
> X his mark
> Omanhene Agona

Witness to mark
(sgd) Tim A. Coleman. The Assistant D.C., Swedru

It should be said in passing that the police could not completely
prevent a riot during the installation ceremonies. Kojo Nyarko, the
exchief, is believed to have slapped one of the elders supporting
Kobina Botwe. An attempt on the life of the newly installed chief
failed when the gun aimed at him misfired.

It is clear, I believe, from the above cases in Agona, that, contrary
to proverbial assertion, the British administrative agents were not
necessarily free to dabble in tribal politics (though there are examples of this), intrigue between the chiefs and their councillors, and
make themselves "king-makers." The asafo companies, as we have
just noticed, still had some voice which carried weight in the affairs
of the traditional states. There was certainly much cooperation between the chiefs and the D.C., especially when it served the interests of both partners.

This does not mean that the system of indirect rule was beyond
modification in the direction of progressive administration, particularly when the growing number of educated people and wage earn-
ers in the towns began to feel that somehow their interests were not
effectively represented in the existing governmental structure. Thus
seventeen years later, in 1948, we find the Watson Investigation
Commission, which visited the Gold Coast from England to inquire
into the riots of that year, concluding that the whole system of indirect rule should be scrapped and replaced by a more democratic
(reflecting the diverse populations of towns) form of local government, a recommendation later endorsed by the Constitutional Reform Committee of 1949, chaired by Coussey, and implemented in
1952 as part of the new administrative system. Governor Alan
Burns, a strong believer in the policy "let the people decide," with
characteristic insight, put the problem in these words:

As I have said, I think indirect rule an excellent school in which the
difficult art of self-government may be learnt. But indirect rule cannot
be applied to all. It cannot be applied, for instance, to those educated

people who have become divorced from tribal life, and have adopted, perhaps with the Christian religion, a form of civilization which is very much like ours. You cannot set the clock back in Africa, or anywhere else, and you cannot expect the educated African to be satisfied with a Native Administration run by men in whom he has no confidence — illiterate men whom in his heart he despises.[17]

THE D.C., THE CHIEF, THE COURTS, AND LOCAL GOVERNMENT

In the traditional precolonial political systems, the chief performed a multiplicity of highly diffused roles — those of a judge, administrator, priest, war captain, economic entrepreneur, and political leader. With the establishment and extension of British administration and justice, during the Pax, the chief lost some of these functions, and those which remained were symbolic or greatly modified in nature and shape. Thus, the D.C. and later the magistrate's court in Swedru, for instance, displaced the chief as the adjudicator in major disputes, especially those about land and monetary claims, within the chiefdom and within the state. The chief's role as military captain naturally became otiose with the Pax. However, some interpersonal disputes involving, for example, assault, stealing, adultery, land boundaries and sales, and marriage still found their way into the chief's native tribunals which were recognized by the colonial authorities. Although in any particular state these native tribunals were not officially hierarchically organized at first, the omanhene's tribunal was considered the most superior, and appeals from the divisional chiefly tribunal lay there in fact. These native courts were subject to much abuse, as we shall soon see.

We have already observed that among the more serious charges brought by the Agona divisional chiefs against Yaw Duodu VII in 1931 was that concerning his uncompromising attitude toward the divisional courts. He was accused of systematically closing down almost all the tribunals in Agona and then making sure that most cases which could have gone to the few that he allowed to function, such as Nkum, came to his court at Nsaba. The reason for this unscrupulous behavior was, as we saw earlier, quite simple — a desire to monopolize the fees and fines accruing to the courts. The scramble between the omanhene and his subordinate chiefs, for these and other revenues and material resources, not to mention the glory and

17. Burns, *Colonial Civil Servant*, p. 322.

honor accorded a rich and powerful chief, led to many disputes, including the more notorious protracted "stool-cum-land disputes" in
Agona, in which supporters of rival claimants to the stool, often ap-
pealing to different interpretations of custom, came to blows and a
few even lost their lives. Let us consult the statistics on the matter.
As Alan Burns pointed out in a speech to the Legislative Council in
September 1942, between 1931 and 1942 twenty-two paramount
chiefs were dethroned in the Gold Coast and twenty-two other paramount chiefs abdicated, generally to forestall dethronement.[18]
Seven stools of paramount chiefs were then vacant, and in many
states no paramount chief had succeeded in maintaining his place
on the stool for more than a very short time.

In the case of subordinate chiefs, the position was even worse.
Time, energy, and money were dissipated on these disputes. We
have noted that in Agona there were no fewer than five dethronements and one abdication involving paramount chiefs between 1920
and 1931. It is significant to stress that this general political instability and civil confusion was directly the result of attempts to control
key economic resources or avenues to them, such as land, cocoa production, and the collection of court fines. It is also obvious from the
number and frequency of disputes and dethronements that the colonial government under the existing law lacked sufficient power to
control the situation and that, as the Nyakrom-Nsaba dispute and
the Swedru case have shown, the government's decision to recognize one of the contending claimants to the stool was not usually
accepted by the other candidates. Although both parties to a dispute as a rule accepted the offer by the D.C. to arbitrate, the decision was rejected by the losing side as soon as it was made.

Burns's Reforms: The Grading of Courts

Sir Alan Burns, who had arrived in the Gold Coast in 1941 to take
up the position of governor, immediately went to work to reform
the corrupt native tribunal system. In December 1942 he appointed
a committee of seven, five Africans and two European officials, to
consider the constitution, jurisdiction, and procedure of native tribunals. Nearly all the recommendations of the committee were accepted and given legal force by the 1944 Native Administration
Ordinance.

18. Ibid., p. 202.

The most important modifications were the grading of the native courts and the limitation of the powers of the courts of each grade; the relieving of the paramount chiefs of their judicial functions as members of the courts; the reduction in the number of judges sitting in each court; the payment of all fines and fees into Native Administration treasuries which had to be established; and the appointment of a judicial adviser as a "guide, philosopher and friend" to the native courts. The 1944 reforms certainly dealt a tremendous blow to the amanhene of Agona, who lost under the new system much traditional power and influence and were prevented from seizing the fines and fees which should have gone to subordinate chiefs. Before the reform, the members (judges) of tribunals consisted usually, as was the case in Swedru, of the adontenhene or chief of the town, who was the president, the mankrado, the gyasehene, the senior linguist of the chief, other senior elders, that is, the chief's councillors, and a registrar-secretary, all of whom divided among themselves the fines and fees imposed. As the members were many, there was a tendency to impose heavy fines and costs in most trivial cases in order that the judges could receive adequate monetary reward.

Under the new ordinance, the number of judges in a native court was limited, and these received regular "sitting fees" as remuneration, for all fines and fees were henceforth to be paid into Native Administration treasuries. The money thus collected could be used in the development of the local area. A treasury was established for Swedru and the local court was graded "B." The "A" court, highest in the state, was at Nyakrom. In Swedru, the new arrangement slightly democratized the judicial service in that judges, consisting of a panel of three at any one sitting, included in some cases nontraditional members. The Native Authority reforms, the recommendations for which were made by the Coussey Constitutional Commission of 1949 (associated with the emergence of the modern political party), further reduced the chief's authority.

THE CHIEF, LOCAL GOVERNMENT, AND THE
RISE OF POLITICAL PARTIES

At the end of the last chapter, I made the observation that the future political drama in Swedru, and for that matter in the Gold Coast, was to be played increasingly in an environment of social and economic protest.[19] What made politics in the Gold Coast (Ghana) exciting and explosive and lent it an appearance of radicalism was the fact that economic and political relations continued to be increasingly heavily colored by economic considerations. What was relevant was not political responsibility but economic freedom, not political consensus but a community of economic and material well-being.

The emphasis on economic interests, which were also power interests, had directly produced the Fante Confederation of 1868–71 and later, in 1897, the Aborigines' Rights Protection Society (ARPS), both of which had been supported by Agona and other Fante chiefs and their educated lawyer subjects, many of whom were close relatives of the chiefs.[20] It is significant to note that these organizations, especially the ARPS, had as their major raison d'être serving as a link between the traditional rulers and the colonial government. They were designed as a move to improve the economic position of the chiefs and lawyer collaborators vis-à-vis the administration and foreign business or commercial interests. They were never conceived as political organizations advocating a complete break from British imperial connection, but they were to cooperate with the colonial authorities in securing reforms by "constitutional means and methods" and in promoting "the interests and advancement of the aborigines of the Gold Coast in any lawful manner whatsoever." At this stage, it was perhaps obvious to the members, both the chiefs and lawyers, that the colonial system, if pushed a little, would serve their interests better than any. For instance, the ARPS fought to preserve the stool lands, the material basis of their traditional power and prestige.

The West African National Congress was founded in March 1920, largely through the inspiration of the late Joseph Casely Hayford, M.B.E., of Cape Coast. Unlike the ARPS, it concentrated most of its efforts on demanding the creation of job opportunities in the public and judicial services for the rising educated urban "middle class"

19. The peoples of the Gold Coast, unlike those of some oriental societies, were not as a rule prepared to take refuge in some transcendental spiritual kingdom (for example, the ascetic impulse that makes a virtue of suffering a hardship, a dominant feature of normative-Hinduism in India) in the face of harsh economic realities.

20. The two organizations may be considered as expressions of neotraditional economic nationalism (they have been hailed as the forerunners of modern Gold Coast nationalism).

and "financial control in the Legislative Councils" by Africans. Although all these organizations spoke, in the name of the people, of the necessity of effective African representation to articulate the wants and aspirations of the common people in the streets and villages, it is clear that what was at stake was the satisfaction of emergent class-individual or status interests. Thus, despite the fact that the chiefs did cooperate with the lawyers in the recent past, when in 1926 the lawyers saw their interests hurt by the government's creation of the Provincial Council of Chiefs to deal directly with administration of customary matters, the executive committee of the ARPS moved at once and resolved that "no Paramount Chief shall attend any of the Provincial Councils or accept nomination to the Legislative Council, since the presence of any Paramount Chief at any of these Councils would involve a breach of the native constitution"; yet the chiefs of the provinces defended and attended their provincial councils.

However, these same chiefs and their subjects who derived their income from cocoa sales were quick to protest against the British Government and refused to sell their cocoa when, between 1928 and 1932, the period of the Depression, the value of cocoa harvests declined and the revenue dwindled to almost one-half, a case of economic distress bringing about reactions affecting the politico-administrative system. Again, in 1937–38, there occurred the famous cocoa holdup and boycott when the farmers of the colony and Ashanti, acting in opposition to the monopolistic purchasing pool of the European firms, brought the economy of the country almost to a halt. The Nowell Commission endorsed these grievances.[21] Here tribalism was definitely irrelevant.

Then again, in 1941, a few days after the arrival of Governor Alan Burns, the government railway and harbor workers in Sekondi-Takoradi went on a sudden strike, despite the fact that with their consent their demand for wage increases and other concessions had been referred to an arbitrator.[22] There was sabotage and disorder in Takoradi, followed by sympathetic strikes and some disorder in

21. Padmore, *Gold Coast Revolution*, p. 56, describes the holdup as "mass emotional upheaval . . . and . . . the first instance of unanimous popular action throughout the Colony and Ashanti together."

22. The harbor workers' strike marked the beginning of active political agitation of Gold Coast trade unions against colonialist economic exploitation, and of their direct involvement in the struggle for economic and political freedom.

other parts of the Gold Coast, which were later suppressed by the police, who made arrests.[23]

In 1948, Nii Kwabena Bonne III, a famous Ga chief, organized a country-wide boycott of European and Syrian shops to force these foreign firms to reduce the exorbitant prices they were charging for essential commodities consumed by Africans, such as milk, corned beef, and Manchester print cloth. This anti-inflationary movement sparked the famous looting of shops, which went on mainly in the principal towns of the Eastern Region and in Kumasi, Ashanti. In the same month, on 28 February 1948, the representatives of the exservicemen's union marched on the Castle, the residence of the governor, to present a petition asking the governor to redress their grievances — to provide jobs for demobilized soldiers. The Watson Commission of that year, like the Nowell Commission, endorsed substantially the economic nature of the protest and drew special attention to the general indebtedness of the mass of the population, the cocoa farmers.

What should be stressed here is that all these demands, demonstrations, and protests were organized by ad hoc committees that represented class or group economic interests but claimed they operated in the name of the people. It is these occasional but regular economic protests which give primary meaning to the politics of the Gold Coast and Ghana. In a sense, this pattern of economic politics is somewhat institutionalized.[24] People saw long-term political achievement primarily in terms of the cost of living index. Whenever real income was generally considered high, for example, when the producer price of cocoa was high relative to the cost-of-living index, people were hardly receptive to political activities. Political involvement tended to be more symbolic and normative than instrumental at this time.

When, therefore, the first political movements — sometimes referred to as political parties even during the initial stages — specifically, the United Gold Coast Convention (UGCC) and later the Convention People's Party (CPP) were formed, they had to rely

23. Burns, *Colonial Civil Servant*, pp. 186–87.
24. Amazingly enough, what was objectionable about Chinese and Russian presence in Ghana in the 1960s was what a majority of the people considered the inferiority and shoddiness of their goods, rather than the fact that they were communists. Political ideology as such was not the most crucial factor. Only when ideology is perceived as affecting economic well-being is it a crucial factor.

almost wholly (but not entirely, it should be stressed) on the direction of economic interests for support. They could not provide any overarching ideology beyond promises of economic prosperity for all.[25] In this context ideologies are largely irrelevant. The fragility of this was to become increasingly apparent to politicians, who could not, in a poor country, but fail to live up to those promises. No wonder, in the course of harsh economic deprivation over time, almost anybody who is daring enough can emerge as a "savior" and later achieve "charismatic" attributes if he immediately succeeds in bettering the economic situation.

This essentially utilitarian politics was appreciated by a man who had both the training and the temperament to do so. That man was the late J. B. Danquah, John Stuart Mill scholar of the University of London and "the doyen of Gold Coast politicians." In his very obscure exercise, *Liberty of the Subject*, he stated under the fourth of the Seven Postulates of the Gold Coast Races Nationalist Movement that "the state represents the National State insofar as there is a progressive identification of State interests with the interests of the Gold Coast races [tribes], and not otherwise." [26] This predominantly laissez-faire attitude is quite consistent with what is generally acceptable to a majority of the people. The Youth Conference which Danquah and some other intellectuals had convened in 1930 was neither a political party nor a nationalist political movement in terms of its appeal, but just a gathering of some educated Gold Coast men to exchange ideas on economic and social problems.

It is no accident that when the UGCC was formed in 1947 at Saltpond in the Central Region, the executive (at least on paper) of this new nationalist movement was made up mainly of old and young lawyers. Mr. George ("Pa") Grant, ex–Legislative Council member and financier, was chairman. These young men (ages thirty to fifty), as later events were to prove, were nothing but ambitious "scholars" eager to improve their economic circumstances by a political career under the umbrella of nationalism. But the chiefs were

25. Since in Ghana a sharp normative breach never really occurred, given the accommodationist capacity, what was generally expected of any leadership was the "use" of extant norms to achieve commanding heights of economic betterment for individuals and communities, whatever the structure of government.

26. What this often amounts to is that sovereignty of the state is considered meaningless except when State power is used to further the interests of dominant socioeconomic groups.

quick to realize that they might be fighting a class, not a nationalist, battle. Pa Grant complained that "the chiefs led or misled by certain ambiguous collaborators with the imperial power neither could make up their minds whether to swim with the people or sink with imperialism."

That the chiefs should have been hesitant about throwing their weight behind the intellectual lawyer-politicians, after a fashion, is significant in that they were not prepared to sink with anybody. It might have been obvious to them that there was no guarantee that following the new men who favored self-government "in the shortest possible time" would necessarily serve their interests. In Swedru, the largely illiterate Kwahu petty traders and store owners especially had come to rely heavily on the European firms for what to them was generous credit advances and commissions, and they were afraid that self-government might involve the closing down of European firms and the repatriation of the Europeans.

The UGCC was to remain an organization on paper only until Nkrumah arrived from London in December 1947 to take up the post of secretary in 1948. He immediately began "a drive in earnest for members." As the Watson Report (Appendix 12, Colonial Reports, no. 231) put it with much candor, Nkrumah was largely successful, initially, at any rate, because he "endeavoured to enlist under their banner everyone who had a public or private grievance against the Government and to seize upon every complaint, great or small, which might inflame a population avid for excitement." [27] The riots and looting of 1948 provided the political fuel. It was under these circumstances that the Coussey Constitutional Commission of forty Africans was asked to make proposals for a new constitution. The very composition of the commission was to be attacked, for the members were handpicked by the governor, Sir Gerald Creasy, and included many chiefs, representatives of traditional interests, and lawyers. (The Commission had succeeded in uniting the old and the new elites of paramount chiefs, lawyers and professional men.) The conspicuous absence of representatives of other major interests — farmers, industrial workers, laborers, petty traders, market women, and youth — was seized upon by Nkrumah, who had him-

27. Although national politics was certainly important, the country-wide excitement and agitation could not obscure the real nature of the protest: the largely communal, group, or individual economic self-interest.

self been excluded despite his increasing popularity, to further his political aims.

Nkrumah, in breaking with the UGCC and founding the CPP on the Committee of Youth Organization, in June 1949, made capital of the "fraudulent" constitutional proposal and spoke to the people in class terms. He reiterated that the UGCC was controlled by wealthy businessmen and lawyers who were not interested in "immediate S.G. for the people." At this time, self-government (S.G.) was presented as the only and unfailing means to economic bounty for the common man. The CPP was for the interests of the urban workers, artisans, market women, fishermen, farmers, junior clerks, and teachers – the masses, unrepresented on the Coussey Commission. It should be recalled that it is these sections of the population which between 1929 and 1949 had, without the benefit of party political leadership, sought through both organized and spontaneous protests to better their economic position. It could be inferred from their past behavior that to these people political parties and political ideologies were meaningful primarily to the extent that membership conferred economic and social advantages. This accounted for the popularity of the CPP between 1949 and 1963. It is an irony of history that when Nkrumah was establishing his political kingdom in Ghana, if not in Africa, his followers and henchmen were mostly interested in building an economic paradise for themselves in their local constituencies.

When the Coussey Commission report of 26 October 1949 was published, the CPP could boast of relatively well-established branches throughout the colony and Ashanti. The consequences of this network of organizations for social and political integration became obvious even in the early 1950s. In November 1949, in Accra, the national capital, the CPP underscored the cleavage between itself and the UGCC by calling, along with the Trade Union Congress (TUC), the Ghana Representative Assembly, which was attended by many organizations, including cooperatives; trade unions; farmers' organizations; educational, cultural and women's societies; and youth clubs. The council of chiefs, the UGCC, and the ARPS refused to attend. This refusal to attend was to be a watershed in the political development of the country. It marked a breach which was never to be healed until the military coup of 24 February 1966 abolished by decree membership of political parties and politics. The Assembly resolved that the Coussey Report and the governor's statement thereon were unacceptable. The people of the Gold Coast wanted immediate self-government. The Assembly drew up a memorandum outlining the structure of central and local government they would like to see incorporated in a new constitution. Among the recommendations were a bicameral legislature and a three-tier local government and the abolition of the office of the D.C. It is interesting that in 1956 Nkrumah ridiculed the Opposition Party's demand for the establishment of two houses of assembly.

Nkrumah went a step further in his political aim. He declared "Positive Action" from the midnight of 8 January 1950. This political campaign of nonviolence and noncooperation in the Gandhian tradition was, like the demonstrations before it, given fillip by independently planned open economic protests, such as the march of ex-servicemen in some of the principal towns, including Swedru, of the Gold Coast. The "Positive Action" coincided with the strike of Government meteorological workers which had started earlier and was backed by the TUC. Nkrumah and the CPP succeeded and were henceforth on a political journey of no return: "Forward Ever — Backward Never." Yet even at this early stage, success was purchased at an extremely high price and was largely attributable, as we shall see later, to the strategic economic role of the CPP-controlled CPC (Cocoa Purchasing Company).

It has been necessary to examine in some detail the socioeconomic background of the political developments going on throughout the Gold Coast. It offers a better perspective for a fuller appreciation of how the Agona reacted to or helped generate these forces of national importance. In the succeeding chapters we shall be preoccupied with tracing the changes in local government, which had started with the Burns reforms of 1946, and how these affected the chief. We shall at the same time continue with a consideration of the role of political parties in local and national development.

5 THE CHIEF, LOCAL ADMINISTRATION, AND THE MIGRANT

Briefly, *local government* may be considered as that authority which is concerned with the management of the affairs of a local area or unit. Until the Local Government Act of 1951, under which new and modern local authorities were established, the management of the affairs of Swedru had been handled by a native authority under the system of indirect rule, with legitimate authority firmly in the hands of the adontenhene – the chief of Swedru and his elder councillors. In so far as Swedru remained largely Agona, relatively rural, illiterate, and descent-based, the system of native administration might very well suffice and even help, as Lucy Mair has argued, in the period of transition from tradition to modern colonialism.

But with the increasing urbanization of Swedru, particularly after 1948, and the associated influx into the town of migrants from all over Ghana and from other West African countries, social control and local government under the existing arrangements became increasingly difficult and complex. Even in 1948, Swedru was a thriving and bustling nodality, a real crossroads where people of various ethnic backgrounds came to trade, to get education, perchance to be converted to Christianity or Islam, to work for a living generally. By 1960, Swedru was not only ethnically heterogeneous – the Fante, the Kwahu, the Levantines, the Hausa, the Guan, and others, were all, as we saw in chapter 3, present – but occupationally diverse and specialized. These changes created problems of local administration as many people, by reason of their education or ethnic background or both, though they respected the chief, felt strongly that they had a right to participate in the management of the affairs of Swedru, which after all were as much their affairs as affairs of the indigenous Agona. Some went so far as to argue that, though they were strangers, they had a better claim to Swedru, "the migrant town," "the town of strangers" (descriptions acceptable to and used by the Agona themselves), since they were the ones developing it and not the Agona, a "lazy and unprogressive bunch."

Under these circumstances, how was social control exercised, how was peace and order, the prerequisite to any efficient administration of local affairs, maintained? How was the society integrated? Perhaps we should distinguish at once between formal and informal types of social control operating through various kinds of sanctions.

SOCIAL CONTROL AND SOCIAL INTEGRATION

At the formal level there was the Native Authority system with its police and its tribunal or court; there was Agona customary law which embraced the beliefs, values, and religion of the people. The presence of the Government Police, English common law, and the magistrate's court supported in most cases the native system and strengthened social control. Again, as Busia has shown for Sekondi, it is true that the Agona may have been outnumbered by the migrants, yet they still form an important group which maintains a tradition of tribal discipline and authority.[1] Thus, until very recently, migrants in Swedru were expected to abide (and generally did so) by the custom prohibiting work on farms on Tuesdays; and prohibiting women during their menstrual periods from stepping in the Akora River to fetch water for cooking and drinking, and washing on Wednesdays; and prohibiting their swimming, bathing, or washing in the river.[2] We have already discussed the commercial importance of Swedru and the large role played by migrants, such as the Kwahu, Levantines, and Europeans, in trade and commerce. Whenever the ohene of Swedru "goes to the village," all stores, European and non-European alike, are expected to (and, on the whole, do) close down for a day or two as a sign of mourning to honor the de-

1. K. A. Busia, *Report on a Social Survey of Sekondi-Takoradi* (London: Crown Agents, 1960), and *Social Implications of Industrialization and Urbanisation in Africa South of the Sahara* (Paris: UNESCO, 1956).

2. Significantly, the praise-name of the river or, more appropriately, river god, Aku (Eku), was *Akora aku pantanpran, ofaa ahoho* — that is, "the great Aku of the Akora River, he who drowns only 'strangers.'" This expresses adequately the control mechanism involved. Migrants were afraid and strongly warned their children never to swim or wash in the river for fear that they might drown. In fact, there were a few cases on record of such drowning. There was even the supporting consideration that only members of the Agona asafo companies could save or retrieve a drowning or drowned stranger.

ceased chief. Any store or market open for business on these days is liable to be looted with impunity by the Agona youth.

I have mentioned the local branch of the national police system, with its "bullying" escorts, and the colonial law and justice working through the D.C., the chief, and the magistrate's court. A very effective negative sanction was the court fine and imprisonment or detention in the police cells. People were ashamed to be arrested, on whatever grounds, by the police — in fact, it was a social disgrace. Many, therefore, avoided behavior likely to lead to indictment before the courts. The law and its enforcement certainly contribute toward order and peace in Swedru.

There is, however, much evidence to show that during the initial years of in-migration, interethnic hostilities, particularly between the Pepefo (Hausa) and the Agona or Fante, were rife and led occasionally to street fights. There is no doubt that much of the problem here was linguistic, and perhaps, economic.[3] In many of these fights the common accusation by the Agona was, *Pepefo nte asem ase* ("Pepefo are not reasonable"), that is, "They don't seem to understand what we are saying." But as soon as most migrants, or their children, for that matter, began to adopt and use the host language, the quarrels or conflicts, instead of leading to physical assaults, led more often than not to patterns of obligatory joking relationships. This brings me to a summary consideration of informal types of social control. I shall argue that the informal joking relationships function as a mode of social or interethnic integration, at least helping to prevent a total breakdown of social relations.

ETHNIC STEREOTYPES AND SOCIAL CONTROL

The obligatory joking relationship (the duty to return a verbal abuse or attack only with verbal attack, and thereafter to part amicably!) is based on insults derived from what one ethnic group perceives as the objective qualities of another. That the insults do not usually lead to open fights is largely the result of, among other things, a strong sense of identification of the migrants with Swedru —

3. As the only butchers, the Hausa monopolized the sale of livestock — sheep, goats and cattle. Swedru came to depend almost completely on the Hausa for their daily meat supplies and for the livestock which play such a crucial role in traditional ritual sacrifices and ceremonies. As Mohammedans, Hausa Malams were consulted by the Agona and others for Koranic charms and amulets believed to insure success in trade, commerce, and politics.

they are all Swedrufo — and the realization, rare in other places in West Africa, that all the ethnic groups need and depend on one another for social and economic betterment. The migrants summarize the position thus: "We are in Swedru to work for a living," or "We are in Swedru to make money and not to fight among ourselves."

The objective qualities by which ethnic groups are perceived and stereotyped include eating habits, sexual habits, style of dress, religion, personality characteristics, and so on. All the migrants agree that the Agona are lazy, lack industry, are poor, and that their girls are "encouraged" by their mothers to "prostitute" themselves to scrape a living. The Kwahu are undoubtedly materialistic and put money before everything else; they even sacrifice their children and wives at the altar of money. They are frugal, *Kwahufo pepeefo*. They are skilled traders and wealthy. The Ewe (often confused with the Anloga or Awuna) are thieves, *Ayigbe dzuro*. They dabble in sorcery and evil medicine, *wotu nduru*. They are murderers. The Ga are considered quarrelsome, big-mouthed, and bullies. The Hausa smell, and they are unclean. They are those enjoined "to wash their anus" before they eat their favorite dish (*kokonte*), a reference to the Islamic ritual of washing during prayers. The Ashanti are proud, boastful, and unsophisticated compared to the coastal Fante.

The coastal Fante are polished, "Europeanized," especially in their food habits, educated, yet poor compared to the Kwahu or Ashanti. The inland Fante, the Gomoa-Ekumfi complex, are litigious, rural, rustic. *Gomoanyi* summarizes in derogatory terms their attributes. The Nigerians, Alatafo (more appropriately the Yoruba), are the snail eaters, *Alata wawe ngwa*. They are considered dirty, they live in overcrowded rooms, and they are frugal like the Kwahu. The Indians are clannish, heathens, believers in charms, and they use magic to attract customers to their stores. The Levantines, or the Syrians, as they are locally called, do not wash and have pungent onion smells on their bodies. They seduce local girls and force them into prostitution. It is not uncommon on the street corners of Swedru to see a group of people of different ethnic backgrounds using some of the stereotypes described above to hurl abuses at one another for some time, or tease one another, and then quickly turn to other subjects of mutual interest — the cost of living, or how their football club is faring in the national league.

Again, fairly durable bonds of unity among the diverse ethnic

groups are created by common membership in voluntary associations and by interethnic marriages, concubinages, or "irresponsible"
heterosexual relationships of friendship. It is common knowledge,
for example, that at the Zerikin Zongo quarter or ward there are
many Fante women (precise statistics are wanting) who are married to Pepefo and have adopted the Islamic religion, and equally a
few Fante men married to Hausa women. Such unions are not in
general considered despicable. A well-known local Indian merchant, who lived and died in Swedru, married a Fante woman from
Cape Coast. A very influential Lebanese trader in town married a
beautiful certificated female teacher from Agona Nsaba. As one un-
married Agona woman of about twenty-six tersely put it, "I go with
whoever [men wherever they come from] is able to maintain or look
after me properly." I am sure many girls share her view, judging by
what goes on in Swedru. This point immediately takes us to the nature and patterns of economic interdependence among ethnic
groups.

ECONOMIC NECESSITY AND SOCIAL INTEGRATION

Swedru is a commercial town set within a large rural hinterland.
It is relatively modern compared to the surrounding towns. As we
have seen, its modernity, such as it is, did not develop out of local
roots.[4] Rather, the Kwahu, the Levantines, and other migrants are
the principal agents of modernization in Swedru.[5]

In any case, in a very crude way, it may be argued that the populations of Swedru are polarized or specialized on the axis of those in
primary production and those in secondary and tertiary production.
The Agona in Swedru (and in the immediate surrounding hinterland) constitute a majority in the former category while the latter
category is made up predominantly of migrants or strangers. The
Agona and the stranger migrants are therefore constrained by the
structure of occupational specialization into symbiotic economic re-

4. In fact, a majority of the 19.8 percent Agona in Swedru (1960 census)
were still mostly engaged in primary production of foodstuffs, producing either
for the market or for subsistence.
5. In 1960, it is significant to note that of the population of Swedru, as many
as 30.0 percent had been born in another town in the Central Region; 19.3 per
cent had been born in another region in Ghana; 11.2 percent had been born in
another country in Africa. These figures do not, of course, include the many
children of migrants who had been born in Swedru, nor do they include the
crucial Indian, European, and Levantine population.

lationships. This picture, it must be admitted, is too simple, for it does not account for the few Agona in the tertiary sector and the many Fante in the primary sector of the town economy. Yet the message it carries of the economic interdependence of the various ethnic groups in Swedru is generally valid.

D. Grove and L. Huszar have classified all Ghanaian towns, on the basis of variety and level of services, into six types in a descending order of relative modernity.[6] Grade I towns are the most modernized; grade VI, the least modernized.[7] What I should like to emphasize here is the diversity of the ethnic backgrounds of the workers and, more significantly, the over-representation of migrant groups in this relatively modern tertiary sector (see chapter 3, for instance). No doubt, this over-representation of the Fante, the Ga, and others, is partly a reflection of the local demographic structure and partly of the somewhat superior education and entrepreneurial skill of the strangers.

The other major bond between ethnic groups is that based on a complex and extensive system of indebtedness and patronage which is the very fabric of the socioeconomic life of the people of Swedru. In an important sense, credit giving, also considered a social service, expresses the economic symbiosis of the diverse populations of Swedru, their economic interdependence. In Swedru, as in many other commercial towns throughout the country, almost anything — food, clothing, automobiles, even the services of prostitutes — may be bought on credit by almost anybody, without reference to one's ethnic background or credit worthiness, though very bad risks are generally known and avoided by potential creditors. It is not my intention here to go into detailed discussion of the intricacies of inter- and intra-ethnic indebtedness. The topic would certainly merit a complete chapter. Rather, my objective is to draw attention to some

6. D. Grove and L. Huszar, *The Towns of Ghana: The Role of Service Centers in Regional Planning* (Accra: Ghana University Press, 1964).

7. Swedru, as a grade III town, typically has the following functionally specialized institutions or services which link the locality with the regional and national levels of the state: district commissioners' offices, police stations, post offices, rest houses, gas stations, UAC or GNTC wholesale outlets, main-road junctions, local courts, hospitals or health centers, and banks. A government treasury is typical of grade III towns but there is none in Swedru, though it has a "municipal" bus service, something typical of grade I towns — e.g., Accra. It should perhaps be indicated that Swedru has an important daily local market and other services that attract many people in the central region to Swedru every day.

of the more enduring social and political consequences flowing out
of the economic transaction.

It appears that debts, whatever the amounts involved, are, as a
rule, not readily paid when due. The reasons for this are as varied
as the people and amounts concerned. Clearly, in a majority of
cases, the debtors may not have the wherewithal to meet their obligations. Yet there is much evidence to support the consideration
that in many instances failure to pay is deliberate and sometimes
even expected. The provision of credit or lending in whatever form
is interpreted by the receivers as a social service, a friendly aid from
wealthier and financially more fortunate "relatives" or close friends.
Thus, demands for repayment are usually met with appeals, often
phrased in kinship terms, by the debtor ("son" or "nephew") to his
creditor ("father" or "mother's brother") asking the latter to have
mercy on him. The important thing to note is that such appeals are
made *whether or not* the ties are from the same ethnic group. The
debtor-creditor relationship may assume, over time, features of patron-client ties in which the debtor as client, instead of paying his
debt, is perhaps merely seeking indefinite postponement of the time
for the settlement of the amount outstanding, may give obligatory
gifts in kind annually to the patron-creditor, and even on occasion
perform certain services for him "free" (a reversed form of mediae-
val scutage?).

It must be pointed out at once that nonpayment of debts may,
and in a number of cases does, lead to court action. Even so, many
end up as bad debts, particularly on the death of the original creditor, but the social bond established by indebtedness between the
families of the creditor and debtor at times remains for a number of
generations. An examination of the Returns to the Registrar of the
Circuit Court, Cape Coast, of criminal cases and other matters decided by or brought before the local court of Swedru during the
month of June 1965 provides illustration of the type and number of
cases concerning nonpayment of debts that come before the court.
It should be noted that the cases include both old and new ones.
The numerical distribution shown in table 5 is particularly striking.

The cases that come under the rubric of debt recovery include recovery of "personal loans" and of what the Returns describe as "account due/owing," "balance of money owed," "goods sold," and
so on, emphasizing the commercial nature of the transaction. It
is interesting to observe that the Colonial Reports, from 1949 to

TABLE 5 SWEDRU LOCAL COURT CASES AND
MATTERS DEALT WITH IN JUNE 1965

Nature of Case	Type of Case	Number of Cases
Debt recovery	Civil	30
Assault, disorderly behavior, breach of the peace	Criminal	12
Sanitation hazard	Criminal	14
Failure to pay property rates, local levy, Truck tickets	Criminal	14
Adultery	Civil	2
Suit for damages	Civil	1
	Total	73

NOTE: The official Returns report 46 criminal cases and 43 civil cases, for a total of 89.

1954, which I consulted reiterate that "in urban areas, most of the civil cases coming before the Native Courts concern *debt recovery*" (my italics). The amounts of the debts to be recovered in the 1965 example, when the native courts had been replaced by local courts, ranged from as high as £100, the statutory limit, to as low as £1 6s. Of the thirty cases, thirteen involved amounts less than £10; eight involved amounts from £10 to £25; four involved the recovery of from £25 to £50; and five from £50 to £100:

Less than £10:   13 cases
£10 to £25:   8 cases
£25 to £50:   4 cases
£50 to £100:   5 cases
Total: 30 cases

Yet, the cases before the courts represent, as I have said before, just a small fraction of the total number of debts to be recovered in Swedru in any one month. This, I think, demonstrates, if nothing else, the goodwill, trust, and mutual tolerance developed over time among the various ethnic groups in Swedru. Reference has been made to the common "ethos" of the migrant groups that they are in Swedru "primarily to work for a living and make money," and not to fight among themselves. The storekeepers and retail traders, among them, aim at profit making and do take advantage of their customers. But they are not necessarily ruthless. The Indian, Kwahu, and Fante traders I interviewed all admitted, for instance, that they would have recourse to the courts only as a last resort. It is noteworthy that many creditors under certain extenuating circumstances — such as deaths in the family of the debtor, which normally entail expensive funerals; failure of the business or unemployment of the debtor; sudden sexual interest shown by the creditor in a female relative of the debtor — may forgo the financial claims on their debtors. Since this amounts to generous patronage or money gifts, the creditors thereby gain higher social status and prestige.[8] The consequences of the attitude of compassion among some businessmen in Swedru (and in other towns throughout Ghana) for rapid economic development are yet to be assessed; its implication for social integration is no doubt clear.

A powerful but subtle instrument of social control is undoubtedly public opinion, which makes families and individuals, migrant and non-migrant alike, avoid being branded as troublesome, antisocial, wicked, or the like. The woman who is always quarreling with her neighbors is considered a "witch" and the social ostracism which the term still conjures is enough negative sanction. A few cases, selected at random, of people suing for damages in the local courts should suggest to us the power of public opinion and the desire for neighbors to be in good social standing in their communities.

Case No. 1
Madam Plaintiff v. Mr. Defendant: Defendant is sued for putting Madam Plaintiff "into fetish," to wit: "You will die whenever you drink River Akora or step into it." The accused was fined £3 or sentenced to one month's imprisonment.

Case No. 2
Mr. Plaintiff v. Mr. Defendant: A case of adultery. Plaintiff sues for £100 damages "to admit plaintiff's wife in your bedroom and to allow the plaintiff's wife to cook or prepare food for you as husband and wife" (note the social definition). The case was adjourned and later settled out of court.

Case No. 3
Mr. Plaintiff v. Mr. Defendant: Defamation of character. Plaintiff sues for £50 damages: "You Mr. . . . (the Plaintiff) with ugly face, have you got money? [You are poor.] This foolish work [hard work, little pay] you're doing, do you think you're somebody [rich and important]; all of your families are useless bleed [*sic*, breed] children without having one

8. There is another consideration. According to one Indian merchant, "Some just don't have the money [to pay their debts], and moreover, the 'go-come,' 'go-come' [reference to adjournment] of the court is time consuming and therefore bad for business."

to care for them. Foolish man." The case was struck out and later settled out of court.

Case No. 4

Mr. Plaintiff v. Mr. Defendant: Defamation of character. Plaintiff sues for £50 damages: "You good for nothing fellow. Extortionist person like you who when [you] marry into a family . . . cast a strain into such a house; never shall I give my daughter . . . to you for [in] marriage except [you'll have to] marry . . . your deceased wife." The court awarded £10 10s. plus costs to the plaintiff.

Case No. 5

The State v. Mr. X: "You chief and elders of Agona Asafo with your boreheads [baldheads]. It is our money that you steal in running your chieftaincy." Mr. X is accused by the police, representing the state, of insulting the traditional rulers in words likely to disgrace them. The defendant, Mr. X, was fined £10 or sentenced to two months' imprisonment with hard labor.

Case No. 6

Madam Plaintiff v. Madam Defendant: Defamation of character. Plaintiff sues for £50 damages: "A dirty and senseless woman. A witch, with scratches on her skin." Plaintiff was awarded £10 plus costs.

Case No. 7

The State v. Mr. Y: Mr. Y did intentionally and unlawfully expose defamatory or insulting words against Madam X with the intention of annoying, irritating, or disgracing her to wit: "You are a foolish and stupid woman. O dirty woman whose vagina is full of water." £4 was awarded to the aggrieved woman. Note that here public opinion was acting through the officers representing the state.

All the cases above, selected from Returns to the Registrar of the Circuit Court from Swedru between 1961 and 1966, illustrate what has already been observed, that one avoids as far as is humanly possible acts, words, or attitudes that would stigmatise one in one's community. An Akan proverb has it, "Death is better and more honorable than social disgrace."

A young Agona tailor (about thirty-five) from a reputable lineage in Swedru (his mother's brother is the famous wealthy land and cocoa owner, Otabir) added another dimension to the question of interethnic unity and social integration when he said:

The Agona like foreigners. Why? Because the Agona are in the main so preoccupied with their own petty intra- and interfamily and lineage jealousies, disputes, and selfishness that they would rather help the foreigner succeed in life than their own relatives. Do you know that very recently when the Swedru Omnibus Transport Corporation was looking for an experienced tailor to give the contract of making the uniforms of drivers and conductors and conductresses to, and someone suggested me, it was an Agona man who dismissed the suggestion, because he knew that the contract, if awarded to me, would have made me richer and better than he is, and that the contract was finally given to a foreign tailor? Maybe we Agona have got used to relying on foreigners for everything, to develop our resources for us, even at our expense, because perhaps we considered ourselves adehye [persons of freeborn matrilineal descent] and above manual labour and physical exertion; for example, we gave our fertile lands to Gomoa farmers in return for the small share of a third of the produce of the land. We alienated our lands in Swedru or mortgaged them for a song to European firms and Kwahu, Lebanese [Syrian], and Fante traders and property developers. Now we cannot but rely on them [the migrants] for our very livelihood and existence.

A certain amount of disunity among the Agona, which to some extent forces them into the arms of the migrants, is again illustrated by one significant incident. I was once discussing with some local people the question of succession to the then vacant adonten stool of Swedru. The Swedruhene died a few weeks after my arrival in the field. The king-makers were obviously having some difficulty in finding a suitable candidate.[9]

I asked one Agona man in his forties what he thought. He said flippantly, "This is not a matter for me, it is a matter for the Asona abusua [the Asona matri-clan]. I am not Asona and I don't care who succeeds Nana Botwe." This attitude, I later realized, was very widespread, and was expressed on numerous occasions by various Agona people.

I think my Agona tailor friend hit the nail on the head when he emphasized that the indiscriminate sale of lands belonging to the traditional state, division, or lineage to strangers (migrants) has greatly contributed to the economic and social dependence of the Agona on the Fante, Kwahu, Ashanti, and others. Indigenous power was decisively based, as the gyasehene pointed out to me, on the control of lands and their resources. The very close relationship between chiefship and land and religion has been amply demonstrated in this and other papers. The alienation of Agona lands could not but wrest from the Agona people in Swedru their major source of wealth and power in society. Although lands so transferred have in many instances been redeveloped for modern commercial and private buildings, it is a case of exchanging a principal and almost un-

9. In April 1968, Kwaku Donkoh, a twenty-six-year-old refrigerator mechanic, the grandson of the late Nana Botwe, was enthroned as Nana Botwe II.

failing avenue to wealth, social honor, and political power for a few ready pounds or baskets of farm produce.

THE PERSONALITY OF THE CHIEF, ETHNICITY, AND LOCAL GOVERNMENT

In the preceding sections, I have discussed some of the crucial and salient social factors which make for relative peace and order, a sine qua non for stable local administration, in Swedru. I have considered the role of tribal authority, the law and the courts, informal public opinion, cross-cutting and multiple membership in voluntary associations, the economic interdependence of ethnic groups, and the strong belief shared with the colonialists that it is peace, not fighting, which brings about economic prosperity. What I did not discuss, a very important element indeed, is the role of the chief as a person (with a personality), in contradistinction to his office, as an integrative force in Swedru.[10]

Peter Lloyd and others have shown convincingly that the personality of the chief does influence the exercise of chiefly functions.[11] He may enlarge, diminish, extend, twist, modify his traditional functions in new and unexpected directions. The chief could be as despotic or autocratic as Nyarko Eku I or as democratic as the late Kobina Botwe of Swedru. I hope to argue that Nana Botwe, adontenhene of Swedru from 1932 until his death in 1967 made a personal contribution, both directly and indirectly, to the peace, prosperity, socioeconomic development, and interethnic solidarity in the town. Two important circumstances of his early adult life made him fit to perform the role of mediator between tradition and modernity on the one hand and between the various ethnic groups on the other.[12]

Although Botwe knew he might one day become the chief of Swedru, as a young man, illiterate but ambitious, he left the royal surroundings of his home (it is not clear whether this occurred be-

10. Although in Akan society, office (the stool) and the person of the chief are inseparable, it may be necessary at times to separate them in thought and in action to assess and appreciate the relative contribution of each.

11. Peter C. Lloyd, "The Political Structure of African Kingdoms: An Exploratory Model," in *Political Systems and the Distribution of Power*, Michael Banton, editor (Boston: F. Praeger, 1965).

12. The eldest daughter of the late chief described her father as *obrefo*, a term that connotes knowledge of the outside world, experience, and cosmopolitanism.

fore or after the divorce of his mother), which at the time offered
limited possibilities, to seek his fortune and self-improvement elsewhere. He was aware even in the early 1920s that without money
and adequate resources chieftaincy is meaningless. He became a
migrant worker or wage laborer, like many of the inhabitants of
Swedru today. He worked for a time at Osonase near Oda as a laborer in the timber forests and yards. Thence he went to the mines
of Tarkwa and Aboso, where conditions were considered better,
and worked as a sawyer laborer until his recall home in the early
1930s to be the chief of Swedru. The time he spent in the ethnically
heterogeneous mine communities of Tarkwa and Aboso was certainly educative. There he must have gained an appreciation of the
problems of the migrant — the kind of appreciation that, in a good-
natured man such as he, was most likely to lead to tolerance of and
sympathy for migrants of all tribes.

   The other circumstance is that, like a majority of the inhabitants
of Swedru, he was an "ethnic puzzle," whose precise tribal background and affiliation was difficult for outsiders to determine. Incidentally, ethnic puzzles may contribute toward social integration by
acceptance of multiple ethnic memberships. Nana Botwe's mother,
after her divorce, is believed to have remarried, this time not an
Agona from Kwanyako (where many Gomoa Fante have been
"Agona-ized"), but a man from Ekumfi Adam. His stepfather was
therefore Fante. Since the Agona and the Fante attach nearly as
much importance to the father tie as to the mother one (every
child, male and female alike, belongs to the asafo of his father) the
Fante, the most important single ethnic group in Swedru, could not
help claiming Botwe as a fellow tribesman. There are many people
in Swedru today, especially the non-Agona, who still hold that the
late Botwe was Fante.[13]

   An elderly Kwahu trader, who incidentally happened to be on
very friendly terms with the eldest wife, Amokwandoa, of the late
chief, asserted rather seriously, soon after our discussion with
Amokwandoa concerning the possible successor to her late husband,
that the late chief's father was a Kwahu. What impressed me in its

---

13. In fact, it is popularly claimed that when in 1931–32 Kobina Botwe was
fighting hard for the stool of Swedru against the counterclaims of Kojo Nyarko
and his group (see chapter 2), the Fante of Bebianiha supported Botwe to the
hilt, threatening to fight his Agona opponents! These Fante, it is believed, later
assisted the chief in a series of litigations over land rights.

significance was not the truth or falsity of the claim but the fact that he believed in it and was influenced by it, along with other Kwahu, in his relations with the chief. The Kwahu trader went on to tell me how some of the more prominent and wealthy Kwahu traders had regularly made the chief gifts of money. In one case a double-barreled gun, a prestige item, was presented to him by the late Yaw Booh, who was described by the gyasehene as *guahene* – ("chief of traders"). The Kwahu trader ended by saying, "The chief treated us very well and did everything in his power to help us."

Not only did the chief assist the strangers as far as possible, but he officially honored from time to time those migrants who made special contributions to the socioeconomic development of Swedru, by conferring on them the traditional status of supi (military commander). Thus Chahal, a Lebanese trader, who has made huge investments in buildings in Swedru and so on, was made supi in the early 1950s by the chief. Two related observances in connection with the death of the chief in early 1967 are particularly telling in their expession of the bonds between the various ethnic groups in Swedru and of the respect accorded the chief.

After the rumors of the death of the chief had been generally confirmed, for a day or two, traders, market women, and storekeepers closed down their shops, stalls, and booths. This was done partly as a sign of mourning the chief's death, partly for fear of incurring the negative sanction of Agona tribal authority (threats did abound that markets and stores that opened for business would be looted), and partly out of respect for the chief, who was, after all, the chief of all Swedrufo. The second observance concerns the ceremony of Monday, 20 March 1967 (unusual in the history of Swedru and Agona, according to the elders of Swedru), called "paying the sick chief a visit in his village." [14] The chief had been interred. The day was declared a public holiday in Swedru. Nobody went to work. All the heads of the various ethnic groups and their members were represented and gathered in their mourning clothes – black, red, dark brown, dark blue – near the Labour Office, a few minutes away from the royal cemetery. They all danced, drank, and wept to honor Botwe.

On this occasion, what particularly struck me was the Akan garb

14. Remember that the euphemism for the death of an Akan chief is "the chief has gone to the village."

of the head of Zongo (considered the principal stranger ward in Swedru and other places), that handsome, sedate, former employee of G. B. Ollivant and Company, Ltd., and Hausa wage laborer, now Zerikin-Malam Isifu Darfi. As the zerikin later told me, "I felt Agona enough on that day to mourn the chief not in the traditional flowing Hausa robes, but in Akan-style toga. After all, we are all one people!" As one Ashanti man admitted, "Malam Darfi was the most impressive chief that Monday."

The cultural unity of all the Akan, wherever they may reside, was also given expression when I asked two old women, one Kwahu and one Ashanti, why they were shedding so many tears. They replied, "We are both nananom [grandchildren] of the late chief, because in our various chiefdoms we happen to be the grandchildren of the chiefs. It is as if our grandfathers, the chiefs, were dead. We must therefore mourn with our Agona 'sisters' and 'brothers.'" With this, let us now proceed to a consideration of the position of the chief in the changing structure of local administration in Swedru, that is, from the 1946 reforms of Governor Alan Burns to the National Liberation Council changes of 1966.

6 KOBINA BOTWE, THE NEW SWEDRU URBAN COUNCIL, AND PARTY POLITICS

It has been argued that Nana Botwe, the chief of Swedru for thirty-five crucial years, was an important link between the precolonial remote past (insofar as he occupied the stool of his remote ancestors), the colonial immediate past, and the post-colonial, or modern, present, having himself witnessed the emergence and growth of political parties, the political independence of Ghana in 1957, the progress to and achievement of republicanism in 1960, the one-party system of 1964, and the military coup of February 1966. The significance of his long rule is that his person, more than his office, provided a majority of the people of Swedru with a sense of identity with the town of which he was the traditional head and of continuity in a rapidly changing environment. Yet no one was more aware of the significance of the changes than the chief himself. From about 1952, with the development of such new political institutions as political parties and elected councillors (which were reflected in the Burns reforms of 1946 in the setting up, for example, of centrally controlled Native Authority treasuries), he saw power and authority slipping fast out of his hands. Soon those elders and chiefs who stood to gain by preserving the old system — the gyasehene particularly, but not Nana Botwe — were to become centers of conservative status-class opposition to the new order.

The functional grading of native courts, the establishment of Native Authority treasuries (whose accounts after 1948 were subject to audit and half-yearly inspection by the Government Audit Department), the payment of sitting fees to court panels whose number was drastically reduced, and the relieving of the paramount chief of his judicial functions not only were consistent with the increasing bureaucratization of government along modern lines in the late 1940s and early 1950s, as illustrated by the administrative changes and the emergence of modern political parties, but did much to reduce administrative corruption and therefore some of the friction

163

between the omanhene and his subordinate chiefs prevalent in the 1920s and 1930s. Still, the reforms were destructive of the old order as a system.

Until 1952, local administration in Swedru was in the hands of a subordinate Native Authority, subordinate since the Swedru administrative unit was not coterminous with the Agona traditional area. The Native Authority was a traditional body consisting of the chief assisted by a council of elders and subchiefs who were, generally speaking, representatives only of the original Agona wards of Swedru and not of the growing non-Agona urban migrants. One ethnic group, the Agona, arrogated to itself the right to represent all other ethnic groups in town, whatever their combined number and differing interests.

The colonial government did not interfere, as we have seen, in the selection of the chief, but controlled only the appointment of statutory Native Authorities, institutions absent in the Central Region of the Gold Coast (Ghana). The Native Authority of Swedru, like those in the other areas of the Colony, was charged with the maintenance of law and order in the Swedru area.[1] In the carrying out of this limited function, which included the making of bylaws, particularly sanitary ones, and the imposition of the hated annual basic rate (the levy or "lampool"),[2] the authority was given supervision and guidance by the D.C. resident in nearby Winneba.

The composition of the Native Authority was identical with that of the native tribunal (before the 1946 reforms) on which the chief and his elder-councillors exercised judicial functions.[3] The omanhene represented the people of Agona at the higher interstate level of authority,[4] the Central Provincial Council of Chiefs, which in turn sent members to the highest all-colony council or authority, the Joint Provincial Council of Chiefs (see figure 9), a body which was

1. This function was made easier by interethnic tolerance and by an agreeable chief, among other considerations. See chapter 5, for a discussion of the general welfare of the inhabitants.

2. *Lampool* is a corruption of the French *l'impot*.

3. It is worth noting that the zerikin Zongo, the head and representative of the Zongo, the principal "stranger" quarter, was perhaps the only non-Agona member of the Native Authority and also of the Agona State Council, the highest-level native authority in Agona, whose president after the 1931 Bewes settlement was the omanhene of Agona, Nyarko Eku of Nyakrom.

4. See *Winneba Sub-District: Supplement to Guide to Local Authorities, Traditional Authorities and Native Courts*, issued by The Government Agent, April 1953.

to act as an electoral college for the first Gold Coast elections in 1951.

In 1947, the Agona State Council had twenty members. In 1953, however, membership was reduced to fifteen and consisted of:

Members Declared By Office	Present Occupant
Omanhene, Nyakrom	Nyarko Eku IX
Adontenhene, Swedru	Kobina Botwe
Gyasehene, Swedru	Kofi Amponsah II
Nifahene, Asafo	Yamfo Asuako VII
Twafohene, Bobikuma	Yaw Buabin VIII
Benkumhene, Abodom	Osam Dadzi VII
Kyidomhene, Kwanyako	Kwan Kum III
Banmuhene, Nyakrom	Kwesi Krampah
Ohene, Duakwa	Kojo Amuakwa II
Ohene, Nkum	Kwesi Assan VII
Ohene, Nsaba	Vacant
Ohene, Kwaman	Opaaku Yeboah III
Omankyiame, Nyakrom	Emmanuel Dufu
Zerikin Zongo, Swedru	Malam Isifu Darfi II
Chief, Mankrong	Kobina Mensah

A careful inspection of the above list shows three significant changes from that of 1910 (see chapter 1, p. 45), namely (1) the over-representation of Swedru (including the seating of the zerikin Zongo, a Hausa) and Nyakrom, which points in a sense to their relative importance in the Agona state; (2) the transfer of the banmuhene from Duakwa to Nyakrom after the 1931 Bewes settlement; and (3) the Nsaba vacancy, which demonstrates the difficulties in the Nsaba division and the continuous intransigence of the elders of Nsaba in their rejection of the 1931 settlement.

It has been pointed out that, for administrative purposes, the Gold Coast until 1951 was divided into the Colony, Ashanti, and Northern Territories and that each of these was administered on behalf of the governor by a chief commissioner. The Colony, like the others, was further divided into provinces and districts. A province was under a senior D.C. and the subdivisions of the province, the districts and subdistricts (for example, the Winneba subdistrict in which Swedru was included) came under D.C.'s and assistant D.C.'s. The D.C.'s, in addition to their numerous judicial and political duties, were, after 1949, when local development committees or town boards were established, the chairmen of these committees or boards. The development committees (organs that were to be reformed and misused in the 1960s) and the town boards had two main functions. In the first place, they were to bring together for effective executive team work the field staff of all Government departments and representatives of all important local interests. In the case of Swedru, the important interests were commercial (represented by the UAC managers and other heads of firms) and traditional (represented by the elders). Second, they were to promote self-help in local communities by providing limited financial assistance where the community was prepared to give free labor. The development committee and the Swedru Town Board were to play an important role in the growth of Swedru in the subsequent years.

THE COMING OF THE SWEDRU URBAN COUNCIL (SUC)

Under the Elections Ordinance of 1950 (passed by the Legislative Assembly), Swedru as an administrative unit was not delimited an electoral district. Instead, Agona as a whole was made one of the five rural electoral subdistricts within the Winneba rural electoral district. The others were Gomoa Adjumako, Gomoa Assin, Efutu, and Obutu. Each rural electoral district was to be responsible for sending two members to the National House of Assembly. For the 1951 elections, however, Agona, mainly because of its population size, became a separate electoral district entitled to one representative in the Assembly, and the rest of the Winneba district, consisting of Winneba town or Efutu, Obutu, and the two Gomoas, constituted another electoral district entitled to only one member in the Assembly. We shall discuss the elections in connection with our analysis of political parties and representation in a moment.

The urban status of Swedru was officially recognized as late as 1950 when the Select Committee on Local Government observed that "Swedru is a cosmopolitan town" and made the recommendation that the interests of the inhabitants could best be served by the establishment of a local council distinct from that which should be established for the remainder of the Agona state.[5] The Select Com-

5. In fact, if Swedru town were carved out of the Agona state, with a population of 78,491 (1948 census), the committee stressed, "it would not leave a *rural* area too small or too difficult to administer as a separate local authority" (my italics).

mittee was probably at this time concerned mainly with the more obvious urban characteristics of Swedru, especially its "cosmopolitanism," or else the committee should certainly also have recommended, on population size alone, the setting up of a separate authority for Nyakrom and Nkum with a combined population of 8,910 compared to the population of Swedru which was 10,913.

Nevertheless, the committees' recommendation was accepted and Swedru, with approximately 7 percent of the population of the Agona state, became an Urban Council area by the Local Government Act of 1951. The provisions of the act are significant for three reasons: (1) The local government reform of 1951 coincided with the first general elections of representatives to the National Legislative Assembly in Accra; (2) the act transformed the links between the chief and his subjects and brought both under the constant review of the national administration, thereby forging a new basis for national political integration; and (3) the act made political party affiliation a basis for local and national political participation. Each of these factors will be considered in the course of this discussion.

Reference has already been made to the establishment (by a provision of the 1950 Elections Ordinance) of the Agona traditional area as an electoral district responsible for electing one member to the national assembly. This meant that 78,491 ethnically heterogeneous people or, more correctly, the adult members of the huge population, were to elect one of themselves to the Assembly. How was this to be achieved? But for the emergence of political parties, which claimed to represent interests cutting across tribal and ethnic ones, the diverse population would have been faced with an enormous problem in the history of intertribal or ethnic politics. We shall discuss the question of party and ethnicity more fully when we consider the 1951 general election.

The establishment of the Swedru Urban Council by the minister of local government in 1951 introduced a new political figure, the elected councillor. The membership of the new SUC, it must be pointed out, was to consist of twelve elected and six traditional members, that is to say, the Council was to contain both members directly elected by all adult residents and members representative of the traditional authorities which the new Council was gradually replacing, in the proportion of two-thirds of the former and one-

third of the latter.[6] There was provision also for the addition to the
Council, in exceptional cases, of special members to represent commercial or other interests of major importance in the life of the locality. The president of the SUC was to be the chief, the adontenhene, who was to sit only on ceremonial occasions and was to have
no vote. Otherwise, the Council would elect a chairman from its
own number.

THE FUNCTIONS AND POWERS OF THE SUC

Although local and urban councils were to elect members to the
next higher authority, the district council of the region, it is not necessary to go into this here since no district authority was de facto
established for the Western Region, in which Swedru fell at this
time. At any rate, the SUC was given authority under the instrument to exercise all the powers that had been wielded by the Native Authority it was superseding, and the minister of local government was empowered to confer on it additional powers extending
over the fields of public order, agriculture, forestry, regulation of
trade and industry, operation and regulation of markets, land con-
servation, building and town planning, education, and public
health. The Council had power to make bylaws, subject to the approval of the minister, for carrying into effect any function conferred on it. It is clear that, during the initial stages at least, the
SUC had functions which differed only slightly from those exercised
by the more rural Agona Local Council, the sister body. The more
important consideration, however, is that the door was now wide
open for strong centralized control of local administration by the
minister, who now had almost unlimited power to dictate what was
good, in terms of the national interest, for any particular local area.
But the power need not be abused.[7]

The new administrative structure introduced into the Council yet
another new figure — the civil service official, the employee of the

6. It is interesting to note in this connection that in the proposals for a constitution for Ghana submitted to the Constituent Assembly through the NLC in
1968 it was suggested that the composition of a local council should be determined in the proportion of two-thirds traditional and one-third popularly
elected representatives.

7. It must be indicated that, under the new system, state councils (wholly
traditional bodies) were to be completely separated from the new local authorities and were empowered by ordinance to discharge a number of functions related to native law and custom.

central or national government. It deserves mention that before the establishment of SUC the Native Authority staff had been recruited almost entirely locally and some staff members, such as Timothy A. Coleman, onetime registrar, were the immediate relatives of or had important kinship ties with the chiefs and elders. Their education and training, which did not go beyond the Standard VII, depended almost wholly on facilities provided by the local mission school. The standard achieved was not high, and efficiency of these "bureaucrats" cannot have been high either. To improve the administrative capacity of officials, particularly senior officials – clerks to councils, assistant clerks and treasurers, for example – for their new tasks, a Local Government Training School was opened in Accra in November 1951. The school has proved invaluable to officials of SUC, as they themselves admit.

Again, the customary bonds between the chief and the people gave way under the 1951 act to new statutory links between elector and elected. Although in Swedru, unlike other areas, the elected councillor did cooperate with the official to a large extent, some of the councillors had difficulty in appreciating their real role, which was often confused with that of the politician elected to serve in the Legislative Assembly. Some had a strong urge for power, which brought them into conflict with the traditional members. This was to be expected, for as McLaren realistically argues, all the three roles in the new situation, the roles of the councillor, the elector, and the official, were "hurried into their places by the momentum of political events and there was no time for each to appreciate properly the role of the others." [8] What McLaren was perhaps not aware of was the constant struggle, as time went on, of the elected councillors, especially those with strong CPP connections, to use their positions to personal-financial and other advantage.

Before we consider in any detail the functions, social composition, and other characteristics of the SUC, it would be appropriate and illuminating to discuss first the rise of political parties and their role in local and central government. This approach has chronological validity. The first elections for the new SUC had to wait until April 1952, and the first meeting of the Council was on 12 August 1952. The first Legislative Assembly elections, on the other hand,

8. C. A. McLaren, "Local Government Training in the Gold Coast," *Journal of African Administration* 9, no. 2 (April 1957): 63.

were held on 8 February 1951, and the Assembly met for the first time on 20 February 1951. The political parties therefore had to fight the national elections before the local elections associated with the setting up of new councils. The party preceded the Council.

THE CPP AND THE 1951 GENERAL ELECTION

The development of Gold Coast nationalism, which dates back to the nineteenth century, and the progress toward political independence and its eventual attainment in 1957 have been the subject of extensive scholarly study and analysis.[9] Some commentary, however, is in order. Still one of the most comprehensive accounts of the development of nationalism in the Gold Coast and in other African countries is James S. Coleman's "Nationalism in Tropical Africa."[10] For Coleman, the factors involved in the rise of African nationalism(s) were very complex and sometimes indistinguishable; yet, as far as they could be teased out, they were: (1) economic — for example, the introduction of the cash-nexus and the rise of new classes; (2) sociological — for example, urbanization, education, and social mobility; (3) religious and psychological — for example, Christian evangelization and stress of equality of the races; and (4) political — for example, the forging of territorial individuality by creating national boundaries within which the intensity of social communication and economic interchange had become greater than it was across territorial borders, and the introduction of self-government as a goal of British colonial policy (perhaps after World War II?).

Whereas it would be empirically naïve to ignore the relative contribution of each of the four factors cited in the nationalist process, it would be equally a misreading and misinterpretation of the facts to claim that the four variables, economic, sociological, psychoreligious, and political, made qualitatively and quantitatively similar contributions. Many observers, particularly political scientists, in keeping with the "primacy of politics" syndrome, have continued to

9. See D. Kimble, *The Machinery of Self Government* (London: Penguin, 1953), and *Political History of Ghana*; Hodgkin, *African Political Parties*; David Apter, *Ghana in Transition* (New York: Atheneum, 1963); and Dennis Austin, *Politics in Ghana* (London: Oxford University Press, 1964), to name but a few obvious ones whose brilliant efforts need not be repeated here.

10. In *Independent Black Africa*, William John Hanna, editor (Chicago: Rand McNally Co., 1964), pp. 208–34.

see African nationalism almost entirely as a national political phenomenon — the struggle for independence from foreign rule, the building of national political consensus through the dominant or one-party, and so on — and have neglected local politics.[11]

Gold Coast nationalism was primarily economic. Politics, or the power to decide how economic resources are to be distributed, who is to get what job, and the like, was seen initially by many as perhaps the only effective means, given colonialism, to the real national "good," economic power.

I therefore emphasize the predominance of economic factors for a number of very valid and realistic reasons: (1) The actors, both leaders and the led, saw their political movements in increasingly economic terms — new economic opportunities, new avenues for status mobility, and the associated economic advantages; and the social prestige and power related to wealth possession. (2) National economic exigencies and hardship, serious in a poor country, generated a kind of national political consciousness insofar as people identified control of wealth with control of political power. In this sense, politics and economics were inseparable, or confused. (3) Political power was not sought for its own sake; even Nkrumah's "Seek ye first the political kingdom" was only a means to all the good material things which "shall be added unto" Ghanaians. People were more eager for the rewards of power holding. Any political ideology which did not produce significant economic improvement was therefore irrelevant, even dangerous. (4) Political relations seem to have had no meaning except in terms of property and wealth.

Coleman was near to the point, however, when he concluded his analysis by saying that "in fact . . . nationalism where it is most advanced [for example, in the Gold Coast] has been sparked and led . . . by those who in terms of *improved status* and *material*

11. Of course, the historical significance of nation-building in Ghana cannot be taken for granted. My emphasis on local politics does not negate the importance of *national* politics. In fact, the one cannot be properly and realistically understood except in terms of the other. It is generally recognized by African political leaders, whatever their ideological position, that national governments must be firmly based on the support of the ordinary people at their local levels if they are to acquire a genuinely national dynamism. Herbert J. Spiro, editor, in *Africa: The Primacy of Politics* (New York: Random House, 1965), p. 7, attempts an explanation of this somewhat misplaced tendency thus, "African leaders . . . at home and abroad, continue to act upon the assumption of the primacy of politics."

standards have benefited most from colonialism; in short, by those who have come closest to the Western World but have *been denied* entry on full terms of equality" (my italics).[12]

Like Coleman, the report of the Watson Committee appointed to investigate the riots and disturbances in some urban towns of the Gold Coast in 1948 — disturbances which the CPP was to exploit to build its foundations and organizational strength — saw the underlying causes as broadly economic, political, and social and, like Coleman, quickly pointed out that "there is often no clear dividing line between them [the causes] and they are frequently inter-related." The committee's difficulty becomes clear when under their political factors we read that demobilized soldiers were opposed to authority because on their return they expected a "golden age," and also that people resented the "growing concentration of certain trades in the hands. . . of Syrian merchants"; or, under social factors, we read of the "fear of wholesale alienation of tribal lands leaving a landless peasantry" or "low standards of houses for Africans compared with those provided for Europeans," and so on — considerations that are obviously primarily economic. It must be noted in passing that it was no accident that the committee selected for special emphasis in its report the heavy indebtedness of cocoa farmers (a fact to be continuously exploited by the political parties) as a potential source of disturbance.

Yet somehow the Select Committee agreed with many and recommended that the only panacea for the national economic ills lay in constitutional reforms and political change. In a sense, the recommendation should not have come as a surprise, for in the past almost every economic crisis in the Gold Coast (Ghana) had been associated with a strong and vocal demand for changes in the political system or of political leaders. In this connection, political parties become important.

The CPP in Swedru: The Hard Times

Toward the end of chapter 4, a preliminary attempt was made to sketch out the circumstances which led to the founding of the CPP, the "illegitimate child of the UGCC," by Nkrumah. There it was indicated that the correction of economic grievances was

---

12. Coleman, *"Nationalism in Tropical Africa,"* p. 220.

foremost in the minds of those who seriously hailed the CPP and condemned its "bad parent body," the UGCC, which was presented publicly as standing for the selfish interest of lawyers and powerful and wealthy traditional rulers. Throughout its initial campaigns, the CPP was careful to play on this somewhat self-created image of opposing class-material interests by reiterating that it stood for the common man or the masses (terms that remained unanalyzed and proved increasingly meaningless) as against the wealthier members of the society, who were not sure whether to "swim with the people" or to "drown with imperialism."

The CPP was founded in Accra in June 1949. On 7 August 1949, a branch of the party was formally inaugurated in Swedru by Nkrumah in person.[13] Before the inaugural meeting, however, a group of young men, dedicated, as one of them put it, to "removal of imperialist economic abuses and exploitation," had been holding informal discussions at the Ghana College, a secondary school run by Miss Cole-Benjamin, a well-known Sierra Leonean midwife resident in Swedru, about the best strategies to adopt to reverse the hard times they felt had been deliberately created by European colonialists and European managers of firms and short-sighted local chiefs who collaborated with them. Trade unionism and strong collective bargaining and strikes were seen by members of the group as one strategy; another was Africanization of the public service and senior positions of European firms. Some of the members of this group were to become the foundation members of the CPP in Swedru.[14]

13. Yaw Ampadu (a young Kwahu teacher and trader who was later to become one of the most prominent members of the CPP in the Central Region), responsible for the collection of the entrance fee of one shilling a head at the inaugural meeting, recalled that he collected about thirty pounds that day. This means that at least six hundred people were in attendance at Frimpong's Yard to hear Nkrumah. Of course, hundreds waited outside just to have a look at him.

14. By 1950, this group of party men included Cecil Forde, a Sierra Leonean journalist-teacher of Latin and English at the Ghana College and a relative of Miss Cole-Benjamin; Ablorhdepey, an Ewe who had come to Swedru in 1939 as a storekeeper of the UAC, and who had resigned to become a petty trader and, in 1950, a teacher of mathematics at Ghana College; J. A. Arthur, a Fante clerk at the Swedru post office; Moore, also Fante, a one-time clerical employee of the Swedru post office, later a teacher at the Swedru Methodist School and now a lawyer; Amoa, a Fante clerical employee of the local post office; K. K. Korsah, a Fante, Chief Driver of Swedru; Ampah, a Fante storekeeper of G. B. Ollivant; Ampadu, a Kwahu trader; Kobbah, a Fante storekeeper; E. S. Quainoo, a Fante store clerk with the PZ; E. K. Bensah, an Ewe dispenser-nurse; F. C. Dodd, an Awutu drug peddler, licensed letter-writer; Addo Sekyi, an Agona

It may be necessary to indicate at once some of the more important social characteristics of the group of party men in the early
days of the struggle. Almost all were migrants and had been in
Swedru for periods ranging from about five to ten years. They were
all educated to the Standard VII level and in a few cases beyond
that. They were mostly clerical workers, storekeepers, and teachers
in junior positions, generally dissatisfied either with their jobs, their
pay, or both, and all were eager to improve their status. Although
these men were not exactly "the cream of Ghana," as the late J. B.
Danquah described the members of the UGCC, they were certainly
not "verandah boys" either.[15] In any case, in Swedru, with a predominantly rural and illiterate population of cocoa-subsistence and
peasant farmers, they provided perhaps the only meaningful leadership in a rapidly changing socioeconomic environment.

   During this early period of the political struggle in the Gold
Coast, there were in Swedru three major organizations committed,
as the members themselves put it, to an economic transformation of
the country through constitutional reform.[16] These were the People's Education Association (PEA), the Kwahu Youth Association
(KYA), and the Swedru branch of the Gold Coast Exservicemen's
Union (GCEU). The PEA came under the Gold Coast University
College Department of Extra-Mural Studies, which had been set up
in 1949 with the object of meeting the very considerable demand
for adult education (Colonial Reports). In 1949, manned by a number of resident tutors and part-time tutors, it conducted evening
classes at a total of twenty-three centers throughout the Colony, including Swedru, in a wide variety of subjects. In Swedru the content of the classes offered and the socioeconomic background of the
student-members were very interesting and indicated in a practical
way the immediate concern of the students, who had the freedom
to choose both the topics for study that interested them, and the nature of their political involvement.

---

trader-farmer; Paul Mensah, a Fante cabbage seller and contractor; Essandoh, a
Fante wood and timber contractor; Yaw Ampadu, a Kwahu teacher-bookseller;
Erskine, a Fante catechist of the English Church Mission; Kofi Agyare, a
Kwahu licensed letter-writer; and Asare, a Fante licensed letter-writer. It is
from this foundation member group that branch and regional executives were
to be elected. Some later became urban councillors in Swedru.
   15. *Ashanti Pioneer*, Tuesday, 19 July 1960, p. 8.
   16. This period (1949–54) is described by Apter as the "charismatic period"
("*Nkrumah, Charisma, and the Coup*"). I shall comment on this characterization
in the following pages.

In a 1955 study of certain aspects of Westernization, as applied to 501 men and 49 women, all students in Accra and fourteen other towns including Swedru, Gustav Jahoda, the researcher, reported the following findings, which are worth noting. (1) The PEA was the equivalent of the Workers' Educational Association of Britain. (2) Most of the members of the PEA had a good command of English and were able to follow serious lectures and to write essays for tutors. (3) In the smaller towns and villages the members were drawn from the literate elite of their community. (4) The median ages of men and women were twenty-seven and twenty-two years respectively. Some three-quarters of the men and nine-tenths of the women fell within the range of twenty to forty years, which in Ghana is the youth group. (5) The men were mostly in clerical jobs (43 percent) or were teachers (39 percent), with a few traders, students, and skilled manual workers. The women were predominantly teachers (74 percent) and clerks (20 percent).[17]

Their educational backgrounds were equally fascinating. In percentage terms, 44.1 percent of the men and 16.4 per cent of the women had had up to Standard VII or Middle IV (the pre- and post-1951 terminal points) of elementary education; 21.7 percent of the men and 65.3 percent of the women had had training at teachers' colleges; 17.6 percent of the men and 2.0 percent of the women had received up to four years of secondary school; 10.8 percent of the men and 14.3 percent of the women had had commercial school or technical school training; 4.4 percent of the men and no women had obtained more than four years of secondary school; 1.1 percent of the men and no women had received university training; and no men and 2 percent of the women did not mention their educational backgrounds. It is of some significance that this distribution would compare favorably with the national urban distribution at the time.

Again, more than 90 percent of the respondents were at least nominal Christians, whereas 3 percent of the men were Muslims and 4 percent belonged to syncretistic sects. Another important fact noted by Jahoda was the total frequency of membership of voluntary organizations: a larger proportion of the PEA members with post–primary school education according to the researcher declared their membership in three or more voluntary associations, such as

17. Gustav Jahoda, "Aspects of Westernisation: A Study of Adult-Class Students in Ghana: 1," *The British Journal of Sociology* 12, no. 4 (December 1961): 375–86.

trade unions, social clubs, political parties. This fact, which is not entirely unexpected and has in fact been discussed by me in relation to social integration in Swedru, needs special emphasis. Important for its immediate consequences for political participation is Jahoda's finding that at least 40 percent of the men reported that they were dissatisfied with their jobs.

It is imperative to dwell a little longer on the PEA study for one important reason, and that is that in the 1950s, the election years, almost all the members of the CPP in Swedru claimed to have been also students (and therefore members) of the PEA in Swedru. All the executive members had been such students. Again in the1950s, the PEA members (even the non-TUC members) had been particularly concerned with trade unionism and in 1953, with the help of C. W. de Graft Johnson, a tutor in economics, had prepared a memorandum on the economic implications to the country of the Volta River Project (VRP) and presented it to the Legislative Assembly. They even organized a rally in that year at the Accra Arena (showing their close association with the CPP) and distributed pamphlets in which they explained in some detail the economic benefits of the implementation of the VRP.[18]

Most of the members of the Swedru PEA in the early 1950s, who formed the bulk of the branch — constituency, regional, and, in some cases, national executives — were, as we have seen, mostly Standard VII school leavers and clerical workers (including licensed letter-writers), teachers, and storekeepers, with a sprinkling of skilled manual workers. This observation is quite consistent with the findings of Jahoda. A few had been to secondary school or teacher training college. What should be stressed especially is the preponderance of urban or modern occupations. The CPP in Swedru thus represented at this stage, at the level of leadership in

18. The political involvement here was surely a far cry from the activities of a bunch of irresponsible youth and "strategic marginals" merely impressed in the early 1950s by a charismatic leader. Of course these groups were dissident but, unlike the chiefs (particularly Ofori Atta of Akim Abuakwa and the Asantenhene) and the older political leaders — e.g., the late J. B. Danquah, who saw any change not spearheaded and controlled by them as a serious threat to the old privilege system — these young men welcomed almost any avenue (not necessarily new normative definitions and behavior patterns consistent with them) to upward socioeconomic mobility. In fact, many chiefs have accepted modern norms when these have assisted them in the maintenance of their socioeconomic advantage. See David Apter, "Nkrumah, Charisma, and the Coup," pp. 765–73.

any case, largely urban interests; hence the emphasis on trade unionism.

Ethnically, it must be said again, the PEA-CPP executive members in Swedru were heterogeneous and basically migrant in origin. In 1950–51, the branch secretary was Ablorhdepey, an Ewe; the constituency chairman was Addo Sekyi, an Agona; the branch chairman was Cecil V. M. Forde, a Sierra Leonean by birth; the vice-chairman was E. K. Bensah, an Ewe, the parliamentary representative of Agona and later Swedru from 1951 until 1966, the year of the military coup d'etat. Cecil Forde, after 1951, became the regional chairman. The other members of the executive, the great CPP organizers, included Kofi Agyare, a Kwahu man and the regional propaganda secretary; F. C. Dodd, an Awutu from Senya Beraku; and Paul Mensah, a Fante, the branch propaganda secretary.[19]

In 1950, a Regional Organization of the CPP was formed in Swedru. This was in consideration primarily of the nodal and central position, geographically, in the region. Swedru is still a center of important road networks. Representatives of all the CPP branches within the Central Region met at the Columbia Cinema Hall to discuss the organization of the party and elect officers. At the meeting Regional Chairman E. K. Bensah, Regional Propaganda Secretary Kofi Agyare (then chairman of the Winneba branch of the CPP), and pro-tem Regional Secretary E. K. Amuakwa (an Agona assistant treasurer of Native Authority) were elected. A Regional Executive Committee including such prominent men as A. B. Ntow and M. A. R. Dennis, both Fante and officers of Amanfopom and Saltpond branches respectively, was also elected. It should be remarked that a regional secretary was later appointed by the National Headquarters of the CPP in Accra. We may note again that the Regional Organization was in time to become so powerful as nearly to eclipse the branch and constituency organizations, especially at general elections, when the aim was on total victory at all

19. It should be noted particularly that from 1949, when the CPP was inaugurated in Swedru, to 1958, when regional commissioners were established in Ghana in keeping with the new administrative structure, the CPP was represented in Swedru at three levels of organization — the branch, the constituency, and the regional organs — though in practice, especially at election times, they functioned close together and were sometimes indistinguishable. Swedru was the Central Regional Headquarters and the constituency center of the CPP.

levels of party and society, including the national level, and when the CPP was expected to function as "one disciplined body."

The second major voluntary organization of any political importance in Swedru was the Kwahu Youth Association (KYA), formed in 1950, the local branch of a national organization. The Swedru branch was formed at the instance of some of the local young and more progressive Kwahu, such as I. G. Asiamah, an exserviceman driver and Ampadu, a storekeeper, "to serve Ghana." It is of some interest to observe that the more prominent members of KYA — such as Yaw Ampadu; Asiamah, the assistant secretary in 1950; and Mr. Ampadu, the cousin of Yaw Ampadu — were all either pro-CPP or CPP members. Toward the middle of 1950, the KYA asked Kofi Agyare, then branch chairman of the CPP in Winneba and later the regional propaganda secretary, to accept their invitation to be the chairman of the association, which he did. Soon after, the KYA merged with the CPP.

The third major organization in Swedru was, of course, the local branch of the Gold Coast Exservicemen's Union (GCEU), whose leader and chairman was Paul Edua, an Agona dental technician. The local branch, however, was more than a Swedru organization, since it drew members from all over the Agona state. With some validity it could be described as an Agona union since the members were predominantly Agona with a few Kwahu and Fante. Much has been written on the role of exservicemen in the development of nationalism in Africa.[20] Sir Alan Burns, the governor of the Gold Coast from 1941 to 1947, who in my estimation understood very well the Gold Coast mind, pointed out with much political realism that the most pressing need of the people of the Gold Coast was for economic development because, as he indicated, "economic freedom is an essential preliminary to political independence."[21] In any case, political independence ought to bring about economic progress and hence economic freedom.

Burns lamented the fact that, when the Gold Coast troops came home from Burma and East Africa and were demobilized in 1946, the colonial government could not deal adequately with the many

20. Coleman, "Nationalism in Tropical Africa"; Watson Committee, 1948; Eugene T. A. Schleh, "Post-Service Careers of World War II Veterans: The Cases of Gold Coast and Uganda," paper presented in New York to the African Studies Association, Thursday, 2 November 1967.

21. Burns, Colonial Civil Servant, p. 209.

problems that arose and was unable to start on the planned development works which alone would "have provided occupation for thousands of demobilised soldiers" and would perhaps have changed the course of the political history of Ghana.[22]

THE EXSERVICEMEN'S MANEUVRES IN SWEDRU:
POSITIVE ACTION, A PREELECTION DEMONSTRATION

We have already had the chance to see how the CPP, in association with the TUC (an organization which even in the initial stages was to provide the CPP with "ready-made" support), had on 20 November 1949 in Accra convened the Ghana Representative Assembly which had resolved, among other things, that "the Coussey [Constitutional Commission] Report and His Majesty's Government's statement thereon are unacceptable to the country as a whole" and had therefore demanded that "the people of the Gold Coast be granted *immediate* self-government, that is, full Dominion Status within the Commonwealth of Nations based on the Statute of Westminster." The Representative Assembly had also asked for the convening of a Constituent Assembly to consider the constitutional proposals presented by the CPP. We should recall here that the Coussey Commission did not include Nkrumah and representatives of the people who had been agitating for economic changes leading to mass economic improvement, as J. B. Danquah, leader of the UGCC, admitted. Thus, "it is a historical fact that not one of the 40 Ghanaians on the Coussey Committee, the cream of Ghana, took part in the formation of the CPP" and of the forty only two, J. A. Braimah (Kabachewura) and Hon. Nana Sir Tsibu Darku IX, Kt., O.B.E., later "accepted an office of profit in the CPP government." [23]

If the demand for the Constituent Assembly was not conceded, the CPP threatened to embark on a nation-wide campaign of "Positive Action" based on Gandhi's philosophy of nonviolence, noncooperation. The Positive Action was accordingly launched on 8 January 1950. The exservicemen's union — whose national secretary, C. A. Duncan, was jailed at the time of the Positive Action for writing seditious articles — had also resolved, as Paul Edua indicated, that unless its demand for jobs and back pay was met, its members would join in civil disobedience throughout the country. What a

22. Ibid., p. 208.
23. *Ashanti Pioneer*, Tuesday, 19 July 1960, p. 8.

majority of the people who really did not care for positions of political power were interested in, then and in the future, was amelioration of economic hardship. That was the limit of their political interest. This fact came out clearly in my conversations with men and women, especially the illiterate, in Swedru during my research.

Paul Edua, the leader of the Swedru GCEU, whom I interviewed extensively, claimed with some justification that the success of the Positive Action depended very much on the activities of the soldiers in Accra and elsewhere. The exservicemen planned to march on Positive Action Day to Osu, Accra, to demand their back pay and employment from the Castle, that is, from the governor. In Swedru a more modest but effective plan was adopted by the union. The leader, Paul Edua (who at this writing is in his fifties and whose modern two-story residence on the Oda road is characteristically named "Burma House") told me in a personal interview what exactly happened in Swedru.

On Friday, 1 January 1950, as the chairman of the Central Region Exservicemen's Union, I sent a dispatch rider [reminiscent of the war years] to the various towns and villages of Agona asking the members of the union to meet at Swedru. Remember that curfew had been ordered and Swedru declared a curfew area by the D.C., but it was not imposed. The governor had declared a state of emergency; public meetings were forbidden; mail was opened and censored and freedom of movement was restricted. The executive members of the union then included Yaw Kodua, a Kwahu sterling soldier; Kwame Paintsil, an Agona divine healer from Kwanyako; Kwame Nyarko, an Agona driver from Abodom. The exservicemen duly met secretly in Swedru on that day, on a cocoa farm near the PWD [Public Works Department] on the Oda road.

Kodua and I were, of course, the chief organizers and speakers. There was a quick executive meeting and the necessary strategy discussed and immediately adopted by the rank and file. It was stressed that the march on which we were about to go was to be peaceful and orderly, and no drunkenness was to be tolerated on the part of any soldier [a harsh prohibition since most soldiers ordinarily drank quite a lot]. The whole idea of the march [this needs a particular stress] was to frighten the European commercial firms [e.g., UAC and GBO] in Swedru to submit to reduce the high prices of important consumer goods or force them to close down their stores. We also felt that the presence of the exservicemen in their battle uniforms on the streets would be enough to frighten people to go Positive Action, refuse to buy from the Europeans. It would force the D.C. to take serious notice of their economic demand.

In the morning of that Friday [9:00–10:00 A.M.], 8 January 1950, about 400 soldiers from all over Agona marched accompanied by war songs and cries from the Oda road, proceeded by the UAC [see town plan, figure 4], stopped there for a while, and shouted out the familiar cry of united effort, "Twoo-oo-o Boi, Yeeee-ee-i." The UAC and the Swedru market nearby closed down immediately as expected, and scared sellers and workers rushed home. From there we marched down by Yaabamu Street via Bebianiha to Zongo singing, *Soldier ei yei ya ko aba oo yei*. . . . ["We are the soldiers who have returned from active service overseas . . ."]. At Zongo we were met by the assistant commissioner of police, Mr. Robertson, an Englishman, on a motorcycle. Robertson informed me that the D.C., Mr. Morey, who was then with Bensah, chairman of Swedru CPP, wanted to see me. I replied that I could not see the D.C., not until the next day in any case. We continued our march through the Commercial Street via the police station to Aboso [a small town just outside Swedru in the south]. On our way back, we were accosted by Robertson and the D.C. near the district magistrate's court at Nsawam. It was here that the D.C. tried to persuade me to go to the relay station of the Gold Coast Broadcasting Department, near the Swedru Rest House, to announce on the air, asking local people to go back to work. I refused to do this. I informed the D.C. that I was not a radio announcer and at any rate that the march and the singing was in connection with the death of a fellow exserviceman who had been killed in a truck accident on the Oda road. I then advised the D.C. to see instead the chief of Swedru, "who owned Swedru," about the strike of workers and the opening of the market.

At this time there was a lot of confusion as a huge crowd had gathered. Then a plainclothes policeman I quickly identified suggested to me amidst the hustle and bustle to slap anyone who annoyed me. The idea was to get me to behave violently or in a disorderly fashion to provide grounds for my immediate arrest. I, of course, ignored such a foolish demand. Then the showdown. This, to many Swedru people, was one of the biggest political triumphs in colonial history. The crowd which was milling about, seeing what they considered as the audacity of the soldiers, shouted, hooted at, and booed the D.C. and the assistant commissioner of police. The D.C. in desperation rushed to the ahenfie and asked the chief to beat the gong-gong [the traditional way of announcing the decision of state to the public] ordering the people to go back to the market to sell and return to normal. Civil disobedience continued. There was no one to beat the gong-gong. The D.C. was booed again and again. The police were helpless; in any case, everybody was for cheap consumer items. The D.C. thereafter returned to Winneba, without restoring peace and order, and in the next day we received the sad news that he had shot himself dead.

It is still not clear why the D.C. committed suicide. Rumor had it that he killed himself after gambling away all his money that night, or that he had misused money earmarked for the construction of a railway line in Swedru, or, most probably, that he was so ashamed of the showdown of the soldiers in the previous day, as he was believed to have assured the governor in a dispatch that he could deal with any disturbance in his district, that he could not face living.

After this historic exercise at Swedru, Mr. Kodua, my colleague, left for Accra, where he became one of the brains behind the successful ex-servicemen's demonstration there. Kodua was later arrested and jailed for a year for his part in the positive action. Our bold action really influenced the pace of political development in the country. We contributed our share. It is a pity Nkrumah had to disappoint us in the long run, bringing us back into economic poverty.

This clear statement needs no comment except to emphasize, as we have done before, that when the majority or a significant section of the population really decided to have their way — as was the case during the protracted Nsaba-Nyakrom dispute, fully explored in the preceding pages — the D.C. or the colonial officials were in almost all instances helpless. Again, the exservicemen's demonstration was popular mainly because it seized upon major economic grievances which many people felt at the time. The action of the soldiers was taken independently of CPP control or direction, except to the extent that the CPP had declared formally a Positive Action. We may now turn to the 1951 general elections. Why did the CPP win? How did it win? Let us find out.

THE ELECTION STRATEGY OF THE CPP
AND ITS OPPONENTS

A discussion of any election should, I think, begin with an analysis of the law or rules governing voters and candidates for whom they will be voting, for an electoral success or failure will generally depend on how fair the rules are and the extent to which the political actors understand and abide by the rules. The 1951 general elections were the first of their kind in Gold Coast history and the consequences were far-reaching.

Article 9 of the Elections (Legislative Assembly) Ordinance of 1950 prescribed that every person, male or female, would be entitled to be registered as an elector (in the case of the Swedru area) for a rural electoral subdistrict and, when registered, to vote at the election in such subdistrict of a member of the electoral college for the rural electoral district — every person, that is (1) who was a British subject or a British-protected person; (2) who had, at the date of his application to have his name entered on the register, attained the age of twenty-five years (later changed to twenty-one years; see Colonial Report, 1951), the onus being cast upon the applicant to satisfy the registration officer or his assistant, the D.C. or the assistant D.C., as the case might be, about his or her age; (3) who had resided within the rural electoral subdistrict for a period of at least six months immediately before the date of his application to have his name entered on the register; and (4) who, being liable thereto, had paid the local Native Authority rate or levy, as the case may be, for the current or preceding year. The last prescription had the effect of disfranchising many potential voters.

Apart from not fulfilling the above requirements, people were disqualified from voting (1) if they had been sentenced to a term of imprisonment exceeding one year and five years had not elapsed since their release, (2) if they had registered in any other constituency, and (3) if they were certified lunatics. The effective period for the organization of the elections was about six months and began with the delimitation of constituencies in September 1950. The boundaries of constituencies were, in general, coterminous with boundaries of existing administrative districts and subdistricts. Each rural electoral district was divided into subdistricts, as we have noted, each designed to contain about one thousand inhabitants or more (see Ewart Report, 1950). In the Winneba rural district there were two broad subdistricts, the Winneba-Gomoa area and the Agona area. It was provided that each subdistrict would elect by universal adult suffrage *one* person as its representative to the electoral college, which in turn would elect *one* member of the Legislative Assembly.

Since the elections, in which a combination of the electoral college and universal adult suffrage were used — direct and indirect methods — were the first in the Gold Coast, there were naturally certain difficulties that had to be overcome somehow by any person or group of persons desirous of an electoral success. The problems were in essence associated with (1) the novelty of universal suffrage combined with election by secret ballot in the rural areas; (2) a high rate of illiteracy producing serious limitations on electoral communications in general; and (3) the shortness of the time for the *political* education of the electorate in the meaning of the elections. Nevertheless, some of these difficulties were turned to great advantage, especially by the shrewd CPP organizers who oversimplified the complex issues involved and proclaimed ad nauseam that the CPP was a mere instrument in the hands of the people for attaining high cocoa prices, good jobs, and general welfare. These were considerations every Ghanaian understood very well. All the rural primary elections were to be held on the same day, 6 February 1951, and the successful candidates were to meet in electoral colleges by 8 February 1951.

ECONOMIC DISTRESS AND POLITICAL MOBILIZATION:
"CIPPIPPIFICATION" AND THE CORNED
BEEF ELECTIONS

From the day of the inauguration of the CPP in July 1949 to the formal opening of the Central Regional Headquarters in Swedru in early 1950, the executive members both at the constituency and regional levels had worked very hard in the formation of branches in the rural areas. In each of these areas, the idea was to get hold of a small group of relatively well-known persons to dedicate themselves to party work whenever the need arose. The process of extending the presence of the CPP in all areas throughout the country was appropriately named in the 1950s "Cippippification" (CPP-ification), a term that denoted as much political as "religious" conversion to CPP, to identify emotionally with the CPP. This had involved the touring day and night of the towns and villages of the central and other regions of Ghana by a small but dedicated group of party activists amongst whom two in particular stood out: Kofi Agyare, then the Swedru-based regional propaganda secretary for the Central Region and former branch chairman of the Winneba CPP; and E. K. Bensah, regional chairman and the CPP candidate for Agona.

Entries in the private diary of Kofi Agyare, which was kindly made available to me, demonstrate the seriousness with which the party business was taken and conducted. He worked indefatigably around the clock, holding rallies in towns and villages, giving public speeches, explaining CPP policies on trucks to passengers, and meeting chiefs and elders, clan heads, and headmen.[24] On a typical day, he would travel to Oda, forty-two miles away, give a series of lectures and talks in about four or five towns in the area, return to Swedru, attend a party executive meeting, then proceed

---

24. Although quite a few of the big paramount chiefs were bitterly opposed to Nkrumah and the CPP, many lesser chiefs supported him. It would therefore be misleading to argue that "traditionalism" symbolized by the rule of the chief was necessarily pitted against Nkrumah in a "charismatic dialectic." See Apter, "Nkrumah, Charisma, and the Coup," p. 765.

immediately to Bawjiase, an important market town seventeen miles away, and deliver campaign speeches in at least three other towns and villages, after which he would meet village chiefs informally for discussions of party aims.

Agyare, at this writing in his fifties, a quiet, unassuming, and honest man, obviously a good Christian, had followed Nkrumah because he "held fire" and because his cause was just, socially and economically. Agyare was convinced, like many at the time, of Nkrumah's organizational ability and his sincere belief that only immediate self-government would bring about the widely demanded economic transformation of the country. In Agyare's words, "Nkrumah was preaching and teaching towards the real thing" and "at the beginning we were all with the spirit of God, no *abosomsem*-heathenism. We were all moving with God; fasting and praying sometimes for three good days, during which occasions Nkrumah was in some instances present."[25] Nkrumah's leadership was aided by another factor, his tribal background. The point here is not that he was more acceptable to all the ethnic groups because he hailed from an humble tribe. Nkrumah is an Nzema, and it is still popularly believed that the Nzema are capable, with the help of witchcraft, sorcery, or charms, of supernatural feats. It was even believed at the time that Nkrumah had powers, for example, to vanish at will. This belief, however, does not seem to have influenced people's electoral choices.

This Cippippification, of course, had characteristics of political evangelization for an economic end. Yet, from the point of view of a majority of the CPP rank and file, the "real thing" was nothing but the immediate (with self-government) elimination of unemployment and high cost of living and the bringing about of a better price for cocoa and the Africanization of "European appointment" — a very down-to-earth approach to politics and political involvement. The political campaigns of E. K. Bensah and his group, led by Addo Sekyi, P. C. Dodd, and many others, were equally effective. The main issue was cocoa price and jobs.

E. K. Bensah was one of the early members of the CPP in Swedru, though by no means a foundation member, having joined it during the early part of 1950. A suave, smiling, smooth Ewe dispen-

25. It needs stressing that Agyare, a letter-writer at the time, like most of the minor clerks who joined the CPP saw the party as the best avenue to upward socioeconomic mobility.

er-nurse, he was born on 26 March 1912 and was educated at the Bremen Mission School Keta in Trans-Volta Togoland. He passed the Civil Service Examination in 1929 and entered the Government service as a qualified government pharmacist and nurse. The principal problem of the CPP (or of any party, for that matter) in Swedru and many other places was, in the circumstances of the times, MONEY to finance elections. Most of the early members, though not exactly poor by national standards, could hardly afford substantial contributions to the party. In Swedru, party dues were sixpence weekly and a penny a meeting. The money thus collected was used in buying gasoline for the propaganda vans. Bensah's financial circumstances were somewhat different and his popularity in the 1950s, in fact, was in no small way attributable to his conspicuous generosity to the party and people in Swedru in a period when the potential payoffs for generosity to party and people were practically unlimited. In Ghana there is a widely held belief that every man has a right to reap the full rewards of his investment, whatever its nature.

In those years, when there were few qualified nurses and still fewer medical practitioners in the country, he certainly had enormous opportunity to make a fortune — in fact, to exploit the people, as many druggists still do. But this, as we shall see, Bensah did not do. Bensah was by education, occupation, and opportunity a member of the "new class." Bensah came to Swedru in 1945. After seventeen years in the government service, he resigned in 1948 and in the same year, having inherited the practice of his deceased elder brother, also a pharmacist, established his own flourishing pharmacy and dispensary, the only one in Swedru. In keeping with his bourgeois leanings, he opened in early 1950 a grocery, beer, and fancy goods store, with his nephew as the storekeeper. Clearly, despite his generosity, he was not averse to making money — in fact, money making was directly related to his openhandedness.

Bensah joined the UGCC in 1948 but later, realizing that the UGCC had no prospects for anyone, became a member of the CPP. He had a slight advantage in party circles over Cecil Forde, the Sierra Leonean party chairman, who had initially been suggested as a candidate for Agona. Forde could not speak Fante or any of the local tongues and, in any case, when the time came for nomination of party candidates, he was sick. The language problem did not prevent Forde, as we shall observe in due course, from holding high

party office. Bensah, clearly a member of the new elite, was prominent in Swedru as an active member of the Swedru Town Board,
concerned with local social and economic development; of the
Swedru Lawn Tennis Club, made up of European commercial managers and Europeanized African officials and managers; of the
Dancing Club and the PEA; and he was patron of a local soccer
club. Despite his relatively high status, he was very close to the ordinary illiterate men.[26] He was their good "doctor." His fees were
considered not excessive and he attended to people around the
clock. He even on occasion gave free injections and treatment to the
poor.

These were qualities appreciated by all and were to stand Bensah
in good stead politically. From the point of view of party organization, he was indeed useful. He had independent means and was
wealthy and influential in Agona. In 1950, he was one of the few
people in Swedru who owned cars. He lent his Morris car to the
party for party propaganda purposes. His residence, perhaps the oldest two-story building in Swedru, stands at the junction of the
Commercial and Owani roads. The first floor room below was given
to the CPP for use as both branch and then regional headquarters.
His beautiful Nzema wife and he played host to Nkrumah (himself
an Nzema) on his many visits to Swedru and the Winneba district.
Bensah's assistance to, and therefore investment in, the CPP did not
end here. As one of his party lieutenants observed,

He would hire a truck or van for party campaigns [Mr. Essandoh, who
worked closely with Bensah, also occasionally made available one of his
trucks for party use]. He drew, with the help of other party "field workers,"
a chart for the establishment of a network of party branches throughout
Agona.
    Party meetings were held regularly on Fridays at the Ghana College or
in Mr. Thomson's house. Sundays were devoted mainly to opening of new
party branches. Most of the branches in Agona and elsewhere in the Central Region were inaugurated by Bensah in person and his lieutenants
[Paul Mensah, F. C. Dodd, etc.] between 1950 and 1953. This was good
training ground; it familiarized him with the local conditions and he
became acquainted with the influentials in villages and towns, people
who were particularly useful during elections. Sometimes a group of
people would come to Swedru to Bensah and request that a party branch

26. This is of much political importance. Much of the early unpopularity of
Danquah and most of the UGCC leadership was due to the fact that they were
generally perceived as unapproachable, aloof, and pedantic.

be established in the village or town and Bensah would readily oblige. This was a very important political asset.

In Swedru there was, therefore, a group of men who, though small in number, were energetic, enterprising, and ambitious and who were prepared to sacrifice money and time to party activities.[27] And these were the men who were to inherit the earth with each electoral success of the CPP. Bensah was the Parliamentary representative for Swedru for fifteen consecutive years, from 1951 to 1966.

How the CPP Won the First General Elections

In the 1950s, two broad classes or economic interest groups could be discerned in Agona. In the first category were traditional chiefs and elders, who in most cases were landlord-cocoa farmers; the cocoa-brokers or middle men, who in some cases were cocoa-farmers as well; the rich Kwahu and Fante traders, who were mostly owners of medium or large-size stores and themselves landlords who invested a great deal of money in house building; European and African managers of European commercial firms; and various wealthy people with independent means. These were the people most likely to support the colonial system or who, at any rate, were more concerned with demands for immediate economic reform than for political change. In the second category were the new urban classes — clerks and storekeepers, teachers, ministers and priests, drivers, skilled and semiskilled wage-earners, and the heavily indebted small-scale cocoa farmers and the unemployed school leavers, people generally dissatisfied with their economic lot. Kojo Essilfie, a strong NLM executive member, described this group who welcomed changes in the political system as a means to economic self-improvement, as "rascals and rogues." It is very misleading to refer to them as "verandah boys," as some observers have done, for the

27. Every new organization, to survive, needs a cadre (whatever the nature of their commitment), a group more or less permanent, forming a nucleus for expansion as the need arises. In this regard I find Apter's argument ("Nkrumah, Charisma, and the Coup," p. 766), brilliant as it is, difficult to accept, at least as it applied to Swedru and the Central Region. Between 1949 and 1954, the so-called charismatic period, the CPP party officials, on their own admission, were little concerned with transforming the pattern of normative life and public behavior (short of casting one's ballot). The colonial framework minus the "white colonial master" was largely acceptable. Nkrumah himself did not push any normative changes until after 1960.

real verandah boys in Swedru were the Hausa or Pepe porters and night watchmen, who were to remain largely nonpoliticized. The members of this second category were more likely to support the CPP.

For a number of tangible reasons, the 1951 elections could hardly be considered the first real test of CPP organizational strength and mobilizational ability. The literature abounds with mostly a priori statements about the very successful mass mobilization of the CPP. The CPP was seen as a mass-party. It had a mass following. The 1951 election results do not warrant such conclusions. First, no other party had had time to organize for the elections. The obvious alternative party, the UGCC, was still dazed after what Danquah described as "the unholy trick of a national split" by Nkrumah. Second, the whole country was more or less unified in its demand for the immediate correction of economic hardships reflected, for example, in price inflation, unemployment, the compulsory cutting of cocoa trees. In any case, there had been a series of country-wide strikes and demonstrations, especially in the towns, which had in the main been organized and led independently of the CPP. In fact, one CPP member admitted that "after all, the 1951 elections were not as hot as those of 1954, which were the hottest." And finally, many people did not vote.

In a sense, the combination of both direct and indirect elections — by the electoral college system — were an immediate help to the CPP, the only well-established organization with nation-wide branches. Little wonder that most of the electors chosen to go to the electoral college were generally elected on the only real "party ticket," that of the CPP. The members of the Agona electoral college were, as a rule, not subjected to vigorous canvassing by rival candidates. As we have seen, Bensah, the CPP candidate for Agona, and his men had combed the rural towns and villages, made important contacts, treated many despite the fact that treating was an electoral offense, persuaded, exhorted, begged, even pushed primary electors to vote CPP long before the actual elections, and had even allegedly bribed a few local influentials. Nana Kum, a strong and famous anti-CPP man in Swedru, alleged with some confirmation by a local CPP man, that "on the eve of the elections, Bensah transported members of the electoral college to Winneba, where they stayed for the night, and there gorged [them] with corned beef, kenkey and schnapps," and tried by a combination of bribery and treating to influence them to vote for him. In the morning of 8 February 1951, Bensah is believed to have brought them back to the Swedru Boys Industrial School, where the elections took place. "Unfortunately," Nana Kum complained, "Bensah's opponent couldn't reach them." Bensah won.

Swedru (Agona) was among fifteen constituencies in which there were straight fights between two opponents.[28] In Agona, the rival candidates were E. K. Bensah (CPP) who was nominated by (1) Joseph M. Ansah, a produce buyer of Kwaman; (2) Nana Prah III, head of Nyego stool family, Duakwa; and (3) Sekyi Addo, trader of Swedru. Note that, despite the fact that Bensah was an Ewe tribesman, all his nominators were Agona. The other candidate was Dr. Kuta-Dankwa, an Agona registered medical practitioner from Nyakrom, the seat of Agona paramountcy. Incidentally, Kuta-Dankwa's wife was English. Dr. Kuta-Dankwa was nominated, quite significantly, by (1) Nana Kobina Botwe, the chief of Swedru; (2) Timothy A. Coleman, secretary of the Swedru Town Board and a lineal relative of the chief of Swedru; and (3) Titus K. Aduamoa, state secretary of Agona State, Swedru.

From the occupations and ethnic backgrounds of the nominators of the candidates, it is clear that it was scarcely a straight fight between Agona traditional tribalism and cocoa conservatism (represented by Dr. Kuta-Dankwa) and urban nontribal radicalism of Standard VII school leavers (represented by E. K. Bensah). Although it is obvious that Dr. Kuta-Dankwa's support was more tribally based than that of Bensah — Kuta-Dankwa is Agona and had the weight of Agona traditional authority behind him — there is no doubt that Bensah was the one who was playing "home," in the sense of his familiarity, against Kuta-Dankwa, who was "away," because he was relatively unknown to many people and thus the visitor on the political soccer field. Few people knew him and many did not even know about him, for Kuta-Dankwa had then only very recently returned home from Britain.

The effect of the presence of Kuta-Dankwa's English wife in those days on social communication, and the social distance it must have created, could not but have worked against Kuta-Dankwa politically. Again, after all, Bensah was himself in his own way the people's "doctor." Also, Kuta-Dankwa's organizational base was def-

28. *Government Gazette*, 1951.

initely weak or even nonexistent and, what is more, he fatally centered most of his campaign on Swedru, perhaps forgetting that the
rural vote was the more important. Like most independent candidates without a solid organization to boost their image Kuta-
Dankwa had little or no popular appeal and was a complete novice
in the political game. No wonder Bensah won by as many as twenty-
seven votes (forty-two to fifteen).

It should not be forgotten that, in the final analysis, the CPP won
the 1951 election because it alone promised convincingly what those
who voted wished to have — higher prices for their cocoa and the
rejection of the compulsory cutting of diseased cocoa trees. The
non-fulfillment of these promises, not to mention the corrupt operation of the CPC set up to help indebted farmers with much needed
advances, was to become one of the major issues of the 1954 and
1956 general elections and led directly to the emergence of the
National Liberation Movement in Swedru and Ashanti. As we mentioned earlier on, many people either could not or did not vote
in 1951 for a number of reasons. In the first place, the qualification
that to be a voter one must be a ratepayer led to many disqualifica-
tions, as very few Agona in Swedru and elsewhere had actually
paid their local rates. Again, some even believed wrongly that registration was a prelude to more taxation or associated with the hated
cutting of diseased cocoa trees, a measure which had been introduced by the colonial government to prevent the deadly swollen
shoot disease from spreading to healthy cocoa trees. Many, therefore, refused to register and to vote. The CPP in some known cases
deliberately fostered this fear among Swedru people in particular.

During the period between the first general election of 1951 and
the second one of 1954, at least eight political parties, excluding independents, sprang up in the political scene. This phenomenal
mushrooming of political parties during the three years could be related to a number of economic considerations.[29] The CPP had dem-

29. The emergence of CPP independents (and other independent candidates) was not an isolated phenomenon. The period 1951–54 also witnessed the
phenomenal growth of "political parties" at local and national levels. What
this meant, if anything, was not the negation of charisma, nor did it illustrate
necessarily the weakness of CPP organization (see Apter, "Nkrumah, Charisma, and the Coup," p. 772). Rather, it demonstrated (1) that the CPP was
not meeting, obviously, the socioeconomic needs of certain individuals and
groups, including members of the party; (2) that charisma was largely irrelevant
even in 1951, since a majority of the independent candidates were never CPP

onstrated to many people the financial advantages of party leadership. The cost of living in the country was still high despite a slight reduction. The pegging of cocoa prices at 72 shillings per load of sixty pounds for four years in order to combat fluctuations of price on the world market was seen by some farmers as a sign of trouble ahead. Table 6 attempts to capture the trend of cocoa prices paid to farmers from 1938 to 1966. The average year-to-year fluctuation in payment to farmers was 19.3 percent computed for 1947–48 to 1960–61. The introduction by the government of a "New Deal" for cocoa at the end of 1951, which consisted of higher compensation for diseased trees voluntarily removed, accompanied by intensive propaganda pointing out to farmers and to the whole industry the dangers of not cutting, was hailed as fraudulent. It must be remembered that the CPP and Nkrumah in the 1950 political campaigns had totally rejected in principle the cutting of cocoa trees. As Nana

TABLE 6 MONEY PRICES PAID TO COCOA PRODUCERS,
1938–1966

Financial Year	Price	Financial Year	Price
1938–39	7s. 10d.	1952–53	70s. 0d.
1939–40	8s. 4d.	1953–54	72s. 0d.
1940–41	7s. 0d.	1954–55	72s. 0d.
1941–42	7s. 10d.	1955–56	80s. 0d.
1942–43	6s. 11d.	1956–57	80s. 0d.
1943–44	7s. 3d.	1957–58	72s. 0d.
1944–45	11s. 9d.	1958–59	72s. 0d.
1945–46	14s. 6d.	1959–60	60s. 0d.
1946–47	27s. 6d.	1960–61	60s. 0d.
1947–48	40s. 0d.	1961–62	54s. 0d.
1948–49	65s. 0d.	1962–63	54s. 0d.
1949–50	45s. 0d.	1963–64	54s. 0d.
1950–51	70s. 0d.	1964–65	54s. 0d.
1951–52	80s. 0d.	1965–66	30s. 0d.

SOURCE: Adapted from W. Birmingham, I. Neustadt, and E. N. Omaboe, editors, *A Study of Contemporary Ghana*, vol. 1, *The Economy of Ghana* (London: George Allen and Unwin, 1966), p. 382.

NOTE: The price paid to producers, in shillings per load is the net of voluntary contribution to development plan and compulsory savings.

members, and those who were had joined the party for clear-cut economic and status advantages, and not because they were heavily committed to something as unreliable as the leader's charisma. Of course, traditional symbols and myths were deployed to express socioeconomic interests which could and were articulated using European (or a combination of European and traditional), symbols, ideologies, and norms.

THE NEW SWEDRU URBAN COUNCIL AND PARTY POLITICS

Kum argued, "Nkrumah had told us that when a tree was sick or diseased it needed treatment and cure of the sickness and not destroyed or killed as the colonialists would have it." Some farmers had voted for the CPP because of Nkrumah's stand on the cutting of cocoa trees. The government had also established the Cocoa Purchasing Company, and the financial benefits to whomever controlled it were obvious to a number of shrewd political entrepreneurs.

Again, in 1953 assemblymen (M.L.A.'s) in the Gold Coast were receiving a salary of £960 per annum, and the government proposed an annual salary of £1,500 for the leader of the official parliamentary opposition.[30] Ministers were earning even more, over £2,000. The plums of political office were certainly very attractive.[31]

It is apparent from the list that "going to Assembly" did improve the financial position of all but a handful of the assemblymen. Many teachers were thus made middle-class people, something they had long dreamed about. It stands to reason that the "ins" should have fought hard to cling to their "sweet" plums of office and that those outside should have tried equally hard to get in. In 1951, the average age of the assemblymen was forty.[32] Bensah, the representative for Agona, who was later made ministerial secretary, was thirty-nine. The fact that many of the assemblymen were young men — some of whom, like Bensah, had made heavy investment in the CPP — made a great number of them envision many years of a life of leisure, prestige, and wealth in the Assembly.[33]

We may note also that between 1951 and 1953 there were eleven ministers and an equal number of ministerial (parliamentary) secretaries. This represented over 25 percent of the whole Assembly of eighty-four members. Almost all of the 25 percent were CPP members. The rewards of political office were clearly unevenly distrib-

30. Kimble, *Machinery of Self Government.*
31. The 1951 Legislative Assembly consisted of the following: 15 chiefs; 14 school teachers (two of them being ministers of religion); 12 merchants; 7 Native Authority employees; 6 professional politicians; 5 lawyers; 5 pharmacists; 4 farmers; 4 civil servants; 3 journalists; and 1 each of carpenter, engine driver, house agent, letter-writer, doctor, postal agent, retired army officer, and university lecturer. J. H. Price, *The Gold Coast Election,* West African Affairs Pamphlet no. 11 (London: The Bureau of Current Affairs, 1952).
32. Kimble, *Machinery of Self Government.*
33. According to the 1948 Gold Coast census, a majority of the educated people — the potential assemblymen — were between twenty-five and forty-five years old and very few were between forty-five and sixty-five years old.

uted, even in the House. Politics had become not only power, but a
means to wealth and further power. So far, there was hardly any
ideological emphasis – either socialism or other – in sight. Party
representation or membership on the basis of political beliefs and
values – political ideology – was largely irrelevant. The motivation
was still greatly economic, or the involvement instrumental. No one
was more aware of this "middle-class" interest than Nkrumah. He
had warned the CPP leaders against accumulation of wealth and os-
tentatious behavior while they were M.L.A.'s. He had even gone
further and had suggested that, in order that the CPP M.L.A.'s
would live humbly instead of being allowed to be overtaken by private economic interests, all the M.L.A.'s should surrender their salaries to the party and draw instead an agreed remuneration from
party funds "to avoid class conflicts." [34] This was the insoluble di-
lemma that beset the CPP throughout its history.[35]

34. Kwame Nkrumah *Autobiography of Kwame Nkrumah* (London: Nelson
and Sons, 1957), p. 139.
35. See Appendix for CPP/UGCC election manifestoes for the 1951 general
election.

7   PARTY POLITICS
SUC and the Chief

The CPP had won the 1951 general election with an impressive majority. In 1952 it was again to win — as if to convince its opponents of its strength — over 90 percent of the seats in the newly formed local councils throughout the country. In simple numerical terms, the CPP had indeed shown its superiority over all other political groups. Notwithstanding these electoral victories, it would be misleading to attribute these early electoral successes to effective mass political mobilization. I must anticipate here a little bit some of my eventual conclusions by emphasizing that the CPP or, for that matter, the NLM or the United Party (UP), never really got down to the basic task of mass political (nonelectoral) mobilization. An attempt in this direction was made by the CPP, especially after 1964, with Nkrumaism offering the obvious ideological push. Yet the aim never seriously went beyond the comfortable seats of the Kwame Nkrumah Ideological Institute. The real job of mass political socialization never got under way. Until 1964 the CPP was, at the local-urban or rural levels, without a systematic and clear political ideology (it was still being worked out) that could provide the normative backing for effective mass mobilization in the national or party interest. Even here, when the actual education field work began, the transmitters of the ideology could not go beyond such hackneyed, but parochially attractive, promises as immediate supply of free pipe-borne water, hospitals and so on.

How could the CPP have won the 1954 and 1956 general elections without a large politically mobilized following of loyal party members on whom it could call whenever the occasion demanded? The answer, as I shall show in a moment, is quite simple. It lay first in the simple-majority electoral rule. Second, by entering the political field first, the CPP had all the advantages and some of the disadvantages of the pioneer. It found itself in the midst of a pool of economic and social grievances which skillful leadership might ar-

195

ticulate and exploit. Nkrumah was quick to realize the far-reaching
political consequences, and he and his field organizers kept reiterating that "the people want their grievances redressed." [1] Again, the
obvious venality of a poor people with middle-class orientations
was to be turned to great political advantage. Finally, from the
point of view of the urban jobless (and the clerk who was dissatisfied with his low income and limited chances of upward occupational and social mobility) and the poor cocoa farmer (habitually in
debt but whose increasing material wants could be met by a higher
cocoa price), the CPP was capable of a number of feats: providing
shortcuts to high bureaucratic office and creating highly paid jobs,
thus satisfying the mobility aspirations of many; transferring the
control of the world price of cocoa to local farmers (the Cocoa
Marketing Board [CMB] and the Cocoa Purchasing Company
[CPC] were formed to cater to this); and establishing open avenues
to wealth, power, and prestige. The CPP approach was seemingly
effective because it was direct, simple, locally meaningful, and nationally relevant.

In a commercial society where people were already economically
conscious and highly mobilized economically, perhaps the only
meaningful way of getting people to act politically was through further economic mobilization — "economization" — instead of politicization. The CPP won because to a number of voters between 1951
and 1960, when there was something approaching genuine democratic elections, it really mattered very little to those who cared to
vote (and many did not) under whose leadership the "good life"
was attained.[2] In Ghana a leader's charisma is directly related to
the popular effectiveness of his economic performance. In any case,
we know that in the Gold Coast there had always been special interest (economic) groups who had from time to time either protested against or cooperated with the colonial government in the
name of economic improvement. The fact that this could have been
done in any regular way without formal aggregation of interests by

1. There were two different but related economic demands here: (1) The
demand for the general improvement of the community (the town) — that is,
the demand for better schools, hospitals, clinics, good drinking water, and
roads; and (2) the demand for higher wages and salaries, for higher real income, and for better conditions of service. Nkrumah, *Autobiography*, p. 116.
2. This reminds me of the two cases of the woman in 1951 and the farmer in
1954 who asked the polling assistant in Swedru whether it made any difference
in which box they dropped their ballot papers!

political parties is significant.[3] Thus, when the CPP assumed leadership of the various interest groups, such as the TUC and the PEA, in the 1950s and 1960s, the party could not destroy completely the independent bases of these groups.

In any case, the socioeconomic and political atmosphere of the times was not conducive to the development of political parties with carefully formulated national ideologies. Almost everybody was preoccupied with self-government as a political means to an economic golden age. Until 1960, three years after independence, Nkrumah was still, perhaps for tactical reasons, careful about propagating his brand of "socialist" ideology. As a result, his so-called bourgeois intellectual opponents — Dr. J. B. Danquah, Akuffo Ado, and others — lacked an effective political platform on which to assail the CPP. In any case, for most of the time, the opposition groups were themselves concerned with internal conflicts and bickering about who should be the leader. In the 1950s, Nkrumah could claim that "by forming the Convention People's Party and so introducing into the country the party political system, the foundation stone of parliamentary democracy was laid."[4] He went on to declare elsewhere that the 1951 local government reforms were to give local people the opportunity to participate actively in the management of the affairs of their localities. As yet there was no serious concern with normative reorientation or restructuring of society. The emphasis at this period was still on the democratization of the colonial structure, that is, on making the colonial structure serve more effectively the socioeconomic needs of the population.

THE NEW LOCAL GOVERNMENT STRUCTURE

We have discussed in some detail how the increasing immigration to Swedru and urbanization have made it somewhat obligatory to broaden the base of local representation. The migrant ethnic groups (Fante, Kwahu, etc.) were not represented on the Native Authority of Swedru and the educated Agona had begun to consider the representation by his illiterate elders as very unacceptable. The whole basis of local administration was questioned. Some had found the traditional authorities inefficient, corrupt, and unprogres-

3. Even in 1967, though for different reasons, some people in Ghana were quite seriously demanding a "no party" system.
4. Nkrumah, *Autobiography*, p. 108.

sive. The D.C. represented colonialism, which nationalist economic agitation was seeking to eliminate. The new local government structure was therefore intended to produce authorities at the local level which would be both democratic and efficient. The new system was to provide opportunities for "the majority of the people to contribute to and participate actively in that sphere of government which most immediately affects their everyday life." This was "therefore the only sure foundation on which to base a democratic system of central government." [5]

THE 1952 SUC ELECTIONS AND THE CHIEF

In the 1952 SUC elections (the six traditional members apart), the introduction of the party system had meant the election of the Council members on the basis, to some extent, of party affiliation. At the national elections, Bensah (CPP), the representative for Agona, had fought, as we noted, not a political party, but an independent candidate who nevertheless did perhaps represent traditional and Agona interests. The extent to which tribalism constituted a primordial political force in Swedru and in Ghana is still to be assessed. The expression of new politico-economic interests through the manipulation of traditional symbols, myths, beliefs, and praise-names is neither "tribalism" nor "retribalization," since in many instances individuals and groups are merely searching for more effective and meaningful ways to articulate their demands in a changing socioeconomic environment. In all societies tradition provides a set of ready-made deployable symbols and concepts which exhibit indigenous and borrowed elements and are redefined and reinterpreted to adapt to the changing environment. It has been argued that, at the local level in particular, the party system may have fewer advantages and many disadvantages. The advantages include the possibility that councillors would take more interest in the work of the Council and the further possibility that members would be well organized and would decide together, after serious discussion of issues, before the Council meets. The disadvantages are that party members may be forced to subordinate local needs to the national interest as defined by the Central Committee at the national capital. Fortunately, this need not be an either/or case, for

5. Colonial Report no. 250: Statement by HM Government on the Report of the Committee on Constitutional Reform.

local people may from time to time be called upon to sacrifice
the local good in the national interest. Where there is one party dominant (the case in Ghana from 1960–64) or a formal one-party
state (Ghana after 1964), however, local participation in politics
may become of only theoretical interest, and, where this occurs, the
chairman of the Council as a party functionary, and a party caucus
may dictate policy (sometimes formulated elsewhere) and even decide on points of detail.

The Position of the Chief in the New Administration

Before we consider the election and the composition of the new
SUC, it may be in order to discuss briefly the position of the chief
in the new local government structure. The Local Government Ordinance, enacted in 1951 and brought into operation after the 1952
local elections, affected the chief in two vital areas: (1) his power
and authority in the native state or division of which he was the
head and, where the new administrative area was not coterminous
with the native division, his authority in the administrative area
also; and (2) his control of economic resources, a control which
added much to and sometimes stabilized his authority. With respect
to the first area, the chief and his traditional council lost all their
administrative functions and powers and were limited to the declaration of customary law and arbitral proceedings — that is, the settlement of minor informal disputes and the determination of "local
constitutional disputes" (disputes relating to chiefly affairs and
chieftaincy). In Swedru, though it could be argued that the chief
and his councillors still commanded respect and some loyalty, it
would be a gross misreading of the facts to claim that the chief
wielded much actual influence. The emergence of the political
party, for example, had forced the chief and his elders to take sides
in the political sphere — the chief supporting this and a few of his
elders supporting that party — and even to be involved in the secular and "dirty game" of party politics instead of acting, as in the
past, as a neutral source of social integration and local political
unity.

It is true that the Swedruhene was never a card-carrying member
of any of the political parties, yet it was clear from his actions that
his sympathy was on the side of the forces and factions that were

opposed to the CPP. In the 1951 general election, he emerged as the principal nominator of Dr. Kuta-Dankwa, the Agona candidate who lost a straight contest to Bensah, an Ewe and the CPP official candidate; also, when the NLM was inaugurated in Swedru in 1955, it was in his palace (ahenfie) that the ceremony was performed. The local branch of the NLM was blessed with chiefly legitimacy. The chief consequently lost much of what respect and influence he had enjoyed among many of the migrant, and many local Agona, youth. The second area relates to the control of resources.

We have indicated how the wise and very articulate gyasehene, Yaw Amponsah II of Swedru, had pointed out categorically that chieftaincy was synonymous with four interrelated elements: the oath, adjudication, control over the disposal of lands, and control of people — "grandchildren." These four factors at once defined and sustained chiefly power and authority. They were all, he had argued, sources of wealth or money without which chieftaincy was rendered powerless. To remove or destroy them is to destroy chieftaincy itself. The gyasehene was aware of the effect on chiefly status of the changes in native administration brought about since 1944, particularly the effect of the establishment of treasuries. Although the chief was deprived of much income, derived especially from exorbitant fines and court abuses, the gyasehene insisted that "the lifeblood of chieftaincy was not completely sapped," for the importance of the chief's oath was still recognized, fines were still imposed, and the chief and elders were given honoraria for sitting on cases as panel members. The post-independence measures, however, were to change all this.

Land was mentioned as an important ingredient in the indigenous political system. The Akan devotion to land is by now very well established. The land is closely bound up with ancestors and ancestor worship. It is a source of the "good life" — abundance of harvest, wealth, life, and hence chiefly authority. When management of local affairs was in the hands of Native Authorities composed of chiefs and their councils, agreements were signed by chiefs who had titular rights over land as stool holders, assigning the revenue from this source to the Native Authority of the area. This followed the setting up of native treasuries. Since the chiefs received monetary remuneration from the native authorities of which they were members, the difficulty of persuading them to give up their rights could in most cases easily be overcome.

REMUNERATION OF CHIEFS AND THE LAND QUESTION

The chiefs were generally content with having control over their own salaries, which they received as Native Authority members as a substitute for the land revenue that would otherwise have accrued to them. The exceptions were the chiefs, such as Ofori Atta of Akim Abuakwa, who controlled lands rich in minerals or cocoa. In any event, the land revenue was by custom *not* a personal right. It was difficult in practice, however, to distinguish in this case a personal from a communal right.[6]

With the enactment of the Local Government Ordinance in 1951, it was necessary for a formula to be found for dealing with stool land — that is, land which by custom the chief held in trust for the people. Here we are concerned not with lands owned by families or by individuals in their own right. Briefly, the major provisions made in the ordinance required consent to be given by the local government council to any disposition of right in stool land and all revenue from stool lands to be deposited with the Council for payment to the accountant general, with subsequent division between the Council and the stools concerned. The division was to be made in accordance with an agreement between the parties — which, in the case of Swedru, as the gyasehene indicated, were the chief, the stool, and the government — or, in default of such an agreement, in proportions determined by the minister of local government. In Swedru, there seems to have been little difficulty over obtaining agreement on the division of land revenue, particularly since there was very little revenue derived from stool lands. In some cases the chief made available to the Council stool lands for local development projects at a small compensatory fee. Lands thus acquired were redeveloped in the interests of the local inhabitants.

In many parts of the Gold Coast what specifically constituted

6. In the Agona area the allowances given to the various ranks of chiefs were as follows:

a. The omanhene (paramount chief): £50 per month, plus £20 per annum for traditional festivals.

b. The Swedru adontenhene: £15 per month, plus £12 per annum for festivals.

c. The gyasehene of Swedru: £8 per annum for festivals ("for tobacco," according to the gyasehene).

d. The tufuhene of Swedru: £5 per annum festival allowance. Thus, while the paramount chief was receiving a total of £620 per annum, the new M.L.A. was paid £960 per annum plus certain allowances. This unfavorable comparison contributed to the reduction of the chief's influence almost everywhere.

land revenue had created some problems, for the term *revenue* included any valuable consideration, and *land* included the ground itself and "virtually everything below it [mineral resources] or attached to it." This question is, however, of academic interest here, since in Swedru there was no significant land revenue to demand considerable verbal attention. The existence of the problem elsewhere deserves some mention, nevertheless. What was of political import was the centralization of economic control in the office of the minister of local government. Despite this, the chief's rights over the disposition of land in the Akan areas continued to be recognized, although subject to some control by the central government; and, again, the right of the chief to a portion of the revenue from land became more firmly entrenched, though after 1960 the entrenchment was greatly modified.

THE MEMBERSHIP OF THE SUC: ETHNICITY OR PARTY MEMBERSHIP?

Under the new act, therefore, the chief lost all his administrative functions; politically he lost much of his power, especially when his economic position was drastically weakened; and judicially he retained only his customary and arbitral duties. Some attention has already been paid to the overall effect of the Local Government Act of 1951 on the role of the chief in the political affairs of his locality. I mentioned the introduction of the elected councillor; the civil service official, whose official behavior was primarily regulated by the impersonal norms of centralized and hierarchically organized local branches of a national bureaucracy; and the free elector, as the new and important political actor. In the new setting, the Swedruhene became the ceremonial president of the SUC, with neither official duties nor vote. Although a symbolic link of the past with the present was maintained by the added institution of one-third traditionally appointed members, who were all educated, it ought to be emphasized at once that the traditional representatives did not necessarily speak for or in the name of tradition. The traditional chief-president was to some extent isolated from his subject-councillors, elected and appointed. The chief was illiterate, and local political leadership was transferred to a new elite of education. What was left in the hands of the chief and elders was reduced, but still significant, social influence in their wards.

Let us now look at some of the social characteristics of the new urban councillors. Here I am concerned with five factors — occupation, education, ethnicity, party, and age.

Occupation

Of the eighteen councillors of the SUC who served from 1952 until 1958, when traditional representation making up a third of the Council was abolished, eight were or had been storekeepers or store owners, that is, petty traders. This represented almost half the total number of councillors. The storekeepers of the European firms were sometimes described as clerks.[7] The remaining ten councillors comprised the following: two elementary school teachers, two Malams, one Anglican catechist, one shoemaker, one building contractor, one exchief, one licensed letter-writer, and one cocoa farmer. In a sense, the distribution reflected the differential politicization of occupational groups and the desire to participate actively in local political decision-making. Unlike the politicians at the national level, the local councillors were at this period interested mostly in the sense of power and prestige that membership conferred. Their interest was in the maximization of *status* and *power*, not in the economic advantages — maximization of wealth — which were fewer at this level. With the introduction of local D.C.'s (somewhat a contradiction in terms) after 1959, emphasis on wealth became salient.

Education

All the councillors, including the six traditional members, had had some elementary education. In fact, almost all had finished Standard VII or Middle IV. Council deliberations were held in English, and the ability to understand and communicate in English was essential. The two Islamic Malams had had an impressive Arabic education, and one councillor had had secondary school education. The most educated of the members was the man who was chairman of the Council for almost eight consecutive years. The man was Cecil V. M. Forde, the Sierra Leonean journalist and former teacher of Latin and English at the now defunct Swedru Ghana College.

7. Jahoda (see pp. 175–176) found the largest single concentration of PEA students in this group (43 percent), the group with the greatest political involvement.

Ethnicity

The ethnic composition of the Council was very interesting and partly, but only partly, followed the pattern of ethnic distribution in Swedru. There were one Sierra Leonean, one Ga, two Hausa, seven Fante, and seven Agona, though four of the Agona were not from Swedru. They were indigenes of other Agona divisions or towns. But for the relative importance of political party affiliation, the Agona would have been over-represented. The fact that there was not a single Kwahu or Ashanti on the Council should not be surprising. The Kwahu in particular were generally more preoccupied with matters of trade and commerce than with political management. In any case, most of the Kwahu traders were illiterate and considered Council duties burdensome and distracting. They were, on the whole, satisfied with the tremendous informal social influence they wielded as a result of their obvious affluence.

Party

Of the twelve popularly elected members, no fewer than nine were CPP members. The three others were either independents or, on most issues, anti-CPP. Of the six traditional members (appointed by the Agona State Council), almost all were either anti-CPP or independents. This point should be particularly noted. It should be observed en passant that the independents, by virtue of their so-called neutral position, could strategically influence voting by selling their votes. Independent status could therefore prove financially profitable.

At any rate, despite the nationalist agitations, the so-called mass mobilization of the CPP at the local and national levels, and all the effective organization and powerful electoral machine, there were about the same number of CPP members as nonmembers in the new SUC. The groups of independents were as conspicuous at the local as at the national level. However, the fact that the CPP was able to capture the two most important offices, those of the chairman and the vice-chairman, and the chairmanship of the all-important Finance and Staff Committee for nearly eleven years continuously, when there were relatively free elections in Council to these offices, is very significant. Even so, many did not vote in local elections.[8]

8. The chairman had three major functions: (1) he presided over meetings

Age

The age distribution of Council members was equally interesting in that it was quite consistent with the distribution in the Legislative Assembly. The emphasis at both levels, local and national, was clearly on youth (which in Ghana refers to "energetic" people between twenty and forty-five years of age). In the case of the SUC, except for one member who was under thirty, most of the councillors were between thirty-two and forty-five years old, the average being forty-one years. With this general socioeconomic background, we may now turn to the first three years of the Council's existence and see how it functioned, noting in particular whether or not issues were discussed and voted upon on party lines.

THE POLITICAL PARTY: LOCAL DEVELOPMENT

For purposes of this discussion, local participation in national politics and in the politics of the Swedru area may be said to have passed through three broad phases, the end of each phase being marked by increasing centralization or monopolization of political and economic power by the CPP, as reflected in the growing importance of executive decision-making, at both the local and national levels, and the decreasing participation by the electorate except through the symbolic ballot which in Swedru lacked popular appeal. In Swedru, the initial phase extended more or less from the first general election until about 1958, when local elections were last contested on something approaching open-party basis; the second phase lasted from 1958 until 1961, when the CPP completely monopolized the Council — all councillors were CPP members; and the third phase was from 1961 to 1966, when the Council was dissolved following the military coup d'etat of February 1966 and the CPP

---

of the Council, kept order, and saw to it that the standing orders (rules made by the Council about the conduct of its business) were obeyed; (2) he was the ceremonial head of the Council, entertaining visitors on behalf of the Council; and (3) he was at once the representative and the servant of his Council and town. Although he had no powers of his own, he could initiate and influence decisions on policy and in fact could become powerful by firm leadership. It was his duty to see that the Council did its work smoothly and maintained a good relationship with its officers, the electorate, and the minister of local government. In a sense, therefore, he was an important link between the local and the national levels.

was proscribed.[9] It ought to be noted that the beginning of each phase also coincided with the elections for new local councils and that there was at least one general election, national referendum, or national plebiscite in each phase. All the phases were linked or mediated by elections and the activities of the national party system, which after 1955, in Swedru especially, was to provide the major framework for political participation, particularly through the leadership of the CPP.

The initial phase was certainly the most crucial phase. It contained three importatnt general elections — those of 1951, 1954, and 1956 — and ended with the political independence of Ghana in 1957.[10] The party had a majority following, having won over 90 percent of the Council areas at the local elections of 1952. In the first phase, perhaps the party "stocktaking" period, the CPP was preoccupied with the definition of the functions and powers of the new urban councils and the assessment of the party's relative strength at the local level; and nationally the CPP concerned itself with the reexamination of party aims and objectives, the rewarding of friends, and the punishment of enemies. The end of the phase marked the introduction of the Preventive Detention Act and the Avoidance of Discrimination Act that made it illegal for sectional parties — those based primarily on religion, tribe, or primordial loyalties — to exist, a measure which weakened rather than strengthened open opposition groups. Since both opposition groups and CPP members inevitably had to use traditional symbols, images, and the idiom of kinship to articulate and advance their new politico-economic interests, the CPP was in effect forcing the opposition either to join the CPP or to cease existing.

The minutes of the SUC show the major concern of the councillors at the time: the delimitation of the areas within which the new local authority and the court B of Swedru had jurisdiction, and the composition of the court panel; the exact role of traditional mem-

9. The military coup and the period following it, that is, until the general election of August 1969, may be considered a phase, the fourth.

10. Locally, despite CPP victory at all the polls which in every case put Bensah in the Legislative Assembly (a victory that, from the point of view of the branch or constituency and regional [central] organizations, both centered in this period in Swedru, marked not only the effective establishment of the CPP at all levels of society — the village, town, regional capital, and national capital — but also the establishment of the CPP as a dominant party), the party continued to work harder.

bers (who were not necessarily native Agona or illiterate) vis-à-vis the elected members; and ways of raising local revenue and its expenditure on local development. One is definitely impressed at this time with the absence of division or conflict on party lines and the democratic participation at general meetings and committee discussions. But this was hardly surprising: the Gold Coast until 1957 was still a colony and there were in any case very few plums of office to be fought for at this level. The fact that party considerations were not particularly salient in the SUC was significant, given the fact that political parties and factions were much in evidence at the local and national scenes.

The new SUC met for the first time on 12 August 1952. In the opening address, the president, the chief of Swedru, said among other things that "by the zeal and patience and loyal sense of public duty the councillors will prove themselves worthy of the trust reposed in them by the electorate." The government agent (G.A.), who had replaced the colonial D.C., read a message from the minister of local government congratulating the "hard and useful" work done by the old Native Authority. In his address, the G.A., a senior civil servant, now the liaison between the Council and the central government at the district and regional levels, advised councillors to set aside "party feelings" and work in harmony, and to appoint statutory bodies. He suggested that the SUC and the Agona Local Council (ALC), the two local authorities set up in Agona since 1951, appoint a joint committee to share the Reserve Fund of fifteen thousand pounds and to discuss the distribution of the Native Authority staff.[11] The G.A. further warned that Swedru should try to avoid the misunderstandings which had arisen in many parts of the country between the new councils and the chiefs.

Cecil V. M. Forde, Sierra Leonean, now chairman of the Regional Organization of the CPP, was unanimously elected chairman of the new Council. Another CPP executive member, Duker (Fante) defeated Ambaa (Agona), eleven votes to four, to become the vice-chairman. It is again noteworthy that, of the eight members appointed to the all-important Finance and Staff Committee, six were CPP or definitely pro-CPP. Perhaps it was this effective control of the central locus of local policy decision-making that encouraged

11. It should not be forgotten that, before 1952, Swedru was a subnative authority in the native authority area of the Agona traditional state.

the new chairman to promise in his address to work "without fear or favour and without resort to nepotism," a promise which was to become increasingly difficult to keep, especially during the second and third phases. Perhaps the chairman's declaration was partly motivated by the realization that the 1954 general election was in the offing and the CPP needed to mobilize all the support it could get, and partly by the fact that the CPP could hardly count on a decisive majority in the Council.[12]

In any case, Forde seems, at least for a time, to have lived up to his promise of nonfavoritism, for the G.A., in February 1953, was able to describe him as "calm, polite, and very patient to appreciate every councillor's point of view." Let us at this point turn to the Council meetings to see if we can find any evidence for the agent's contention. At the 19 September 1952 general meeting, a motion by E. S. Quainoo (a Fante CPP executive member) seconded by Isaac Yankson (another Fante, a pro-CPP member) to delete the name of Kyiame Kweku Nyame from the native court B panel list was defeated by five votes against eleven. Kyiame Kweku Nyame, it should be indicated, was the senior linguist of the chief of Swedru. The defeat of this otherwise simple motion was significant. It demonstrated that during the first phase the CPP did not have enough support to have things its own way. In fact, in the 1953–54 election of officers, the Council voted for an Agona exchief, Osam Duodu, noted for his anti-CPP stand, as vice-chairman of the Council.[13] At this stage of the game, the "traditionalists" still had considerable support.

It is important to observe, as a measure of the centrality of particular issues, that between 1952 and 1956 most of the motions, irrespective of their sponsor, were unanimously carried in almost every case.[14]

12. It should be mentioned in passing that Forde was later appointed the general secretary of CPP at the National Headquarters in Accra in 1955 and therefore became a member of the all-powerful Central Committee of the CPP while still chairman of the SUC. The problem which this raised at the local level, despite the obvious integrative functions, will be discussed later.

13. In the 1956 general election, he was the principal nominator of Anyan, the NLM candidate.

14. At the 19 September 1953 meeting the following motions, for example, were unanimously carried: (1) "Since the Akora river is the only source of drinking water in Swedru, a penalty of not less than £1 be imposed on persons found bathing and washing in the river." This, incidentally, represents modernization of social control, through the infliction of monetary penalty. In the past,

It is clear from the records that the noncontroversial nature of the issues voted upon, their welfare orientation, and emphasis on local development contributed in no small measure to the unanimity with which they were accepted. Thus all the councillors, irrespective of their ethnic background or political affiliation, were agreed in 1953 that, by reason of the commercial importance of Swedru and the fact that there were many workshops which "will need the study of technical subjects," it should petition the central government to establish a technical school in Swedru. The Council was ready to provide land.

The relatively high degree of consensus over policy decisions achieved by the councillors in committees and at general meetings did not necessarily mean that party affiliation was completely irrelevant. Neither did it reflect a peaceful adjustment of all claims, as between the Council and the Agona State Council, the Council and the ALC, or between it and the central government, to name only a few possible parties to probable disputes.

THE SUC AND THE ADJUMAKO COUNCILS: A CASE OF TRADITIONAL RIVALRIES?

The immediate problem that faced the SUC on its establishment was the administrative status in the new structure of Aboso and Bensu, two little Gomoa-Fante towns on the old Sekondi-Takoradi road, just at the southernmost outskirts of Swedru and, in fact, indistinguishable physically from it. The twin towns had been incorporated in 1952 in the Swedru planning area and, in accordance with Gazette no. 40, the Adjumako State Council was to appoint one or more representatives for these towns on the SUC. Of course, the in-

---

tribal sanction against polluting the river was primarily religious. (2) "To encourage Mass Education Literacy, children between 5 and 14 who are not in school should attend night schools in Swedru." It is interesting that the only night school, then as now, was the one run by Miss Cole-Benjamin, the aunt of Forde, at the Ghana College. (3) "That any person under 14 should not visit drinking bars, dancing halls, cinemas." (4) "That the Chairman, two councillors, and the Clerk of Council should represent the Council at the official opening of the Gold Coast Sports Stadium in Accra and the Council be the sponsor." In April 1953, the motion that "in view of the swarming influx of people into this town [Swedru] and the comparatively small number of good houses to accommodate the newcomers, this Council petition the Minister of Housing to create a Housing Loans Board for the Swedru urban area to ease the housing problem that confronts the community" was also unanimously carried.

habitants of Bensu and Aboso were to pay their local levy to the SUC instead of to the Gomoa-Adjumako Local Council, a poorer council. In terms of rational town planning requirements and the interest of the inhabitants of the twin towns, this was not a bad thing at all. The annual basic rate of eight shillings per male and four shillings per female (over eighteen years of age in both cases) was one of the lowest local rates in the whole Gold Coast. The SUC area had more modern facilities. Yet the very suggestion was enough to revive latent traditional animosities and rivalries. We have had occasion to discuss fully the defeat of the Agona by their neighbors, the Gomoa-Fante, in the seventeenth century and the subsequent subjection of the former by the latter, as a tributary state until 1899. To most of the Gomoa, the acceptance of the inclusion of Gomoa towns in an *Agona* authority structure would be tantamount to reversal of roles, to defeat. The attitude of the Gomoa was therefore understandable, especially when some Agona still claim that Aboso and Bensu areas are all Agona lands.

At the third meeting of the SUC (19 September 1952), R. W. Hayford from Bensu was introduced as an observer and was to attend all future general meetings of the Council, in accordance with section 41 of the Local Government Ordinance, 1951. When asked about the collection of arrears of Native Authority–local council levy in Bensu and Aboso, Hayford pointed out that the levy collectors from Gomoa-Adjumako came to Bensu to collect them, but the tufuhene, who obviously favored the joining with Swedru, turned them out. A letter dated 11 September 1952 from Gomoa-Adjumako Local Council protesting strongly the inclusion of Bensu and Aboso in the Swedru Planning Area was read. It should be noted that Hayford's "representation" was still unofficial, and he therefore had no vote in the Council. To correct this, the SUC advised Hayford to get Aboso and Bensu people to bring pressure to bear on the Adjumako State Council to appoint a traditional member to represent the twin towns on the SUC. Meanwhile, to anticipate, and as a gesture of the desire to incorporate the two towns in the SUC area, fifteen pounds and twelve pounds were included in the 1952–53 estimates of SUC to meet the cost of classroom furniture and equipment for Aboso and Bensu schools respectively.

Bensu was prepared to join Swedru. The Aboso Odikuro (headman) and elders were also ready, after persuasion and pressure, to go along with the SUC. In March 1953, however, Asafo ("Supi") Kojo

Mensah (captain of the traditional military company), the asafomma (company members), and others at Aboso disassociated
themselves from Odikuro, the head chief, and his elders and protested against levy being paid to SUC. The SUC retaliated by re-
moving the Aboso primary school to Bensu. Aboso still refused to
join SUC, but Afransi and Obuasi chiefs and elders, and Gomoa
people, in April 1953, petitioned SUC for inclusion, hoping for
faster local development that way. The petition could not have
been serious, because of the geographic location of the towns —
Afransi and Obuasi are both about six miles from Swedru. To solve
the deadlock, the G.A. in Winneba arranged a local plebiscite at
Aboso, Bensu, and Ekroful for 25 January 1954. But a majority
refused to vote. Another plebiscite was therefore arranged. The results of the 23 March 1954 plebiscite indicated that Aboso, Bensu,
and Ekroful were to remain with the Gomoa Adjumako Local
Council.

THE SUC AND THE COURT B

Another problem with which the SUC had to deal was its relationship with the native court B in Swedru — what powers should
the SUC exercise in respect to the court, and should councillors
be panel members. At one of the Council meetings, the G.A.
pointed out that the court B had jurisdiction over the whole Agona
state and not just Swedru. The SUC would be responsible for the
revenue and expenditure of the court, according to the G.A., and a
portion agreed to by a joint committee of the SUC and the ALC
should be taken by the latter. In view of the traditional interchiefdom (town) rivalry and conflicts, the question of the spatial limits
of the power of native courts was hotly contested. The G.A. noted
that it was the right of the governor to appoint fit and proper persons to carry on as panel members of the court. Old panel members
who were also councillors could, however, remain as court panel
members. It is clear that the CPP during this initial phase had no
control of panel membership and therefore of the local court. This
situation was, of course, to change drastically during the third
phase of local and national politics.

The authoritative explanations of the G.A. notwithstanding, a letter from the ALC dated 30 October 1952 protested against arrests
made by the SUC of persons within the jurisdiction of the ALC and
requested that the case of one Kofi Kum Adotemu be transferred to

the latter. Many of such protests were not made solely to protect the rights of the inhabitants of a given council area. Rather, they were motivated by the fact that court cases and fines constituted important sources of revenue for some councils and, where there were abuses, for panel members. Although the governor had the right to appoint panel members, as the G.A. again indicated in May 1954, the SUC had a duty to suggest names for the consideration of the governor.[15]

In May 1954, the SUC, in accordance with its duties, suggested certain names to the governor to be considered for panel membership. The case is cited here for the light it throws on some aspects of the relationship between the CPP and non-CPP members both in Council and outside it, and also between the Council and the central government. There is no doubt that the chairman of the SUC had control over what names were to be sent to the governor for consideration. The list was therefore interesting. Apart from Nana Kobina Botwe, the chief of Swedru, the people recommended were all either CPP members, sometime executive members, or "traditional notables," mainly lineage heads, or community (ward) influentials with possible pro-CPP orientations.[16] The strategy here was that of both informal and formal cooptation of traditional leaders and other local influentials — for example, the giving them of due but, in terms of the exercise of real power, empty recognition. Other methods included patronage, exploitation of tribal conflicts, and sometimes the legitimation of the conflict, as in the Nyakrom-Nsaba dispute when the CPP government in 1958 upgraded the rank of the chief of Nsaba to paramountcy. With these weapons,

15. The SUC was also unclear about where an appeal court would be situated in Agona, if Swedru were given court B. It was indicated by the G.A. that, according to the *Handbook for Native Courts in the Colony, 1956*, the local magistrate's court could be such an appeal court. Appeals from court B therefore lay with the magistrate's court, Swedru.

16. The list of suggested names was made up of Nana Kobina Botwe (chief); Ebusuapanyin Yaw Kuma (lineage head); Osafohene Kobina Moses (lineage head and captain of asafo company); Malam Seidu (an Islamic liman and the brother of the zerikin Zongo [himself anti-CPP]); Kwaw Wompeh (executive member of CPP); Kojo Dei (head of Kwahu community); F. C. Dodd (executive member of the CPP, who later turned against the party because it refused to nominate him for Council elections); F. Y. Addison (CPP member); Yaw Bob (lineage head and executive member of the CPP); Kobina Ansah (Presbyterian elder and friend and neighbor of Bensah, CPP M.L.A.); Yaw Kwaitoo (executive member of the CPP); and K. Kwadufuru (lineage head and CPP member).

which were effectively used by the CPP, the party was thus "a non-traditional wolf under tribal sheepskin." Although these strategies ensured simple electoral successes, they fell far short of mass political mobilization. The CPP was forced into a compromising stance from its very inception.

It must be indicated that of the twelve persons whose names appear on the recommended list of panel members, eight were Agona, two were Fante, one was Kwahu, and the other was Zambrama. We should also remember that the 1954 general election was only a few weeks away and that the CPP needed all the support it could muster by almost any means.

THE SUC, THE CENTRAL GOVERNMENT, AND THE GOVERNOR

The names were not all accepted by the Ministry of Local Government. In August 1954, a month after the general election of that year, the SUC resolved to send a protest to the minister of local government against the inclusion of some persons on the panel of court B who had not been recommended by the Council. The Council insisted that the original list submitted be retained. It is almost certain that the protest was not the result of a bid for local autonomy in decisions affecting the Council and the electorate. It may be seen rather as predicated on the necessity to fulfill preelection promises to influentials who might have mobilized electoral support for the CPP. Copies of the protest resolution were to be sent to the prime minister, Dr. Nkrumah; the governor; the minister of the interior (CPP); the regional officer; the government agent; and E. K. Bensah (CPP), the local M.L.A. and then minister of works. A roster of presidents of panels up to January 1955, prepared by the chairman of SUC (the CPP general secretary), reads as follows: September, Yaw Bob; October, Nana Botwe; November, Yaw Kwaitoo; December, Francis Yaw Addison; January, Yaw Dei. The consideration of party patronage and favoritism could not be mistaken, despite Forde's promise in 1952 against "favour" and "nepotism."

A letter in September 1954 from the senior judicial officer, Accra, to the SUC defined again the relationship between the SUC and the court in no uncertain terms. The judicial officer made the following points: (1) The question of traditional or elected members of the Council had nothing to do with court panels. Members were all appointed, not elected. (2) The SUC was not empowered to decide the appointment of court panels. The Council's recommendations carried no force upon the governor, who was responsible in accordance with Native Courts (Colony) Ordinance, 1944. (3) Two members of the SUC list were rejected because one, F. C. Dodd, was a letter-writer and, as a rule, letter-writers were not appointed. There was no information about the occupation and qualifications of the second person rejected. The SUC replied that it was "aggrieved" because of the deletion of two of the names it had recommended and the inclusion of five names it had not. To this the judicial officer explained that it was necessary to have old and experienced hands on the panel. The five persons, members of the former court (and most probably anti-CPP) obviously met that necessity. As a compromise, the judicial officer advised that the SUC could recommend five literate persons. He pointed out again, however, that the Council's appointment of presidents for the court was not in order. Panel members themselves were to appoint presidents for a year or two, and not for just a month. The president's functions included summoning meetings of panel members and drawing the roster for court sessions. The president was not necessarily chairman at every court sitting. One of the three members sitting at any one time according to the roster should be appointed to occupy the chair.

This lengthy and protracted explanation apparently failed to satisfy the SUC. Some of the councillors, mostly CPP, in fact started interfering with court proceedings, trying to influence the decisions of panel members. Consequently, in February 1955, the G.A. informed the SUC that no councillor had any right to interfere with the duty of the court. The Council could go into the activities of the registrar of the court, but could not ask him any questions about how cases were decided; such questions should be directed to the G.A. It is clear from this discussion that the Council or, more correctly, the CPP chairman had little direct control of the court B at this time.

THE SUC AND TRADITIONAL BODIES

It has already been remarked that the setting up of new local councils after 1951 led to conflicts all over the Gold Coast between the new councillors and traditional authorities. In Swedru, however, respect for the chief, coupled with the fact that there were many Agona members on the Council who in matters affecting their locality and their chiefs were prepared to set aside party feeling, did much to reduce this type of conflict. Again, until the Council building was completed in 1955 and the Council moved in there, the councillors met at the ahenfie, the official grounds of traditional power and authority. The Native Authority police, who were absorbed into the new administrative structure, were also housed there. The native court B also met in one of the sections of the ahenfie. Thus, until the physical break was made by moving into the new Council administrative building at Bebianiha, the councillors had to behave with some restraint toward the chiefs and elders of Swedru.

The first indirect confrontation came in October 1952, when the traditional authorities invited the SUC to a meeting on the question of stool lands and stool holders. There was, for example, the problem of how income from the stool property was to be divided between the new Council and the chiefs. The Council chairman's reaction to the invitation was instructive. He pointed out to the messengers of the traditional body that the SUC as a *statutory* body could not break its order of business against *standing orders* to meet with any other body. The chairman was allowing the two bodies to meet "out of respect for the traditional authorities." He warned, however — and the warning was portentous — that that joint meeting would be the first and the last. Whereupon the SUC adjourned to listen to what the chief and his elders had to say. The SUC later decided to appoint a select committee to discuss the matter of stool lands and chiefs. Again, in 1954, the year of the general election, when party attitudes were becoming more and more crystallized on a pro-CPP, anti-CPP axis, the Agona State Council appointed Messrs. Bandeley (part Fante, part Yoruba Swedru hotelier) and Nana Kum (Fante painter and usurer) to the SUC. They were to fill vacancies created by the decision of Aboso and Bensu to remain with the Adjumako Local Council and by the resignation, on the grounds of ill health, of Nana Kweku Adjaye (Agyei), head of the stool family and a traditional member. These appointments brought the first minor conflict, on party lines.[17]

17. It should be stressed that it was not until 1956 that one could to some reasonable extent speak of the party system in the Swedru area. Until then there was only one party, the CPP, and the various hardly organized opponents of it. Even in 1956, the NLM in the central region was very weak, as R. R. Amponsah, a staunch member, admitted recently in public. (I am, of course,

By the time of the general election of 1954, Nana Kum in particular, and Bandeley to some extent, had emerged as strong anti-CPP men. Nana Kum, in fact, registered as a local candidate on a Ghana Congress Party (GCP) ticket to oppose Bensah, the CPP candidate, but withdrew because he "wasn't ready yet." On 29 October 1954, Nana Kum and Bandeley went in to take their seats in the SUC as traditional members. But the chairman and some others would not seat them. This led to a heated exchange between the new councillors, who insisted they had a right to be there, and the other councillors, who were opposed to their presence. There was much misunderstanding and confusion. Yet underneath it all was the obvious fact that the CPP councillors resented not only the anti-CPP persuasion of Nana Kum, a man of substantial and independent means, but also what some considered the interference of traditional bodies in the affairs of the SUC. Some, as a matter of fact, had called for the total abolition of traditionally appointed members.

The chairman, on account of the somewhat deliberately created bear-garden situation, transferred the Council meeting from the ahenfie to Ghana College (also the meeting place of the CPP). It was thereupon resolved that, in view of the confusion which might again arise during a meeting at the ahenfie (the seat of traditionalism and anti-CPP sentiments), general meetings of the Council should be held at any place within the area of the Council's authority which the chairman would consider suitable. It is not clear how many such meetings were held subsequently outside the ahenfie. Nevertheless, the fact that Nana Kum and Bandeley were finally seated after a week should not blind us to the significance of the incident, which brought face to face, in the open, people representing property and cocoa interests and those who saw their interests as primarily lying in the new bureaucratic expansion created in a large measure by the CPP.

referring to the discussion by Dr. Busia, Apaloo, Dombo, R. R. Amponsah, et al., on "The Role of the Opposition, 1954–1956" on 17 May 1967 at the University of Ghana, Legon.) In Swedru, the NLM or the UP was to remain a "cadre" party, even a debating club, with scarcely any organization at all, in the hands of just two principal men — Nana Kum and Kojo Essilfie (about whom more will be said later). What little support these men or their party got, for instance, at elections was based not on organizational effort or other formal criteria of membership of the NLM but on social or psychological identification with what these men represented at the moment. What is important here is that formal party membership was not a sine qua non of political behavior. This makes the analysis of political party affiliation at times difficult.

The SUC, Local Finance, and Special Interests

In April 1953, Britton, the senior G.A. in the district, visited the SUC and reviewed a number of problems in connection with the large development projects, such as a modern town hall, streets, and a new market, which the Council envisaged. The G.A. then pointed out that the Council, like most others in the Gold Coast, lacked the resources to enable it to implement its projects and be able to stand on its feet financially. He therefore suggested the introduction of property rates, something that had proved very beneficial to councils in England. As if to make the new rate more acceptable, Britton praised the Swedru Brass Band for winning first place at the Central Region Coronation (of Elizabeth II) band competition held at Cape Coast and then urged the SUC to give the ratepayer the visual evidence of the benefits he received from the tax he was called upon to pay. Bennet, the G.A. at the Regional Office, Cape Coast, supported Britton and stressed that, without rating of immovable property, the Council could not undertake any development works. Swedru was still without clean pipe-borne water, a fact that proved very handy as a common propaganda tool at the 1954 general election.

The new SUC building, constructed with a building grant of two thousand pounds from the central government, was opened on 7 May 1955 by the minister of local government. On 17 June 1955, the Finance and Staff Committee of the Council met to discuss, among other things, the imposition of property rates in Swedru. The meeting was not open to the public. Yet news had got around long beforehand — thanks mainly to the traditional and Agona members that a meeting to *approve* the new property rates was scheduled for that day and that those who were against it had every right to go there to protest. This undoubtedly was civic irresponsibility on the part of the councillors, who more or less had organized the demonstration. Civic and national interests are for many people still hard to understand except in terms of individual or group interests. Many people accordingly went to the Council Hall and strongly protested with asafo war songs the introduction of the new rates. There were some members of the Swedru asafo company among them. A representative group of landlords and other immovable-property owners also congregated there and managed to demonstrate their dissatisfaction before the G.A., who was himself attend-

ing the Finance and Staff Committee meeting that morning. The
demonstration, though without clear leadership, was so strong,
noisy, and unruly that the deliberations of the committee could not
go on and had to be postponed.
The chairman of the Council later extended to the G.A. the regret
of Nana Botwe, president of the Council, and of the Swedru asafo
company, who were believed to have spearheaded the demonstrations. Bandeley, the honorary "Supi" of the Swedru asafo and traditional member of the SUC, submitted that there were asafo songs
but no member of the asafo company, to his knowledge, took part.[18]
All the same, the point had been registered. There was no doubt
that Bandeley and Nana Kum and a few others like them, as property owners, were against the introduction of property rates and
may have even privately organized the protest. They were themselves members of the Agona landlords association. In the 1956–57
financial year, the SUC passed the property-rate ordinance in the
face of further protests and angry demonstrations. The Agona landlords association, still adamant, had recourse to the law "that only
tyrants may use to abuse." The landlords may be considered for
some purposes as a group conscious of their class interests. Their
economic interests in this case certainly overrode their civic-eco-
nomic responsibility. The SUC was sued. This action was remarkable and demonstrated again the primacy of narrow individual or
group conservative economic interests. Messrs. Lynes and Cridland,
a British law firm, represented the SUC. Judgment was given on
18 January 1957 in favor of the SUC at the cost to the Council of
£226 17s. 7d.!

THE CPP, THE 1954–1956 GENERAL ELECTIONS, AND
THE STRUGGLE FOR LEADERSHIP IN THE SUC

Between 1953 and 1958, our first phase of politics, there were two
outstanding political features at both the local and national levels.
The first was the static nature of political, or electoral mobilization,
reflected in the fact that almost the same number of people voted in
each of the general elections, and none of the parties could substantially improve upon the number of votes it received, despite the
apparent strength of the CPP electoral machine and the obvious

18. Here again traditional symbols, songs, and gestures provided a ready-
made idiom for the articulation of modern economic interests of both literate
and illiterate members of society.

weakness of the organizational base of non-CPP factions. The second feature was the increasing control and malversation of national economic resources by the CPP, as evidenced by the operation of the CPC.[19]

The 1954 general election, according to most observers of the local and regional scenes, was the most fiercely contested of the three relatively free elections in the country.[20] But it would be misleading to claim that the political contest was on anything like strong party lines. Here again about half (see tables 7 and 8) the qualified adult population of Swedru did not vote. Again, until the military coup of 1966 which ousted Nkrumah and dissolved the CPP, the CPP was the only nationally organized party in the country in contradistinction to the ad hoc local and regional factions or groups, representatives of sectional interests, all allied opponents of the CPP, and independent candidates. Despite their differential but colorful party labels all saw going to the Assembly as the best means to advance their economic and other interests. In fact, the fierceness of the electoral contest was not really due to party organization, though the party machine helped to some extent, but the inordinate scramble on the part of already highly motivated individuals and groups for seats of profit in the Legislative Assembly, a fact well attested to by the number of independent candidates who stood for elections and were returned (see tables 7, 8, 9, and 10).

Although between the first general election in 1951 and the second one in 1954, a period of three years, no fewer than eight "parties" in addition to the independents had sprung up, it is doubtful that any group of these could have organized themselves on a coalition basis as opposition party in the Assembly. The annual salary of fifteen hundred pounds to the Opposition leader would have proved too attractive for the leaders of minority parties to agree on a common leader. In fact, after 1957, when the Avoidance of Discrimination Act forced the minority parties into the United Party, their parliamentary weakness was the result of incessant struggle among the leaders of the component parties and, of course, of individual "crossing of the carpet" to the CPP.[21]

19. The CPC is discussed along with party finance in the first section of the next chapter.
20. It may be said in passing that elections under ideal conditions might have perhaps produced fewer voters.
21. Among the proposals submitted in 1968 for the New Ghana Constitution was the provision that the office of member of the National Assembly should

The electoral rules themselves, as we shall see in a moment, directly encouraged the growth of ad hoc parties and populism.[22] These "instant" parties, unlike the CPP, lacked either the money, organizational skill, or the time to move outside their places of birth, and the few — such as the Moslem Association Party (MAP) or the Ghana Congress Party (GCP), which in Swedru were really the same thing — that tried to organize on a more than local or regional basis found it extremely difficult to invade what they considered somewhat exaggeratedly as "CPP territory." The GCP meetings in Swedru, for example, tended to be nothing more than an occasional assembly of a small group (the core group was not more than four) in the home of a local patron. When the NLM replaced the GCP in Swedru in 1955 (in anticipation of the 1956 election), one of the members of the executive committee of four, Kojo Essilfie, the propaganda secretary,[23] admitted that the NLM imposed no membership fees. The party card cost two shillings and sixpence, but very few people held party cards. The major source of finance was the individual contributions of Nana Kum. Kojo Essilfie claimed that about two hundred men and women attended their election rallies, hardly enough for an electoral success, but rallies are scarcely reliable indicators of successful party mobilization. All in all, Essilfie could name only about forty people as regular supporters of the party they represented. Yet more than one thousand voted for non-CPP candidates at each election, a fact that made party organization seem somewhat redundant.

For purposes of the 1954 election, a *political party* was defined by governmental ordinance as "any group which intended to contest more than one seat" at the general election. Thus, if two or three persons pooled their meager resources and contested two or three seats in a region or district, they constituted, legally, a political party! This certainly provided a very shaky basis from which to assail the CPP. The CPP, by a relatively disciplined nation-wide organization, better financial resources than other political parties, the tactics of treating and patronage, and, to some extent, the popularity of the leader, Kwame Nkrumah, had captured the imagination of

not be a paid office. Certain allowances, however, would be paid. *Know Your Constitution* (Accra: State Publishing Corporation), p. 7.
    22. Apter, "Nkrumah, Charisma, and the Coup," p. 765.
    23. The other members were Osam Duodu, chairman; Nana Kum, treasurer; and Amo Ntiforo, secretary.

the small but growing "lower-middle class" of minor clerks, salesmen, semiskilled wage workers, lesser municipal functionaries, and
teachers as the party of economic opportunity and of the future.
As we have already noted, this group in Swedru consisted of people who were in the main propertyless and dissatisfied with their
jobs because they were ill-paid. They were the votaries of the PEA
who would seize on any opportunity at all to improve their socioeconomic status, to enter the "embrace of privilege" and economic
power. These people were quick to realize, especially after the 1951
election, that political power was the primary force or means that
created better economic chances and hence largely determined
one's social prestige. They were also quick to notice the unmistakable reciprocal relationship between political power and economic
and social power. The desire for economic and social mobility
through political action comes out clearly when we examine and analyze not only the number of people who stood for the 1954 election
but their occupational backgrounds as well. The 104 Assembly seats
to be contested were distributed regionally as follows: 26 for Northern Territories; 19 for Ashanti; 13 for Trans-Volta Togoland; 39 for
the Colony; and 7 for the Municipalities: 3 for Accra, 2 for Kumasi,
and 1 each for Cape Coast and Sekondi-Takoradi.

On the whole, 323 people contested the 1954 election. This means
that throughout the nation there were slightly over 3 persons, on the
average, for each seat. In the Awutu (Central Region) constituency
there were 5 candidates for a single seat, and of these, 4 were independent candidates and 1 a CPP, the candidate who was returned.
In Swedru, there was a straight fight between Bensah (CPP) and
Coleman (independent).[24]

It is noteworthy that about one-third of all the candidates were
clerks and teachers, and slightly over one-half the number were clerks
teachers, and salesmen, the group who suffered most, in terms of

24. The socioeconomic background of the contestants was interesting. Of a
total of 323 candidates, 66 were teachers and 56 clerks. There were 29 merchants (wholesalers, storekeepers) and 26 petty traders. Twenty were farmers;
16 barristers; 13 politicians; 11 contractors; 10 journalists; 9 chiefs; 9 letter-
writers; 5 each of pharmacists, pensioners, ministers of religion; 4 each of sur-
veyors, druggists, nursing dispensers; 3 each of ministerial secretaries, transport
owners, drivers, and private businessmen; 2 each of medical practitioners, house-
wives, engine drivers, court registrars, and accountants; 1 each of dental technician, printer, telegraph inspector, tailor, planter, timber broker, gold mining
prospector, produce buyer, blacksmith, and bailiff (*Your Government*, Daily
Graphic Publication). See Appendix for professions of the 1951 Assembly.

self-evaluation, from relative economic deprivation in the modern
urban setting and who saw status and economic improvement
through the exercise of political power as members of the Legislative Assembly. In Swedru the contest was between Coleman, registrar
for the Agona Native Authority, a contractor, a lineal relative of
the chief of Swedru, and a former member of the Swedru Town
Board, and Bensah, a politician, a pharmacist-dispenser, and an Ewe
man who had also served on the Town Board.

All 323 of the candidates had had up to Standard VII education.
No less than 30 had had post-secondary school training. There were
at least 16 barristers and 2 medical doctors. Of the 11 cabinet ministers, all CPP in 1954, 5 had had post-elementary school training and
6 had academic degrees. This, I think, is very impressive considering the fact that many have associated the CPP (leadership and followers) with unemployed standard VII school leavers. In fact,
locally it was not the vote of the unemployed (many of whom
could not vote because of the requirement that they should have
paid their local rates) that made the CPP. It was, rather, the vote of
the rural farmers and, to a minor extent, of clerks.

THE CPP IN SWEDRU AND GENERAL ELECTIONS

Between 1951 and 1956, it was the avowed aim of the local branch of
the CPP in cooperation with the central organization of the party,
which had its headquarters also in Swedru throughout our initial
phase, not only to recruit new members but to nip any new party in
the bud before it became a threat to the CPP, a fact that reflected
the monopolizing tendency of the CPP throughout its history. There
were really two types of CPP members, total and verbal,[25] and one
subcategory (core):

The verbal members or fellow-travelers and followers were those
who professed adherence and were accepted by core members as
sincere but took no active role in party activities. They were, as
likely as not, card holders. Some might have become total members.
These exhibited their commitment through deeds. They always
voted CPP, regularly attended party meetings, and canvassed for

25. This follows the formulation of "verbal converts" and "total converts"
by J. Lofland and R. Stark in their analysis, "Becoming a World-Saver: A Theory
of Conversion to a Deviant Perspective," *American Sociological Review* 30, no. 6
(December 1965): 862–75.

party candidates. They were the "deployable agents" or "deployable personnel." [26] From this, a subgroup, the hard core of the party in Swedru, the foundation executives, was recruited. Outside these groups was a broad mass of potential voters who might themselves in time become party members. Since they are primarily unattached or unaffiliated persons, their interest in the CPP, or any party for that matter, was primarily instrumental.[27]

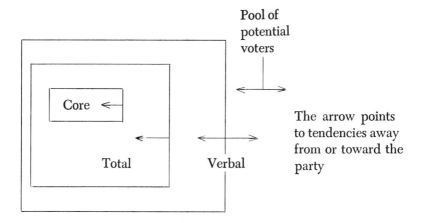

Pool of
potential
voters

Core

Total   Verbal

The arrow points
to tendencies away
from or toward the
party

Although basically, as I shall argue, all the members, total and verbal, were motivated by money and, to some extent, power considerations, they tended in public to speak of their party in terms of the national or transnational interests.[28] The strength of the CPP therefore lay in the fact that it possessed a closely knit executive group, about twenty at any one time, with an inner executive caucus of about seven who were the real local decision-makers, field workers, and organizers. It was especially from this inner group that local councillors were nominated and prospective parliamentarians recommended to the National Executive for selection or appointed by the National Executive as official party candidates. There was no record available to me, unfortunately, of the total size of CPP mem-

26. On the concept of "deployable agent" in social movements see Philip Selznick, *The Organizational Weapon* (New York: Free Press, 1960), pp. 18–29.
27. See the next chapter for a discussion of the three types of political involvement — symbolic, normative-ideological, and instrumental.
28. This should not be read as complete lack of commitment to national goals and to the national interest.

bership in Swedru, not even of those who carried cards and regularly paid dues. I doubt very much if there were more than two hundred such members in any one year. Even if we assume, a very unwarranted assumption at that, that in 1949 all those who paid to attend the inaugural meeting became CPP members and remained members throughout the first period, they could not have numbered more than six hundred.[29]

The coincidence of branch and regional organizations of the CPP in Swedru, and the fact that membership in the party could pay off, generated much CPP activity in town and in the surrounding Agona, Fante, Efutu, and Akim areas. The minutes show that meetings were held regularly, work was planned well ahead of time, correspondence was conducted in a thorough manner, and the symbolic activities — dances, harvests, public rallies, and other fund-raising activities — were held frequently. Although the CPP constitution provided for an annual regional conference, it is obvious from the minutes that sometimes two or even three regional conferences were held in Swedru in any one year or close to one another in two consecutive years. Thus there was a regional conference on 18 December 1954 preceded by a preelection regional conference and followed on 12 February 1955 by another central regional conference. These were in addition to formal and informal regular weekly and daily meetings of the party executive. At the local and regional levels, at least, the CPP was real indeed.[30]

The local branch, which in 1954 became the constituency branch, held regular weekly meetings on Fridays, and devoted Sundays to organizational work — campaigning, opening new rural branches, and distributing propaganda, as we have noted. General (as opposed to executive) meetings were increasingly replaced by the public rally at which all party members were required to be present. In 1954, the Swedru CPP, consistent with its important local, regional, and national role, was fortified with a propaganda van, a Peugeot car with the familiar red, white, and green colors of the party painted on it and the CPP electoral symbol, the "red cockerel," pasted all over it. The van was equipped with powerful loud-

---

29. After 1964, all those who sought governmental employment had to carry a CPP membership card. The effect of this on local CPP membership is clear.

30. The agenda for the December 1954 conference was typical: (1) election of representatives to form the National Executive, (2) party organization, (3) the CPC, and (4) other matters arising.

speakers and amplifiers. Popular gramophone records blared out of speakers and usually drew large crowds to political rallies. With the carnival atmosphere thus created, the entertainment value of this medium to the urban masses was unmistakable and lent to the CPP much symbolic (if deceptive) mass support and appeal. Organized intimidation, through the strategic use of the local police force and "action troopers" — breaking up anti-CPP (and therefore anti-Government!) gatherings — was also a reliable tool in the CPP propaganda kit. All the same, the 1954 electoral battle was fiercely fought.

The area near the post office, Owani, one of the four original (traditional) quarters or wards of Swedru and the home of Kojo Essilfie, was nicknamed by the CPP supporters "Dunkirk," reminiscent of World War II, and so named because it was in this area — the stronghold of "tribal," cocoa, and land interests and of opposition to the CPP — that some of the major clashes took place, with bottles thrown and broken on people's heads and fisticuffs pursued.[31] The other centers of traditional-tribal opposition in Swedru were Ankyease and Kubease. Ankyease is the seat of the chief and the oldest ward, and Kwaku Otu was the ward anti-CPP leader. Kubease, slightly younger than Ankyease and adjoining it, is the place where Mame Dapaa, woman farmer and market seller, was most outspoken against the CPP. They were all against the CPP for many reasons, but the burning ones were directly socioeconomic. They were, in the first place, strongly against what some described as rotten policy for cocoa. They wanted a guaranteed price of five pounds for a sixty-pound load of cocoa instead of the CPP government's control price of seventy-two shillings. Second, they could not tolerate an organization that was seen as antichief and opposed to the traditional system of privilege and status respect. It is in this second connection that the CPP may be considered somewhat revolutionary and radical. Again, as Kojo Essilfie, now in his late fifties, put it, "CPP mmofra no na woye rough" ("the young supporters of the CPP were very uncouth and disrespectful"), an allusion to conflict between generations. The CPP was for the "unstaid youth," and the

31. We could not mistake the influence of the exservicemen here, whose leader, Paul Edua, was at this time a pro-CPP man who in fact had withdrawn his candidature on the persuasion of the Central Committee of the CPP after a promise that the electoral expenses he had incurred would be repaid to him and that he would be the official candidate at the 1956 election.

anti-CPP elements for "respect for old age." [32] Finally, many people, including Kojo Essilfie, were under the mistaken belief that the SUC would take over, under CPP orders, all private lands and farms (*haban*). This was long before Nkrumah started propagating "socialism."

Two preelection incidents in Swedru, one at the Zongo (the Muslim area) and the other at Ankyease (the Agona tribal home), demonstrated the close relationship between the CPP and the Swedru government police, a relationship which I do not propose to examine here except to indicate that there was much evidence to support the claim that the police aided and abetted the CPP and that the undeclared policy of the party that "when persuasion and treating fail, force must prevail" held good. The party had enough financial resources, since it was the government and controlled some of the strategic financial institutions, such as the CPC, to be able to operate on all these fronts at the same time.

Sometime before the 1954 general election, the zerikin Zongo, Isifu Darfi, received a letter from the national headquarters of the newly inaugurated MAP requesting him to meet with his elders and organize a local branch of the party in Swedru.[33] The zerikin accordingly convened a meeting of Malams, Limans, dignitaries of Islam, and his personal friends, including Habu and Adamu, to discuss the matter. The Zongo chief, who admitted ignorance of the implications of political party organization for the Zongo people, advised caution for, as he put it, "Whatever is new should be evaluated carefully before accepting it." The zerikin pointed out to me that, because of "lying and insincerity of politicians," he was not interested in party politics. But Habu and Adamu prevailed on the thirty-six-year-old zerikin to accept the invitation to organize a local branch. Habu and Adamu, of about the same age as the chief, were very ambitious young men who argued that they had nothing to lose and much to gain from party organization. The example of the CPP, the model, was cited. Meanwhile, Nana Kum, a painter and the local money lender, who was one of the bitterest opponents of the CPP, had embarked on the difficult task of organizing a branch

32. The "youth" saw the "old" people as having vested interests in the existing privilege system which largely ignored their political and socioeconomic needs.
33. Note that, as the name implies, the Moslem Association Party was based on religious or confessional affiliation.

of the Ghana Congress Party (GCP) in town. He was at this time both propaganda secretary and sole financier-treasurer. Nana Kum and later Kojo Essilfie, two people whose names are synonymous in Swedru with anti-CPP action, confessed, in the words of Nana Kum, that "the popularity of the CPP, such as it was, was gaining such a *noisy* following that any opposition party could hardly hold a meeting in peace." Opposition party meetings and rallies were met, Nana Kum continued, "with jeers and boos and hooting. We just could not function."

Nana Kum, primarily interested in the defeat of the CPP, approached the zerikin Zongo and his people and asked them to join forces in a common party against the CPP, "the thieves." An agreement was reached. Nana Kum, therefore, obtained a permit from the district police, Winneba (since it was difficult, according to him, to get one from Inspector Harry and his men of the local police station, who were under the thumb of the CPP) for a rally at the Zongo. Nana Kum, the zerikin Zongo, and many inhabitants of Zongo and nearby Dwinhu, the ward of Nana Kum, attended the rally. There was much singing and drumming to draw crowds and to entertain and also to deal with serious party business at the same time.[34] The CPP, as usual, set out to wreck the rally.[35]

In the course of the rally that late evening, the Swedru police came down, having allegedly been bribed by Bensah, the CPP candidate and a friend of the Ewe police inspector, and ordered that the gathering was illegal and should be broken up. The organizers refused to break it up, because they had permission to hold it. Whereupon a trumped up charge of their having abused Kwame Nkrumah (the prime minister) and the CPP with intent to cause riot and breach of the peace was brought against them. Fighting broke out; there was general pandemonium. The outcome was that the zerikin Zongo, his two wives, and eight others were arrested. Five of them, those who had resisted arrest, were later fined ten pounds each at the Swedru Magistrate's Court. Halidu, an Hausa

34. It must be emphasized again that the size of the attendance at these rallies was not a reliable index of the effectiveness of political mobilization, despite statements to the contrary by party leaders.

35. It is interesting to note that Habu and Adamu, after a visit to Accra, where they may have been "bought" by the CPP, had returned to persuade the zerikin that the MAP was, after all, "a hopeless organization." The two thereafter joined the CPP. In fact, Malam Seidu, the zerikin's own half-brother, embraced the CPP.

butcher, soon thereafter presented a live goat to Dr. Nkrumah as a sign that he completely dissociated himself from MAP actions. That was the formal end of the MAP and the GCP in Swedru. Nana Kum pointed out sadly that all that occurred had been possible because the CPP had a rough and ready following and because it had the police in its grips. They could therefore do anything with relative impunity. By the time of the election the GCP, according to Nana Kum, could boast of no more than thirty members! He therefore wisely withdrew his candidature and supported Coleman, the independent candidate.

Another incident, more serious from the point of view of the Agona elders, occurred at the ahenfie, the official residence of the chief, which until 1955 housed the SUC. This time those involved were the CPP action troopers from Bukom Square, Accra, led by Kakabuka ("the fierce one") and Agona traditional authorities. The action troopers had arrived in Swedru from Accra on their way to Apam, Western Gomoa, the constituency of Kojo Botsio, then minister of state and one of the right-hand men of Nkrumah, to make sure by threats or other means that people voted for the CPP's Botsio. In Swedru they were the guests of E. K. Bensah. One Sunday, a day after the arrival of the action troopers and a few weeks before the general election, the chief and his elders met at the ahenfie. Even at this early time the CPP was identified exclusively with the government, and this meeting was considered anti-CPP for a number of reasons; in fact, that was the obvious conclusion to any observer. In the first place, the chief and some of his elders were anti-CPP. Second, Coleman, the Independent candidate, was clearly anti-CPP (though he was wont to change his party affiliation), and he was a member of the Swedru royal lineage and a cousin of Kojo Essilfie, the anti-CPP champion, who was also present at the meeting. The meeting was not tribal as such, for what was at stake was property and land interests.

The action troopers, therefore, attacked the ahenfie, broke up the meeting and destroyed some traditional drums as well as many other things there. There was much fighting in the area of the ahenfie as many Agona, who could not stand the assault on the "traditional notables," joined in. Many sustained injuries from broken bottles and stones which were hurled indiscriminately from all directions. Kojo Essilfie, at the time secretary to Coleman, and a few others attacked Bensah. Had it not been the fact that many Agona young men were either working for Bensah or supporting him, and also that many elderly Kwahu and Fante supported the chief and Coleman, the conflict would have degenerated into "tribal" fights between the foreigners led by the Ewe Bensah and the Agona, represented by Coleman and Essilfie. The police came in to restore order, but only Kojo Essilfie was arrested on charges of assault and fined at the court. Whereupon the nationally famous Swedru Brass Band, a wholly Agona organization (a majority of the members belonged to one matrilineage) which had played on numerous occasions at CPP picnics, both in Accra and Swedru, protested the police and CPP action by composing a number, the words of which constituted an attack on Bensah. Note the form of the protest and the stress on Bensah's ethnic background.

The initial lines of the number and its refrain are very interesting. It starts with: *Bensah ne na awu oo* ("Bensah's mother is dead"), which in the Akan context has the implication that Bensah was virtually an outcast, a worthless person without a home or family; and the refrain, *Oye Oyigbeni, Oye Oyigbeni.* . . . means "He is an Ewe man, he is an Ewe man," in reference to membership in an "inferior" tribe. After the 1954 election, when Bensah was returned for a second time and made a cabinet minister, he reacted to the band's number by preventing them from playing on the streets for months. What this meant was that the police refused the band a permit for most public engagements.[36]

In Swedru, not every non-Agona was CPP, and not every Agona was non-CPP. The struggle in Swedru was primarily, but by no means wholly, over economic interests and, following from these or related to these, power interests. It was a fight between property and nonproperty, between what Polly Hill has called the "rural capitalists" and landlords with investment in immovable property who had protested the introduction of property rates and would later protest the property tax — and propertyless urban and rural wage-

36. It needs remarking that despite the above example of "tribal" political protest, it would be a gross oversimplification to reduce politics in Swedru or elsewhere in Ghana, even in Ashanti, to mere tribalism. Coleman, who seems more a careerist than a tribalist, would, as a nontraditional wolf in a tribal sheepskin, seize on any opportunity to exploit his tribal affiliation — in fact, any affiliation.

workers.[37] There were many Agona young men, Annobil and so on, who were in the executive committee of the CPP.

CPP INTRAPARTY FACTIONALISM

The 1956 general election, from the point of view of the CPP field organizers, was "relatively easy for the CPP." Bensah, the local candidate, in keeping with the CPP idea of "one Ghana, one People," was away from Swedru most of the time, traveling with the prime minister, Dr. Nkrumah, in the Northern Region canvassing for the CPP, and therefore personally took very little part in electoral mobilization in his constituency. All the same, Bensah was returned for the third time with about the same number of votes as the number he polled in 1954 (see tables 8 and 9). After the 1954 election, as one might have expected, the CPP in Swedru, if not throughout the country, was hit by an intraparty conflict over the question of constituency leadership. Party leadership had proved to be economically worthwhile. In Swedru, some of the members of the constituency executive had petitioned the Central Committee of the CPP in Accra that Bensah, who had repeatedly been voted into the Assembly since 1951, should be replaced by a new man. The careerism of a few of the executive members provided the primary motive. One of the men who were very interested in representing Swedru in the national Assembly was Kwesi Armah (the most "wanted" man in Ghana since the military coup), who had come to Swedru in 1955 from Cape Coast, where he had been very active in party work, to assist Kofi Agyare in the propaganda unit of the central regional office. Another was Paul Edua, the leader of the Agona area exservicemen, who had led the local Positive Action in 1950 and had withdrawn his candidature in the election of 1954 on the promise of the Central Committee of the CPP to pay for all the expenses he had incurred campaigning as an independent candidate — expenses amounting to five hundred pounds, according to Edua. If the figure is correct, and there is no reason to doubt it, the CPP must have spent thousands of pounds to win any one election.[38]

37. See Polly Hill, *The Gold Coast Cocoa Farmer* (London: Oxford University Press, 1956), and *Migrant Cocoa Farmers of Southern Ghana* (Cambridge: At the University Press, 1963). For a discussion of property rates, see above pp. 217–18.

38. We should indicate that in 1954 a number of independent candidates, many of them members of the CPP until they were dismissed by the Central

The Central Committee laid down the rule that, where possible, the existing Assembly member should be nominated again; in many other cases, the local constituency organizations were asked to send a short list of names to Accra for the final decision. The electorate or the local constituency had very little control over who their representative should be. The party could, obviously, hardly hope to avoid division on the basis of selection by the Central Committee, especially when the supply of Assembly seats was smaller than the enormous demand for them. In any case, many constituency members felt strongly that they had as good a claim as anyone else to draw £960 in the Legislative Assembly.

The rebel or independent candidates became an early source of split and factionalism in the CPP. By now the improved economic and other status benefits accruing to M.L.A.'s were nationally obvious and hotly discussed, and many men were prepared to fight tooth and nail to join the select, wealthy, and powerful group of M.L.A.'s. According to Paul Edua, the Swedru constituency executive had voted seven against and five for Bensah's nomination in 1955, but the chairman at the time refused the nomination of a new candidate for Swedru because it was not on the agenda. The question of nomination was therefore left until the constituency delegates' conference, held in Swedru two weeks later in the latter part of 1955. At the conference were Nathaniel Welbeck, candidate for Cape Coast, representative of the Central Committee, and acting general secretary of the CPP (until the appointment that year of Cecil Forde, chairman of SUC, as general secretary); and Kofi-Baako, a member of the CPP National Executive, and a representative for Saltpond.

The conference, which had been originally scheduled to take place at the Ghana College, was suddenly transferred to the Taj Cinema Hall, Swedru. Paul Edua alleged, with the insight of an insider, that the transfer was deliberate and gave Welbeck and Baako enough time to influence the delegates by bribes and promises to vote for Bensah when the conference opened. Despite the votes against Bensah by the delegates from Kwanyako, Asafo, and Mensakrom, when Welbeck reminded the delegates that Bensah was the

_____

Committee for opposing the official candidate or as "rebel candidates," left the party. The extreme cases were in Ashanti, where there were twenty official candidates and twenty-seven such rebels. Austin and Tordoff, *Voting in an African Town*, p. 136.

Central Committee's man and that the choice was irrevocable and final, there was an overwhelming "Yes" for Bensah.[39] Most of the opposition to Bensah came from Swedru itself. Bensah's opponents charged that he lacked respect for the local executive members of the party; that he failed to use his position as a minister to aid local social and economic development; that he failed to listen to his Swedru constituents; and that many people in Swedru strongly preferred Cecil Forde, the chairman of the SUC, who was considered more sensitive to local needs.

When Bensah was returned in the following year, 1956, among the first things he did was to weed out his principal opponents — namely, F. C. Dodd, Erskine (who was later brought back and made a D.C.), Essandoh, and Paul Edua — from executive positions and replace them with the younger and more faithful and reliable S. Y. Annobil and R. K. Appiah, former schoolmates, who were to become perhaps the two most powerful CPP members in the 1960s, at least at the district level. It may be more correct, in Paul Edua's case, to say that he left the party.

The 1956 election was a three-cornered fight between Bensah (CPP), Anyan (NLM), and Edua (Independent). The 1956 results (see tables 9 and 10) were little different from the previous ones, as we have noted. The real difference was that Anyan and Paul Edua had to split and share the opposition, non-CPP, votes. The cocoa campaign and NLM traditionalism could not stop the more powerful and reliable CPP electoral strategy, which made many potential voters not bother to vote because it was a foregone conclusion that the CPP would win anyway. The central ingredients of this strategy were perhaps a little electoral malpractice, heavy treating (Bensah spent some money buying table salt, kerosene, corn on the cob, and other basic consumer items for constituents), excessive patronage, and the ruthless self-confidence of members: *nsamanfo betow aba ama yen CPPfo* ("the ancestors will vote CPP") or *wofi CPP mu a ade no ngu* ("if a member leaves or rebels against the CPP, the party does not collapse"). The CPC, which at this time was under fire by opposition members to the extent that a commission of inquiry into CPC activities had been set up, was the major institu-

---

39. It may have been the case, as one CPP official was quick to point out, that Bensah was still very popular outside Swedru, which had as many votes (two) at the conference as the other thirteen or so rural towns making up the constituency and represented at the conference.

tional means for the extensive networks of administrative, farming, and commercial patronage under the firm control of the CPP. Ministers and parliamentarians rewarded their followers with jobs and money, and they appointed their henchmen to manage national development corporations (such as CPC and the Industrial Development Corporation) and boards and committees (such as CMB) which controlled the allocation of contracts, loans, and import licenses.[40] The interests of such people were therefore linked with the interests and electoral success of the CPP, the party in power. No wonder Paul Edua later conceded that he could never have won the 1956 election in Swedru. The following is an example of how the patronage system worked. According to Essilfie, after the CPP electoral victory in Swedru in 1954, Duker and Forde, then chairman and vice-chairman respectively of the SUC and local constituency executive members of the CPP, called on Coleman, who had opposed Bensah, and on Essilfie, Coleman's election secretary and a bitter opponent of CPP, and promised both of them jobs. Essilfie was to have a job at the SUC, possibly as an administrative officer, and Coleman was to be given the contract for the construction of the Swedru secondary school near Asafo if they would first join the CPP. Coleman agreed and was in fact given the contract, but Essilfie, of course, held his stand. Another instance, this time of bribery involving Nana Kum, the other anti-CPP man, needs recounting.

NANA KUM, KOJO BOTSIO, KWESI ARMAH, AND J. A. DIXON: THE BRIBE THAT NEVER WAS?

It should be declared at once that whatever the size in numerical terms of the electoral support that Nana Kum controlled, and this was very small indeed, he was a big thorn in the flesh of the CPP in the Winneba District of the Central Region. Born in 1906 to Chief Amissah, nifahene of Cape Coast, he came with his mother to Swedru in 1923, where he attended the Methodist school, finishing the Standard VII in 1932. From 1937 until 1949 he worked as a painter with the local Public Works Department (PWD). In 1949 he suddenly came into money and became a licensed moneylender

40. This style of politics is quite familiar to Southern Nigerians and many other West Africans. See James S. Coleman and Carl G. Rosberg, Jr., editors, *Political Parties and National Integration in Tropical Africa* (Berkeley: University of California Press, 1964).

(an usurer, in fact — this partly accounted for his lack of popularity in the 1950s). In 1967 he was, on his own admission, worth about sixty thousand pounds in assets and property, particularly buildings. In 1956 he finally decided, having withdrawn his candidature in 1954, to contest the election as an NLM candidate, not in Swedru but at Western Gomoa, against Kojo Botsio (CPP), minister of state in 1954.[41] In 1951, Botsio had been elected unopposed into the Legislative Assembly. In 1954, he had defeated his opponent, the MAP candidate Ismaila, by as many as 2,926 votes. Yet, since the 1956 election was the last pre-independence election, it had its special attraction and must by all means be won by Botsio. The best guarantee of success at the polls was being elected unopposed as he had been in 1951. To insure this, Botsio allegedly sent his close party colleagues, Kwesi Armah (who was then in the Central Region propaganda section of the CPP with Agyare) and Dixon (a Fante UAC storekeeper who had nominated Botsio), to persuade Nana Kum to withdraw his candidature. The "persuasion fee" was sixty pounds. Nana Kum was duly contacted. According to Nana Kum, Armah and Dixon went to his house on numerous occasions about the deal, and so he finally decided to do something about it.

When the two called at his house the next time, Nana Kum informed them that he would accept the money and withdraw his candidature but that they should keep the money until he had formally withdrawn it at Winneba in their presence the next day. In fact, he had only one day left to make the deadline for withdrawal of candidature. Armah and Dixon agreed to Nana Kum's suggestion and left. That same night Nana Kum traveled to Cape Coast, sixty-one miles away, to consult with Amponsah Dadzie, the regional NLM secretary and party candidate for the Cape Coast constituency, and to arrange with the Cape Coast Police for the arrest of Armah and Dixon. He took this long line of action because, "I did not trust the police in Swedru." Bensah's influence on the police was too great, Nana Kum pointed out. Unfortunately, Amponsah Dadzie and he could not recruit policemen from Cape Coast to effect the arrests. The Cape Coast police were clearly also under CPP influence and control, Nana Kum remarked bitterly.

Instead, the superintendent of police at Cape Coast suggested

41. Botsio (B.A., honors) was one-time teacher at the Abuakwa State College. In 1951 he was minister of education and social welfare and was associated with the so-called Botsio Certificate. The certificate was notorious for the

that Nana Kum could achieve his purpose if he would arrange for strong men to effect the capture of the culprits as they handed over the money to him; he should also get a cameraman to take a picture of the transaction and a reporter to record the proceedings, all of which could be used as evidence at the court. This was obviously a very tedious and expensive procedure. Undeterred, Nana Kum hired some muscular Cape Coast fishermen, a newspaper reporter, and a cameraman as suggested, and brought them down to Swedru the same night. It was arranged that Nana Kum's bedroom, which opened into the living room where the transaction was to take place the following morning, would be used as the hiding place of the hired men. The cameraman and the reporter were to observe from vantage points in the bedroom and perform the assigned duties. The strongmen were also to remain at the hiding place and were to rush out at a given signal to capture the CPP victims.

Nana Kum dramatized every piece of the act to me as he reconstructed what was almost a successful play. Kwesi Armah and Dixon came in in the morning with the money as planned. As the money was being handed over by Armah to Nana Kum, the strongmen rushed out at a signal and pounced on Armah and Dixon, who struggled fiercely trying to escape. "Dixon was seized just in front of my house," Nana Kum said, with obvious self-satisfaction. But Kwesi Armah, a younger and more athletic man, was finally captured about a quarter of a mile away. The case was taken to the magistrate's court after the party had been handed over to the local police, but it was summarily dismissed by the court, not surprisingly, on the trumped up grounds that Nana Kum owed Dixon £60 for goods purchased in the latter's store and the money was to defray the debt outstanding. However, the £60 was returned neither to Nana Kum nor to Dixon. Later, Nana Kum learned that Botsio had originally given £200 to Armah for the bribery, but the latter had kept £140 for his own use. Thereafter, it was impossible, according to Nana Kum, to canvass for votes in Western Gomoa. At one point, he was nearly beaten to death, his car was stoned, and the headlights and windshield were smashed by people allegedly hired by Botsio to do the job. Botsio naturally won convincingly, by 3, 317 votes to Nana Kum's 79.

---

ease with which it was obtained; in a number of cases pupils were awarded certificates without having taken any examinations at all, according to popular belief.

THE SUC AND CPP DOMINATION

One of the reasons why Nkrumah continuously stressed the extreme importance of party organization at the local level was, as we have seen, to insure "mass participation in the government" of the country. What this increasingly meant was that a strong local CPP organization was needed "to broaden the basis of support for the leadership" of the party. The party gave leadership and mobilized the people for support of leadership decisions. The party again provided "central leadership," especially during the third phase of politics, to such institutions as the civil service, judiciary, armed forces, police, central banks, government boards, and corporations. This implied, among other things, party control of local government. The CPP never thought of the so-called masses as capable of local or national political decision-making. Their only active participation began with the rallies and ended with the vote. The elected thereafter ceased to be accountable to the electorate for their actions, a fact which was an attribute of the centralizing aim of the CPP.

In the SUC, this policy had meant making certain that the CPP

TABLE 7 GENERAL ELECTION, 1954: RESULTS AND
STATISTICS

Party	Seats	Votes Received	Percentage of Total Votes
Convention People's Party	71	391,817	55 (including 3 seats unopposed)
Northern People's Party	12	53,705	7
Togoland Congress Party	2	21,026	3
Ghana Congress Party	1	32,168	5
Moslem Association Party	1	21,172	3
Ghana National Party	. . .	3,579	1
Ghana Action Party	. . .	285	. . .
Anlo Youth Organization	1	7,375	1
Independents	16	175,593	25
Total	104	706,720	100

NOTE: Total number of voters on Register: 1,225,603 (100%); total number of votes cast: 706,720 (58%).

Electors, at the time of their application to register, must have paid their local authority rates for either the current or previous year. The "previous year" requirement caused a lot of trouble and technical disfranchisement. Interestingly, the Independents received nearly half as many votes as the CPP. The figures in the table are adapted from Ministry of Local Government report (mimeographed).

TABLE 8 GENERAL ELECTION, 1954: RESULTS FOR
SOME SELECTED ELECTORAL DISTRICTS,
COLONY REGION

Electoral District and Candidates	Votes Cast			Electors on Register	Percentage that Voted
	CPP	MAP	Ind.		
Agona				6,289	85
Albert Derbi Appea	....	...	3,037		
Swithin Maxwell Arko	2,332	...	....		
Agona-Swedru				7,585	66
Emmanuel Korbla Bensah	3,156	...	....		
Timothy Augustus Coleman	....	...	1,825		
Western Gomoa				3,380	100
Kojo Botsio	3,153	...	....		
Ismaila, Mugtadir Annan	....	227	....		
Awutu				11,858	58
Alfred Jonas Dowuona-Hammond	3,603	...	....		
Samuel Mensah Herbert Baxter Yarney	....	...	1,502		
Isaac Damoley Baiden-Amissah	....	...	1,249		
Simeon Cobina Abbeyquaye	....	...	376		
Samuel Henry Brew	....	...	186		

controlled the Council through the elected chairman and the vice-chairman, and particularly through control of the Finance and Staff Committee, whose chairman was almost always the chairman of the Council. A second CPP–non-CPP clash, between the Swedru CPP members and the NLM supporters, occurred in front of the ahenfie in the early part of 1955, at the time of the inauguration in Swedru of a branch of the NLM. This clash demonstrated again the monopolistic and centralizing tendencies of the CPP, which were to become more and more pronounced during the second and third phases of politics in Ghana. CPP thugs then had hurled down the NLM flag and had engaged the NLM "Action Groupers" in a free-for-all fight. Present at the inauguration ceremony were Bafour Akoto, Joe Appiah, Victor Owusu, R. R. Amponsah from Kumasi, and Kwow Richardson from Cape Coast. The police arrested the NLM Action Groupers, but they were later freed after R. R. Amponsah and Victor Owusu, both Ashanti lawyers, had pleaded with the inspector for their release, since the action of the Groupers was in self-defence.[42]

Against this background, it is hardly surprising that the election of a chairman of the SUC on 14 October 1955 was so fiercely fought

TABLE 9 GENERAL ELECTION, 1956: RESULTS FOR SOME SELECTED ELECTORAL DISTRICTS, WESTERN (CENTRAL) REGION

Electoral District and Candidates	Votes Cast				Electors on Register	Percentage that Voted
	CPP	NLM	WYA	Ind.		
Agona					11,104	42
W. A. C. Essibrah	3,786	....	...	...		
A. D. Appea	....	872	...	...		
Agona-Swedru					8,762	54
E. K. Bensah	3,472	....	...	...		
J. K. Anyan	....	969	...	...		
Paul Edua	....	....	...	314		
Western Gomoa					5,997	56
Kojo Botsio	3,317	....	...	...		
Nana Kum	....	79	...	...		
Eastern Gomoa					9,509	53
C. C. K. Baah	5,046	....	...	...		
O. Kwow Richardson	....	40	...	...		
Awutu					12,500	33
A. J. Dowuona-Hammond	3,767	....	...	...		
E. O. Tetteh	....	....	...	435		
Cape Coast					14,596	63
N. A. Welbeck	5,744	....	...	...		
K. Amponsah-Dadzie	....	3,437	...	...		

SOURCE: Adapted from *General Election 1956*, LA64, vol. 2, Ministry of Local Government.

NOTE: Omitting five uncontested seats, there was about a 50 percent poll over the country as a whole.

The total number of electors in the Western (Central) Region was 226,911. The CPP was strongest in that region and better organized compared to Ashanti. Out of 111,895 votes cast in the Central Region, 97,063 were for the CPP and 14,832 were for other parties (NLM, 7,109; WYA, 3,898; Ind., 3,825). Out of 224,569 votes cast in Ashanti, 96,968 were for the CPP and 127,601 were for other parties (NLM, 119,533; MAP, 71,565; Ind., 503).

42. It is again significant that the young Agona man who had pulled down the NLM flag and had been knifed in the thigh (he showed me the scar) — he

out between the CPP and the non-CPP–NLM complex. In attendance were Bensah (CPP), representative for Swedru and a cabinet
minister; the G.A. from Cape Coast; the G.A. from Winneba; and
the president, the adontenhene, the chief of Swedru.

TABLE 10 AGONA-SWEDRU CONSTITUENCY, 1956

Candidate	Nominator	Votes Received	Percentage of Total Votes
E. K. Bensah (CPP) Pharmacist-Nurse, dispensing chemist	D. K. Amuakwa Minta Clerk, Duakwa	3,472	73.2
	Sam Kofi Dodoo Farmer, Abodom Kobina Ansah Farmer, Swedru		
Paul Edua (Ind.) Dental mechanic and ex-serviceman	Kwame Atta Farmer, Kwanyako	314	6.4
	J. Arku Cobbah Clerk, Assisim, W. Swedru Samuel Onyame Farmer, Asafo		
J. A. Anyan (NLM) Tutor-teacher	G. F. Osam-Duodu Farmer, ex-chief, Duakwa Alhaji Adam Tailor, Zongo, Swedru Kwasi Kyei Farmer, Asafo	969	20.4

NOTE: Registered voters, 8,762; percentage that voted, 54; total votes cast, 4,755.

Councillors Cecil Forde (CPP) and Osam-Duodu (NLM)
were duly nominated and seconded. The result of the first voting
took many aback: Forde, nine; Osam-Duodu, nine — a tie. Note that
Forde was then the general secretary of the CPP and spent part of
his time in Accra, the national capital, and part in Swedru. Paton,
the G.A. of Cape Coast, explained that according to section 26(3)
of the Local Government Ordinance of 1951, if the Council failed to
elect a chairman it would be in default. Councillors were therefore
asked to think the matter over carefully for fifteen minutes and then
vote again on a chairman. On resumption, the G.A. and the presi-

had done this hoping that Bensah would give him a job he had promised him,
a promise that was never fulfilled — was not arrested by the police.

dent advised all parties to set aside all differences and try to elect a chairman. Everybody, particularly the G.A., was aware that, unless something was done, division in Council on the basis of political party could be disastrous for smooth Council functioning and that there was a possibility of not getting projects discussed and implemented. A second vote again showed a nine-nine tie. The Council was in default and the G.A. informed the councillors that he would notify the minister of local government. The meeting was therefore adjourned until 3 November 1955.

When the Council met after nearly three weeks for a third attempt to elect a chairman, Forde again received nine votes, but this time won because two of the councillors, who allegedly had been bribed, abstained, and Osam-Duodu therefore had only seven votes. The SUC seems, on this evidence, to have been fairly balanced on party lines throughout the first phase, though it is clear that the CPP, through the chairman of the Council, had a decisive edge over the non-CPP councillors and controlled important decisions. During the second and third phases of politics, local elections to the Council virtually ceased, or ceased to have any meaning, for only CPP members had any chance of becoming councillors. As we may recall, when in 1955 Nana Kum lost to E. S. Quainoo (CPP) at the local elections, he was nevertheless returned as a traditionally appointed member, but with the abolition of the traditional one-third membership in 1958, the non-CPP opposition lost its last effective grip on the CPP in the Council. In Swedru the years of virtual one-party rule had begun.

8 THE PROBLEM OF POLITICAL MOBILIZATION, PARTY MEMBERSHIP, AND PARTY FINANCE

The concept of political mobilization or "politicization" is one of the key notions in the analysis of nationalism, political development, and modernization in the new states of Africa and Asia. The concept has been particularly central to David Apter's studies of the social and political changes in Ghana.[1] Closely related to the idea of mobilization is the notion of "personal charisma" and charismatic leadership, classically formulated by Max Weber.[2] This is a force that acts in situations of transition as a *"primary* functional vehicle of institutionalization" (my italics), making political change meaningful, acceptable, or legitimate to the political public."[3] In this connection, the various analyses of Runcinman, Tiger, and Apter of political transformation in Ghana are very interesting, but too generalizing and speculative.[4]

Apter's concern with the problem of how the new states of Africa can be made to hold together as moral entities (Apter, for instance, holds that political life can be understood *only* in moral terms) and his preoccupation with charisma take him directly to the idea of "political religion" as an integrating device in the political development of Ghana.[5] For Apter, political religion consists of "those transcendental ends that define the state as a moral entity," and

---

1. See David Apter, *The Political Kingdom in Uganda* (London: Oxford University Press, 1961), pp. 22–23; *Politics of Modernization;* and especially "Nkrumah, Charisma, and the Coup."
2. Talcott Parsons, et al., eds., *Theories of Society* (New York: Free Press, 1961).
3. See K. Deutsch, *Nationalism and Social Communication* (Boston: M.I.T. Press, 1966), pp. 126–27, on the concept of the "political public" and its relationship to "mobilization."
4. W. G. Runcinman, "Charismatic Legitimacy and One-Party Rule in Ghana," *European Journal of Sociology* 4 (1963): 148–65; L. Tiger, "Ghana: A Charismatic Nation," *Current History* 45 (December 1963): 335–40; Apter, *Ghana in Transition; Politics of Modernization;* and "Nkrumah, Charisma, and the Coup."
5. Geertz, *Old Societies and New States.*

241

Chapter Eight

Nkrumaism was such a religion in Ghana. It should be said immediately that Apter's conceptualization confuses, to say the least, the facts of political change and legitimation of authority in Ghana. But the intention here is not to present a point-by-point criticism of Apter's at times misleading but otherwise provocative and useful essay on the "politics of modernization" in Ghana.[6] Suffice it to indicate that political life in Ghana can best be understood in terms of economic expediency. The "moral culture" of a majority of the diverse peoples (tribes) of Ghana was expressed in the traditional religion centered on forms of ancestor worship. This religion, as well as other beliefs, as I have had occasion to demonstrate, was basically utilitarian in its primary emphasis on life and economic well-being of individuals and groups in this world as opposed to the other, transcendental world. This utilitarian world-view was further reinforced in the colonial situation by the colonialists' preoccupation with the creation in the Gold Coast of "native capitalists" and of a social and cultural system geared to the market and monetary values.

Only those aspects of Apter's treatment of the political development in Ghana that bear directly on my present study will be carefully and critically considered. In his most recent magnum opus, *The Politics of Modernization,* Apter categorizes polities under four major types or subtypes: theocratic, mobilization, neomercantilist, and reconciliation systems. The typology presents us with a framework for a study of political modernization, with examples drawn mostly from Africa and with Ghana as perhaps the prototype. Apter's aim, that is, was to "present a typology of governmental forms and some theories about how they change, meanwhile demonstrating the relationship between these forms and several functional categories." Apter does not posit a unilinear change from one type into another. All the same, one of the sequences by which polities change is the case whereby a mobilization system (perhaps the basic political type) is transformed into a neomercantilist system, and then after industrialization, into a reconciliation system.[7]

The important thing here is that, according to Apter, Ghana under Nkrumah — that is, during what I have defined as the second

6. Consult *American Sociological Review* 31 No. 2 (April 1966): 266–69, and *Pacific Affairs* 39, no. 1–2 (Spring–Summer 1966): 135–44, for critical reviews of Apter's position.
7. See Apter, *Politics of Modernization,* for full exposition.

and third phases of political development in Ghana — was a mobilization system moving toward a neomercantilist system and, hopefully, a reconciliation system. The basic difficulty with Apter's model and the theories of change derived from it is that they are based on insufficient empirical evidence. There are serious errors of fact, unwarranted precategory assumptions, and peculiarities of interpretation so far as Ghana is concerned, as I hope to demonstrate presently. Let us look at Apter's characterization of the mobilization and neomercantilist systems and see how it compares with the empirical data on political change in Ghana.

A mobilization system, according to Apter, is one in which a party or regime engages in drastic and thorough reorganization of the society. The major features of the system are: (1) Hierarchical authority, in which power, instead of being dispersed, is concentrated in the hands of a single charismatic leader who also monopolizes legitimacy. Voluntary organizations are auxiliaries of the dominant political party and act to mobilize consensus in the public. (2) Total allegiance, which means that the party (CPP) demands a fundamental commitment and involvement on the part of the individual. (3) Tactical flexibility, making it possible, even necessary, for the party to alter its alliances, goals, and targets as circumstances demand. The party has a remarkable freedom of action with very little accountability. (4) Unitarism, in reference to the party's devotion to the establishment of new political units which are essentially new, subordinate, solidarity groups. The party itself becomes a "party of solidarity"; hence other alternative solidarity groupings — for example, tribes, ethnic groups, religious organizations — which oppose the aspirations of the party are attacked. (5) Ideological specialization, which means in part that the party often acts on grounds of expediency and necessity, using ideology to give perspective and justification for what already appears necessary. The immediate tasks or government projects are cast in the context of ideological slogans as a form of communication.[8]

Apter proceeds to argue elsewhere that the mobilization system is superior to the reconciliation system in achieving modernization, for it can foster national integration by eliminating primordial loyalties to ethnic, tribal, or sectional groups, which in Ghana were considered to be divisive and to prevent successful mass mobilization and

8. Apter, *Political Kingdom in Uganda.*

hence modernization.[9] However, the mobilization system is transient. Consequently it is not permanent, and eventually, after industrialization is achieved, the reconciliation system, which allows for diverse solidarity groups to compete, is superior. Again, in a mobilization system the government accepts the prime burdens of modernization. The government's economic role leads to emphasis on social mobilization through either the administrative structure or the "party of solidarity," but particularly the latter. The role of the party is reinforced by political religion which through indoctrination establishes and reinforces such new values as hard work and thrift. Ideology itself is often an expression of political religion which converts instrumental values — for example, improving economic conditions — into consummatory or sacred values. Mobilization systems therefore claim higher morality than other systems. Furthermore, Apter asserts that in mobilization systems coercion is high and information low. This, according to him, is an advantage because at the two points of "conversion" from one polity type to another, mobilization systems are "most suitable" in establishing a new polity, and from late modernization to industrialization where *action* and not *information* is crucial.

What does Apter mean by "modernization," "industrialization," "development" in his analysis of political change? For Apter, development is the process by which secular (Western?) norms of behavior are made universal. Modernization is a particular case of development which implies three conditions: (1) a social system capable of constant innovation that embodies among its beliefs the acceptability of change (the institutionalization of innovation); (2) differentiated, flexible social structures; and (3) a social framework to provide the skills and knowledge necessary for living in a technologically advanced world. Industrialization becomes a special case of a modernization or post-modernization system in which the strategic functional roles of the society are related to manufacturing. There is a problem here, not clarified by Apter, concerning the precise relationships between development, modernization, and industrialization. At what stage in Ghana's development could we say she is modernized? What segments of the society must accept innovation for modernization to occur? Since education comes out as a crucial instrument of social change, what percentage of Ghana's

9. Apter, *Politics of Modernization.*

population must be literate in order to have a modernized society and polity? Is the specific content of education relevant? Is it possible to modernize by relying on imported foreign technical and skilled personnel? What happens if education is used, as it is being increasingly used in Latin American and African societies, to perpetuate class advantages and privilege and maintain the status quo? Apter's characterization does not offer unambiguous measures for answering satisfactorily the above questions. We do not know the sufficient and necessary conditions for the emergence of one as distinct from other political types.

However this may be, let us proceed to a description of the second type, the neomercantilist system, and see what light it throws on the political development of Ghana until the military coup of February 1966. It must be said at once that Apter has very little to say about the neomercantilist subtype. This is not surprising for it enters Apter's scheme as a typological stopgap in the rather long transitional period between the institutionalization or routinization of the leader's charisma in the "party of solidarity" and the possible emergence of a reconciliation system. The term *neomercantilism* is borrowed from the economics of mercantilism. Apter explains the unusual use of the economic term to identify a political subtype by referring to the fact noted by Eli Heckscher that classical mercantilism used a mixture of public and private enterprise "in which the critical rationale of economic activities is political." Thus for Apter the neomercantilist society also has a distinctive policy toward the economy. It uses the economy to "support authority." It has been pointed out by critics that such a description would apply to almost any Asian country which was not totalitarian, such as India, Pakistan, Japan, and Thailand.

In the movement toward neomercantilist polity from the mobilization system, instrumental values become more prominent and consummatory values lessen. Individual opportunism and corruption increase as political religion declines. Coalitions and factions tear the ruling party apart and generational conflicts increase. The neomercantilist system is further characterized by less coercion and more information available to the government.[10] Again, in a neo-

10. It should be noted in passing that Apter leaves the definition of "information" rather vague. Does he, for instance, mean a two-way flow of communication between leaders and the led that makes for vertical political integration? Does he mean a free press?

mercantilist system ideology becomes both nationalist and socialist but non-Marxian, that is, "with neomercantilist orientation to government enterprise rather than a Marxian one." Leadership is institutionalized in some form of presidential government. Apter holds that many mobilization systems change into neomercantilist systems, the transformation taking the form of ritualizing leadership by transferring authority from a charismatic leader to a successor and of traditionalizing its consummatory values by making them into a new and effective link between novelty and the past. Apter suggests that this was the sequence in Ghana under Nkrumah. The neomercantilist system makes a specific political contribution as "an agent of unification."

The basic difficulty with Apter's analysis as it relates to Ghana, and perhaps to other states as well, is his uncritical acceptance of psychological and sociological assumptions about the political process in Ghana under Nkrumah, concerning the relationship between the rulers and the ruled, the leaders and the led, which *appear* to be so obviously true as to demand no further investigation. These uncritical assumptions are in reference to the sociology and psychology of charismatic authority and the very notion of charisma that plays such a central role in Apter's work. It is the contention here that Apter's principal types of polity, namely, the theocratic, the mobilization, and the reconciliation, correspond to Max Weber's pure types of authority or domination: the traditional, the charismatic, and the rational-legal or bureaucratic, respectively. As we shall see, Max Weber's statements about the change from one type of authority system into another are more or less faithfully adopted by Apter, albeit in somewhat new terminological dressing.

Max Weber's caution that many empirical cases represent a combination (the mixed types) or a state of transition among several such pure types, leads Apter to introduce subtypes of the three pure types that emerge on careful reading as subtypes of charismatic authority.[11] Two examples of these subtypes are the modernizing autocracies of Thailand and Ethiopia, subtypes of traditional domination; and the neomercantilist systems of Ghana and Mali. Apter agrees with Max Weber almost without qualification that charisma is an instrument of sociocultural innovation, for "its attitude is revolutionary and trans-values everything. It makes a sovereign break

11. Weber, *From Max Weber*, parts 2 and 3.

with all tradition or rational norms." In fact, only the bearers of charisma could integrate "new" laws or values into the circle of what was upheld by tradition.

In its specific application to the political context of Ghana, Apter saw the rise and popularity of the CPP in terms primarily of a single variable, the "personal charisma" of Nkrumah acting as a "primary functional vehicle of institutionalization" of new values and structures.[12] As a charismatic leader in a mobilization system, Nkrumah was seen as engaged in a drastic and thorough reorganization of Ghanaian society, in which traditional authority had no or little place. Thus Apter argues that in Ghana the "party of solidarity [CPP], in attacking tradition, has jostled the public into functionally useful roles for the pursuit of modernization. . . . Modernization has come to require many individual attitudes and forms of social organization antithetical to traditional behavior. . . . Thus, for a time, the Ghana government was unable to make use of traditionalism to support innovation." [13]

There is no doubt that traditionalism, particularly in Kumasi and other places in Ashanti, served as an effective rallying point for opposition against the CPP. It is also true that Nkrumah was against political parties based *solely* on tribalism, religion, or other sectional interests, as we noted earlier, and in fact used governmental machinery to remove individual "difficult" chiefs and replaced them by others favoring the CPP (a strategy quite familiar to historians of colonial government — in Ashanti, King Prempeh was exiled in 1899 for challenging colonial authority). It would be misleading if not wrong, however, to generalize from the Ashanti experience to the rest of Ghana and claim that the CPP was bent on the destruction of traditionalism. In fact, the United Party opposition leaders and their supporters agreed that the CPP was successful largely because as a governing party it used repeatedly the whole machinery of state — the police, district and regional commissioners, the courts, and national financial resources — against all opposition forces and was backed by "*illiterate chiefs* threatening voters with fetich [*sic*] swearing by gods and urging them [their subjects] not to vote for

12. In a recent article, Apter (see "Nkrumah, Charisma, and the Coup") limits the concept's applicability to the period from 1949 to 1954 — the "charismatic period." This limitation does not substantially affect my basic contentions.
13. Apter, *Politics of Modernization*, p. 110.

the UP." [14] In fact, if anything, during all the three phases of political development in Ghana the CPP in Swedru and throughout
Ghana demonstrated its ability to incorporate traditional leaders
and other local influentials through a combination of cooptation,
persuasion, bribery, coercion, and selective appeals to traditional
symbols, rituals and values, within the new national institutions.
David Brokensha finds in his study of Larteh that the town had "a
remarkable syncretic ability to absorb new institutions, so that *even
the powerful CPP . . . emerges* as a Larteh rather than a national
institution" (my italics). What was really happening here was the
manipulation of traditional political disputes by the CPP in the
service of support for national leaders and their objectives. The
CPP in Larteh, like the CPP in Swedru, was both a local and a national institution. The CPP was a compromise organization par
excellence.

What is often forgotten or not realized is that the political development in Ghana, particularly between 1950 and 1966 (but also
even further back), contrary to Apter's developmental sequence,
was characterized by a political process in which individuals and
groups in various local areas supported and voted for this or
that group or political party in terms largely of instrumental values
expressed by individual opportunism and careerism (it was common
for individuals at any one time to hold multiple party cards!).
Other techniques in the political process were "crossing the carpet,"
bribery, corruption, which to some extent may be considered a
normatively oriented behavior, standing election as an independent
candidate against the official party candidate when one is not endorsed by the party (this was very predominant in the 1954 and 1956
general elections), and intraparty factionalism. [15]

14. *Ashanti Pioneer*, Thursday, 21 April 1960. Between 1950 and 1954, the
CPP in the Swedru area worked very closely with traditional leaders. The success of the CPP in the area was due in great part to the support it had from
chiefs and elders.
15. In this connection, it may be interesting to refer to a statement made by
Solomon Odamtten, then national chairman of the UP (the opposition party)
to the *Ashanti Pioneer* on Tuesday, 16 February 1960, a few months before the
presidential election. Odamtten there claimed that he had received phone calls
and had had interviews with important CPP members who had argued with
him that all people with the interest of the country (Ghana) at heart should
organize to oppose the Republic idea. When Odamtten asked them why they
could not come out openly to help the UP, which was against the republican
constitution, they replied: "Old man, because of our belly. We will be

The strength of the CPP lay not *primarily* in the ordinary Ghanian's devotion to Nkrumah on the grounds of his charisma, although one cannot rule out completely the popularity of Nkrumah as a national hero with charismatic attributes. To a great extent the strength of the CPP lay in the ability of both Nkrumah and the party, right from the beginning, to appeal to and mobilize generalized or shared instrumental values derived both from the still-important traditional Ghanaian cultures and the culture of Eurocolonialism by providing, as a government party, economic opportunities, jobs, and a sense of power to all classes of people, particularly the disadvantaged, on the almost sole basis of membership in the CPP. Thus, tribal, religious, or other primordial considerations were obviously made irrelevant. This and other policies of the CPP government — the setting up of the CPC to grant substantial loans and advances to cocoa farmers and the Africanization of the public services — contributed tremendously toward the creation of a sense of national identity and acted as an "agent of [national] unification."

Apter holds that political religion, a distinguishing characteristic of mobilization systems, is a device for national integration. In spite of the importance attributed to political religion, the concept remains vague. This may be because the concept of charisma itself needs to be explored further by Apter.[16] For instance, Apter is silent about the relationship between his political religion and the traditional or church religions of Ghana. The predominance of nominal

---

chucked off from our employment if we come out openly." As if to vindicate the fears of the CPP men whose statement has just been quoted, at a big CPP plebiscite rally held at the Bukom Square, Accra (at which the minister of state for special duties and N. A. Welbeck, acting general secretary of the CPP, had complained that civil servants who had voted against the CPP had had two membership cards — one CPP, the other UP — always in their pockets and produced them severally when challenged), Provençal had warned that "there are so many members of the CPP who are without jobs and those of the civil servants who voted for Danquah will all be dismissed and replaced by CPP men" (*Ashanti Pioneer*, 7 May 1960). The statement is significant whether the civil servants were in fact dismissed or not.

16. We are hardly assisted by Apter's apodeictic formulation ("Nkrumah, Charisma, and the Coup," p. 765) that " . . . charisma can arise in part when the increase in modernity is not met by a proportioned decline in 'traditionalism.' " This scarcely specifies unambiguously either the ratios involved or the necessary and sufficient conditions for the emergence of charisma, anywhere. His claim that Ghana's charismatic leader was part traditional and part modern, a sort of "political centaur," destroys, I think, whatever analytical clarity and usefulness the concept may possess.

Christians in Ghana who are not communicants or who, if they are, adhere strongly to traditional non-Christian customs, leads me to ask specifically who in Ghana adopted the personality cult of the divine Nkrumah so devoutly as to have influenced political development and modernization appreciably, and who accepted the political religion only in form? [17]

What empirical evidence we have indicates that Ghanaians have on the whole displayed a strong sense of commitment to modernity. They have generally accepted with remarkable enthusiasm Western-type education as soon as the material and high status payoffs have been clear to them and have embraced forms of Christianity and a wide range of modern technological skills and techniques. Since 1900 especially, administrative integration, cocoa farming, mineral production in the mines, and commercialization have combined to produce a complex pattern of migration and extensive urbanization and a heterogeneous social and occupational structure, as the Swedru example has shown. These are the factors that have continued to shape the society in the direction of increasing modernity. Ghanaians at all levels of society are committed to achieving economic mobility, a rising social status, and the personal satisfaction of having the wherewithal to meet one's extended family obligations. Fathers achieve high status vicariously and even realistically through the economic mobility of their sons and daughters.

But it is a "conservative" modernity that hardly aspires to creative innovation. It is modernity that aspires to privilege through high-status seeking and is desirous of well-paid and materially comfortable, mostly white-collar, occupations. In a poor or underdeveloped economy such as Ghana's, which hardly has the resources to expand rapidly, this modernist orientation has created institutionalized structural instability, making drastic political change inevitable. It is in this socioeconomic context that political change continues to occur.[18]

17. Apter's contentions ("Nkrumah, Charisma, and the Coup," p. 777) that "party officials formed the charismatic 'nucleus' for whom charisma *meant everything*" (my italics), and (ibid., p. 769) that "dissident marginals with the youth formed the basis for the charismatic following" are, at best, debatable on factual grounds.

18. Nkrumah commented on the situation thus: "Things had moved fast, the feeling of power was a new thing; the desire to possess cars, houses and other commodities that were regarded as necessities by the European population in the country, was not unnatural in people who were suddenly made to

What tied the follower to the political leader was, therefore, not charisma but economic necessity, a reciprocal tie that at times assumed the form of a patron-client relationship (and even the creditor-debtor connection discussed earlier). The relationship held so long as the patron honored his material and economic obligation, and the client his duty to vote at elections and perform various other services for the patron, including ritually praising him in public. Mass political mobilization is hardly possible in this situation.[19] The leadership directly contributed to the largely economic view of politics and reinforced it rather than changing it by responsible political education.[20]

It has been my contention that Apter's mobilization model and the theories derived from it are found misleading and cannot be demonstrated using the facts of Ghana's political development. Apter still has to explain the differential responses to Nkrumah. Was the image of Nkrumah the same among total and verbal members of the CPP (see my usage in chapters 6 and 7) as it was among members of the NLM or the UP? Why were independent candidates able to get nearly half as many votes as the CPP in the 1956 election? Did the independents combined have half as much charisma as Nkrumah? How do we explain the fact that, in the 1960 election, in Nkrumah's own constituency (Accra Central) Nkrumah polled 7,013 votes against Danquah's 4,692?[21] At this point we may

feel that they were being prepared to take over from the European; money, the wherewithal to obtain these luxuries, was tempting" (Nkrumah, *Autobiography*, p. 257). One of his ministers had been accused of accepting a two-thousand-pound bribe.

19. In this respect, I am at one with Anthony Astrachan when he realistically points out that "such 'politicization' as has occurred among Ghanaians has had as its main effect the translation of traditional participation in tribal [and colonial] affairs into a politics dominated by 'bread-and-butter' issues" (*Commentary* 45, no. 3, (March 1968) : 76).

20. In their campaign speeches at the 1960 presidential election, both the late Dr. Danquah (UP) and Dr. Nkrumah (CPP) could not go beyond saying: "I will pay the farmers £G5 a load for their cocoa, which the Government could easily pay even now, and I will give the worker a minimum basic pay of £G15 per month in order to ensure a dignified existence and comfortable standard of living for all the people," and "The test of the future would be the amount of purchasing power put into the hands of the workers and the farmers. . . ." respectively. *Ashanti Pioneer*, 29 June and 1 July 1960. See a comparison of the manifestoes of the CPP and the UGCC at the general election of 1951 in the Appendix.

21. To some of these questions, Apter ("Nkrumah, Charisma, and the Coup," p. 773) would reply that by 1955 charisma was dead in Ghana. In

turn to further exploration of the nature of political involvement in Ghana, examining particularly some aspects of voting behavior since electoral victories were used increasingly by the CPP to show that the "will of the people" was on their side, that it had a mass following, and that the people supported the leadership of the party.

SYMBOLIC-EXPRESSIVE, NORMATIVE, AND
INSTRUMENTAL POLITICAL INVOLVEMENT

An approach based on a modified model of motivational basis of action presented by Daniel Katz may be especially rewarding.[22] Katz states that individuals can be tied into a bureaucratic system in one of three ways or some combination of them. According to him: (1) Symbolic attachment refers to emotionally held attitudes in which the symbols represent absolute values and have a life of their own. They are not means to an end but are ends in themselves.[23] Again, symbolic involvement may have an entertainment value. I have called this type "symbolic-expressive" involvement. (2) Normative involvement on the other hand, says Katz, implies the acceptance of specific legitimate requirements of the system necessary for the system membership.[24] Thus one meets the demands of one's role because one wants to stay in the system, not because one is emotionally attached to signs representing its abstract values. (3) Finally, functional or instrumental involvement has to do with commitment to the system because its demands are instrumental to one's needs. Thus the party member may be committed to his party because it is a group means for dealing with his needs. Katz indicates that such a functional attachment is not limited to bread-and-butter matters. It

---

Swedru — to party officials like C. V. M. Forde, E. K. Bensah, Kofi Agyare, Yaw Ampadu, and Kwesi Armah, who remained faithful to the "cause" — was charisma really dead? Or was there no charisma to begin with?

22. In a recent article, "Group Process and Social Integration: A System Analysis of Two Movements of Social Protest," *Journal of Social Issues*, vol. 23, no. 1 (January 1967), Daniel Katz distinguishes three main types of involvement, namely, symbolic, normative, and instrumental.

23. This in some ways is very similar to Talcott Parsons's expressive orientation, in his expressive-instrumental continuum. About the expressive orientation Parsons writes: "The essential point is the primacy of 'acting out' the need disposition itself rather than subordinating gratification to a goal outside the immediate situation." Talcott Parsons and Edward A. Shils, editors, *Toward A General Theory of Action* (New York: Harper and Row, 1951), p. 348.

24. Normative commitment is not a unitary variable or factor; it may include intellectual, moral, ritualistic, communal, and other considerations.

can also be related to the individual's own values which find meaningful realization in group action which advances his beliefs and attitudes. This latter distinction is between an ideological commitment of a functional character, in which values are translated into specific programs of action, and symbolic attachment to nonoperational goals.

In the analysis of the political process and change in Ghana from 1950 to 1966 (covering the three phases of political development I have outlined) it is necessary to distinguish three types of political publics — that is, political actors or potential political actors — namely, (1) total members of political parties, (2) verbal members, and (3) all the adult population qualified to vote. Corresponding to some extent to the above types, we must further differentiate three broad types of political participation or mobilization: (1) electoral (which was the most crucial); (2) symbolic-expressive (rallies, "picnics," and parades associated with elections); and (3) what may be called doctrinal-ideological (attendance at party national ideological school or at local ideological study groups). The distinctions are important since they draw attention to and explain the differential effects on, or implications for, the political system of specific types of actors and their related forms of political action. The nature of political behavior was also closely associated with types of political involvement, as already defined.

Thus political actors participating in party rallies and parades, whether organized by the CPP or the NLM-UP, were very likely to show highly charged enthusiastic emotional behavior and to have a mass character. The rallies attracted huge crowds, both adults and minors, male and female, and members and nonmembers of the party which had organized them.[25] The behavior at rallies was radical. It was here that party leaders were excessively adulated or abused in songs, "worshipped" or attacked. Many of the interparty (even free-for-all) fights took place during or after rallies. It is significant to note that those who attended, say, CPP rallies did not necessarily vote CPP. In fact the evidence is clear that many did

25. This indiscriminate political participation disturbed some party leaders and, in fact, at a big CPP plebiscite victory rally held at the Bukom Square and already mentioned, N. A. Welbeck, then acting general secretary of the CPP, warned in these words: "We do not want sleeping CPP members. We want active members. *Definitely* some of the people who *attended* our *rallies* are *not* CPP. From now on we are going to count upon party members who attend *ward* meetings" (my italics).

not. Political involvement here was primarily symbolic-expressive and provided participants with immediate emotional gratification. This mass involvement had little to do with functional support for party organization and party objectives or normative redefinitions.

The behavior of voters, whether farmers or wage-workers, on the other hand, evinced much instrumental or functional involvement, as we shall see presently. Here parties and their leaders behaved very much like entrepreneurs who attempted to sell their party and candidates to the voters. Voters acted like consumers who aimed at maximizing their material returns from their votes. A majority of these voters were either verbal members of particular parties or nonmembers ready to sell support to the highest bidder. To these, party doctrines, manifestos, or ideologies were irrelevant. What mattered was the personality or credibility of party leaders and candidates. Total party members, however, behaved more consistently. They attended party rallies and ideological schools and voted always for a particular party. They were more likely to emphasize in public their normative involvement (CPP always, right or wrong). This latter group constituted the party bulwark. Unlike the *total members*, whose party affiliation was known to most constitutents, and most of whom held either executive offices and high party administrative positions or both and were definitely in the minority at all levels of party organization, the *verbal members* — such as the "floating" electors who were in the majority — acted less on the grounds of principle than on expediency. They were therefore hardly reliable political actors.

It must be pointed out again that the analytical distinctions do not make the claim that political participation was either exclusively instrumental or symbolic-expressive or purely normative, nor could it be.[26] It could be demonstrated empirically, for example, that the CPP, despite its nation-wide network of organizations and despite its great appeal, fell in 1966, without much organized protest or resistance, because of its inability, among other things, to recruit or mobilize members having primarily normative or ideological commitment to the party. The same accounted for the relative weakness of the NLM-UP complex. The basis of support in each case was

26. We are interested in the relative primacy of one mode or another of action. Knowledge of the relative primacy is invaluable in assessing the basis of organizational strength and in predicting its capacity to survive. It is also useful in demonstrating the real nature of the empirical behavior involved.

largely instrumental and to some extent symbolic-expressive, types of involvement which have little survival value. Organizations which are more instrumental in orientation will survive *ceteris paribus* as long as they have adequate economic resources to distribute to members. It is interesting to note that much of what Apter calls "political religion" headed by the divine Nkrumah could be described as various manifestations of symbolic-expressive involvement.[27]

Now to the factual account. Here I rely heavily on the committee findings and report of the famous Jibowu Commission of 1956; on the minutes of the Central Regional Conference of the CPP (1955); and on data from extensive interviews with many adults of all walks of life in Swedru, including ex-CPP and ex-UP members and officers, about the basis of political behavior in the region in the recent past.

The Cocoa Purchasing Company (CPC) was established in June 1952 by the CPP Government with an authorized share capital of two million pounds, with the primary object of purchasing cocoa in competiton with other long-established, mainly foreign, buying agents, such as Messrs. Cadbury and Fry. The CPC was also to make loans or advances to assist persons to purchase cocoa.[28] Within three years the CPC became the primary local cocoa-buying agent.

The fact is, when Nkrumah was a political prisoner in 1950, he had discussed with Ashie Nikoi the question of organizing the Gold Coast farmers as an independent body to enable them to bargain collectively for the sale of cocoa. Cocoa is still the mainstay of the national economy, and the Gold Coast farmers are perhaps the most important single group in the country. The Ghana Farmers Congress was formed as a result of the organizing of the farmers, but owing to differences between Ashie Nikoi and Nkrumah over the control which the CPP was to exercise over the Farmers Congress,

27. Symbolic involvement and instrumental involvement may be considered polar opposites on an action continuum. On the basis of the evidence, the symbolic-rally category had little significant consequence for the national political process and change. But the instrumental-electoral category had tremendous consequences for the system process and development. It was in this context that parties became national government, rose and fell, transforming the character of the political system.

28. The CPC was a subsidiary of the Cocoa Marketing Board (CMB) established in 1947 "to purchase, store, export, ship, sell or otherwise deal in cocoa" produced in the Gold Coast, including Ashanti and Trans-Volta Togoland.

there was a split therein. One part followed Ashie Nikoi and became the National Farmers Union, later associated with Opanyin Kwadwo Buor, one of the founders of the NLM in Ashanti. The other followed Nkrumah, was led by Dennis, and became the United Ghana Farmers Council (UGFC). It must be stressed that, because of the huge size of the farming population and the national economic role, particularly, of cocoa farmers, it was clear that he who controlled the farmers or had their support controlled the national political process and its outcome.

There is much evidence for concluding that only members of the UGFC were to be entitled to CPC loans and advances – in short, the UGFC and the CPC, the "atom bomb," were to be instruments of the CPP, the government party. For one thing, directors of the CPC were also members of the all-powerful, highest tribunal Central Committee of the CPP. In 1955, the Jibowu Commission sat to inquire into the allegations, going on since 1953 and later pressed by the NLM, of irregularities against the CPC which included: (1) that the CPC was controlled by the CPP; [29] (2) that funds of the CPC were used for the purposes of the CPP; (3) that the CPC financed CPP organizations by means of spurious loans to fictitious or nonexistent persons, secured by equally fictitious or nonexistent farmers; (4) that only UGFC members, who were CPP members, were given loans;[30] (5) that CPC vehicles were used for CPP election purposes; and (6) that loans and advances were given to influence the 1954 and 1956 general elections.

The CPC operated thirty-eight districts – including a famous, perhaps notorious, one in Agona-Swedru – which administered 1,960 buying centers throughout Ghana. The operation of the CPC in Swedru was very interesting, to say the least.[31] Every adult who was in Swedru between 1952 and 1956 still recalls vividly the hey-

29. The problem here was distinguishing party control as such and control by the party in power. Nkrumah had said that the "proper constitutional position is for the Government of the day to accept ultimate political responsibility for the *disposal* of *public funds* and for the conduct of statutory authorities which are entrusted with such funds." Nkrumah, *Autobiography*, p. 257.

30. The importance of the loans or advances was that they assisted the many farmers throughout the country whose farms had been confiscated as a result of their indebtedness to European-owned cocoa-buying firms and to African middlemen and brokers, to redeem their farms. Note that the 1948 Commission report on the riots of that year had singled out the indebtedness of farmers as one cause of the disturbance.

31. It must be remembered that, until 1958, Swedru was both the local and the regional (Central Region) center of the CPP.

day of the CPC, whose headquarters on the Nsawam road is now occupied by the National Nutrition Board, when, as one Kwahu trader put it, "Trade was very brisk, and you could sell anything at any price; haggling was out in most cases," and the farmer or the pseudo-farmer carrying his briefcase containing *only* one thousand pounds he has just collected from the CPC in loans or advances, was as conspicuous in Swedru as the flow of the Akora River. That the CPC financed the CPP in the Central Region, the stronghold of the CPP, was admitted by both ex-CPP and non-CPP members in Swedru. The independent evidence is also clearly corroborative, as we shall see below. The superior electoral strength of the CPP in the Central Region lay in no small measure in the support given the CPP by the CPC.

The loans docket of James S. Bansah, a Fante driver, who in the 1960s became the CPP chairman for Ward I, Swedru (exhibit 10, Jibowu Commission), shows that a loan of £3,200 out of the sum of £5,500 for which he applied, which was not recommended by the supervisor of Swedru area, was approved and granted on 29 September 1953 by Dennis, because in this case and others "applicants are all very staunch Party [CPP] members in the area." Nevertheless, Dennis was aware of the relative instability of party membership or support based primarily on substantial money grants. In a letter to Djin, the acting managing director of the CPC in December 1953 (exhibit 121), he pointed out very realistically and warned in paragraph 4 that "as politicians having the interest and solidarity of our party [CPP] at heart, we should always have in mind that we *depend mostly* on the *farming community* in this country *for votes* to *remain in power* to enable us to carry out for a *long time* and *successfully* what our gallant and noble leader [Nkrumah] has established for the farmers" (my italics). One point needs to be stressed here, and that is the great reliance of the CPP, or the NLM for that matter, on the farmers, on the rural vote not the urban, to remain in power.

The very close symbiotic relationship between the CPC and the CPP in the Swedru area, and its significance for electoral mobilization and the implication of strong instrumental involvement of political participants as I have discussed it, are again obvious from the contents of other correspondence, this time from the Teacher Okai Farmers Group (Teacher Okai is a small but important cocoa-buying center a few miles from Swedru on the Nsaba road) to Djin, dated February 1955. The contents of the letter (exhibit 126) warrant quoting at some length. Note that the 1956 pre-independence general election was about a year away.

As many of the cocoa farmers in the Swedru districts were disappointed, as no loans could be given them any longer after making [incurring] such expenses, that they were approached by underground workers of the National Liberation Movement [note the similiarity of the strategy of NLM-CPP] in the name of Cadbury [the British buying firm] offering strong promises to pay their loans; (5) that there was a plan from the National Liberation Camp to win the farmers from the Convention People's Party and the CPC. The NLM had succeeded to get [in getting] Messrs. Cadbury and Fry to grant loans to farmers and *all our farmers are being enticed into their* [NLM] *fold with heavy* [money] *advances* which the farmers were using to pay part of their debts involving their cocoa farms.

In fact this action of the NLM was breaking down our Centre and others. *It was a real threat to the general organization of the CPC and the CPC.* It became appalling danger to our Party in power [CPP] and our dear Company – CPC. (6) That as a responsible body now operating, we Teacher Okai Centre Executive [of CPP] decided to combat the situation. We began to hold meetings and devised ways and means of rubbing shoulders with farmers in their villages and even [on their] farms. By this means we came to learn that most of them had taken heavy advances from Cadbury and Fry for which each farmer had secured [pledged] his cocoa farm. (7) That we were able to convince most of them to restore confidence in the CPC upon our assurance that we shall move Heaven and Earth to get their loans paid. That these farmers imposed on us one condition, namely – to give each sufficient advance for refunding same to Cadbury to free themselves from there and to deduct same from their respective loans when paid. (8) That although we had no power to use purchases money for this campaign, yet as the position was such that little *delay on our part would cause heavy damages to our Party in power* [CPP] and the CPC *we became compelled* to storm the weather *by giving out advances* in question and we saw [to] it well that they are [were] paid to Cadbury as refund of the advances reported. Thus we captured Farmers and villages some of which we at once transferred . . . into sub-Centres under Teacher Okai Centre. . . . [My italics.]

In conclusion the Teacher Okai Executive congratulated themselves that they had "*annihilated* them [the NLM] and their plans could not work." The Jibowu Commission later found that, in Swedru alone, about £60,000 given out by the CPC was unsupported by agreements or any loan dockets! In July–August 1955 loans to a total of £175,091 were given out at Swedru, according to the Swedru loan cash sheets. These figures are very significant and astounding for a poor country with limited resources. For the present study the important fact to note is the characteristic behavior of the farmers. It is clear that they were ready to vote for any party which was equally prepared to give them "sufficient money advances" to redeem their pledged farms. The primarily instrumental basis of their political behavior was unmistakable and was even encouraged by both the NLM and the CPP. The point was very well understood by the party leaders, who realized the material rewards of political power.

Lest we need additional evidence, let us turn to the February 1955 Central Regional Conference of the CPP held at the Columbia Cinema Hall, Swedru. Incidentally, this conference was held at least six months before the Jibowu Commission sat. Each constituency branch of the CPP in the Central Region attending sent four delegates to the conference as provided in the Party Constitution.[32] On the instructions of the headquarters in Accra, Agyare was appointed conference chairman.[33]

The constituencies represented at the CPP Central Regional Conference were (1) Agona, (2) Agona-Swedru, (3) Awutu, (4) Eastern Gomoa, (5) North Birim, (6) South Birim, (7) Adjumako-Esikuma, (8) Ekumfi-Enyan, (9) Saltpond, (10) Assin, (11) Abura-

32. The agenda for the conference read: (1) Election of representatives to form the new National Executive; (2) The party's organization; (3) The CPC; (4) Other matters. It was signed by Kofi Agyare, Regional Propaganda Secretary, Swedru.
33. It is interesting that Agyare was at this time employed as a roving supervisor of the Swedru CPC. It merits noting that Agyare admitted in a personal interview with me that he totally disagreed with how the affairs of the CPC were being handled. Agyare pointed out, for instance, that at the end of the March 1954 cocoa season (1954 was an election year) loans given to farmers in the Swedru district and still outstanding amounted to about sixty thousand pounds.
At a meeting of the farmers' executive of the Central Region and senior officials of the CPC, held in March 1954 in Swedru, including Djin (acting managing director), Agyare, and Eduful (loans officer), the farmers were warned that unless the amount outstanding was defrayed no further advances would be forthcoming. It must be indicated that in a number of cases farmers or presumed farmers had been asked to pay amounts in excess of what they had originally received. The reason for this was that when farmers had asked for, say, five hundred pounds as a loan and had been given that amount, CPC loans officers had entered, say, one thousand pounds as the loan given, thus making use of the difference of five hundred pounds. This type of extortion inflated amounts actually going to farmers. Agyare believed that "it was the CPC which brought into being the NLM," perhaps to challenge CPP financial control of CPC and the farmers. Many prominent Ashanti cocoa farmers had been denied advances and loans for one reason or another.

Asebu, and (12) Cape Coast Municipal; absent were Elmina and Western Gomoa. The attendance was impressive and testifies to the interest in the party of the total members in the region and to the organizational effectiveness of the executive of the CPP. The National Headquarters was represented by C. V. M. Forde, the Sierra-Leonean chairman of the SUC and general secretary of the CPP. In attendance were Hon. Kojo Botsio, minister of state and M.P. for Western Gomoa and Hon. Kofi Baako. Botsio's presence perhaps explains the absence of delegates from Western Gomoa. The conference was conducted, it should be stressed, in accordance with the directive and agenda from National Headquarters. The CPP was a fairly centralized organization, with respect to most party decisions.

The conference opened with one of the delegates for Assin taking the general secretary to task for disallowing complaints about the requirement that financial contributions from CPP M.P.'s to the constituencies be made through the National Headquarters. The Assin delegate felt the M.P.'s could contribute directly to the constituency chest. Contributions paid through the National Headquarters rarely got down to the constituencies. The centralized financial control was obviously intended to strengthen the hand of National Headquarters, making the local and regional levels subservient to the national level. After the first speaker, another delegate from Assin, Bobbie-Ansah, took the floor.

> We want to take this opportunity of welcoming our Minister of State and the Ministerial Secretary and to place before the Minister of State the failure of CPC . . . management in the giving out of loans to fulfill the [1954] election promises to our farmers; namely the redemption of their pledged cocoa farms . . . [; that] loans were not forthcoming is breaking down the Party [CPP] and we want to know what our leaders are doing in the matter.

To this Hon. Kofi Baako replied that he and other leaders had already met Djin, who had convinced them that farmers who had received loans in the past had refused to refund them, and so the CPC could not give out any further loans. This, of course, met with strong disapproval of the delegates.

Ampiah immediately retorted:

> There are numerous malpractices in the loans operation which are reacting on the CPP itself and damaging the Party [and with which] Djin says it has no connection.

S. K. Mbroh Eastern Gomoa, took up the issue.

Our brother Kofi Baako cannot convince us. Some of the loans were given out at random. How can a person who does not know our farmers [those who support CPP] be given the power to give them the loans? Some of the supervisors never knew the farmers. We have those who know the farmers very well in our area, but would not be chosen to handle the work. The so-called field inspectors came to kill the farmers and not to save them.

After a few speeches in this vein by other delegates, Bobbie-Ansah moved the following resolution, which was adopted.

Mr. Chairman, I move that in view of the glaring fact that Mr. Djin's CPC management is breaking down the CPP, this Conference does place on record that this state of affairs in our onward march [is] to be deplored, [and that we act] to bring pressure on Nkrumah and other leaders to restore confidence in our farmers.

This resolution was typical of many, and is obviously far from near-emotional acceptance of the leadership of a charismatic ruler. Here shrewd calculation of economic interest was at the basis of party and electoral support. It is again significant that at the meeting of the Working Committee of the CPP in the Central Region in Swedru (held soon after the Regional Conference), Kwesi Armah strongly deplored the fact that there were fewer CPP members working in the CPC in Swedru and suggested that arrangement should be made to have more CPP members on the staff of the CPC.[34] In this way, party finance, which had hitherto depended mainly on proceeds from harvests, concerts, dances held throughout the region, contributions by M.P.'s, membership fees, and other personal contributions, all of which added up to a small sum, could be greatly assisted.[35]

THE STRATEGY OF THE ELECTORAL CAMPAIGN AND THE POVERTY OF MASS MOBILIZATION

At this stage, we may consider the electoral strategy that was adopted, particularly by the CPP field organizers, for the light it

34. The meeting was attended by Mary Koranteng, Kwesi Armah (the controversial ex-Ghana high commissioner in London), S. K. Mbroh, P. C. Awittor, and Kofi Agyare. The committee unanimously endorsed a unitary form of government in a memorandum to the Select Committee on Federal Form of Government and Second Chamber Legislature, appointed by the government.

35. Incidentally, one of the party executives in Swedru alleged that Kwesi Armah, later on in 1957, left the country for the U.K., taking with him all the proceeds of a dance held in Swedru in honor of the late George Padmore!

throws on the nature of political mobilization and the political process. I would like to suggest at once that elections in Ghana, as I have argued, were generally non–issue oriented. Using Fenton's categories, political participation in Swedru had always been predominantly reward- and "job-oriented," with people competing and voting out of a desire for jobs, benefits, contracts, and other personal or community material gains (where there was a strong communal spirit) rather than because of a concern for public policy or the national interest as such.[36]

It should be mentioned that quite a lot of men and women in Swedru participated very actively in party politics just for the fun of it, for ceremonial entertainment, or for ego fulfillment, a condition which prevailed especially in the context of "Super-monster" rallies, party processions, and electioneering. But ultimately only a plenitude of patronage sustained the political process.

The Problem of Basic Party Education

The strategy adopted by party organizers and campaigners, both CPP and NLM-UP, at the local levels during election years and interelection periods largely ignored party ideological education. Effective transmission of educational content of any kind takes time and energy and demands continuous reinforcement of what is learned. Ghana's "Age of Ideology," 1960–65, produced many books, such as *Neocolonialism, the Last Stage of Imperialism*, mainly written by Nkrumah and inflammatory articles on socialism in various national newspapers and the *Spark*. Yet the few Ghana-

36. See J. H. Fenton, *People and Parties in Politics* (Glenview: Scott, Foresman and Co., 1966), pp. 51–77. An example of a case in which communal considerations influenced political decisions and behavior flowing from them would be the resolution of confidence in W. A. C. Essibrah as Agona candidate for the Legislative Assembly, sent to the Central Committee of the CPP by the majority of the fifteen members of the CPP executive of the Agona Western Constituency, dated 30 March 1954. When the resolution was made, six other CPP members had already filed their applications as candidates for Agona. In the resolution it was emphasized that an "overwhelming majority" of the constituents "have already felt the good work" of Essibrah, who as president of the Nyakrom Town Board "has built a modern market, lorry park, dispensary and a Methodist Girls' Boarding School for Nyakrom." The petitioners reminded the Central Committee that "despite our hatred [as loyal CPP members] for tribalism" they considered any person, Agona and non-Agona alike, who had not been living with the people "a real opportunist come only to sap the juice out of the Agona(s)." The resolution was accepted and Essibrah, an Agona, became the official CPP candidate for Agona Western in the 1956 general election.

ians who could read *and* understand the contents paid little heed to them. Many were convinced that socialism did not apply to the daily circumstances of life in Ghana. A majority of the population are illiterate, and they knew from experience, along with the workers and farmers, that what really mattered in Ghana was how much money one had available at any moment. They were more interested in the price paid to cocoa farmers and wages than in socialism. They could not see the immediate connection between socialism and the price of cocoa. Where a relationship was seen to exist, it was reversed. In a letter to the *Ashanti Pioneer*, for 1 July 1960, when Ghana became a republic, a citizen asked rather characteristically: "If Ghana is all that rich [paying her M.P.'s £150 a month, including allowances] . . . why can it [the good salary] not be extended to all her citizens. . . ?[37] That indeed will mean real Freedom for all. If we must work towards social Freedom [socialism] then something *must* be done for the poor worker and farmer through whose toil and sweat the country derives her huge revenue. We hear of developments taking place here and there but *where* are they in reality?" (My italics).

What party education went on in CPP study groups, which met infrequently in Swedru, was unsystematic, haphazard, and irregular. The district party education secretary admitted that he could not devote much time to education work. But he could have devoted more time to ideological communication if, like his counterpart at the regional level, who was receiving over one thousand pounds per annum, he had been remunerated. All the same, the minutes of the education secretary indicated that the few times the study groups met (in theory there was to be at least one meeting a week), with no more than thirty people attending each time, discussions were centered on some of the most recent speeches of the president. One of these was the famous "Dawn Speech" of 1961 in which the excessive financial interests of ministers and M.P.'s were severely attacked, and the address at the formal opening of the national Kwame Nkrumah Ideological Institute at Winneba, fifteen miles from Swedru.

The sixty-one-page, catechism-like *The ABC of Socialism*, prescribed as basic reading, was obviously hardly read, judging by the number of unsold copies in the possession of the district education

37. The basic problem is certainly how the national income was distributed or allocated to citizens, who make up classes and other socioeconomic groups.

secretary in Swedru, in 1967.[38] Although the education secretary attended the periodic ideological refresher course for all party education secretaries at the Ideological Institute, he frankly admitted that "we were ourselves confused as regards what was being taught, perhaps it was only Nkrumah who knew what it was all about."

But everybody knew what elections were all about. Consequently, a consideration of the electoral process and how the party electoral machine worked in practice would be fruitful. In Swedru, despite the strong emphasis by the CPP on a united national solidarity front and the party's attack on tribalism and primordial loyalties, in reality CPP (and NLM-UP) electoral mobilization took the practical form of exploiting ethnic-tribal solidarities and similar ties or conflicts by using chiefs, elders, and community influentials as brokers or mediators wherever possible. Traditionalism was therefore incorporated, albeit uncomfortably and even with embarrassment, into the very foundations of the new process of national integration.

Chiefs, local influentials, and notables were carefully and judiciously coopted both formally and informally into the local and national party bureaucracy, sometimes as executive officers. Many of the clan and lineage elders in Swedru became party chairmen in their various wards; however, the party saw to it that, whenever kinship and party interests conflicted, the latter came first. The primary basis of national integration through the CPP bureaucracy was that the party as a national organization made the national cake a real one to which the Ga, the Nzema, the Ashanti, the Talensi, and all the tribes of Ghana had a right to and received an adequate share of, thanks to such practices as excessive patronage — provided, of course, that they respected "good CPP organizational lines." I have considered electioneering and voting as both processes of political participation and mechanisms of unification through individual memberships and the networks of party organization and leadership.

It goes without saying that Swedru, as a center of both local-constituency and regional organizations of the CPP, played an effective mediating role between the surrounding rural areas and the national capital and that the very mobile national party executive

---

38. Leo Huberman and Sybil H. May, *The ABC of Socialism* (copyright by *Monthly Review*, New York; reprinted in Accra, Ghana: Government Guinea Press, Ltd., 1953).

forged durable links (or merely reinforced already existing ones) between the region, of which Swedru is the ecological and functional center, and the national society.[39] By the model of Bailey, the rural, the constituency-regional, and national political arenas all converged on Swedru through party organization and leadership action.[40] The various levels may therefore be thought of as truly a single socio-political system. C. V. M. Forde was at once the chairman of the Swedru constituency organization of CPP, chairman of the SUC, and general secretary of the CPP.

We have already discussed how party functionaries had traveled throughout Ghana in the 1950s "Cippippifying" the country. The equation was "one people, one party, one nation, one destiny." I mentioned that one of the notable figures in this nationalist effort was Kofi Agyare, a Kwahu who in 1954 was the CPP regional propaganda secretary, Central Region, Swedru. About five weeks before the 1954 general election, on 6 May 1954, to be exact, Agyare received a letter, one of many, from the regional secretary of CPP, Eastern Region, at Koforidua requesting propaganda and electioneering assistance to insure the success at the election of the official CPP candidate for the New Juaben constituency in the Eastern Region.

Kofi Agyare, by now nationally conceded to be one of the most experienced party propaganda secretaries in the country, accepted the Eastern Region invitation. Although Nkrumah was still the country's popular "show boy," the background information requested by Agyare from his counterpart in the Eastern Region, on the basis of which his Eastern campaign was waged, demonstrated beyond any doubt the poverty of charisma as a mobilization and integrative device and the relative efficacy of carefully calculated, shrewd, and realistic procedure. All the way through, the CPP had to fight a fierce and at times ruthless battle, relying mostly on the redoubtable weapons of patronage, spoils, and the state machinery such as the police, and depending for leverage on the skills of its organizers, such as Agyare, for victory at elections.

The questionnaire sent to the regional secretary at Koforidua by

39. Some of the national party executives, such as C. V. M. Forde, were residents of Swedru.
40. S. G. Bailey, *Politics and Social Change: Orissa in 1959* (Berkeley: University of California Press, 1963).

Agyare was interesting. Immediate information was wanted on the following:

1. What are the special difficulties in the constituency and in the region?

2. What are the difficult areas in the constituency?

3. What is the nature of the personal relations between (a) the candidate and the executive of the CPP, (b) the candidate and the chiefs and elders, and (c) the candidate and the electorate?

4. Who are likely to contest the candidate in the constituency?

5. Who are agents or likely agents of the CPP candidates' opponents?

6. What is the strength of other parties in the constituency and what is the basis of such strength?

The point about the above questions raised by Agyare is that they were all perceived as obstacles to successful electoral mobilization and must be carefully and thoroughly dealt with if one wanted to be elected.[41] Let us now go back for a moment to take another look at party rallies and their relationship to political mobilization.

The "Super-Monster" Rally and the Political Process

One phenomenon in the political context — apart from the activities of the familiar noisy propaganda van of the political parties and individuals exhorting the electorate to vote CPP, NLM, or for Mr. X — which attracted observers of political behavior was the party rally. In fact, the size of attendance at the largely urban political rally was considered as an index of the popularity of a party and even as popular demonstration of the legitimacy of the authority of the ruling party. To some, especially the participating leadership and the executive officers of the party, the rally was the highest form of political expression and involvement. And so it was, but it was bound to its own immediate situation. Here it was said that the rank and file became acquainted with the national and local leadership.

There is a kernel of important truth in all this, yet it would be grossly misleading to claim that most of the participants at these party rallies were there to seriously approve of party leaders or help them make significant national political decisions. We have already noted the statement by N. A. Welbeck, acting general secretary of

41. Incidentally, a similar questionnaire was used by me to probe certain aspects of political behavior in Swedru.

CPP in 1960, that many of those attending CPP rallies were against the CPP. Again, anyone familiar with conditions in West African societies knows the relative centrality of outdoor life and how easy it is to draw large crowds — provided, of course, that there is recorded music or singing and drumming. That music, song, and rallies, like the ubiquitous CPP "picnics," went together cannot be denied.

In most instances, the rally was considered a social event at which the behavior that mattered was primarily social and ceremonial. Participation in politics here was at best symbolic-expressive, in terms of the definition already given. In any case, many of the attendants were too young to vote. It is again an undeniable fact that the huge crowds, at either the Arena or Bukom Square in Accra; Chapel Square in Cape Coast; Olympia Park in Swedru; and Abbey Park, Kumasi, were all assembled by their skillful leaders (who believed in their tremendous ability to draw crowds) only to be informed enthusiastically what had been decided already and to be asked for their symbolic approval. In the highly charged emotional atmosphere of the rally there was little room for rational debates and development of rational solutions to practical problems facing the nation and the people. The whole scene had elements of a play in which the principal political actors, the party leaders, played up to the gallery, the mass gathering, many of whom were not even qualified and registered voters. No argument was tolerated. An incident at a CPP rally held in 1952 at the Olympia Park, Swedru, will illustrate the hortatory-declaratory nature.

In a pre–1951 general election speech in Swedru, Nkrumah is believed to have declared his stand against the compulsory cutting of cocoa, a measure aimed at preventing the spread of the deadly swollen-shoot disease that was killing cocoa trees in Ghana. Nkrumah knew the cocoa farmers were against the compulsory "destruction" of their primary source of wealth, status, and livelihood. It is claimed that farmers voted for Nkrumah because of his stand on the swollen-shoot question. When Nkrumah was elected and became the Leader of Government Business, however, he changed his mind and supported the so-called New Deal for cocoa, which to the farmers was not different from compulsory cutting. As we may recall, the New Deal consisted of higher compensation for diseased trees voluntarily removed. Nana Kum, an anti-CPP figure in Swedru, took Nkrumah to task at a subsequent post-election CPP victory rally on the cocoa question. He demanded an explanation from

Nkrumah about why he had deceived the people. The way Nana
Kum was dealt with was typical. Nkrumah, of course, did not even
attempt to explain his apparent inconsistency. He merely called
Nana Kum onto the raised wooden platform from which leaders
spoke and asked him to repeat his question over the microphone,
which he did. Then Welbeck, CPP National Executive member and
from the same town as Nana Kum, asked the crowd to boo the latter. Nana Kum was accordingly and uproariously booed. When the
crowd expressed anger, as the above example shows, it was spontaneous, and if anything it was only to push the leaders to get on with
whatever they, the leaders, had promised to do. CPP rallies usually
began with a very loud "freedom" song, followed at times by the
Christian hymn "Lead Kindly Light." The hymn gave the rally a
solemn or ritual flavor. The crowd roared and shouted and clapped
to whatever the leaders said. This was hardly an effective and lasting way of mobilizing people for responsible support of national political leadership and leadership decisions. Nkrumah rose and fell
not because of waning charisma or the unsuccessful routinization of
it, but primarily because of the difficulties created in the support
base, its fragility. Emotional outbursts were soon spent, leaving only
the certain but exhaustible patronage. Rallies could scarcely act as a
vehicle for the institutionalization of new norms and of legitimation
of new authority.

Popular demonstrations, public adulation of national leaders —
call these "political religion" — were, after all, symbolic-expressive,
even ritual, acts which had little capacity to cope with a national
economic crisis that hit at the very roots of graft and patronage and,
of course, severely affected people's material well-being.[42] Nkrumah's regime relied too much on party patronage and instrumental
popular mobilization. When the basis of patronage suffered, the regime lost its friends.[43] In Ghana, the social revolution, which received greater momentum with the introduction of cocoa as a cash
crop, has continued to be a revolution primarily of rising materialis-

42. I agree with K. A. B. Jones-Quartey when he observed that "the political structure will break down and politicians [be] swept out of power *only* if
and when economic and social progress suffers a severe setback." K. A. B.
Jones-Quartey, "Institutions of Public Opinion in a Rapidly Changing West
Africa," in *Africa, The Dynamics of Change*, K. A. B. Jones-Quartey and H.
Passin, editors (Nigeria: Ibadan University Press, 1959), p. 165.
43. The regime's enemies were equally embittered by a tottering economy,
inflation, arbitrary and almost indiscriminate arrests and detention, and suppres-
sion of popular criticism.

tic expectations which are intolerant of frustrations based on economic deprivation. Insofar as greater control and conspicuous consumption of wealth remain the primary basis of achieving high social status and prestige in Ghanaian society, and as high status-respect continues to be the primary goal of social action, the struggle between classes and groups of people to accumulate and subsequently consume wealth to maintain or achieve high social status will ever remain. For Ghanaians still lack the ascetic impulse, associated, for instance, with Hindu *Weltanschauung*, which makes a virtue of material suffering and hardship.

In the next chapter I shall discuss the one-party state in Ghana, its structure and process, from the perspective of Swedru.

9 THE ONE-PARTY STATE
Structure and Process

In the last chapter, I made a strong case, on the basis of our evidence from Swedru, against the explanatory usefulness of some of Apter's categories, particularly his notion of "charisma" and "political religion" in the analysis of the political development in Ghana under Nkrumah. It was demonstrated that the crucial ties between Nkrumah and the CPP leadership on the one hand, and the rank and file of the people on the other, were not based primarily on the "highly personal experience of heavenly grace . . . and the godlike strength of the hero," Nkrumah — a consideration that would be especially relevant in mass religious movements. (We should be careful not to confuse the Ghanaian love of pomp, royalty, and social ceremony with the charisma of leadership.) Rather, these ties were based on what I have called group or individual fundamental instrumental commitment to the party and goverment. It is, therefore, narrow if not fallacious to argue, as Bretton does, that Nkrumah's personal rule was the "sole unchallenged repository of power, influence and coercion in Ghana" until the military coup.[1]

What is often not realized is that the D.C.'s at the local level and the regional commissioners (R.C.'s) at the regional level sometimes wielded and exercised "tyrannical" power which Nkrumah could not control and often did not approve of. They even made, with relative impunity, policy statements which were often in conflict with what Nkrumah had publicly announced.[2] The fact is still that the CPP and Nkrumah survived, that the leadership of the party was legitimate, as long as they succeeded in meeting effectively the

1. H. L. Bretton, *The Rise and Fall of Kwame Nkrumah: A Study of Personal Rule in Africa* (London: Pall Mall Press, 1966).
2. Witness the incessant warnings at CPP conferences and executive meetings, particularly between 1961 and 1965, that "policy statements are presidential," "conflicting unauthorized statements are harmful," and that "no statement is valid without presidential or cabinet approval." Thus, CPP officials did not always function merely as "derivative agents" of Nkrumah.

economic and material demands of the small-scale farmers and workers on whom the CPP depended for votes. (It is interesting to note that Nkrumah saw mass political participation primarily, perhaps even only, in terms of their exercise of the franchise.)

We divided the political development of Ghana between 1950 and 1966 into three broad phases: (1) 1951–58; (2) 1958–61; and (3) 1961–66. So far we have dealt more fully with the first phase and only sketchily with the last two. In this chapter and in the next we take up the last two phases and indicate with case materials that the most outstanding feature of this latter period was the CPP's increasing dominance at all levels of society, through the de facto and de jure elimination of almost all constituted, *open* opposition (represented by the UP), the control of society and economy by the party, and the CPP's culmination in a legal one-party state in 1964.

At the local level (in Swedru), in any case, the development with the most drastic consequences for the local population was the embarkation in 1961 by the government on an ambitious program for enlarging state (or party) control of the economy and breaking the hold on it of British and other European interests. The government's intention was given adequate and clear expression in a letter to the SUC (no. SCR. 0359), marked "confidential" and signed by the acting secretary to the cabinet.

I am commanded by Osagyefo, The President, to inform you that the Bank of Ghana has been empowered to hold, on behalf of the Government, all the sterling or foreign exchange reserves of the Central Government, Local Authorities and Statutory Boards and Corporations.

The aim was "to bring about a *centralized* economic planning" and "to *control* external budgetary expenditure" (my italics). There were now four sectors of the national economy, all of which were controlled in various ways by the central government: (1) the state sector, (2) the joint state and private sector (this was to ensure direct government participation in the profits of private monopolies), (3) the cooperative sector, and (4) the private sector.

The private sector, made up principally of Euro-American, Levantine, and other foreign firms and business concerns, was controlled through high taxation, restrictions on repatriation overseas of profits, and control of imports through the difficulty of obtaining import licenses. In fact, some of the firms were taken over by the government and the owners compensated. This happened in the

case of A. G. Leventis and Commonwealth Trust, Ltd., with
branches throughout Ghana, which became in 1962 the Ghana National Trading Company (GNTC). All the measures were deemed
necessary in the national interest.[3]

I have already discussed the heavy reliance of the local Kwahu,
Fante, and other petty traders and storekeepers on European firms
for generous credits and goods advances which made it possible for
the traders to stay in business at all. The fact that the UAC could
not import easily the merchandise to restock its inventories meant
that the African traders were not able to receive the goods advances
they needed so badly. Stores grew emptier and emptier; trade fell;
and commerce, the very life blood of Swedru and the outlying
areas, suffered tremendously. Consequently, many of the migrant
traders who were forced out of business, resorted occasionally to
hoarding and trading in the black market or left Swedru for Accra-
Tema, where trade and commerce still remained relatively brisk.

The government's imposition of property *tax* (this should be distinguished from the local property *rate* paid to the urban council)
made matters worse financially for these traders, many of whom
were also property owners. The alienation of this class of people
from the CPP was complete.

The GNTC, "The People's Shop," which should have assisted indigenous petty traders in Swedru (and could have, since it was in a
better position to import goods), failed in that duty. The management was controlled by the D.C. and the local CPP executive. Re-
ceipts for obtaining goods were to be signed by the local manager
and approved by the D.C., the most senior executive member of the
CPP at the district-local level. GNTC became a source of CPP patronage. Only the supporters or members of the party and friends
and favorites of the D.C., who often personally supervised the distribution of essential but scarce goods, could hope to receive them.

When the CPP "traders" obtained the goods, they usually resold
them to eager and waiting customers at from 100 percent to 300

3. In Swedru, the restrictions on and the difficulties of obtaining import license by the large European firms — UAC, GBO, etc. — led especially in the
third phase to a reduction in the scale of operation of these firms. They limited
their operation to those places — such as, Accra and Tema — where they were
certain of enjoying comparative advantage. The UAC, for example, closed
down its wholesale outlet in Swedru and transferred to Tema the workers who
were willing to move. Those who could not move, for family and other reasons,
lost their jobs.

percent profit. The customers in turn retailed the merchandise at still more exorbitant prices to other retailers before it finally reached the consumer, who had to pay an inflationary price for the items. The closing down of Cadbury and Fry and other European cocoa-purchasing agents by legislation in 1962 also pushed many of the African middlemen and cocoa brokers working for these firms out of business.

Again, in January 1961, a letter from the regional office, Cape Coast, to the SUC notified the urban council that the government had taken over administration of all stool lands in the region and had appointed an administrator of stool lands.[4] The power to collect all stool land revenue, inclusive of — and this was very important — any part formerly considered as the stool's share, was now delegated to local authorities with the "request" that all such monies were to be paid into the government treasury. This was almost the straw which broke the chiefs' backs.[5] Through fiscal and monetary control, the CPP government hoped to achieve unanimity by monopolizing all power and authority, including the bases of power and authority.[6]

The chiefs and elders were aware that their authority and influence were intricately bound up with the amount of local economic resources they could control and use in generating local socioeconomic development. The chiefs lost power and influence to

4. Note that, under the Local Government Act of 1961, the minister of justice became responsible for local government. The minister had power to delegate some of his powers in respect of local authorities to regional commissioners, who normally approved estimates of local authorities on behalf of the minister of justice. D.C.'s also advised local and urban councils.

5. The interesting fact is that the government was clearly aware of the financial-economic basis of the chiefs' power and authority. In fact, during the third phase, allowances paid to intransigent chiefs by the central government were very irregular.

6. At the 2 June 1967 post-coup meeting of the Standing Committee of the Agona Traditional Council, held at the palace of the gyasehene in Swedru, the following motions (unanimously carried) reflected some of the crucial trouble areas in the relationship of the traditional council with the central government:

a. Monthly allowances to chiefs to be paid regularly. (In the second and third phases such allowances were all but suspended.)

b. The reinstitution of local police under local councils. (The role of the local police in local authority finance will be discussed presently.)

c. The introduction of cocoa surtax in the traditional area to boost local socioeconomic development.

d. Increase in the price of cocoa paid to local farmers (and all other farmers).

e. The cessation of unauthorized persons' purchasing cocoa.

the extent that they and the people came to rely almost totally upon the central government as the source of economic development and material rewards.

The monopolizing tendency of the CPP during the second and third phases was total. It embraced not only the economic (though the economic was fundamental), but the social and political realms. In Swedru, control of social and political activities was even clearer. It began with the destruction of the relatively competitive urban council elections, which until 1958 had been familiar facts of life in town — at least in theory if not in practice. Apart from an occasional uncontested ward, all the twelve electoral wards had been more or less contested between 1952 and 1958, resulting in a slight CPP majority. Put another way, between 1952 and 1958, with the presence in the council of members appointed by traditional authorities and members popularly elected, all the major class-status interests in Swedru had a chance of being effectively represented. This was to change after 1958, as we shall soon see.

There is no doubt that from 1957, Independence Year, until about the end of 1962, the increase in the influence of the CPP throughout Ghanaian society was incontrovertible. This could be explained partly in terms of the attraction of power and the associated money, and partly in terms of the great socioeconomic reform, symbolized by such features as more schools and hospitals, first-class roads, the implementation of the Volta River project, better price for cocoa, and increased Africanization of higher civil service, which meant more money available to the people of almost all walks of life for a better standard of living. There was (and still is) a strong desire in the population to be on the winning side. At the national level this tendency was reflected in the hurried and confused "crossing of the carpet" in the national Parliament.[7]

In the midst of this national euphoria, generated by the apparent unlimited opportunities for socioeconomic mobility for all — in any case for the supporters of the CPP, a party which was identified, at the time of independence, with infinite power to create such opportunities — the CPP could rush through a series of acts with little or no challenge (opposition criticism was either feeble or brushed aside). These acts were to have telling consequences on the

7. Krobo Edusei, the government chief whip, was thus able to exclaim in the House rather serio-comically, amid laughter, "When I wave my wand, you see the opposition members falling to the government side."

social, political, and economic lives of the people at the local, regional, and national levels in the years ahead.

To begin with, in 1957–58 the traditionally appointed members were abolished from the local councils. The Agona (Colony) Local Council and the Nyakrom-Nkum Urban Council were also established in anticipation of the Greenwood Reform of Local Government Structure (1959), to satisfy the conflicting demands in Agona of Nsaba and Nyakrom. The historical roots of the Nsaba-Nyakrom dispute have been fully explored. As a result of the changes, the membership of the Swedru Urban Council was reduced to twelve popularly elected members. This, as we can see, destroyed the last legitimate basis of traditional, property-class, and therefore NLM, GCP, MAP, or UP opposition to the CPP.[8]

In the 1958 SUC elections (elections were triennial), the allied groups opposed to the CPP made their last stand. But it was a feeble stand. This was to be expected, for many people in Swedru, including, of course, the heavily indebted small-scale cocoa farmers, and especially youths, represented by the clerks, junior teachers, and wage-workers saw the CPP as doing what those opposed to the CPP might not do (that is, create economic opportunities for all) because of what was perceived as selfish, narrow class interests of opposition members. Three of the wards – E, J, and K– were originally contested. R. K. Essilfie, however, a bitter enemy of the CPP, a UP member, and a candidate for Ward E, in order both to avoid what was clearly an obvious defeat (his opponent, CPP candidate had been returned continuously for the ward since 1952) and to make virtue of necessity, fell on kinship ties as the only reason for the last-minute withdrawal of his candidature.[9]

At the time of the 1958 elections, therefore, only Wards J and K, both physically adjacent and both traditionally associated with anti-CPP action, were contested. The results, shown in table 11, were a foregone conclusion. They are presented here for the light they throw on the irreversible trend (the CPP motto was: "Forward Ever, Backward Never") in local and national political behav-

8. In 1955, for example, Nana Kum, the archenemy of the CPP, had contested the J ward election and had lost to E. S. Quainoo, the CPP candidate, but had been returned immediately as a traditional member.

9. In a letter dated 14 October 1958 to the clerk of council, SUC, Essilfie wrote that he had "been adviced by my uncle" not to contest as J. K. Amakyi, the other candidate, "is my cousin."

ior, in which the determination of the CPP to monopolize all political, social, and economic power in the nation was unmistakable.[10]

In Ward J, perhaps the most populous area in Swedru (the delimitation of wards has no relation to population size, density, or territoriality), slightly over 22 percent voted. In Ward K, the Zongo Muslim quarter, the flimsy battle almost ended in a tie; yet for the first time in an open election (also the last), a CPP candidate tasted defeat in a local election.

TABLE 11 SUC ELECTIONS, 1958: RESULTS

Ward	Number of Electors	Candidates	Party	Votes Received	Election Declared
A	491	E. B. Mensah	CPP	. . .	Elected unopposed
B	560	F. A. Botchey	CPP	. . .	"
C	573	D. Sackey	CPP	. . .	"
D	599	S. Y. Annobil	CPP	. . .	"
E	385	J. K. Amakyi	CPP	. . .	"
F	465	K. Annan	CPP	. . .	"
G	385	C. V. M. Forde	CPP	. . .	"
H	632	E. P. Aggrey	CPP	. . .	"
I	864	C. K. A. Dufu	CPP	. . .	"
J	939	E. S. Quainoo	CPP	190	Elected
		Nana Kum	UP	20	. . .
K	512	Malam Seidu Darfi	CPP	101	. . .
		Alhaji Adam	Ind	115	Elected
L	518	A. K. Afful	CPP	. . .	Elected unopposed

NOTE: Total number of electors in Wards A–L, 6,923.

Even here the defeat could be easily explained. The CPP candidate, Malam Seidu Darfi, is half-brother of the zerikin (chief) Zongo, Isifu Darfi. The former's mother, like the father, was Wangara. The latter's mother was Hausa. According to the zerikin,

10. The number of registered electors for each ward is not available for 1958. The 1962 figures given in table 11 in parentheses provide us with a very rough idea of the size of potential voters in each ward. The number of registered voters in Swedru for the 1956 general election was 8,762. In that year the percentage poll was 54 percent. There were at least two things striking about the 1958 local elections: the paucity of people who actually voted in those wards — J and K — where there was a contest, and the probable number of voters on the electoral register. Given the overall increase in the population of Swedru between 1950 and 1960, we would expect a figure higher than 6,923 for 1958 if a register of electors for that year was available, and if all those qualified to vote had been actually registered.

when their father died in 1952, Seidu fought tooth and nail to succeed their father as the chief of Zongo on the principal grounds that his (Seidu's) mother was the eldest wife of their father, who had made the difficult journey with him from the north. Unfortunately, Seidu's mother had lost all her children in their infancy. Their father, fearing that he might never have a male issue to succeed him, had consulted a Muslim priest who had foretold that he would have a son by a non-Wangara wife. Accordingly, their father had married Isifu's mother, an Hausa, and had begotten Isifu. Seidu was born a year and a half after the birth of Isifu.

In Hausa and Muslim custom, male primogeniture is crucial, and Isifu, supported by the huge Hausa community, was made zerikin Zongo in 1952. Malam Seidu had, it seems, never been satisfied with his own leadership in the mosque and had, in fact, since stood opposed to anything that his senior half-brother accepted. The zerikin was no doubt sympathetic to the MAP and the NLM cause, and he even told me that the CPP threatened him with detention in 1965 unless he threw his full weight behind the CPP. Alhaji Adam, though he contested as an independent candidate, was nevertheless, for the UP, having in fact nominated Anyan, the NLM candidate, for the Swedru constituency at the 1956 general election.[11] In any event, Swedru Zongo was always associated with opposition to the CPP. But here again, out of a tentative figure of 512 electors, only 216 voted.

Another thing striking about the 1958 urban council elections is the number of CPP candidates who were returned unopposed. About 83 percent of all their candidates were thus elected. This fact was related to many people's attitude toward local and national elections. Many a man strongly believed that it was pointless to fight the CPP at elections, for the CPP would win anyway. So why bother to oppose? The CPP was already in 1958 a party of consolidation and solidarity, instead of a party of representation in Swedru. In the next urban council elections (1961–63), a CPP candidate, Issaka Alabi, was returned unopposed — as a result, mainly, of threats — for the Zongo ward. In the J ward, there was similarly no opposition. Nana Kum, the only person who would have had enough courage to contest, was detained in 1961, as we shall soon observe.

11. Alhaji Adam is a fairly wealthy tailor and prominent Islamic leader. "Haji" is a title acquired by a Malam who has made the pilgrimage to Mecca.

From 1958 onward, it became increasingly difficult to find a legitimate stand for the opposition parties. The CPP was steadily and successfully (though the progress was not easy) monopolizing all authority in the country. The UP, made up of NLM, NPP, Togoland Congress, and MAP, came into being with the passage of the Avoidance of Discrimination Act in 1957, which made it illegal for the so-called sectional parties to exist. From the CPP point of view these parties, based solely on tribe or religion, threatened the whole structure of governmental authority, this despite the fact that between 1951 and 1956 the CPP itself had to rely heavily on some local chiefs and tribal elders for success.

By 1958, the Preventive Detention and Deportation acts were passed, which further restricted any serious protest or criticism against the CPP government. In fact, during our second phase, which ended in 1961, the CPP in Parliament made a series of enactments that seriously impaired the freedom or relative autonomy of local authorities and brought local administration firmly under central government, and therefore CPP, control. Of the various acts and instruments, the following were of particular local and regional significance: Agona Nsaba Paramount Chief (Recognition) Instrument, 1958; Houses of Chiefs Act, 1958; Chieftaincy Act, 1961; Stool Lands Control Act, 1959 (1961); the transformation of G.A.'s into politically appointed D.C.'s in July, 1959; and the establishment of local courts under the Local Courts Act, 1958, and the Local Government Act, 1961. We have already discussed the series of measures taken by the central government since 1961 to bring the nation's economy under centralized direction. How did these acts and measures affect political participation in Swedru, local government, local administration of justice, and so on?

Despite Kojo Essilfie's withdrawal of his candidacy for the 1958 local elections and Nana Kum's defeat at the elections, the two men had continued to criticize openly the strong-arm methods of the CPP. Each in his own way had condemned the Preventive Detention and Deportation acts as tyrannical. Nana Kum especially had abused and challenged the Swedru executive officers of the CPP. His public behavior was considered not only "insolent and treacherous" but also "not conducive to public good," a phrase which became increasingly handy in CPP government circles. It should be stressed that many of the hard-core opponents of the CPP authority were wealthy men of independent means who resented the new "political capitalists" created by CPP administration.

POLITICAL DETENTION OF KOJO ESSILFIE AND NANA KUM

In August 1960, Kojo Essilfie received and accepted an invitation from the UP headquarters, Kumasi, in Ashanti to attend a party rally at the Abbey Park.[12] The rally had scarcely begun when three police patrol cars pulled up and the policemen asked them to stop the meeting on the orders of the prime minister, Dr. Nkrumah, or else face general arrest. The meeting was thereupon immediately transferred to the palace of the twafohene, a chief of Kumasi, and there went on without further incident. Essilfie returned to his native town, Swedru, after the urgent meeting, which had discussed and adopted, among other things, strategies to get UP members out of detention.

On his return he apparently tried to organize people in Swedru to raise funds to combat the CPP through legal action for the release of the UP detainees. On 19 October 1960, he was arrested without charge by the Swedru police and transferred to the Winneba police station, from where he was taken to the James Fort Prisons, Accra, on 20 October 1960.[13] He was later moved to the Ussher Fort Prisons. Although Essilfie was not formally served with detention orders, it was clear to him that he was in prison as a political detainee. According to my informant he was in detention until the 24 February 1966 military coup, having served a term of five years, four months, and two weeks.

The other Fante opposition leader in Swedru, Nana Kum, was similarly dealt with, but he was luckier. He was arrested on 8 November 1961, just about the time of the visit of the Queen of England to Ghana, obviously in the interest of "national security," taken to Winneba, the Swedru district police headquarters, and thence to Cape Coast, the Central Region police headquarters, on 9 Novem-

12. At this time, R. R. Amponsah, Apaloo, and Bafour Akoto, the senior linguist of the Asantehene and popularly considered the founder and leader of the NLM, all of whom were members of the United (opposition) party, were serving preventive detention on various charges including treasonable activities against the CPP government.
13. There he saw some of the leading members of the UP — such as Bafour Akoto — and some sixty others.

ber 1961, where he was detained in the castle. After about a week, unlike his colleague Essilfie, he was formally served, along with two other persons, with detention orders. He was detained until 6 May 1961 and then released. It is interesting to observe that, after being served with the order, Nana Kum petitioned, in his own words, "the Osagyefo personally," admitting that "I am a member of the UP but I do not know of any crime that I have committed or any wrong done and so I beg to be released." [14]

While individual opposition party leaders were being controlled by detention and deportation, in some cases traditional leaders — chiefs and elders — were prevented from participating directly (as citizens) or indirectly (through their power to appoint local councillors) in "modern" politics. The CPP government sought to keep them out of politics, at the same time preserving their indigenous rights relating to customary matters, and ceremonial dignity in new Traditional Councils and Regional Houses of Chiefs.[15] Although the House of Chiefs might participate in the procedures by which certain rules of custom could be modified, its role was purely advisory. Cases involving paramount chiefs were heard by judicial commissioners appointed by the CPP government. Houses of chiefs in each of the six regions (now nine) into which Ghana was divided for administrative purposes dealt with such matters as disputes over chiefly succession and precedence, but all their decisions had to have the approval of the president. This was the colonial governor's powers all over again in a new Republican clothing.

Chiefs might not accede to office without the president's confirmation; he had power to install, depose, exile, or recognize any chief. This, of course, is similar to the formal power vested in the governor in the colonial days, as has been remarked already.[16] But

14. Later on in the year, at one of the CPP ward J meetings at Dwinhu, Nana Kum alleged that R. K. Appiah, then D.C. for Swedru, openly boasted that he had ordered his detention and went on to caution that unless Nana Kum changed to CPP, he (the D.C.) would see to it that he was detained again. The power wielded by the D.C.'s at the local levels during the third phase was ineffable.

15. The minister of local government and then the minister of justice were vested with wide powers relative to the chiefs. The minister, for instance, had power to assign the chiefly institutions any functions deemed fit.

16. We may recall that under the new Native Administration reforms of 1946 the chief was not "necessarily the Native Authority recognised by the Governor" and that when "the people themselves cannot agree as to the election of a chief, or where the chief and his council prove incompetent to perform the

whereas, at least in the Central Region, the governor rarely exercised this power, by the Agona Nsaba Paramount Chief (Recognition) Instrument, 1958, the head of state exercised such right in Agona, despite protests from the only legitimate paramount chief in Agona at Nyakrom. The 1958 recognition therefore gave the Agona people two paramount chiefs and therefore two traditional councils, at Nyakrom and Nsaba, where traditionally only *one* had existed.[17]

It is true that, under the 1960 Republican Constitution, chieftaincy as such was "guaranteed and preserved," but it is equally the case that the sphere of functional competence of chiefs was limited to ceremonial and customary duties (what Governor Alan Burns called "priestly" and "civil" functions), including settlement of disputes and general arbitral proceedings involving amounts not greater than fifty pounds. In the past the chiefs had received revenue from stool lands – the stool's share – and certain allowances from the government. The new Stool Lands Control Act of 1959 (1961) wrested this financial advantage from chiefs and impaired the autonomy of local authorities. What was even more damaging from the point of view of the local Swedru Urban Council was the absorption of the Native Authority police into the central government police system. With the establishment of the SUC in 1952, the better qualified Native Authority police, according to the assistant clerk of council, had been sent for training at Elmina, at the Government Police Depot, with the object of detailing them after their training for duty in the SUC area. This did not happen.

Under the old-system the Native Authority police had not only succeeded in keeping order in town but court fees and fines derived from their arrests of delinquent hawkers, truck drivers, market women, and others, had contributed enormously to the local authority treasury. Basic rates, hawking and market tolls, and lorry park fees were paid regularly and readily, for failure would invariably lead to arrests and detention, followed by payment of fines and rates plus costs. The clerk of council lamented that, as a result, truck drivers, with no police to arrest them, avoided using the Swedru bus and taxi station to avoid paying for tickets. Instead, they used space adjacent

---

functions of a Native Authority, the Governor has power . . . to *appoint* other persons as the Native Authority" (Burns, *Colonial Civil Servant*, p. 204).

17. It is interesting to note that the NLC after the 24 February coup withdrew the 1958 recognition (see NLC Decrees 112 and 136), but in April 1968 restored the recognition!

to filling stations in town. It was difficult for the new plain-clothes revenue-enforcement officers to tap this important source of revenue to the council (see tables 12 and 13). The loss of revenue affected local administrative autonomy, and the implementation of much needed development projects.

TABLE 12 1955–1956 FINANCIAL YEAR

Estimated Revenue (£)		Estimated Expenditure (£)	
Annual rates	2,350	Administration	2,813
Native courts	1,930	Treasury	853
Lands	81	Native courts	867
Fees and tolls	4,775	Police	1,138
Licenses	735	Prisons	8
Interest	51	Agriculture	250
Miscellaneous	. . . . .	Forestry	. . . . .
Grants-in-aid	2,399	Medicine	. . . . .
Transfer from reserve fund	. . . . .	Health	2,549
Education	1,513	Education – primary, middle,	
Total	13,834	and night school	2,825
		Recurrent works	1,059
		Other	62
		Total	13,795

NOTE: 1957–58 financial year estimated revenue, £ 46,744, estimated expenditure, £ 45,983; 1958–59 estimated revenue, £ 28,355, estimated expenditure, £ 27,906. The much-resented property rate was introduced during the 1956–57 financial year.

The council in Swedru, unlike councils in many other towns had proved itself quite efficient under its able clerk, T. H. Mafo, and financially viable, in any case until it lost after 1961 some of its more stable sources of revenue. The financial viability of the SUC and its efficient administration had in the past led little towns such as Asafo, Bensu, Obuasi, and Afransi to seek to come under the council area of Swedru for development planning purposes, if for nothing else.[18] The estimates of the SUC for the 1955–56 financial year, which would be compared with the 1962–63 one, may throw some light on the financial position of the council before and after 1961.

18. Its financial viability, a very crucial index, was further proved by the fact that the 1959 Greenwood recommendations for local government reform in the country did not affect Swedru. The status and structure of S UC were not changed in the interest of more efficient and viable administration as many others had been.

TABLE 13 THE CLERK OF COUNCIL'S MODIFIED
PRESENTATION OF UP-TO-DATE REVENUE
CHART: DETAILED BREAKDOWN,
ITEM 68, 1962–1963

Head	Estimated (£)	Actual (£)	Balance (£)
Annual rate	2,980	2,429	551
Annual arrears	50	9	41
Property rate	7,000	6,487	513
Property arrears	300	207	93
Court fees	450	+ 479	0
Court fines	1,350	1,093	257
Bailiff service	150	144	6
Market	5,150	+5,448	0
Slaughterhouse	500	442	52
Cattle pounds	80	64	16
Bus and taxi stations	6,250	4,500	1,750
Cattle kraal	20	10	10
Marriages and divorces	1	0	1
Births and deaths	10	9	1
Public cemetery	30	25	5
Town hall	400	247	153
Palm-wine sellers	30	26	4
Herbalists	100	+ 108	0
Hawkers	1,350	265	1,085
Palm-tree tappers	25	20	5
Total	26,256	22,012	4,543

The great dependence of SUC on fees and tolls, annual basic
rates, and native court fines and fees is obvious from table 12. These
are what I have called stable sources of revenue. Note that this was
before the introduction of the local property rate. But, as we can
see from table 13, the 1962–63 figures, the reorganization, throughout the nation, of the judiciary in accordance with the Local Courts
Act of 1958, its implementation in Swedru in 1960, and the withdrawal of the native police from the urban council system led to
financial losses to the SUC which made it almost impossible for the
council, without substantial grants from the central government, to
embark on new development projects or even to meet other urgent
recurrent expenditure, such as buying new pans for the removal of
night soil or street repairs.[19]

19. It is interesting to note (table 13) that in the 1962–63 financial year, of
the estimated revenue of £6,250 from truck parking tickets, only £4,500 was

PARTY POLITICS AND LOCAL GOVERNMENT REVENUE

Consequent upon the reorganization of the judicial system in 1960, the local courts were placed in the charge, in most cases, of politically appointed lay magistrates who were removed from the jurisdiction and control of local authorities.[20] In 1958 the principal cases or offences dealt with by the Swedru native court were: (1) traffic offences, including loading passengers contrary to Section 2(1) of SUC (L.P.) rules of 1946, failure to buy bus and taxi station tickets, and obstruction; (2) hawking without license; (3) fouling of water, specifically the Akora River; (4) aggravated assault; (5) threatening; (6) stealing; (7) selling outside the market; (8) refusing to pay levy (basic rate); (9) practicing native medicine without license; and (10) breach of the peace. Fines and fees imposed in connection with the above offences constituted an important source of SUC revenue.

Although in 1958 the clerk of council, SUC, had drawn attention to certain anomalies in the operation of the local court, the court was yielding a modest but important monthly average revenue of £150. This healthy financial situation was to change after 1960. In 1958, the clerk of council had noted the slacking of staff attached to the local court B and the "unfair treatment suffered by poor litigants." This, he had observed, had caused the public to lose interest in the native court. Again, at times, accused persons fined by the native court paid their "fines" to some policemen when they were in custody instead of to the issuing clerk. But both the G.A. and the clerk of council felt that, on the whole, the court was a "very satisfactory" one.

The operation of the court became less and less satisfactory from 1960 on for a number of reasons. Despite the fact that under the new arrangement the SUC lost complete control of the local court and the minister of justice was vested with the sole power "to appoint, promote, transfer, . . . dismiss and control local court magistrates," the SUC was made responsible for all the pay (£960 per annum) and allowances (£9 15s. monthly car maintenance) of the

realized; and of the estimated revenue of £1,350 from hawkers, only £265 was collected; representing a loss to the council of £2,835 on the two items.

20. According to one estimate, the central government control of local courts represented a financial loss to the councils of about one hundred thousand pounds per annum. A. S. Y. Andoh, "Local Government and Local Development in Ghana," *Insight* 2 no. 1 (February 1967) : 46.

local court magistrates and the staff and for providing them with court houses and other accommodation, furniture, books, and "other things for proper execution of their duties." Court fines and fees were also to go to the central government. (In 1965 the central government took over the payment of the salaries of local court magistrates.) The financial burden to the SUC is obvious. To worsen matters, for the first four months of the existence of the new local court under Mrs. Charlotte Abakah, a fully qualified barrister-at-law and a former magistrate of the Swedru (higher level) magistrate's court, the court had already incurred a deficit of £94 16s. 1d.

As a result of the unusual deficit, the chairman of SUC, Forde (then a member also of the national executive of the CPP and resident mostly in Accra), accused the local magistrate of failure to impose heavier fines.[21] Replying to Forde's unwarranted criticism, Mrs. Abakah pointed out, rather insightfully, that "there is a period in the year [in] which the people of Agona as farmers devote more of their time in farming than on litigations" and that, if Forde were resident in Swedru, he would know that "most of the people would prefer to go to jail rather than pay heavy fines." The situation deteriorated after 1962 when, as a result of their growing power, the local D.C. and the R.C. increasingly arbitrated cases which normally should have gone to the courts.[22] This notorious practice grew when the Local Government Act, 1961, made local government areas coterminous with parliamentary constituencies. The constituencies were under the direction of local D.C.'s, politically appointed agents of the central government, who were all dedicated total members of the CPP.

THE D.C. AND THE SUC

The relationships between the D.C.'s (known in the colonial days as "the little governors of the bush"), the Swedru urban councillors, and the council officials are worth reconsidering briefly here, particularly for the period 1958 to 1964, the year of the legalization of the one-party state. From 1958, few non-CPP men dared contest a

21. In fact, it appears that there was pressure on Forde from the Swedru CPP executive officers to replace her with a political appointee. Accordingly, she was later replaced by a lay magistrate.

22. R. K. Appiah (D.C.) and J. E. Hagan (R.C.) were particularly notorious for bringing administration of justice and local and regional government under firm political control.

council election, which until 1964 was in principle contestable.[23] Public attendance of council general meetings, which had never been substantial, decreased to a trickle.

From 1960 going, party politics and administration became intricately intertwined. This no doubt had serious and untoward consequences for administrative efficiency, locally. As Max Weber has argued, there are certain important prerequisites for the efficient working of administration, namely, the existence of an established procedure for dealing with a problem, and the existence of an established hierarchy of responsibility for decisions. I submit that in Swedru the line between party decisions and administrative decisions of the urban council became exceedingly blurred during our third phase, as the D.C. emerged as a very powerful party man and government agent all in one. Unlike the D.C.'s of the colonial era, the D.C.'s of the 1960s were mostly people with little or no administrative experience — Standard VII school leavers whose only qualification was either their total commitment to the CPP or a recommendation from a minister or an R.C., or both. In some cases, the post of D.C. was "purchased" outright.[24]

In Swedru, the power of the local D.C., R. K. Appiah, for instance, was obviously almost without limit. Between 1962 and 1966, he was seen to have arrogated to himself some police duties, including the arresting, personally, of drivers who, he claimed broke traffic rules. He made decisions which sometimes went against important decisions taken by the SUC; he settled cases which should have gone to the courts. He was even believed to order the local chief about. There was therefore much friction between the D.C., who believed he had the authority to make all public decisions affecting Swedru, on party considerations and by personal whim,

23. Thus, for example, on 26 July 1963 the clerk of council informed the councillors that at the close of nomination of candidates for the by-election in Wards F and J, two CPP members were the only persons who had filed their papers. They were to be returned, therefore, unopposed!
24. An instance of this was the case of Boniface Iddrisu Oppong of Swedru, a man who could not speak English, but who in 1962, after the disruption of his trading business, approached the R.C. of the Central Region, J. E. Hagan, for appointment as D.C. of Ankaase. Oppong allegedly paid four hundred pounds to Hagan, who demanded the money "to cover the expenses involved in getting the post for him as he [Hagan] would have to consult a lot of 'big men.'" *Daily Graphic*, Tuesday, 17 January 1967. Oppong did not get the post. It must be mentioned that the post of D.C. commanded an annual salary of twelve hundred pounds, a bungalow, various allowances, and fringe benefits.

and the councillors and council officials, who felt the D.C. was invading their territory of administrative responsibility. The conflict between the D.C. and the chairman of council and his councillors was, however, partly a reflection of the familiar intraparty factionalism, fights, and jockeying for positions of wealth and power that had characterized the CPP throughout its life.

In a letter to the SUC from the regional office, Cape Coast, dated 9 October 1961, it was observed that the minister of interior and local government's attention had been drawn to "disagreements between local authorities and D.C.'s with respect to their *respective spheres of responsibility* in *Local Government*" (my italics). Conflicts of that character, the letter continued (with the insight of a Max Weber), were apt "to hamper smooth and progressive local government administration," that is, they would impair efficient administration. The letter concluded by urging the parties concerned to observe Circular no. LAC 6/60 and to conduct themselves in such a manner as to "reduce to an absolute minimum the incidence of friction." The recommendation is interesting. At least there was an appreciation of the necessity of separating party decisions and administrative decisions.

Circular no. LAC 6/60 from the minister of local government defined the respective functions of D.C.'s as administrative links between the local government and the central government and councillors and officers of urban and local councils. What made the relationship difficult in Swedru was the personality, inexperience, and limited education of the D.C., Appiah. The circular also defined the primary function of chairmen of councils and councillors as the making of "decisions on policy." In practice, this meant increasingly, except in minor instances, decisions taken or approved by the R.C. The duty of the councils' officers was, the circular continued, to carry out the policy laid down. And it was the responsibility of all councillors to attend committee and council meetings to consider and arrive at such policy decisions. The councillors should not, however, interfere with the proper execution of these decisions by the officers.

It was the duty of the D.C. to insure that the officers implemented the councils' decisions and maintained a satisfactory standard of administration. The D.C. was to act in close consultation with the chairmen of councils and, whereas the D.C. might attend

council meetings as ex-officio member, he should not interfere with
the decisions of the council; yet the D.C. was authorized to countersign checks issued by the council and signed by the chairman and
treasurer of the council. The financial control in the hands of the
D.C. and the sense of power he enjoyed as a senior member locally
of the CPP proved too flattering for the D.C. to respect the stipu-
lated spheres of competence. Backed by the enormous power of the
CPP, the D.C. could do virtually anything, arrogate to himself the
making of decisions of policy, and interfere in the actual execution
of the policy taken by him.

The structure and function of the CPP in Swedru explain why the
provisions of the circular as laid down by the minister of local government could not be met, not easily, at any rate. Organizationally,
Swedru had always held a unique position. Until 1958 it was at
once a branch, constituency, and regional center of the CPP. From
1961, Swedru had two levels of organization, the branch (ward)
and the district. The twelve electoral wards into which Swedru is
divided each constituted a chartered branch of the CPP with executive officers, chairmen, and other officers. The Swedru structure was
more in line with what obtained at a municipality than at an urban
area. The district-level organization was made up of the D.C. and
his party officers, elected every two years by delegates, two each,
from the ward-branches. In practice, the D.C. was not elected by
the district conference but was handpicked by a high official or the
president himself. Appiah was chosen by Bensah, M.P. for Swedru
and minister, a very close friend.

The district executive of twelve members constituted perhaps the
most important group of persons in the Swedru urban area. But, of
course, local decisions were effectively controlled by an inner band
of about five people who held special positions in the party district
executive, headed by the D.C. This group controlled the election
(or, perhaps more accurately, the appointment) of chairmen and
vice-chairmen of the urban council, and the important District
Working Committee, considered the policy-making body of the district executive.[25] It is significant that no fewer than seven of the
twelve urban councillors since 1958 had been members of the Dis-

25. On 28 June 1962 the District Executive Committee, for example, put the
following matter before the SUC for necessary and immediate action—
"putting 'K' ward Zongo under priority in the 1962/63 development project."

trict Executive Committee of the CPP in Swedru. Of course, all councillors had to be CPP stalwarts.

The social characteristics of the inner group, the core of total members and the party, and so administrative decision-makers, are worth noting.[26] Before doing this, it must be indicated that, after 1964 especially, though policy decisions were considered presidential — with the implication that only the president had the right to determine matters of policy — one of the day-to-day problems of the CPP and the government was the many decisions and policy statements issued at the regional and local levels, most of which seriously contradicted presidential policy pronouncement.[27]

The party decision-makers in Swedru were (1) R. K. Appiah, D.C., (1962–66), a Gomoa Fante in his middle thirties, who was educated at the Swedru Methodist Middle School, a CPP member since 1950, and a former store boy for Norris Court, a Syrian; (2) Yaw Ampadu, district education secretary (1964), Swedru delegate to the national executive meeting of CPP in 1965, a Kwahu in his late thirties, who was educated at the Swedru Methodist Middle School, a former teacher, now storekeeper, who joined the CPP in 1949; (3) S. Y. Annobil, chairman of the SUC (1964–66), an Agona in his late thirties, who was also educated at the Swedru Methodist Middle School, a former PWD messenger who had joined the party relatively late (in 1956), but a friend and classmate of Appiah and Ampadu; (4) E. B. Mensah, vice-chairman of the SUC (1962), later district organizer of the Ghana Young Pioneers, a Fante in his middle thirties, who was educated at the Winneba Methodist School and was a very close friend of Appiah; (5) and E. S. Quainoo, chairman of the SUC (1961–63), later D.C. of Potsin, a Gomoa Fante in his late thirties, was also educated at the Swedru Methodist School, joined the party in 1950, and was a storekeeper of the Swedru PZ. These were the power holders, but the local inhabitants

26. Most decisions affecting the locality — which, it must be stressed, should be in line with the basic party policy and program laid down either at the Party Congress or, more realistically, by the Central Committee — were taken by the "core group."

27. There was little the president could do in that respect except warn people against such statements in the future. The minutes of the 1965 Central Regional Steering Committee (the regional counterpart of the District Working Committee) Conference at Cape Coast indicated the prevalence and concern about such "unauthorized" decisions by R.C.'s, D.C.'s and other party men. Even within the CPP, the president was hardly the "sole repository of power and influence."

would agree that Appiah, Annobil, Ampadu, Quainoo, and Mensah exerted power in that order. The first four were the CPP members who were detained in 1967 by the NLC. Appiah and Annobil were considered particularly powerful because of their closeness to E. K. Bensah, parliamentary representative for Swedru and for many years minister of works.[28]

Annobil indicated that most of the party and council decisions in Swedru were made informally outside council or party meetings — on the streets, in beer bars, or wherever the inner group might find themselves together.[29] Then, when the party executive met, the decision of the group was presented for comments and approval a procedure that was a mere formality. At any rate when, say, Appiah and Annobil decided on an issue, and stuck to their decision, there was very little the others could do. Debates in the council or district executive meetings were mostly statements of approval of D.C. or R.C. decisions. Annobil went on to indicate some of the various means by which the cohesion of the inner group was maintained, one of the most effective being the appointment of a member to an important CPP office whenever he was seen as growing cold toward

28. It is important to stress the fact that all the above party men were (and still are) very close friends. As Annobil put it, "No one could penetrate our solidarity as great mates." When I asked him why everybody in town, including his friends, thought he was influential he answered, "I am not afraid to speak out. I am a go-getter. People therefore asked me to make suggestions they themselves were afraid to make, particularly at council and party meetings." The ability to speak forcefully is a factor in leadership recruitment.

29. An example of how council decisions were taken and traditionalism manipulated by the CPP to advance party interests is to be found in the SUC minutes for 5 August 1963. The meeting was to discuss how best councillors — all CPP members — could contribute in the forthcoming Akwambo festival of the Agona. The clerk of council reminded the councillors of the usual practice of paying "homage to the Adontenhene" in the form of cash and drink gifts. Councillors decided that each would contribute one pound for the purpose. Whereupon, S. Y. Annobil announced that he had already been *appointed* a member of the "Akwambo planning committee" (which had been formed without the knowledge of most of the councillors). Annobil pointed out that money had already been voted to purchase drinks for the occasion and that councillors' cash gifts should be used solely to defray the expense which would be incurred by the chiefdom. Annobil's suggestion was naturally accepted without argument. The Adontenhene's letter to the SUC asking permission to declare 7 August 1963 a holiday to enable council employees to participate in the Akwambo celebration was read and approved. Finally, the clerk of council was asked by councillors to create a head in the Estimates to provide money in the future for the Akwambo so that councillors might be exempted from personal contribution!

the party, especially if the member happened to be influential locally.[30]

Upward mobility within the CPP power hierarchy from the local angle is diagramed in figure 10. The D.C., it was common knowledge, wielded enormous, almost unlimited, *actual* power in his locality and he was notorious in its exercise. In Swedru, D.C. Appiah was particularly guilty of misuse and abuse of power.[31] All traditional and local councils in the area had to submit all addresses intended for the president first to the regional office and only through him. All self-help projects in the SUC area had to *first* receive his sanction. This made council debates and decisions redundant or useless. The D.C. publicly insulted the chief but equally publicly procaimed to build a new, modern palace for him if only the chief would work with him. Note the personalization of authority.

D.C. Appiah attended most of the urban council meetings as an ex-officio member, but found himself interfering with the proceedings and decisions of the council. No wonder, councillors in 1963 and after refused to contribute to or lost interest in debates which only led in a number of cases to the unwilling acceptance of the D.C.'s personal decisions. On 30 January 1963, as the council minutes show, the naïve D.C., unaware that his imposing behavior in council might have something to do with the waning interest in debates in council, warned that "all councillors should in future try to contribute to debates at meeting and not to sit mute in the hope of getting their allowances." The fact was that their contribution to debates would not seriously have affected decisions taken by the D.C. Sometimes the D.C. even ignored important council policy decisions by making counteracting decisions.[32]

One councillor, in a rather belated protest, told me that whenever

30. The example in Swedru was when Ampadu, the district education secretary, wanted to leave the party and was immediately nominated by Annobil — without the former's knowledge, of course, of the motive behind it — to represent the district at the national executive conference at the Flagstaff House in Accra in 1965.

31. Between 1962 and 1966 — that is, in our third phase — he held the whole of the Swedru town to ransom. He is alleged to have confiscated private lands and forced rich people to put up building for his private use (the case of Mensah and the land in Bebianiha was an example).

32. For instance, in order to increase the council's revenue, the council decided sometime in 1963 to direct all entertainment promoters to engage the Swedru Town Hall for all such functions. The D.C. made this ineffective by signing permits for entertainment in private houses.

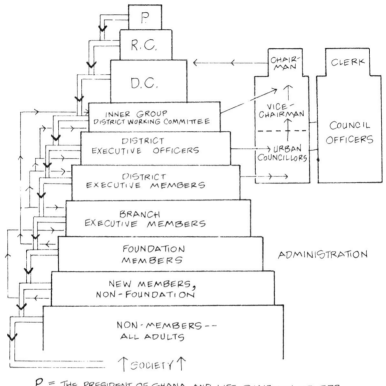

P = THE PRESIDENT OF GHANA AND LIFE CHAIRMAN OF CPP

RC = REGIONAL COMMISSIONER

DC = DISTRICT COMMISSIONER

DOUBLE ARROW ————————→ = FLOW OF INFLUENCE AND CONTROL.

SINGLE ARROW ——→———→ = DIRECTION OF UPWARD POWER MOBILITY.

POWER WAS DETERMINED BY:

(1) DATE THE PARTY WAS JOINED AND THE CONTRIBUTIONS (FINANCIAL SERVICES) TO THE PARTY,

(2) OFFICE HELD IN THE PARTY AND THE PERCEIVED LOYALTY TO THE PARTY AND NATIONAL LEADER,

(3) LEVEL OF THE OFFICE IN THE HIERARCHY OF POWER,

(4) SPECIAL PRESIDENTIAL AND OTHER FAVORS.

Fig. 10. The Power and Influence Hierarchy of the CPP, Swedru

the D.C. attended the council meetings "he dominated them." This clearly affected attendance. In August 1964, the D.C. further warned councillors sternly that those who failed to attend meetings "may not be *re-elected* [appointed] at elections" (italics mine). Such was the extent of D.C. Appiah's actual power. Attendance continued to deteriorate and from 1 January 1965, councillors were offered inducement of 10s. per sitting to attend meetings (the chairman received £180 per annum).[33] There is evidence that the measure greatly improved attendance of council meetings.

Another incident in 1964 demonstrated the nature of the D.C.'s control of various types of decision-making. On 26 March, 1964, the chairman of the SUC, Annobil, a member of the inner group, *informed* the council that, with the consent of the D.C., the young men in Swedru had formed a vigilante group known as *Nsamangoro* ("the games ghosts play"). He explained that the aim of the group was to patrol the town in the night to assist police in arresting thieves and other criminals. It is worth pointing out that the group was already in operation when the chairman brought its existence to the attention of the council. It was clear that the D.C. and the chairman had alone taken this important decision. The council endorsed the formation of the group as a good move but regretted that some of the members had been molesting innocent people and that prominent people in town were being forced to give "gifts" to members of the group. The council pointed out that the organization was voluntary and that any acts of violence or threat that would tarnish the good name of the council and the town should be discouraged.

It was obvious in the above instance that a majority of the councillors was against the formation of the Nsamangoro group, but they dared not oppose the decision of the D.C. and his very close associate Annobil, the chairman. After a lengthy discussion, the council recommended that the executive members of the organization be invited to meet with the council to discuss the aims and the violent action of some of the members of the vigilante group. The chairman agreed to this, but the meeting never took place.

The D.C.'s control did not stop on the floor of the airy, horseshoe-shaped council hall. It went beyond to the tidy office of the hard-working, intelligent, and highly dedicated clerk of council,

33. Previous to that, the chairman received four pounds and the councillors two pounds as monthly allowances or honoraria.

Chapter Nine

one-time headmaster of the Swedru Presbyterian Middle School. Here two examples may suffice. In 1964–65, the Ghana Farmers Council, through the Ministry of Agriculture, sent a sum of money to the clerk of council as bonuses to the cocoa farmers of Nyamendam village. The money was to be used to help the farmers as deemed fit by the council. Councillors suggested that the money should go into the construction of either a feeder road or a school. The D.C. overrode this wise recommendation and demanded the check (after all, he was empowered to countersign all council checks before they could be honored) from the clerk of council and decided to take the necessary action himself. The clerk admitted to me that there was nothing he personally could do. He handed the check over to the D.C. and it is anybody's guess what happened to the money. The second case was even more gross and portrayed a serious lack of sense of civic responsibility.[34]

The almost tyrannical exercise by the D.C. of his powers affected almost everybody in Swedru. He could order at will the Swedru market to be closed for the day so that market women would attend rallies; he allegedly obtained goods from local stores and refused to pay for them; he controlled the distribution of goods at the Swedru GNTC, as we have seen. He also controlled the police and the courts. At the end of 1964, the D.C. was appointed chairman of the all-important Tender Board of the SUC, which considered, evalu-

34. The public, whose interest — particularly socioeconomic — the council was supposed to represent and serve, had to suffer and be inconvenienced through the selfishness and stupidity of two men. The men were W. Y. Eduful, Permanent Secretary of the erstwhile CPP-controlled and owned Publicity Secretariat, which had responsibility relating to the publication of books, newspapers, and the like "in the national interest"; and Appiah, D.C. Eduful is a native of Swedru. To hold a funeral befitting his deceased sister, Eduful, a very important CPP national figure, caused to be pulled down the old and tumbledown switch (wattle and daub) and corrugated iron sheet family dwelling and replaced it with an ultra-modern structure with terrazo floors, louvred windows, baths with water heaters, fully equipped kitchen with metal sinks, large refrigerators, coolers and other modern conveniences on the same piece of land, near the Swedru old SAT cocoa shed. The building, which is estimated conservatively to have cost about £6,500, took only a few months to construct. Unfortunately, the dignity of the beautiful tenement was tarnished by the presence a few feet away of public latrines serving the people of at least three adjacent wards. Misusing his powers, he "ordered" the clerk of council through the D.C. to shut the public latrine throughout the period — about four days — of the mourning, to spare the mourners an unpleasant odor. The inconvenience to the poor inhabitants without private toilet facilities in their homes cannot be overemphasised.

ated, and granted contracts to tendering contractors. The other members of the board were the chairman of the SUC; the local government inspector; and the clerk of council, who was the secretary-recorder; and the district engineer or works superintendent of the Ghana National Construction Company. It is popularly alleged that the D.C. used his position to get contracts for his friend, "tribesman" Hewton (in 1967 considered the wealthiest person in Swedru). It is believed that, through the D.C., Hewton met the all-powerful R.C. of Cape Coast, J. E. Hagan. Hewton admitted before the Jiagge Assets Commission that he was a party to a fraudulent deal with the regional commissioner of the Central Region, Hagan, in which he received eighty thousand pounds on a mere one-thousand-pound contract![35] It was primarily the financial mismanagement of this nature that finally brought down the CPP government. This was what produced the mass pauperization and made ordinary citizens ready to transfer political allegiance to anybody or any system that promised alleviation of what was *perceived* as mass economic poverty.

The D.C. finally controlled the SUC through his direction of the town development committees. The D.C. had delegated power to appoint either the chief or the chairmen of the local branches — wards of the CPP — as chairmen of the development committees. The smooth functioning of local administration was thus upset by unnecessary political interference. The very activities of the development committees were meddled with by the D.C., and finally made every form of communal work organized by the committees in the wards of Swedru to be interpreted by the local people as nothing but corvée instead of as voluntary work.[36]

In the next chapter, I consider some interesting but general structural and processual questions raised by the CPP "party-state" experience and attempt to show the relative strength and weaknesses of such a party-state. This is important because, in September 1969, Ghana returned to party politics and civilian rule.

35. *Daily Graphic*, 2 September 1967.
36. In fact, it is popularly believed in Swedru that the huge amount of money given to the D.C. by the central government to cover the cost of laying pipes for the pipe-borne water supply in Swedru was misappropriated by the D.C. who enforced communal labor for the purpose. Note the similarity between the abuse of power by the D.C. in the 1960s and by Kojo Nyarko, chief of Swedru, in the 1920s.

10 THE ONE-PARTY STATE, ECONOMIC FACTIONALISM, AND POLITICAL INSTABILITY

From the almost sudden emergence of the CPP in June 1949 in Accra and its very rapid spread throughout Ghana to its forcible dissolution in February 1966, following the military coup, its organizational structure and to some extent process were affected by one major constitutional change, that of 1962. In effect, there were the two party constitutions, of 1949 to the 1950s (which aimed primarily at the "organisation of the common people, the masses through the leadership of the party for the attainment of Independence") [1] and of the 1960s (which sought the "consolidation" of leadership of the party, that is, "safeguarding popular democracy," and the establishment of a "socialist society" in Ghana and in Africa). [2]

Throughout its existence in Ghana, the CPP was characterized in a most glaring way by a steady and continuous monopolization of political, social, and economic authority and power. It strove to be the nation-state itself, by capturing the supreme and unqualified power to make society-wide and nation-wide decisions of policy. The CPP was to be Ghana and Ghana was to be the CPP. It succeeded, in fact, in dominating the political and then the social and economic scenes by its economic control of "integral organizations," such as the TUC (whose general secretary was a member of the party's national executive), the UGFC, the NCGW, the Ghana Young Pioneers, and the Cooperative Movement, all of which organizations were similar in structure to the CPP and were controlled by it. Thus the party gave general direction not only to

1. K. A. Busia, in *Judge for Yourself* (Accra: The West African Graphic Company, Ltd., 1956), p. 1, recalls that "the CPP was built on the slogan 'Self-Government Now' which was interpreted to include the immediate attainment of independence, and the provision of material benefits for all."

2. Apter has described (in Coleman and Rosberg, *Political Parties*) the former as the "party of representation" and the latter as the "party of consolidation" within a "mobilization system," categories that are somewhat misleading, as we have argued.

workers, farmers (cocoa and foodstuff), market women, and petty traders, but, most important of all from the party point of view, to the youth. But it was a control that was unreliable from the beginning, since it was based primarily on the instrumental considerations of the members of these various relatively independent "solidarity" groups.[3]

Legitimate political power was made directly dependent on *acceptable* economic performance of the party leadership (judged in most cases ultimately by the amount of purchasing power that individuals and class-status groups commanded). What was acceptable, of course, changed as people's conception of economic well-being changed.

With the founding of the Kwame Nkrumah Ideological Institute at Winneba in 1962 for the teaching of Nkrumaist socialism, the CPP also assumed what Nkrumah described as the "central leadership" of the public services and corporations: the national civil service, the judiciary, the armed forces, the police, central banks, and government boards and corporations. The outstanding feature of this central leadership was the substitution in the filling of positions and promotions, in a number of instances, of the *appointive* principle based on party connections for the *elective* and *merit* principle based on experience and qualifications. This was no doubt an attempt to establish firmly a party cadre, the new bureaucrats of party and state administration (committed to rapid industrialization of Ghana) to supplant the bureaucrats of the colonial civil service, most of whom were considered reactionary and conservative and whose primary basis of prestige and social status derived from attachment to colonial bureaucratic norms. This steady monopolization and consolidation of national leadership by the CPP was associated throughout the three phases of political development ending in 1966 with an almost self-perpetuating, almost noncirculating, political elite at each of the four hierarchical levels — branch, district, regional, and national — of party organization, despite the growing membership of the CPP.[4] This phenomenon led to what I

3. All these organizations, it seems, were prepared to exchange their independent bases of political and economic action for the "leadership of the party" only when, *ceteris paribus*, the marginal material or economic returns to them (individually or as a group) were greater than the cost to them of surrendering their freedom of action.

4. In 1962, the party claimed membership of about 1.5 million. The near "self-perpetuating oligarchy" was largely due to the CPP rule that, wherever

have termed the "party corporation." The legalization of one-party
state in 1964 was, in effect, the granting of a de jure recognition to
a state of affairs that had existed especially since 1958.[5]

Party members, therefore, saw themselves as having monopolistic
right over authority in society, economy, and polity. The party was
the state. A letter from the branch secretary (Yaw Ampadu) of the
CPP, Swedru, to the branch secretary of the party at Tema, dated
11 October 1962, illustrates to some extent the "perpetuity" element
in the CPP:

Dear Comrade,
INTRODUCTION OF COMRADE H. G. K. MARTINSON CR/AGSC/4
I wish to introduce . . . who had been an active member of the Great
C.P.P. Swedru Branch for [from] 1953 [to] 1961.
  His business has brought him to Tema. I am therefore recommending
him to you and admit him to your membership. . . .
                     Yours in the Service of Ghana
                     Signed Yaw Ampadu, Branch Secretary

Although the CPP recruited its members from all sections of the
Ghanaian population, there was no doubt at all that it was in itself
exclusive (or "closed") and hierarchically led, with leadership more
or less in the hands of foundation members.

The CPP had initially relied for sheer organizational survival, as
we have already noted, on relatively small numbers of people for
financial contributions and for services as organizers, propaganda
workers, and campaigners. In Swedru the former category included,
among others, E. K. Bensah, M.P. for Swedru from 1951 to 1966;

---

possible, foundation members should have prior consideration for party or state
offices.
  5. The party was a corporation in three related senses: The party was seen
by members and nonmembers alike as a legal "personality." The party was
considered supreme — it was "one disciplined army" having corporate responsibility and identity, with some of the members sincerely believing that the
CPP "will never die." This belief is adequately expressed in the following:
"Forward Ever, Backward Never," the party motto; Provençal's statement
at the 1960 plebiscite victory rally in Accra (*Ashanti Pioneer,* 7 May 1960)
that "we [CPP] can stay for twenty years without calling an election and nobody can say anything"; and "Nkrumah shall never die." The CPP also held as
just that foundation members, believed mistakenly to symbolize the new social
order, had perpetual rights to manage the affairs of the state, which to them was
corporate property in primary economic terms (note the prescription that to hold
a party or state office, members should have been in the party for at least five
years). The party was thus organized "to broaden the basis of *support* for the
leadership," and allegiance to the party was considered identical with allegiance
to the state;

Essandoh; and F. C. Dodd. In the latter category were Agyare, "elected" M.P. in 1965; Addo Sekyi; R. K. Appiah, D.C. for Swedru, 1963–66; S. Y. Annobil, chairman of the SUC, 1964–66; Kwesi Armah, Ghana High Commissioner in London, 1961–65; and Yaw Ampadu, district party education secretary, to mention the most prominent ones.

The contributions by these men and others like them, assembly-men and cabinet ministers, were seen in a majority of cases not just as sacrifices in the national interest (though everybody was proud to be Ghanaian and was proud of Ghana's role in African and inter-national affairs), but also as investments of time and money in the party corporation. The party, as a corporation identified with the state, in any case controlling the state and society, was expected to yield in time to these party-member "investors" or "shareholders" not only substantial material "dividends" but also assured positions on the political board of directors, as R.C.'s, D.C.'s, chairmen of councils, and the like. The president of the state, also the life chair-man of the CPP, became (or was seen as) the trustee, for the whole state, of the property and of almost all other economic resources vested in it. State property became party property — at any rate, the party had almost unlimited power to allocate or distribute the re-sources as it thought fit. The authority to distribute national eco-nomic resources was the primary basis of the party's supreme power. Having no other immediate authority with which it must share the exercise of power, the CPP was accountable only to itself or, indirectly, to the electorate, whose ultimate rights — the fran-chise and freedom of speech — were becoming increasingly difficult to exercise in any meaningful manner.

In Swedru, the CPP, as I have shown, had initially attracted mostly people who felt that they were suffering from relative economic deprivation and had strong desires for improving their eco-nomic (or class) status.[6] For electoral votes the CPP in Swedru and in many other constituencies depended very much on the small-scale, heavily indebted peasant cocoa farmers in the surrounding

6. They were not necessarily the unemployed and were not the proverbial "verandah boys." Many were individuals who were basically dissatisfied with their relative economic positions and hoped for economic betterment, and so improved status, through membership in the CPP, the only party in 1949 and the 1950s that was seen as being seriously concerned with the economic lot of the relatively poor people — not necessarily unemployed urban workers.

countryside, concerned (as we saw in the previous chapters) with finding money to redeem a pledged couple of acres of cocoa farms. These petty cocoa farmers saw the CPP-controlled CPC as the unfailing source of financial aid. They accordingly voted CPP.[7]

The real "verandah boys" in Swedru, the Zongo "lumpen proletariat" of Mosi, the Fulani, Wangara, and others, many of whom were seasonal migrant laborers, were wont to vote for MAP-NLM complex on the grounds of religious or primordial interests, rather than for the CPP, if they participated actively in politics at all. Yet the CPP remained immensely popular among minor clerks, minor salesmen or storekeepers, semiskilled workers, and lesser municipal functionaries — some of whom, as we have seen, provided party leadership, especially at the local and regional levels. Their interest in the party was rational and their commitment instrumental. For a people who had neither the educational qualification to become lawyers or doctors in the foreseeable future nor the financial or kinship resources to become cocoa magnates, the only possible avenue to power and wealth, that is, to upward social and economic mobility, was the party.

But the government party could not go on forever creating employment opportunities for this or any other group of a rapidly expanding party following, nor could the government keep rewarding materially its many "friends" of fortune without a substantial rate of economic growth or at least a high and stable international price of cocoa.

DECLINING ECONOMY AND POLITICAL INSTABILITY

Public funds were limited and scarce, relative to the numerous alternative demands made on them.[8] Nkrumah himself was aware of

7. The large-scale "rural capitalists," whose cocoa farms were at least twice or thrice the size of the national average of about six acres, and who had made substantial investment in huge modern, middle- and upper-class urban housing, were generally anti-CPP, as were the Kwahu and Fante traders, who bore the brunt of local property rates and national property taxes. The large-scale cocoa farmers were more concerned about the increase in the price of cocoa paid to farmers and the abolition of property taxes and compulsory savings. Nevertheless, almost all the farmers believed, somewhat erroneously, that the CMB's policies were designed only for the prosperity and benefit of cocoa producers. The point still is that, because of the dominant role of revenues derived from cocoa in the national economy, the sectional interests of farmers have to be weighed against national economic objectives.

8. It was clear, for instance, that through the government's establishment

the necessity of continuous hard work, in order to increase economic output in terms of a substantial rise in the gross national product, as the only way to economic and therefore political stability. In 1961 he therefore launched the "Double-Action" year and, in 1962, "Work and Happiness," associated with the ambitious Seven Year Development Plan which obviously had little effect on industrial and agricultural productivity.

Between 1961 and 1963 the great structural transformation in Ghana related to huge government spending — construction of roads, schools, hospitals and other government services, and the attendant enlargement of economic opportunities — resulted in monetary expansion which in 1963, as many people in Swedru attest, began to exert powerful inflationary impact on the economy. Import restrictions and anomalies in the issue of import licenses led to serious shortages of key consumer goods (including indispensable farm implements, such as cutlasses and hoes, and imported food) for which effective demand far outstripped supply as a result of the increasing money income in the hands of the workers. This produced further price inflation and the demand for more money across the board, as real incomes fell. In Swedru, trading stores, both African and European, grew emptier for reasons which have already been discussed; hoarding and black marketing rose. Nationally, the protection offered against cumulative inflation by large foreign reserves owned by Ghana no longer existed.[9]

The situation grew worse and by 1965 it was hurting almost everybody. There was no increase in the daily wage rate in this period, and price inflation no doubt upset middle-class incomes as well. Living standards went down and the CPP began to lose its popularity among many. In 1961, the introduction by the government of compulsory savings as one of the measures to control in-

throughout Ghana of the Workers' Brigade, a construction corps organized on a somewhat para-military line (which had been used both in the national interest and in the purchase of support for the CPP and had absorbed thousands of unemployed school leavers, male and female, thereby reducing drastically semi-skilled unemployment), the workers in fact had received out of public funds salaries for work which in most cases they had not actually done. The organization, concerned primarily in the production of food, did so little productive work that it became a constant drain on national reserves and profits.

9. According to one calculation, real wages for unskilled workers in Accra (and, from my informants' crude estimates, in Swedru as well) declined from an index of 119 in 1960 to 89 in 1963. See Tony Killick in Birmingham, Neustadt, and Omaboe, *Study of Contemporary Ghana* particularly chapters 3 and 5.

flation led, understandably, to strikes of workers in parts of Ghana. Many who could not protest openly grumbled and mumbled as ministers and high party officials engaged themselves in competitive spending on scarce consumer items to which as important personages they had prior rights of purchase. Some traveled to Europe to shop, using public funds they had lavishly misappropriated. The resentment against this new privileged class of party men was only human. After all, their uncurbed local spending (the basis of their high status, prestige, and power in society), fed into the inflationary spiral and worsened the lot of the common man, the minor clerk, teacher, or laborer, who had supported the party but was forced to rely on a meager real income to make ends meet.

Despite this, the CPP officials and leaders, from the president down through the party hierarchy, continued the process of self-enrichment, as the recent commissions of inquiry reports indicate (making allowances for misrepresentation and exaggeration). As members of the party jockeyed themselves into the best financial positions, intraparty factionalism increased. Unfortunately for all concerned, world price of cocoa fell drastically. So serious was the fall that the government was forced to embark on yet another politically risky measure. It could, and did, cost the government its very legitimacy. In July 1965, a year after the legalization of the one-party state, the government fixed the gross producer price per load of cocoa (sixty pounds) at £2 0s. compared with the 1951 price of £4 0s. per load and the 1954–58 guaranteed minimum (irrespective of fluctuation in the world price) of £3 12s. From the £2 0s. in the face of rising cost of living, the farmers were to pay a "voluntary" contribution to national development plan at the rate of 6s. per load of cocoa plus a compulsory contribution of 4s. per load of cocoa, making a total contribution of 10s. per load. This important decision was taken in consultation with representatives of the United Ghana Farmers Council Cooperatives (UGFCC), many of whom were not farmers but party men.[10]

Thus by 1964 the CPP government had lost many of its supporters. In Swedru a sizable number of the minor clerks of the post office and the PWD, semiskilled workers of the electricity corpora-

10. In *The Ghana Coup* (London: Frank Cass, 1966), A. A. Afrifa talks about opposition of farmers to a government under whose rule their "money was being squandered by so-called Secretaries, chief farmers and a host of brigands who had never held a hoe in their lives."

tion, rediffusion station, and so on (except those who held party office of profit) and also the small-scale habitually indebted cocoa farmers were now bitterly against the CPP. It is therefore against this background of a rapidly and steadily declining national economy, party desertion, and potential breakdown of the political system that the legalization of the one-party (CPP) state should be assessed.

THE CPP AND THE NEW BASIS OF LEGITIMATION

Having lost much of its popular appeal and authority (based primarily on instrumental commitment) and so its very legitimacy, the CPP reacted, in the true spirit of the political monopolist, by rhetorically seeking a new legal and ideological basis of its right to govern. The fact that there was a mock national election in 1965 at which even CPP members who had attempted to oppose or contest the official party candidates had been penalized supports this view. (Tanzania, a one-party state, had allowed this sort of opposition.) The 1964 act made the CPP the only *legal* party, with the obvious implication that CPP political decisions were now legally unassailable by dissident factions, and there were many, outside the party, as all legitimate criticism must come from within the party itself. The corporate identity of the party was now clarified by law for all.

The CPP was now convinced of unflinching loyalty from those for whom the party had manipulated promotions, salaries, and conditions of service, and of support from the national army and police (many of whose senior officers unfortunately identified with the old colonial privilege system) and from the new presidential guard (a small but very well-equipped standing army) for both the party and the president. The CPP, therefore, now believed strongly that it had finally created the conditions for its perpetual structural survival even in the face of protest in an increasingly impoverished society. To the ordinary consumer, it was becoming more and more difficult for the government to explain the economic problems facing the nation just in terms of the necessary, but perhaps too rapid, socioeconomic developments implemented throughout the country and which had consumed a substantial proportion of the national reserves abroad. The loyalty of the army to the party was particularly crucial, as later events were to demonstrate.[11]

11. At least one prominent member of the CPP as recently as 1962 was very

In any case, the legal one-party state was seen by the CPP as the only way by which members, leaders, and officials of the party could hope to cling to their vested power and monetary interests in a period when the possession of a large amount of money was the only way, however circular, to beat the rising cost of living and maintain a decent standard of living.[12] Those who supported the legalization of a one-party state were mostly motivated by their narrow economic interests as a new elite of party and state functionaries and not by their commitment to national socialism. It could be argued, however, that the emphasis on the ideology of socialism in the 1960s was an attempt by the CPP leadership to push a population faced with chronic economic hardship and strain to deny the existence of the hardship outright by legitimizing it in terms of the higher values of socialism and rapid industrialization of Ghana.[13]

The one-party state in Ghana, contrary to popular belief, was not dictated by the demands of traditional Ghanaian cultures — though we could not rule out completely the possibility of the influence of

---

aware of the possibility of a military coup d'état in Ghana unless precautions against its occurrence were taken. In the course of a now almost forgotten debate in Parliament on 11 June 1962 on the Armed Forces (Amendment) Bill, Second Reading (1962) Hanzard: 691), F. E. Tachie-Menson, CPP member for Denkyera, insisted that the minister of defense be included in the proposed Chief of Staff Committee of which the president as supreme commander was to be chairman, and that the minister of defense act as the chairman when the president was not present at its meetings. This was necessary, because all the other members of the committee were members of the armed forces. "Experience in some countries has taught us that Heads of some Armed Forces usually make an attempt to stage a coup d'état." To this Kofi Baako, minister of defense, had exclaimed, "Not in Ghana." Ignoring Kofi Baako's remark, Tachie-Menson went on to argue with concern that, if the chief of Defense Staff were to chair such a meeting in the absence of the supreme commander, "It will be very dangerous for us." Tachie-Menson was proved right, though for different reasons, in 1966.

12. In fairness to the party leadership, particularly Nkrumah, it should be strongly emphasized, for a more complete picture, that political survival in Ghana for the CPP was a necessary condition for pursuing the long-term national economic development of rapid industrialization of the country to which Nkrumah was genuinely committed. That Nkrumah failed to achieve his economic objectives was partly due to the terms of international trade, which since 1960 had been particularly unfavorable to Ghana, and partly to economic miscalculations, mismanagement, and the corruption of public officials and party men.

13. It must be said, incidentally, that there is no reason to believe that the NLM-UP opposition would have behaved any differently (they might have used a more subtle method) if they had seized power. There is every indication that they would have clung like leeches to their class interests.

some elements of these cultures and of the culture of colonialism. I have in mind here authoritarian tendencies in the public behavior of leaders and *seniores priores* practiced at all levels of society, and even the sheer materialist emphasis. These factors insured the relative acceptance of the one-party state. But Marxist-Leninist influence on Nkrumah must have contributed to its development.

Perhaps modern politics in Africa is dangerously unstable because people are more aware of and preoccupied with competition for class, community, or individual material interests, whether such competition is couched in the name of the national interest or not. The consequences of this acquisitive action for national stability are hardly considered. Personal or group economic sacrifice is still a distant value in most African countries. It is only by mass or popular commitment (including that of the national leadership) to economic sacrifice that the circumstances for national political stability would be established.[14] This, of course, would categorically require new normative definitions and reorientations consistent with an "ideology of sacrifice," and even acceptance of a certain degree of relative economic deprivation and hard work as inevitable in developing economies with our present level and rate of economic growth.

Let us at this point turn to a brief consideration of the CPP organization in Swedru after 1962 to see if some of the functional features of control, perpetuity, and monopoly, mentioned above, were present at the operation of the party at this local level. Figure 11 illustrates what the CPP, as a structure of political decision-making, looked like from the local level.

THE PARTY STRUCTURE AND PROCESS: THE REVISED CONSTITUTION

By 1962, when the revised constitution of the CPP was introduced, the party had emerged as the most ubiquitous and most dominant party in Ghana. The party stood at the very center of the common life, reaching out on the one hand into the state structure, of the legislature and the executive, civil administration, the army, and the judiciary, and reaching out on the other into the socioeconomic structure of professions, occupations, churches, trade unions, and

14. Euro-American finance and industrial capitalists would have to adopt a more humane posture in their dealing with Africa. It would be imperative for them to pursue policies genuinely beneficial to African economies and societies.

various forms of community life. The party, like its child – political independence and the republic – was now the common possession of all Ghanaians; it loomed over the life of everyone residing in Ghana. The party was thus their national pride as well as shame, their source of pleasure as well as pain. Whether it was the "Common People's Party" or the "Corrupt People's Party" (both descriptions were apt to a large extent), it was the national party and was known and accepted as such by every child and parent, villager and townsman, foe and friend, Talensi and Ashanti alike.

The party, despite the ambivalence of attitude toward it in some sections of national society, was the symbol of national unity, based not so much on political consensus (though elements of this were present) as on its economic triumphs and failures, a condition found also in the colonial situation.[15] The CPP helped create a new national political community in three important senses: (1) It had a monopoly over the legitimate use of force. (2) It was the center of national decision-making that was able to affect the allocation of resources and rewards throughout the national community. The pre-independence Ashanti bid for a federal form of government does not contradict this.[16] It is interesting to note in this connection that people were more conerned about *how* resources were distributed than *who* distributed the resources. (3) The CPP emerged as the superior focus of political identification for a large majority of the politically aware citizens. The nation was therefore, relative to many African nations, highly integrated.

The 1962 party constitution and the new party organization reflected, according to the president, the new task of the party, which "coupled with the role which our country [Ghana] plays in international affairs makes it necessary for the organisation of our party to be streamlined and strengthened to enable it to cope with the new responsibilities Ghana is committed to discharge." The president observed that if "inner party democracy" and "self-criticism" were

15. National unity, after all, is not just a state of mind. As Karl Pearson correctly points out, "You cannot get a strong and effective nation if many of its stomachs are half fed . . ." (see Karl Pearson, *National Life from the Standpoint of Science* [London: A and C Black, 1905], p. 54).

16. As K. A. Busia puts it, "Federation is a unity of equals. We want the Northern Territories, Ashanti, the Colony and Togoland, each to be able to manage as much of its own affairs as possible, and at the same time . . . each contributing to the greatness and well-being of our country." *Judge for Yourself*, pp. 4–5.

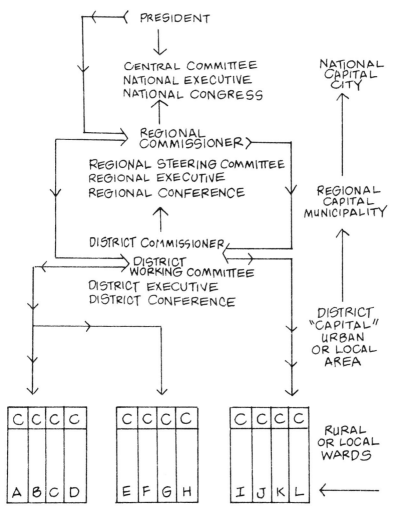

PRESIDENT

CENTRAL COMMITTEE
NATIONAL EXECUTIVE
NATIONAL CONGRESS

NATIONAL
CAPITAL
CITY

REGIONAL
COMMISSIONER

REGIONAL STEERING COMMITTEE
REGIONAL EXECUTIVE
REGIONAL CONFERENCE

REGIONAL
CAPITAL
MUNICIPALITY

DISTRICT COMMISSIONER

DISTRICT
WORKING COMMITTEE
DISTRICT EXECUTIVE
DISTRICT CONFERENCE

DISTRICT
"CAPITAL"
URBAN
OR LOCAL
AREA

C	C	C	C
A	B	C	D

C	C	C	C
E	F	G	H

C	C	C	C
I	J	K	L

RURAL
OR LOCAL
WARDS

A–L IN THE LOWER BOXES REPRESENT THE ELECTORAL WARDS OF SWEDRU WHICH ARE ALSO BRANCH ORGANIZATIONS OF THE PARTY.

C IN THESE BOXES REPRESENTS CHAIRMEN OF THE BRANCH ORGANIZATIONS.

Fig. 11. The Party as a Structure of Political Decision-Making, 1962–1966

practiced, it would follow that all decisions of the party were decisions of the entire membership. Democracy would then be at its
plenitude throughout *all* levels of the party. This was what the new
party structure was to achieve.[17] The president further emphasized
that "to understand the ideology of our party is to appreciate the
need to improve the well-being of the greatest number of
people."[18] This was certainly the most important statement, from
the point of view of the general population, since it reinforced what
was their primary concern. Ghanaians understood the "ideology"
very well. It was, in fact, the only message everyone, in whatever
class or status, would appreciate: "the well-being of the greatest
number of people." This was to be the acid test of the right of the
CPP to govern.

PARTY ORGANIZATION

Briefly, the new organization of the CPP (figure 11) had four hierarchically arranged structural levels, namely, the national, the regional, the district, and the branch, the branch being the most basic
organization. The branch was established in most of the towns and
villages of Ghana, giving the CPP a truly national character. The
party wings, the socioeconomic categories or groups such as the
TUC, the Co-opM, and the UGFCC, constituted integral parts of
the party and all members of the party ipso facto belonged to one
or another of these wings. The organization of the wings was mod-
eled after that of the parent party — they too had national, regional,
district, and local branches.

Although the 1962 constitution provided that "every village or
town other than a municipality or a city shall constitute a branch
and shall have a charter," Swedru, which is neither a city nor a municipality, also had a district organization within the confines of the
urban area. This perhaps should not be surprising, for apart from
the large and dense population concentration of Swedru and from
the fact that the urban council had in fact asked for the status of
Swedru to be changed to that of a municipality, the town, as we
have seen, did play in a number of respects a unique role in the history of the party and the political evolution of Ghana as a whole.

Each of Swedru's twelve electoral wards, therefore, constituted a

17. *West Africa* 22 June 1963.
18. Ibid.

party branch with a charter. Here, the branch was managed by an eleven-member branch executive committee which was, in theory, elected annually at a general meeting of the branch, in keeping with the party constitution. Again, theoretically, at the branch level the important members were the (ward) branch chairman, the branch secretary, the branch education secretary, and the branch treasurer, with the chairman as the most important figure. The other members of the branch executive were the propaganda secretary and six others. In practice, however, the ward-branch executive including the chairman were not freely elected and had no real power. In fact, they were really not elected at all. Instead, in Swedru they were carefully handpicked by members of the next higher level organization, the district executive committee (DEC) and particularly by an agreement between the "inner group" — the district chairman (who represented all the branch chairmen and executives at the district level), the D.C., and Annobil (who became chairman of the SUC in 1964–66 and who was one of the most powerful and influential members of the local party cadre).

This pattern of party leadership recruitment by appointment or cooptation is very interesting and was found, as a matter of fact, at all levels of party organization. In consonance with its tacit policy of informal and formal cooptation the party, in practice, managed to coerce the involvement of "communal heroes," "traditional notables," socially influential characters, and other possible loci of opposition in the various wards.[19] Through this mechanism of leadership recruitment, the party hoped to confer legitimacy to party decisions and commands and to insure the essential stability and processual continuity of the party in Swedru, in the region, and in the nation.

As a number of party ward-branch chairmen pointed out to me, the chairman and his branch executive had only token powers to make binding decisions. The authority to make decisions for the town and wards was the preserve of the D.C. and his personal friends and colleagues, the party cadre, who worked most closely on major issues affecting Swedru with the equally handpicked district executive committee. Between 1962 and 1966 almost all the

19. In the activities and symbolic leadership of the party at the ward level, there were, for example, Kwaw Wompe, the elderly driver; Kofi Desu, lineage head; and Kwame Anto, the influential Ashanti Kente-cloth weaver for Ward J; and the late Yaw Booh, the wealthy Kwahu trader; and late Kwesi Damprani, the successful Ashanti prestige furniture maker and carpenter for Ward G.

branch chairmen agreed that D. Sackey (the chairman for Ward C)
was, as "head" of all the branches and the district chairman of the
party, the most important figure at the ward-branch level.[20] It must
be noted that almost all the branch chairmen were illiterate or semi-
literate ward "elders" and this fact clearly affected their role as
branch leaders.

One of the branch chairmen pointed out, without any satisfaction,
that being a ward chairman was expensive in time and money, a
view shared by many. Unlike the members of the regional executive
committee, members of the branch executive (and the district executive, except the D.C. and one or two others) were not paid. Instead, they were forced to spend their own money to hire bands
and other entertainers during CPP functions. This was a constant
source of friction and intraparty factionalism between local party
leaders and regional party officers.

The branch chairman went on to describe for me a typical "election" of a ward chairman, which was usually held, if possible, in the
yard of the house of the outgoing chairman or of the prospective
candidate, or at a convenient open ground in the ward. A week or
sometimes a day before, and again on the day of the election the
CPP propaganda van would be called at the instance of the ward
councillor, himself an important party man who had been asked to
do so by the D.C. and the council chairman. The van would announce over its loudspeakers throughout the town where and when
the election would take place and ask all the members of the particular ward to attend. People were sometimes informed through
the local announcement of the Ghana Broadcasting Service. Similar
announcements were made before council elections. At the meeting,
the D.C., who was really there as an ex-officio member and who
had no vote or veto, would open the meeting by stating that it was
high time the branch elected its chairman and other executive members. There was to be an election of new officers every year.

One of the young men, who had been previously primed, accordingly would then nominate a ward influential, such as a trader or a
lineage head. It did not matter whether the person nominated was

20. Throughout my conversations with some of the branch chairmen, they
kept referring, with some exaggeration, to the near-omnipotent power of R. K.
Appiah, D.C., though they were quick to note significantly that the R.C., then J.
E. Hagan, had more power than the D.C. and that the D.C. had to take orders
from him.

present at the meeting or not. The person nominated would have to accept the nomination without protest because, especially after 1964, it was considered unpatriotic to decline the offer of a party office. After the nomination there was usually unanimous approval of the nominee. The same procedure was carried through until all the executive members had been "elected."

TABLE 14   MEMBERS OF THE 1964–1966 SWEDRU CPP
DISTRICT EXECTIVE COMMITTEE

Name, Ethnicity, and Age	Education (Elementary)	Party Office
Daniel Sackey, Fante, early 50s	Apam Methodist	Chairman
S. B. Duker, Fante, middle 50s	Saltpond Methodist	Secretary
Yaw Mensah, Akim, middle 40s	Swedru Methodist	Treasurer
Yaw Ampadu, Kwahu, late 30s	Swedru Methodist	Education Secretary
R. K. Appiah, Fante, middle 30s	Swedru Methodist	D.C., ex-officio
*E. K. Bensah, Ewe, middle 50s	Keta Bremen	M.P.; minister, ex-officio
*Yaw Kwatu, Agona, middle 50s	Illiterate, foundation member	Member
K. Acquah, Agona (?)	Swedru Methodist	Member
F. A. Botchey, Fante, middle 50s	Winneba Methodist	Member
S. Y. Annobil, Agona, late 30s	Swedru Methodist	Member
E. B. Mensah, Fante, middle 30s	Swedru Methodist	Member
*Nana Aba, Fante, late 30s	Trader	Member
*Adjoa Duabah, Fante, middle 30s	Trader	Member

NOTE: Ages listed are 1966 estimates; exact ages are not available.
*Members who had not been urban councillors between 1958 and 1963.

The ward-branch chairman, among other duties, supervised communal labor, the sweeping and cleaning of the ward, and general duties concerning sanitation. The chairman could take some initiative in the carrying out of these responsibilities. One ward-chairman of the CPP complained bitterly but helplessly that ward duties which were supposed to be *voluntary*, but were not, interfered with his business. He pointed out, "We were 'yes' men, who obeyed orders from above" — from the D.C. — "and carried out decisions taken from above." A beggar's democracy indeed.[21]

21. It should be observed that the town development committee — made up of the D.C., chairman of the SUC, the chief (who had very little to say), a

The ward-branches annually (not biennially, as stiuplated in the party constitution) sent two delegates each to the district conference to elect the district executive committee, which in Swedru consisted of at least twelve members. Here again, only the appointees of the D.C. had any chance of being "elected." Table 14 lists the 1964–66 members of the Swedru District Executive Committee of the CPP.

For roughly the same period, 1963–66, the councillors of the SUC were the following: [22]

Ward A	*E. B. Mensah
Ward B	J. E. Baiden, vice chairman
Ward C	*Daniel Sackey
Ward D	*S. Y. Annobil, chairman
Ward E	J. K. Amakyi
Ward F	*Yaw Ampadu
Ward G	P. K. Bentil
Ward H	E. P. Aggrey
Ward I	Kingsley Oppong
Ward J	S. K. K. Wilson
Ward K	Isaka Alabi
Ward L	A. K. Afful

D.C.'s for the Swedru area were:

Awittor, Winneba, 1959–60
A. A. Korsah, Agona, 1960–61 (deceased)
T. K. Anison, Agona, 1961–63
R. K. Appiah, Swedru, 1963–66

SUC members who were also members of the district executive committee held these two positions despite the party constitutional provision that a councillor "shall not hold party office, paid or unpaid" though he could be a member of the executive as unofficial member. Daniel Sackey was not only a member of the district executive but also district chairman and a councillor.

The rule that executive officers at any level of party organization must have been members of the party in good standing for at least

_____

civil servant, and other handpicked private men and elders — was responsible for making decisions relating to the general development of Swedru.

22. (*) indicates councillors who were also members of the district executive at about the same period.

five years previously, unless the central committee decided otherwise, was clearly adhered to in practice in Swedru. This in part accounted for appointed officers instead of genuinely elected ones.
This, of course, led to the self-perpetuating character of local and
national leadership. In Swedru, people like Annobil, Appiah, Duker,
Ampadu, and Sackey were expected always to be among the local
party leaders. It also meant that local party men like E. K. Bensah
and C. V. M. Forde, serving in executive positions at the national
level, must continue to do so. It must be remembered that these
local leaders were mostly foundation members. They were the crucial local party cadre. This was why, according to Yaw Ampadu,
Yaw Kwatu was appointed executive member. It is true that as a lineage head he could be useful, but Yaw Kwatu was, most important
of all, a foundation member.

In theory it was the ward-branch of the party which elected one
of its members to the SUC as a councillor for the ward. Here again,
since in practice the district executive of the party supervised
branch council elections, the D.C. in particular and other members —
for example, Annobil — of the district executive greatly influenced
the elections. It is generally agreed in Swedru that whenever the
D.C. was present at these elections his man was always elected. It
should have been clear from the foregoing also that meetings of the
ward to elect its councillor and meetings of the ward-branch of the
CPP to elect its executive were somewhat difficult to distinguish by
the local people. For one thing, both sets of meetings were heavily
controlled by the D.C. and his district executive and not by the
adult residents of the ward as citizens, qualified electors, and rate
payers. Even as ordinary party members, they really had no, or very
little, say in the election of their own representatives.

Whenever the ward councillor, for instance, wanted to meet the
ward and inform it of decisions taken by the council which affected
the particular ward, he first of all informed the ward-branch chairman of the CPP, who made the necessary arrangements for the
meeting. This is interesting, for though not every ward resident was
a CPP member — for example, Nana Kum held his ground in Ward
J — decisions affecting the ward were communicated through a rally
organized by the CPP. It must be said, however, that in 1964
every citizen became in theory a CPP member.[23] The time and

23. I remember somewhat naïvely asking one illiterate driver in Swedru to

place for ward meetings or rallies were announced throughout the town, as we noticed, over the loudspeaker (most of the time by J. K. Owusu, a staunch CPP man) of the CPP propaganda van or over the local relay station of the Ghana Broadcasting Station, in Fante, Twi, or Hausa. Local administration was inseparable, especially from 1963, from local party organizations.

The most important group of the district executive committee of the party was the district working committee, which was in fact the executive organ of the party at the local level. It was perhaps the most active committee and it actually met, as the minutes and personal interviews indicate, at least once a week. It should be stressed, however, that in whatever capacity and under whatever name the district executive committee functioned, it was the supreme decision-making body at the local level. The district executive committee made decisions for the council and put its decisions to the council in terms of appeals, recommendations, and orders. However they were couched, the decisions were almost always adopted by the council. The SUC had a duty, as a body of citizens and party men, to take the necessary action on those decisions.[24] The council was also to inform and explain the adopted decisions to their ward members through rallies and meetings organized by the CPP ward-branches.[25]

---

name all the members of the local CPP whom he knew or knew about. He smiled and said, "We were all members of the CPP. No one had a choice not to be."

24. From 1958, all councillors were party men. This was insured by the Local Government Amendment Act of 1962, sec. 2, articles 34 and 52. The act made public officers, members of the armed forces, teachers of elementary or secondary schools, and heads of corporations ineligible as councillors. But members of the Young Pioneer Movement, TUC, UGFC, Co-operative Farmers Association, Workers' Brigade, and National Council of Ghana Women were not disqualified from becoming councillors, since their organizations — controlled or established incidentally by the CPP — had not been constituted by an act of Parliament as public services of Ghana in accordance with Article 51 of the constitution.

25. The following is an example of one of the decisions of the district executive committee. On 28 June 1962 a letter from the District Executive Committee (DEC) to the SUC put the following matters before the council for necessary action:

"(a) Dwinhu Road: House No. J 56, owner be approached and advised to demolish building as the place [of the building] dangerous to traffic;

"(b) Ward K, Zongo: The Council to place K under priority in 1962/1963 development programme for Swedru.

"(c) Market sheds: Some sellers, notably cassava, erecting small [unauthorized] sheds which, if not checked, would invite others to do same."

The district working committee — that is, the DEC, constituted for certain specific functions — consisted of the district chairman (Sackey), the district secretary (Duker), the district education secretary (Ampadu), chairman of the SUC (Annobil), and the D.C. (Appiah), an ex-officio member. The committee formulated plans for the smooth working of the party. It was the local policy-making body par excellence for the district. The decisions and policy reached at the annual district conference of the party — decisions which, as we noted, had to be in line with the broad policy and program laid down at the national party congress, the congress decision itself being invariably the decision of the central committee of the party — were in practice formulated by the working committee for the approval of the district conference. Copies of district decisions were then sent to the office of the regional commissioner for his information. The working committee also had a duty to see to the implementation of major decisions taken either by the regional steering committee of the regional executive, affecting the whole region, or by the central committee of the party at the national level.

There was also the district advisory committee at the local level. This committee was set up in Swedru on the instructions of the central committee to deal with some of the problems of intraparty conflict and factionalism. In Swedru the committee was a response to the difficulty in November 1962 over who should be elected council chairman. As I indicated earlier, the post of council chairman was very important in the party power mobility. The office of chairman was a crucial stepping-stone to higher party office, such as that of D.C., R.C., or member of the national executive. Between 1962 and 1966, no fewer than three past chairmen of SUC were made D.C.'s. On 12 January 1962, when Kobina Annan was elected chairman of council to replace E. S. Quainoo (who had been appointed D.C. for Eastern Gomoa, the election of vice-chairman was contested by E. B. Mensah and A. K. Afful. E. B. Mensah was elected, five votes to three.

On 17 November 1962, when Kobina Annan likewise vacated the post of chairman on his appointment as D.C. for Swedru, E. B. Mensah, vice-chairman, was slated for the vacant post in accordance with established local party convention; however, for various reasons, many of the councillors and some of the members of the district executive committee did not approve of Mensah as chairman. Many preferred Afful, but Appiah, a very close friend and fellow "tribesman" of Mensah, pushed Mensah's candidature. All the same, when the council met on 29 November 1962, A. K. Afful was elected, five votes to three. J. K. Amakyi was elected vice-chairman. In January 1963 Appiah was appointed D.C. for Swedru. It was tacitly agreed by the DEC and councillors that Mensah should have his chance at the November 1963 election of chairman of council. But there was a new difficulty. S. Y. Annobil, member of the local party cadre, was also very interested in the position of chairman. There was much innerparty fighting behind the scenes. The D.C. (Appiah), a close friend of both candidates, was for a time helpless. He appealed (passing the buck, in a sense) to the central committee for a solution. The answer from the central committee was the setting up of an advisory committee, made up of the DEC and the councillors, with the district chairman as its chairman. He had a casting vote.

The advisory committee met annually, soon after the election of councillors, to discuss the election of a chairman of council. When nominations had been made and various views about the candidates heard, the councillors retired from the meeting and the election of the chairman was made by the district executive officers on the advisory committee. Thus the election of chairman was no more by councillors. In November 1963 the advisory committee decided to appoint S. Y. Annobil as chairman and J. E. Baiden, councillor for Ward B, as vice-chairman. Through the recommendations of D.C. Appiah, E. B. Mensah was later given the more important post as district organizer of the Ghana Young Pioneers.

It should be pointed out again that between 1963 and 1966 the CPP at the district, regional, and national levels was increasingly and seriously perturbed by intraparty factionalism, squabbling, and petty jealousies, as individuals struggled and undermined each other to get higher party and state offices commanding higher remuneration. This problem was intensified by a declining national economy and the relative inability of the party bureaucracy and the state apparatus to absorb the growing number of self-styled party activists, this despite the increased membership of the 1965 corporate parliament to 198.

PARTY FACTIONS

The district working committee and its regional counterpart, the steering committee, and the district advisory committee were, as we have just observed, created to deal with some of the perennial problems of conflict and factionalism besetting the party. Innerparty factionalism and conflict took a number of forms. There was conflict between the local constituency M.P. (mainly resident in the national capital) and the D.C. (the locally based party-government functionary, responsible to the president), between the salaried regional education secretary and the unsalaried district education secretary, between the appointed chairman of council and the neglected candidate for the post, between ideological socialist activists and nonactivists, between foundation members and party cadre and the new members considered opportunists, careerists, and time servers. The struggle was fierce.

It was in this atmosphere of large-scale opportunism, careerism, and time-serving that the results of the constitutional referendum of 1960 (by which Ghana became a republic) and the referendum of 1964 (by which Ghana was transformed into a legal single-party state) should be assessed and evaluated. Both referendums were characterized by serious anomalies, made possible, partly, through intimidation but to a large extent through the last-minute rush of some to over-declare their unswerving commitment to the party in power, "Our Party." [26]

The 1965 central committee decision to enlarge the composition of the National Assembly from 114 to 198 could hardly solve the problem of intraparty conflict with which it was partly designed to deal. For in 1965, the national failing noted by Nkrumah in his fa-

26. In Swedru, for instance, though the minister of justice's and the regional office's figures for registered voters at the time of the 1964 referendum were 16,715 and 16,581 respectively, 17,256 voted "yes" and none voted "No" (cf. *Results of the Referendum*, January 1964, Central Region regional office). The discrepancy shown by the additional votes of 541 and 674 respectively could only be accounted for by the fact that some people voted twice or even thrice and that some who were not on the voters' register, especially secondary school boys, also voted. The Central Region achieved the highest percentage of "yes" votes (98.23 percent) in the whole of Ghana, thus living up to Bensah's (M.P. for Swedru) description of the Central Region as the "stronghold" of the CPP (Central Region Steering Committee meeting, 1965 minutes). The 1964 election had the effect of technically disfranchising the electorate and making the electoral process, characterized by "one man, one vote," at all levels of society obsolete.

mous Dawn Broadcast of 8 April 1961 — when the president lamented that M.P.'s were pursuing "a course of conduct in direct contradiction of our party aims . . . tending by virtue of their functions and positions to become a separate social group aiming to become a *new ruling class* of *self-seekers* and *careerists*" (my italics) — was still with the party at all levels as it always had been.

Some of the issues raised by E. K. Bensah, M.P. for Swedru and cabinet minister, in his address at Cape Coast referred to above, need citing here. The regional steering committee meeting held in Cape Coast in 1965 was attended by the following party officials from Swedru: E. K. Bensah, M.P.; R. K. Appiah, D.C.; S. Y. Annobil, chairman, SUC; H. M. Cornelius, national executive member (later replaced by Ampadu for the national executive meeting in Accra); R. E. Amos Duker, district secretary, Swedru.

Bensah in his opening address noted particularly the frequent conflict between D.C.'s and M.P.'s of the Central Region and remarked that whenever "there was a disharmony between a District Commissioner and a Member of Parliament, a Regional Commissioner in serving as an arbiter, more often than not decided in favour of the District Commissioner." Remember that the R.C. and the D.C., and not the M.P., were considered the two most senior party officials at the regional and local levels. It is not surprising that the R.C. was inclined to favor the D.C. in settling a dispute between the D.C. and the M.P., who was mostly resident in Accra and certainly out of touch with local and regional problems. All the same, Bensah was right in thinking that this undermined the efficient running of the party in the region. The new regional commissioner for the Central Region, T. H. Korboe, also made in his inaugural address the significant point that "we should not allow petty jealousies to divide our ranks" and remarked (as late as 1965!) that ideological or party value mobilization was still very weak, a point I have belabored throughout this study. Korboe admitted that "Ghana is now a one-party state but there is still a *lot* of work to be done. We *have to* educate the people adequately on the Party's ideology" (my italics). This was no doubt the basic weakness of the party.

It is very interesting to observe the seriousness with which the question of intraparty disputes — and not, it should be said, innerparty democracy based on constructive criticisms, outlined as a feature of the new party structure — was discussed and various solutions recommended. At the meeting of the D.C.'s of the Central Region held on 27 April 1965 at Cape Coast, the regional capital, the D.C.'s there assembled suggested the employment of the branch executive committee, which until now had practically no powers at all, the district working committee, and the district executive committee at the local levels "for the solution of political issues within the districts"; and employment of the district conference, also hitherto powerless, "for the solution of other difficult problems that beset the district after which the regional working [steering] committee could be informed." The nine or so D.C.'s further investigated and reported to the general secretary's office in Accra, for disciplinary action, complaints against party members who had attempted to contest some of the party's official candidates nominated by the central committee at the 1965 "election." (All candidates were returned unopposed!).[27]

It was again noteworthy that the meeting strongly urged members to read carefully and abide by the instructions in the *Party Chronicle* under various headings, including (*a*) "Democratic Centralism" and (*b*) "Avoid Factions." The attention of the D.C.'s was also drawn to "Instruction from the National Headquarters Secretariat" of the CPP expressing "its abhorrence to direct communication by certain individual party members to the President for employment" instead of writing, as should have been done, to the general secretary of the party.[28] This was an explicit and formal attempt by party officials to come to grips with some of the major difficulties facing the party. The meetings emphasized, among other

27. The following is a concrete example of the issue of party members contesting official party candidates. In the 1965 "election," J. K. Smith-Mensah, assistant regional organizer of the Ghana Young Pioneers, had tried to contest the election — in his own words, "to comply with the wish of my people [of Asebu State] to represent them in the National Assembly" — against the late Eddie Ampah, the official party candidate. What Smith-Mensah, who had in fact seriously campaigned in Asebu State, did not realize was that the electorate, under the new party structure and ideology, had very little choice over who should represent it. The electorate had only the right to approve candidates appointed by the central committee of the CPP.
Realizing later the seriousness of his antiparty decision and behavior, Smith-Mensah was forced to withdraw his candidature and to apologize to J. E. Hagan (R.C., Central Region) and Eddie Ampah, the party candidate, in words reflecting his instrumental commitment to the party. Smith-Mensah said in a letter to the R.C. "it was not my intention to kick against the supreme policy of the party which gives me *my daily bread*" (my italics). This attitude was typical of many members of the CPP.
28. *Party Chronicle*, vol. 2, no. 2, p. 1.

things, the respect for party procedural rules and command chains, which were being set aside.

It should be indicated that the various committees set up, which were essentially district and regional executive committees in various functional capacities, to resolve local and regional party conflicts did not necessarily succeed in settling most of the interpersonal quarrels and disputes of "comrades" over high office. In Swedru, for instance, quite a few of the party district executive members felt that they were better qualified to hold responsible party posts than the D.C., Appiah, who was considered incompetent and ill-educated but who commanded an annual salary of about £1,200, a bungalow, legitimate and illegitimate allowances, and fringe benefits.[29]

Just as the district organization was the branch organization writ large, the regional and national level party organizations were also lower level organizations writ large in each case. The party was a well integrated organization, structurally speaking, with members (officers) from below represented at each of the levels immediately above it up to the national level. Thus, some of the branch executive members formed the district executive, some district executive members in turn made up the regional executive, and some regional executive members were appointed to the national executive. The word *some* refers to a necessary caution, for the central committee or the president did in practice, on occasion, appoint directly from the local level party members to serve on the national executive. C. V. M. Forde was appointed in this way.

At each of the levels above the branch – that is, district, regional, and national – there was one man or official who held the greatest power and in fact controlled to a large extent his executive members. At the district level, he was the D.C., the local man; at the regional level he was the R.C.; at the national level, the man was the president. In keeping with the hierarchical structure of the party, the D.C. was under the R.C., the R.C. under the president, and both the R.C. and the D.C. were controlled by the president. The president wielded supreme and final power over all. It must be quickly

29. Incidentally, the term or title *D.C.* was somewhat a misnomer, for the D.C. in many instances was responsible for just one town, not a whole administrative district comprising many towns and villages, as was the case in the colonial days and until the 1960s.

stressed, however, that in practice — since local people were in daily contact with the D.C. and the R.C. and not with the president — it was the former people particularly who were associated with tyrannical power and abuse and misuse of power. It is often said in Ghana by disinterested Ghanaians that the president should be sympathized with, since he had no effective way of controlling the atrocious behavior of his ministers, R.C.'s, and D.C.'s. Obviously, Ghana under Nkrumah was not a very centralized "democratic centralism." [30]

For example, the regional commissioner for the Central Region, J. E. Hagan, became so powerful, according to the Jiagge Commission, that "he did things which even the Government he served could *not* do." [31] The R.C. arrogated to himself the powers of judge, jury, politician, administrator, all in one. This meant that he controlled at the regional level all the public institutions associated with those roles. Hagan himself admitted before the Jiagge Commission inquiring into the assets of CPP ministers and others that he heard "over 3,000 cases and even settled cases which the Courts could not settle." [32] Although he had no power to award contracts over one thousand pounds, Hagan, as we noted earlier, entered into a fraudulent deal with Hewton of Swedru in which the latter received eighty thousand pounds on a mere one-thousand-pound contract. Hagan manipulated variation orders in such a way that projects that had been valued under two thousand pounds cost over eighty thousand pounds. Like the D.C. in Swedru, the R.C. used his party position to acquire illegally private property in land. During the last phase of CPP rule, the party bosses certainly became more and more unresponsive, in the face of harsh economic realities, to the dire economic needs of the people they claimed to represent. Instead, the party leaders proved themselves more self-centered, more self-elective, more self-opinionated, and more self-seeking. This alone accounted for the overall popularity of the military coup

30. Wallerstein notes, in connection with party structure in Guinea and Mali, that "behind the facade of a one-party regime grows up a de facto acceptance of decentralised political power; thus in effect buying off 'local' elites both politically and financially." "The   New Elites of French-Speaking West Africa," *Journal of Modern African Studies* 3, no. 1 (May 1965) : 17. Something similar may have occurred in Nkrumah's Ghana.

31. *Daily Graphic*, 7 September 1967.

32. *Daily Graphic*, 2 September 1967.

of February 1966 and the acceptance (at least during the first year of the coup) of the coup leaders as the new "economic saviours." [33]

I have shown that instrumental involvement, which in the Ghanaian case was directly tied to political legitimacy based on economic performance and well-being, was particularly fragile and unreliable as a basis of political participation in a poor, developing, and controlled economy characterized by sudden ups and downs.

It is predictable that any political structure in Ghana will, in the short run, remain highly unstable until the ideal of individual and group economic sacrifice (even the acceptance of a certain level of economic deprivation as inevitable for a majority of the population) and of hard work has been generalized and internalized or accepted as normal by a significant section of the national population, particularly the leadership. Nkrumah and the CPP failed and fell largely because socialism or Nkrumaism, which Nkrumah stood for and propagated, was in a concrete sense too un-Ghanaian for it called for too much economic sacrifice and industry. The ideology was, as we have seen, incomprehensible to many – including the CPP leadership – whether they described themselves as socialist activists or not. Against the obvious fact of Ghanaian socioeconomic life that stressed elitism and, the value of individual, family, or class material accumulation, generous consumption, and material well-being achieved, if possible, with the minimum of effort, Nkrumaism was understood only by people whose party positions created opportunities for personal accumulation of wealth. I submit that this attitude is a serious problem in Ghanaian public life and accounts for much of the graft and economic mismanagement in public and private life.

33. On the basis of the evidence from Swedru as presented and discussed in this and in the other chapters, the assertions by Zolberg following Ernst Benjamin that the "omnipresent CPP was in reality very hard to find (*Creating Political Order: The Party-States of West Africa* [Chicago: Rand McNally, 1966]) and by Dennis Austin ("Opposition in Ghana: 1947–1967") that the "party [CPP] . . . [was] more nominal than real" should be seriously reconsidered. It is interesting that Austin had in 1959 ("The Ghana Government," *Africa South*, 3, no. 3 (April–June 1959): 90–96) spoken of CPP's reality in terms of "powers of organization," its "disciplined central committee, its rough and tough organizers and nationalist mass following." In a way, the reasons for the characterization by Zolberg and Austin (1967) are still unclear to me. What led to the apparent easy collapse of the CPP at the time of the coup was not "unreality" of the party, but the "reality" and nature of the commitment – what I have termed instrumental commitment – of most party members to the party.

A young postal agent in Swedru told me bluntly in an interview that "the average Ghanaian is not really interested in politics. What concerns him is abundance of food, enough clothing and money, for himself and family." Perhaps he was right, for were not traditional politics and religion and the "politics" of colonialism, each in its own way, primarily materialistic and utilitarian? What do I mean? I mean, and this has been the central thesis of the present endeavor, simply that throughout the political history of the peoples of Ghana, from the heyday of traditional politics represented by the chief and his elders, through colonialism represented by the governor and indirect rule, to the era of one-party state under Nkrumah and the CPP, the primary basis of politics has continued to be instrumental. Material interests have been related to and controlled by shared values that stress, as the primary end of political action, material and economic benefits, directly related to matters of status and prestige, to individuals and groups, or the removal of general or individual economic deprivation.

Any system of domination that fails to do this is bound to lose its legitimacy. In this connection, we may recall the conversation, still relevant, between Nkrumah and the colonial secretary, Saloway, with the latter trying to dissuade the former from embarking upon the politics of Positive Action (based on Gandhi's philosophy of non-violent protest) in 1950. "Now take India, for instance," said Saloway, ". . . the Indian was used to suffering pains and deprivations, but the African has not that spirit of endurance . . . the people here [in the Gold Coast] will let you down — they'll never stick it." [34] In February 1966 the people deserted Nkrumah because they could stand no longer what they perceived as harsh economic deprivations. [35] The CPP and Nkrumah lost their legitimacy.

Perhaps we should conclude this chapter by quoting from the text of a speech delivered by President Nkrumah at a rally held in the National Assembly in Accra on 12 June 1965 to mark the sixteenth anniversary of the CPP. Nkrumah's own view on the matter — the centrality of materialistic concerns of citizens in relation to the state and to other aspects of society — is interesting.

Comrades, in order to attain our noble and desirable ideals [economic progress, welfare, happiness] for Ghana and Africa, we must face up to

34. Nkrumah, *Autobiography*, p. 116.
35. To add insult to injury the CPP denied the Ghanaian population the customary freedom to demonstrate against their economic plight.

those *defects* and *deficiencies* that militate against their realisation. . . .
Far *too many* of us seem to think that the mere *acquisition of wealth*,
irrespective of how it is acquired, is the *supreme goal* in life. Those who
strive to lead decent lives relying on their honest work are reviled and
scoffed at.

This reminds me of something I heard only the other day. Two persons
were conversing about money and one of them mentioned with disapproval the practice of certain public men making money dishonestly. His
companion, even though he agreed that it was wrong to make money by
dishonest means, nevertheless replied: "Oh yes, I agree, but I still *respect*
a man with money."

Take another instance of utter disregard for public property. A lady
returned to her house and found a man standing behind a mango tree
with a basket load of mangoes which he had plucked from the tree in the
compound. Thereupon the lady asked him: "Why did you take these
mangoes when they don't belong to you?" The man promptly replied:
"But this is a Government bungalow . . . it is for the Government." You
see, Comrades, there is, I am afraid, a *dangerous tendency* for people to
think that Government property *can be made use of freely* instead of protecting it as state property.[36] [My italics.]

Ironically, chiefs, governments and parties have had to encourage,
both directly and indirectly, this "dangerous tendency" in the society in order to survive at all.

36. Supplement, "Ghana Today," 16 June 1965.

11 CONCLUSIONS

In the preceding chapters, I have attempted to explore systematically, on the basis of data from Agona-Swedru, the nature of political and economic relationships as it affects national integration and national stability in Ghana. Swedru, like the state of Ghana, of which it is a part, was seen as a product of a long but continuous process of economic and social change largely associated with Euro-colonial contact and domination, a process which in turn led to major changes in political relations.

In the whole process of national unification, economic factors were considered of crucial significance. The exercise of power, chiefly, colonial, and party, was seen as a major means of achieving, protecting, and advancing individual, family, and status-class or group economic and other material advantages and interests. The struggle for power between groups – chiefs and the new elites, new elites and colonial rulers, and so on – was primarily a struggle in relation to the possession of wealth and its distribution and consumption to achieve or maintain high social status, prestige, and social privilege. In this politico-economic competition, individuals and groups had manipulated, whenever suitable and to their advantage, a variety of symbols, beliefs, images, and ideologies, some clearly traditional and others European in origin, to advance their interests. A particular set of symbols and ideas deployed by a group or party in any one situation seems to have depended on (1) the social characteristics of the rival party and how that party is defined; (2) the mutual definition of the struggle and the social characteristics perceived as relevant to the struggle; (3) the extent to which a particular group or groups have exclusive access to specific as opposed to generalized symbols and myths. This is what lends, in the context of social change, a flavor of "tribalism" to much of the clearly modern political and economic competition in Africa.

In Ghana (and in many other African states as well), where high

325

status is basically defined increasingly in terms of material possessions and wealth or their control and use, power struggles to
achieve control of wealth are particularly compelling and almost inevitable. Changes in power relations tend to reflect, to a very large
extent, changes in the control, distribution, and generalized consumption of wealth. One basic problem that power holders therefore have invariably to cope with is how to use their power to accumulate wealth despite competition from other groups and, once accumulated, how to hold on to wealth in the face of the social necessity to consume it.

In Swedru and elsewhere in Ghana, the introduction of cocoa and
monetization not only led to economic changes, but also affected
the status, power, and authority of chiefs.[1] Many chiefs were forced
to acquire cocoa farms in order to maintain their status and power,
which were threatened by a new group of wealthy commoners. I
have indicated that chieftaincy not backed by material resources
and money is largely powerless. To illustrate this we noted how the
new wealth produced a new and powerful group of men and women
and a consequent shift in political power away from the chiefs
to the elites of education, of trade and commerce, and later (in
1949 and after) to the political parties, especially the CPP.

The political party (CPP) in fact became the single most powerful group in Ghanaian society, for, once it had become the government party, it exploited all the power available to a national government in relation to the control, possession, and distribution of almost all the resources in the country. Membership in the dominant
and, since 1964, the only party, therefore became one of the best
means to power, wealth, and certainly high social status.[2]

The socioeconomic advantages related to power make power
struggles acute, as those who have power want to hold on to it. This
creates great problems of political instability in the new nations of
Africa. Insofar as the national army supported the ruling party, the
legalization of the one-party (CPP) state in Ghana, for instance,

1. Brokensha, *Social Change at Larteh.*
2. Particularly for those who either had no other avenue to wealth or who
strongly felt relative economic deprivation. Brokensha, writing on Larteh, I
think comes to a similar position when he says, without following its implications through, that "the main factors which separate people arise from
shortage — whether of money, land or prestige: the brongs [wards] both pre-
cipitate conflict from these factors. . . . " Ibid., p. 102.

whatever else it may have meant, was undoubtedly the best way for the party leadership to insure the maintenance of the exercise of power and the retention of the rewards of power.

Brokensha interprets the establishment of two separate CPP branches at Larteh in 1959 in terms of the Kubease people's argument that "they were accustomed to have separate institutions and that they have been overshadowed by the Ahenease people." [3] This may have been the case, but it is also obvious, from similar examples in Swedru, that what was at stake was not only the prestige of the ward but also power and the related monetary and other rewards which accrued to CPP leaders throughout the country. Here as elsewhere custom was used in the service of nontraditional economic and power interests.

Commenting on politics in Ghana (1960–63), Brokensha notes for Larteh that "nationalism and political independence have been factors of minor importance, and even the powerful CPP has to contend with the strong localism emerging as almost a Larteh institution." [4] This "strong localism" was associated with the "ascendancy of Larteh values" illustrated, according to Brokensha, by the prominent position occupied by the chiefs and elders, and by the beating of traditional drums of the Kubeasehene at a CPP rally in 1961.

The apparent *ascendancy* of Larteh traditional values may have to be qualified. Although these values seem certainly stronger in Larteh (where the population is more homogeneous or less urbanized, and primordial attachments to lineage, clan, and ward more salient) than in Swedru (where the population is more heterogeneous and where there is a stronger sense, among all ethnic groups and others, of identification with the town and nation), the prominent position given to chiefs, and traditional notables at CPP rallies, a nation-wide phenomenon common in Swedru, was largely an attempt by the CPP to use the respect for chiefs and local influentials, through strategic formal and informal cooptation, to mobilize people in the service of or support for national (CPP) goals.[5] It is true

3. Ibid., p. 124.
4. Ibid., p. 266.
5. The fact that the people of Larteh expressed their new politico-economic needs *in terms* of "traditional values" in the face of changes detrimental to the old system of power and privilege precisely made nationalism of *major*, and not of minor, importance in Larteh.

that elders, and subchiefs were on CPP branch committees throughout the country but these branch committees hardly influenced, initiated, or helped make party decisions. The real power holders and
decision-makers at local levels, as we have shown, were the D.C.'s
and R.C.'s, who were both national figures.

I have spoken of a strong sense of local and national identity in
Swedru. This may be directly related to the degree of urbanization,
commercialization, and ethnic heterogeneity, which has produced a
strong awareness of mutual economic interdependence and the
town's links with the national level. If this is so, one may expect to
find in Ghana regional and local variations of the sense of local and
national identity. Associated with the sense of local and national
identity in Swedru, and to be found across the nation, is that of
"Akan-ness" among many groups. Brokensha even speaks of "Akani-
sation of the Guan political organization" in Larteh. Of course, being
Akan is much more than having a blackened stool as a symbol of
chieftaincy.

·On the question of national unity, the CPP as a "party of solidarity" was one of the major agents of national unification. It appears
that, even at Larteh, particularistic style of political articulation
was supplanted by membership in the CPP, and CPP candidates
seem to have had better chances than non-CPP members of becoming local councillors, a case which had an extreme development in
Swedru, where after 1958 all urban councillors were members of the
CPP.

The CPP evinced much organizational flexibility and achieved
through its leadership a great measure of national integration. This
made it possible for the party to meet the special demands of particular areas while at the same time pushing its national goals
through with considerable success. The CPP never lost its national
perspective despite possible variations in local party organization.[6]
The organizational adaptability of the CPP, common with most formal organizations, was instrumental in the achievement of organizational goals.

The CPP was no doubt a party of mass mobilization. But mass
mobilization is a composite concept embracing different types of action. The CPP was quite successful in mobilizing masses to the polls

6. The Larteh chiefs were the first to accept CPP membership cards, according to Brokensha.

and to party rallies, but it failed in its attempt to mobilize people to accept party ideology of socialism or Nkrumaism.

Group or personal contribution to the nation and economic sacrifice in the national interest are still very much distant values in most African countries. What Africa needs, then, is a new ideology of sacrifice.[7] The present generation of Africans — both the leaders and the led — will have to make economic sacrifices, however painful, to insure economic abundance and political stability for future generations. In the last analysis, we have to learn to lift ourselves by our own bootstraps.

I have argued throughout this analysis that political participation in Ghana is primarily an expression of economic interests. In this final section the nature of five major types of economic interests and motivations will be spelled out: (1) Individual, which may — directly or indirectly — include family or lineage but rarely ethnic interests. (2) Class or sectional interests — the interests of socio-economic groups — such as landlords and *rentiers*; cocoa farmers; the old civil service bureaucrats; lawyers and doctors; the old professional elites of education; party bureaucrats; religious groups, and other associations. This group of interests is perhaps the most dominant in the political process. (3) Community or local-regional interests — such as the demand by local and district councillors for better welfare amenities for their villages, towns, wards, cities, or district or for regional autonomy. (4) The national interest — such as the demand for overall rapid industrialization of the country or for "neutrality" in international politics. (5) Pan-African interests — such as the obligation to assist colonial countries in Africa to gain their political freedom or the establishment of good relations with other African states. These interests are never, or rarely, mutually exclusive. They may combine in a complex way in motivating any specific political behavior. At the local levels, the first three groups of interest, except among the elite of education, tend to predominate.[8]

In Ghana, the CPP as a national party was used by the party

7. In fact, more often than not kinship, "tribalism," local particularism, even party membership, become handy weapons used to advance individual or group selfish economic interests, as against the national interest.

8. It is important to note that the differing groups of interests may be expressed or advanced in terms of the *same* set of symbols, rituals, metaphors, ideas, and beliefs. A sophisticated analysis of symbolism is therefore absolutely necessary if a *meaningful* account of the non-Western political process is to be attained.

leadership and rank and file to achieve the political independence of
Ghana in 1957 and as a vehicle for political liberation of colonies
in Africa. Nationally, the CPP was also successfully employed
as a device for the implementation, particularly between 1956 and
1964, of remarkable national economic and social development of
Ghana. Although a very careful and sophisticated cost-benefit analysis would be required to detail the real contributions of the CPP
and, of course, the economic, social, physical, and psychic costs of
these contributions, it is hardly controvertible that the CPP policies
made possible unprecedented structural transformation of Ghana.[9]

Between 1957 and 1963, Ghana utilized her foreign reserves in
the development of her economy (and in assisting other African
territories — such as Guinea and "freedom fighters" of Angola, Mo-
zambique, and Southern Rhodesia). In 1963–64, for example, Birmingham, Neustadt, and Omaboe indicate that the total central
government expenditure was estimated at £144 million.[10] Thirty-
six percent of this amount was earmarked for social services —
education and health — which were either free or heavily subsi-
dized by the government. No doubt this pattern of public expenditure later created heavy strains on the national economy, yet it was
clearly motivated by the public or national interest. Even here, the
later economic problems were partly the result of bottlenecks in the
system of decision implementation and partly the result of the drastic fall in the world price of cocoa, Ghana's major source of revenue.[11]

The problem of balancing national economic interests and sectional, class, or individual interests is perennial in any society and is
particularly acute in a developing nation like Ghana, in which the
true end of politics continues to be primarily wealth — the accumulation and conspicuous consumption of wealth to achieve or maintain high social status and prestige. Thus, despite the CPP's nationalism, the party became increasingly, until the coup of February

9. As Birmingham, Neustadt, and Omaboe, *Study of Contemporary Ghana*,
p. 21, put it, "With government also passing into the hands of a party [CPP]
charged with *exceptional dynamism* this lead [in gaining political independence]
was translated into *concrete achievement* in the spheres of *economic* and *social*
development" (my italics).
10. Ibid., p. 28.
11. Directly or indirectly, a large part of the total government revenue comes
from cocoa, made up of cocoa export duty, local duty, income tax, farmers'
contribution to National Development Plan, grants by the CMB, expenditure by
CMB on general national development, and loans to the government out of
CMB reserves.

1966, the articulator of narrow class and individual economic
interests — that is, the interests of the new class of party cadre or
bureaucrats who were displacing the old class of professional colonial elites of law, medicine, administration, army, and police. The
CPP, as a class of relatively young people representing — among
others — a new order of political entrepreneurs and party office-
holders, was faced with a constant bitter and violent struggle with
members of the old "middle class," some of whom had been the
founders of the UGCC and later the NLM-UP complex. Internally,
the CPP was torn by factionalism as some members tried to push
their interests at the expense of others.

The "class war" took the form of CPP attacks on the very basis of
the high social status and prestige of the old elites of scholars,
wealthy chiefs, and professional men by popularizing education to a
large extent and by redistributing wealth. By building more secondary schools and colleges and by granting generous government
overseas scholarships, the CPP made it possible for children of poor
and illiterate parents to have access to superior education. By creating the huge party bureaucracy with a national network of
branches, it made it possible for "verandah boys" to become high
state officials and wealthy men, thus attaining high social status and
privilege.

The prestige of the old civil service was set against that of the
new, dynamic CPP, which increasingly controlled the civil service.
New and broadly based channels of upward socioeconomic mobility, with access to the old symbols of prestige, were thus created by
the CPP. The continued existence and protests of the old professional elites, however, many of whom had to join the CPP to maintain their privilege and status, proved to be a continued thorn in the
flesh of the CPP, for the "Old Guard" was ready to take over at any
time from the CPP and reestablish their former glory and privilege.
The coup of February 1966 made this possible.

Although the necessity for the CPP to build and maintain a party
cadre led the party to huge economic consumption, to many cases
of individual self-enrichment, and to national impoverishment, it is
still doubtful whether the NLC, in its three-and-one-half-year rule,
really succeeded in matching the national economic and social
achievements of the CPP.[12] It now appears that the NCL was more

12. Ghana returned to a modified form of civilian rule after the general election of 29 August 1969. An elected parliament from which the government is

concerned about the interests of professional groups — lawyers, university lecturers, commissioned army and police officers, doctors, and businessmen — than members of the rest of society.

We must use every means in our power to wean people away from the notion that the most important thing in life is money and that the true end of politics is wealth.[13]

---

drawn took over from the NLC in September 1969. A three-man presidential commission consisting of two senior army officers and a senior police officer will remain for sometime.

The economic policy (if there was one) of the NLC has been bitterly criticized for not tackling the serious problems of mass unemployment (which has continued to rise since the coup) and the rising cost of living.

The test of the present civilian government of the Progress Party (which won 105 of the 140 parliamentary seats!) under Prof. K. A. Busia, a noted anthropologist, will be the extent to which the members concern themselves primarily with either "class" or party interests — the enjoyment of local and national fruits of office or with the drastic reduction of unemployment, the reduction of prices of essential goods and basic foodstuff, and so on. National political cohesion will continue to depend largely on both rapid economic progress (itself dependent among other things on hardwork and cooperative economic effort and sacrifices at all levels of society) and the sincere belief held by people of all ethnic, religious, or regional groups that they have a stake in the economy of Ghana.

13. Prof. E. A. Boateng in the *Ghanaian Times*, Tuesday, 28 May 1968, p. 9.

APPENDIXES

Appendix A

GLOSSARY OF ABBREVIATIONS

ALC	Agona Local Council
ARPS	Aborigines' Rights Protection Society
CFAO	*Compagnie Française de L'Afrique Occidentale*
CMB	Cocoa Marketing Board
CPC	Cocoa Purchasing Company
CPP	Convention People's Party
D.C.	District Commissioner
DEC	District Executive Committee
G.A.	Government Agent
GBO	G. B. Ollivant, Ltd.
GCEU	Gold Coast Ex-Servicemen's Union
GCP	Ghana Congress Party
GNTC	Ghana National Trading Company
Ind.	Independent (election candidate)
KYA	Kwahu Youth Association
MAP	Moslem Association Party
MBE	Member of the British Empire
MLA	Member of Legislative Assembly
NCGW	National Council of Ghana Women
NLC	National Liberation Council
NLM	National Liberation Movement
PEA	People's Educational Association
PWD	Public Works Department
PZ	Paterson Zochonis and Co., Ltd.
R.C.	Regional Commissioner
SAT	Swiss African Trading Company
SCOA	*Société Commerciale de l'Ouest Africain*
SG	Self-Government
S.N.A.	Secretary for Native Affairs
SUC	Swedru Urban Council
TUC	Trade Union Congress
UAC	United Africa Company
UGCC	United Gold Coast Convention
UGFC	United Ghana Farmers Council

UGFCC	United Ghana Farmers Council Co-operatives
UP	United Party
UTC	Union Trading Company

Appendix B

GLOSSARY OF STANDARDIZED NAMES

Places names and names of tribes appear under various spellings and descriptions in the historical literature. These names have been standardized for easy reference and identification.

Agwana
Ahgoona   Asianti   = Ashanti   Nsarba
Aguna   Asante   Nsabaa
Agona   = Agona   Ashanti   Nsabah   = Nsaba
Agoona   Nsabang
Aghunah   Goomooh   Nsaba
                               Gomooa
Swordru   Akron   = Gomoa
Swaidroo   Gomoa
Swaidro   Gomua
Swedur   = Swedru   Gomuah
Soadru
Swadur   Nyarkrome
Swedru   Nyarkroom
                               Nyakrom   = Nyakrom
Fantee   Dumto
Fantin   Odumto
Fanti   = Fante
Fante
Fantsi

Appendix C °

THE MANIFESTOES

It is interesting to compare the manifestoes of the two major political parties, which were issued to the public a few weeks before the elections took place. The CPP Manifesto, of approximately four thousand words, was entitled "Towards the Goal," and was liberally bespattered with slogans, many of them cf a faintly biblical flavour (e.g., "Seek ye first the political kingdom, and all things will be added unto it"). The UGCC

°Material for this appendix is drawn from J. H. Price, *The Gold Coast Election*, West African Affairs, no. 11 (London: Bureau of Current Affairs).

Manifesto, "Plan for the Nation," was a more modest document of approximately 2,800 words. The following table compares their views on many questions at issue.

Towards the Goal (CPP)	Plan for the Nation (UGCC)

I. Constitutional

The Coussey Committee let the country down by prolonging white imperialism. The C.P.P. will fight for self-government NOW ("self-government" being defined as Dominion status within British Commonwealth).	The present constitution is a watered-down version of the Coussey recommendations; it is "a step, but not our last step, in the struggle for self-government," which must be achieved "by all legitimate and constitutional means."

II. Political
A. The Chiefs

An upper house of the Legislature, known as the Senate, shall be created for the Chiefs.	The Chiefs must, in spite of themselves, be saved for the Gold Coast, by removing the Governor's power to grant or withdraw recognition from Chiefs recognized by their people.

B. Central Government

(i) Universal adult suffrage at the age of 21; (ii) Direct elections, with no property or residential qualifications for candidates seeking election; (iii) Chiefs to sit in the Senate, not the Lower House.	Remove civil servants from the top level of "field administration," and place the character and structure of the civil service under the control of the Assembly. Civil servants must cease to be the "Civil Masters" of the country.

C. Local Government

(i) Supports the Coussey recommendations, together with improvements wherever desirable; (ii) Local government servants should receive gratuities and pensions in same way as civil servants do.	(i) Opposed to the setting up of Regional Administrations modelled on the Eastern Nigerian system. (ii) When the reports of the committees on Local Government are published, the U.G.C.C. will promulgate its views. Until then, it adheres to the Coussey recommendations and the minority rider on Regional Councils.

D. Courts, Justice, and Police

(i) A commission, including experts from Britain, should plan a unified judicial system, with cheap and speedy justice;

(ii) Police should be organized into one national force. Pay and conditions should be improved.

E. Economic

A five-year Economic Plan for social and economic development to afford the people an increasingly higher standard of living:

(i) Immediate materialization of the Volta hydro-electric scheme;

(ii) Railway lines to be doubled and extended;

(iii) Roads to be modernized and extended;

(iv) Canals to join rivers;

(v) Progressive mechanization of agriculture, modern transport and marketing techniques, and improvements in social services for farmers;

(vi) Special attention will be given to the swollen-shoot disease (of cocoa), farmers will be given control of the Cocoa Industry Board funds, mortgaged farms will be redeemed, production will be encouraged, agricultural colleges and scholarships will be established, and a country-wide chain of grain silos will be built;

(vii) The timber industry will be controlled and expanded, afforestation will be undertaken, anti-erosion measures and large-scale irrigation will be instituted;

(viii) Canning factories and cold storage plants will be provided to help the fishing industry, and also to meat, dairy, and poultry industries;

(ix) Industrialization will be carried out with all energy;

(x) Prices, freight charges, and discounts will be regulated;

(xi) A National Bank will be set up to control the economy of the country.

A Ten-Point Programme – "to ensure that the optimum diffusion of private enterprise and ownership of property shall be developed alongside the maximum attainment of personal liberty, within the framework of the WELFARE STATE":

(i) An end to Government's extravagant spending and appointments, and to the lowering of the dignity of the Chiefs;

(ii) An end to the political officers system and to the 'Go-Slow' policy in education;

(iii) A reduction in the importation of light manufactured goods, which should be manufactured locally under a five-year plan;

(iv) A national bank;

(v) An active and adequate road building programme;

(vi) Scholarships for industrial and technological training to show results within five years;

(vii) The raising of the standard of living, improvement in housing, water supply, primary education, health, lighting, clinics, literacy, and culture;

(viii) A five-year plan to cheapen and to better communications and transport;

(ix) The safeguarding of agriculture and land products, a rationalized cocoa industry, diversified agriculture, development of the Volta and of base metals

(x) Development of the rural life of the people.

F. Social

(i) Full employment through the

See Ten-Point Programme above.

expansion of the country's economy and the establishment of labour bureaux;

(ii) Wages to be paid weekly instead of monthly

(iii) Hire-purchase systems to be promoted;

(iv) Education:

(a) A unified system of free compulsory elementary, secondary, and technical education up to 16 years of age;

(b) The University College to be brought up to University status;

(c) A planned campaign to abolish illiteracy;

(d) Teachers to be granted gratuities and pensions on lines of Civil Service;

(e) Scholarships for students studying overseas;

(v) Family assistance;

(vi) A network of recreational facilities;

(vii) A free national health service;

(viii) A high-standard housing programme, together with the re-planning of existing towns;

(ix) A piped-water supply in all parts of the country;

(x) A national insurance scheme;

(xi) Development of broadcasting, a film industry, and enlargement of the postal services.

G. Wages and Means

(i) Hard work by all is necessary to raise the standard of living;

(ii) Even under self-government, taxation will still be levied, but the people will see a return for the taxes they pay.

H. Election Appeal

"This country must send into the Assembly men tried in the furnace of national tribulation and not found wanting. . . ."

". . . elect to the new Assembly the best men for the job, the best men in the true sense, irrespective of party, tribe, religion and class."

Appendix D

PROFESSIONS OF MEMBERS OF THE 1951 ASSEMBLY

	ASSEMBLY						GOVERNMENT		
	Municipal Representatives	Rural Representatives	JPC and AC Members	Northern Territories Members	Europeans	Total (Assembly)	Ministers	Ministerial Secretaries	Total (Government)
Carpenter	...	...	...	1	...	1	...	...	...
Chief	...	...	9	6	...	15	...	...	...
Civil servant	...	...	...	...	4	4	3	...	3
Engine driver	...	1	...	...	...	1	...	...	...
Farmer	...	3	...	1	...	4	...	...	...
House agent	...	1	...	...	...	1	...	1	1
Journalist	2	1	...	...	...	3	1	2	3
Lawyer	2	1	1	...	1	5	3	...	...
Letter-writer	...	1	...	...	...	1	...	...	...
Medical practitioner	...	...	1	...	...	1	1	...	1
Merchant	...	7	2	...	3	12	...	...	...
Native Authority employee	...	1	1	5	...	7	1	2	3
Pharmacist	...	4	1	...	...	5	...	2	2
Postal agent	...	...	...	1	...	1	...	...	...
Professional politician	...	6	...	...	...	6	2	1	3
Retired army officer	...	...	...	...	1	1	...	...	...
School teacher	1	6	2	5	...	14	...	3	3
Stenographer	...	1	...	...	...	1	...	...	...
University lecturer	...	...	1	...	...	1	...	...	...
Total	5	33	18	19	9	84	11	11	22
Minister of religion	...	1	1	...	...	2	*	...	...

SOURCE: J. H. Price, *The Gold Coast Election*, West African Affairs, no. 11 (London: Bureau of Current Affairs), p. 13.

NOTE: JPC=Joint Provincial Council (of chiefs); AC=Asanteman Council

Where a member records two or more professions, for example, "Chief and Farmer" or "Journalist and Politician," he is included in the total for the more important of his occupations (except in the case of ministers of religion, who are recorded under "Minister of religion" and under their other occupations).

"Civil Servants" include (a) one retired senior civil servant, and (b) the minister of justice, who is both a civil servant and a king's counsel and could therefore have been included, alternatively, under "Lawyer."

*The Leader of Government Business holds a theological seminary degree and is said to have been ordained in the United States, although he has never practiced as a minister.

Bibliography

Adams, D. T. *An Elementary Geography of the Gold Coast*. London: University of London Press, 1949.

Adu, A. L. *The Role of Chiefs in the Akan Social Structure: An Essay*. Accra: Government Printing Department, 1949.

Afrifa, A. A. *The Ghana Coup*. London: Frank Cass, 1966.

Alexander, H. T. *African Tightrope: My Two Years as Nkrumah's Chief of Staff*. Boston: F. Praeger, 1966.

Andoh, A. S. Y. "Local Government and Local Development in Ghana." *Insight* 2, no. 1 (February 1967): 42–47.

Apter, David. *Ghana in Transition*. New York: Atheneum, 1963.

——. *The Political Kingdom in Uganda*. London: Oxford University Press, 1961.

——. *The Politics of Modernization*. Chicago: University of Chicago Press, 1965.

——. "Nkrumah, Charisma, and the Coup." *Daedalus*, vol. 97, no. 3 (1968).

Astrachan, Anthony. *Commentary*, vol. 45, no. 3 (March 1968).

Austin, Dennis. "The Ghana Government." *Africa South* 3, no. 3 (April–June 1959): 90–96.

——. "Opposition in Ghana: 1947–1967." *Government and Opposition* 2, no. 4 (July–October 1967): 539–55.

——, and W. Tordoff. *Voting in an African Town*. University of London Institute of Commonwealth Studies. Reprint Series no. 8, from Political Studies vol. 8, no. 2 (June 1960).

Bailey, S. G. *Politics and Social Change: Orissa in 1959*. Berkeley: University of California Press, 1963.

Balandier, G. *Ambiguous Africa: Cultures in Collision*. Translated from the French by Helen Weaver. New York: Pantheon, 1966.

——. "The Colonial Situation: A Theoretical Approach." In *Social Change: The Colonial Situation*, Immanuel Wallerstein, editor. New York: John Wiley and Sons, 1966.

——. "Social Changes and Social Problems, in Negro Africa." In *The Modern World*, Calvin W. Stillman, editor. Chicago: University of Chicago Press, 1955.

——. *Sociologie des Brazzavilles Noires*. Paris: Colin, 1955.

Bealey, F., J. Blondel, and W. P. McCann. *Constituency Politics: A Study of Newcastle-under-Lyme*. New York: The Free Press, 1965.

Birmingham, W., I. Neustadt, and E. N. Omaboe, editors. *A Study of Contemporary Ghana*. Vol. 1, *The Economy of Ghana*. London: George Allen and Unwin, 1966.

339

Black, C. E. *The Dynamics of Modernization: A Study in Comparative History.* New York: Harper and Row, 1967.

Bretton, H. L. *The Rise and Fall of Kwame Nkrumah: A Study of Personal Rule in Africa.* London: Pall Mall Press, 1966.

Brokensha, D. W. *Social Change at Larteh, Ghana.* London: Oxford University Press, 1966.

Brown, E. J. P. *Gold Coast and Asianti Reader.* Book 1. Cape Coast, 1921.

Burns, Sir Alan. *Colonial Civil Servant.* London: George Allen and Unwin, 1949.

Busia, K. A. *The Position of the Chief in the Modern Political System of Ashanti.* London: Oxford University Press, 1951.

———. "The Ashanti of the Gold Coast." In *African Worlds,* D. Forde, editor. London: Oxford University Press, 1954.

———. *Judge for Yourself.* Accra: The West African Graphic Co., Ltd., 1956.

Christensen, J. B. *Double Descent among the Fanti.* File no. 16. New Haven: HRAF, 1954.

Claridge, W. W. *A History of the Gold Coast and Ashanti.* 2 vols. London: John Murray, 1915.

Coleman, James S. "Nationalism in Tropical Africa," *American Political Science Review* 48 (1954): 404–26.

———, and Carl G. Rosberg, Jr., editors. *Political Parties and National Integration in Tropical Africa.* Berkeley: University of California Press, 1964.

Collier, Sir G. R., Sir C. MacCarthy, et al. *Agoona Country in West African Sketches; Compiled from the Reports of Sir G. R. Collier, Sir C. MacCarthy, and Other Official Sources.* Printed for L. B. Seeley and Son, London, 1824. Mimeographed at the Institute of African Studies, University of Ghana, Legon, June 1963.

Cruickshank, B. *Eighteen Years on the Gold Coast.* Vol. 2. London, 1853. Reprinted by Cass of London, 1966.

Danquah, J. B. *Akan Laws and Customs.* London: Routledge and Sons, 1928.

———. *The Gold Coast Akan.* London: 1945.

Dapper, O. "The Akan Forest States." A provisional translation of an extract from O. Dapper, *Beschreiburg von Afrika* (German edition, Amsterdam, 1670) in *Ghana Notes and Queries,* the Bulletin of the Historical Society of Ghana. (Accra), no. 9 (November 1966).

Davidson, Basil. *Can We Write African History?* Occasional Paper no. 1. African Studies Center, University of California at Los Angeles, 1965.

Davis, K., and E. W. Moore. "Some Principles of Stratification," *American Sociological Review* 10, no. 2:242–49.

Dennis, P. C. W. "A Note on Land Revenue and Local Government in Ghana," *Journal of African Administration* 9, no. 2 (April 1957): 85–92.

Deutsch, K. *Nationalism and Social Communication.* Boston: M.I.T. Press, 1966.

Durkheim, Emile. *The Division of Labour in Society.* Translated by G. Simpson. Glencoe: Free Press, 1947.

————. *Professional Ethics and Civic Morals.* Translated from the French by C. Brookfield. London: Routledge and Kegan Paul, 1957.

Ellis, A. B. *The Tshi-Speaking People of the Gold Coast of West Africa.* London: Chapman and Hall, 1887.

————. *A History of the Gold Coast of West Africa.* London: Chapman and Hall, 1893.

Emerson, R., and M. Kilson, editors. *The Political Awakening of Africa.* New York: Prentice-Hall, Inc., 1965.

Etzioni, A. "A Paradigm for the Study of Political Unification," *World Politics* 15, no. 1 (October 1962): 44–74.

Fage, J. D. "History." In *The African World: A Survey of Social Research.* Boston: F. Praeger, 1965.

————. *Ghana: A Historical Interpretation.* Madison: University of Wisconsin Press, 1966.

Fallers, L. "Social Stratification and Economic Processes in Africa." In *Class, Status and Power,* Reinhard Bendix and Seymour M. Lipset, editors. New York: Free Press, 1966.

Fenton, J. H. *People and Parties in Politics.* Glenview: Scott, Foresman and Co., 1966.

Ferkiss, Victor C. *Africa's Search for Identity.* New York: Braziller, 1966.

Fitch, B., and M. Oppenheimer. *Ghana: End of an Illusion.* New York: Monthly Review Press, 1966.

Fortes, M. "Kinship and Marriage among the Ashanti." In *African Systems of Kinship and Marriage,* A. P. Radcliffe-Brown and D. Forde, editors. London: Oxford University Press, 1950.

Foster, Philip. *Education and Social Change in Ghana.* Chicago: University of Chicago Press, 1965.

Geertz, Clifford. *Peddlers and Princes.* Chicago: University of Chicago Press, 1963.

————, editor. *Old Societies and New States.* New York: Free Press, 1963.

Ginsburg, Norton. *Atlas of Economic Development.* Chicago: University of Chicago Press, 1961.

Gould, P. R. *Transportation in Ghana.* Evanston: Northwestern University Press, 1960.

Greer, Scott. *The Emerging City.* New York: Free Press, 1962.

Griffiths, Sir P., and M. J. Watt. *Report on a Visit to Nigeria and the Gold Coast, 1955.* London: Federation of British Industries, 1955.

Grove, D., and L. Huszar. *The Towns of Ghana: The Role of Service Centers in Regional Planning.* Accra: Ghana University Press, 1964.

Gutteridge, W. *Armed Forces in New States.* London: Oxford University Press, 1962.

Hanna, W. J., editor. *Independent Black Africa.* Chicago: Rand McNally Co., 1964.

Harvey, W. B. *Law and Social Change in Ghana.* Princeton: Princeton University Press. 1966.

Hill, Polly. *The Gold Coast Cocoa Farmer.* London: Oxford University Press, 1956.

———. *Migrant Cocoa Farmers of Southern Ghana.* Cambridge: At the University Press, 1963.

Hodgkin, T. *Nationalism in Colonial Africa.* London: Frederick Muller, 1956.

———. *African Political Parties.* London: Penguin, 1961.

Huberman, Leo, and Sybil H. May. *The ABC of Socialism.* Copyright by *Monthly Review,* New York. Reprinted in Accra, Ghana: Government Guinea Press, Ltd., 1953.

Jahoda, Gustav. "Aspects of Westernisation: A Study of Adult-Class Students in Ghana: 1." *The British Journal of Sociology* 12, no. 4 (December 1961): 375–86.

Katz, Daniel. "Group Process and Social Integration: A System Analysis of Two Movements of Social Protest." *The Journal of Social Issues,* vol. 23, no. 1 (January 1967).

Kilson, M. "Nationalism and Social Classes in British West Africa." *Journal of Politics,* Vol. 20, no. 1 (May 1958).

———. *Political Change in a West African State: A Study of the Modernization Process in Sierra Leone.* Cambridge: Harvard University Press, 1966.

Kimble, D. *The Machinery of Self Government.* London: Penguin, 1953.

———. *A Political History of Ghana: 1850–1928.* Oxford: Clarendon Press, 1963.

Kumah, J. K. "The Rise and Fall of the Kingdom of Denkyira," *Ghana Notes and Queries,* no. 9 (November 1966), pp. 33–35.

Little, K. "The Organization of Voluntary Associations in West Africa." *Civilisation,* vol. 9, no. 3 (1959).

———. *West African Urbanisation.* Cambridge: At the University Press, 1965.

Lloyd, P. C. "Craft Organization in Yoruba Towns." *Africa,* vol. 23, no. 1 (1953).

———. "The Political Structure of African Kingdoms: An Exploratory Model." In *Political Systems and the Distribution of Power,* Michael Banton, editor. Boston: F. Praeger, 1965.

———. "The Yoruba Town Today." *Sociological Review,* vol. 7, no. 1 (1959).

Lofland, J., and R. Stark. "Becoming a World-Saver: A Theory of Conversion to a Deviant Perspective." *American Sociological Review* 30 no. 6 (December 1965): 826–75.

McLaren, C. A. "Local Government Training in the Gold Coast." *Journal of African Administration,* Vol. 9, no. 2 (April 1957): 63–71.

Mair, Lucy. *New Nations.* London: Weidenfeld and Nicolson, 1963.

Metcalfe, G. E. *Maclean of the Gold Coast.* London: Oxford University Press, 1962.

Meyerowitz, E. *Akan Traditions of Origin.* London: Faber, 1952.

Nkrumah, Kwame. *The Autobiography of Kwame Nkrumah.* London: Nelson and Sons, 1957.

———. *Guide to Party Action.* Accra: Government Printing Department, 1962.

Nsarkoh, J. K. *Local Government in Ghana*. Accra: University of Ghana Press, 1964.
Oram, N. *Towns in Africa*. London: Oxford University Press, The New African Library, 1965.
Padmore, G. *The Gold Coast Revolution*. London: Dennis Dobson, 1953.
Parsons, Talcott. *Economy and Society*. New York: Free Press, 1957.
————. et al, eds. *Theories of Society*. New York: Free Press, 1961.
Pearson, K. *National Life from the Standpoint of Science*. London: A. and C. Black, 1905.
Peil, M. "Aspirations and Social Structure: A West African Example." *Africa* 38, no. 1 (January 1968): 71–78.
Price, J. H. *Political Institutions of West Africa*. London: Hutchinson Educational, 1967.
Rattray, R. S. *Ashanti*. Oxford: The Clarendon Press, 1923.
————. *Religion and Art in Ashanti*. Oxford: The Clarendon Press, 1927.
————. *Ashanti Law and Constitution*. Oxford: The Clarendon Press, 1929.
Reindorf, C. C. *The History of the Gold Coast and Asante*. Brown and Nolin, Dublin: Richview Press, 1966.
Richards, Audrey I. *Hunger and Work in a Savage Tribe*. (Cleveland and New York: World Publishing, Meridian Books: 1964).
Rostow, W. W. *British Economy of the Nineteenth Century: Essays*, Oxford: Clarendon Press, 1949.
Runcinman, W. G. "Charismatic Legitimacy and One-Party Rule in Ghana." *European Journal of Sociology* 4 (1963): 148–65.
Selznick, P. *The Organizational Weapon*. New York: Free Press, 1960.
Shils, E. "On the Comparative Study of the New States." In *Old Societies and New States*, Clifford Geertz, editor. New York: Free Press, 1963.
Sklar, R. L. "Political Science and National Integration: A Radical Approach." *Journal of Modern African Studies*, 5, no. 1 (1967): 1–11.
Smith, Rev. J. N. *The History of the Presbyterian Church in Ghana, 1821–1960*. Accra: Ghana University Press, 1967.
Smythe, H. H., and M. M. Smythe. *The New Nigerian Elite*. Stanford, California: Stanford University Press, 1960.
Spiro, H. J., editor. *Africa: The Primacy of Politics*. New York: Random House, 1965.
Tiger, L. "Ghana: A Charismatic Nation." *Current History* 45 (December 1963): 335–40.
Tumin, M. "Some Principles of Stratification: A Critical Analysis," *American Sociological Review*, 18:672–73.
UNESCO. *Social Implications of Industrialization and Urbanization in Africa South of the Sahara*. Paris, 1956.
Vansina, J. *Oral Tradition: A Study in Historical Methodology*. H. M. Wright, translator. Chicago: Aldine Publishing Company, 1965.
Wallbank, W. T. *Documents on Modern Africa*. Princeton: Van Nostrand, 1964.
Wallerstein, I. *Africa: Politics of Independence*. New York: Vintage Books, 1961.

———. "Ethnicity and National Integration in West Africa." *Cahiers d'Etudes Africaines*, 3 (October 1960): 129–39.

———. "Migration in West Africa: The Political Perspective." In *Urbanization and Migration in West Africa*, Hilda Kuper, editor. Berkeley: University of California Press, 1965.

———. "The New Elites of French-Speaking West Africa." *Journal of Modern African Studies*, vol. 3, no. 1 (May 1965).

Weber, Max. *From Max Weber*. Translated and edited by H. H. Gerth and C. W. Mills. London: Routledge and Kegan Paul, 1948.

Zolberg, A. R. *Creating Political Order: The Party-States of West Africa*. Chicago: Rand McNally, 1966.

———. "The Structure of Political Conflict in the New States of Tropical Africa." *American Political Science Review*, 62, no. 1 (March 1968): 70–87.

GOLD COAST AND GHANA GOVERNMENT REPORTS AND PAPERS

Bewes Commission Report, 1931. S.N.A. Papers. Accra: Ghana National Archives. *Colonial Reports, Gold Coast, 1949–1956*. London: His/Her Majesty's Stationery Office. *Ghana Today*, 6 June 1965.

The Gold Coast Census of Population, 1948: Report and Tables. Accra: Government Printing Department, 1950.

The Gold Coast Handbook for Native Courts in the Colony. Accra: Government Printer, 1956.

Government Gazette, no. 40. Accra-Tema: State Publishing Corporation.

1960 Population Census of Ghana, vols. 1–4. Accra: Government Printing Department, 1964. N.L.C. Decrees, nos. 1–130. Accra-Tema: State Publishing Corporation.

Report of the Commission of Enquiry into Disturbances in the Gold Coast (Chairman: Aiken Watson). Colonial no. 231. London: Colonial Office, 1948.

Report of the Commission of Enquiry into the Affairs of the Cocoa Purchasing Company Limited (Chairman: O. Jibowa). Accra: Government Printing Department, 1956. S.N.A. Papers. Accra: Ghana National Archives.

Index

UNESCO (United Nations Economic Social and Cultural Organization), 93n
United Party (UP), 195, 219, 271,
279
University of London, 144
Urban councillors, 203–5
Urbanization, 82–84
reexamined, 107
and reform of native authority,
197
structural characteristics of, 93
of Swedru, 95, 148, 167
Ussher Fort Prisons, 279

Vansina, J., 17n, 19
Verandah boys, 299n, 300, 331
Victoria, Queen of England, and
slave trade, 124
Vigilante group, 293
Villages of Agona, as centers of
cocoa production, 94
Volta River Project, 274
Voluntary associations, 108, 111–13
integrative functions of, 159
and interethnic unity, 152
and social integration in Swedru,
102
Votaries, 110
Voters, qualification and disqualifi-
cation of, 183

Wallerstein, I., 11n, 108, 109n, 321n
Ward-branches, 311–13
Wards (abron) of Swedru, 103

Watson Commission, 143, 145
report of, 137, 172
Wealth, acquisition of, in Ghana, 4,
118, 324
Weber, Max, 119n, 241, 287
Welbeck, Nathaniel, 231
Weltanschauung, Hindu, 269
West Africa, population of, 93
West African markets, 50
West African National Congress,
141
Westernization, aspects of, 175
Winneba (town), 83, 94
Winneba rural electoral district, 166
Winneba Subdistrict, 164n
"Work and Happiness" in 1962, 301
Workers Brigade, 300–301n, 314
Workers' Education Association of
Britain, 175
Workers' strike, 89n
Working Committee
of the CPP, 261
regional, 319

Yaw Duodu Kwasida oath, 33
Youth, 226n, 297
Youth Conference, and Danquah,
144
Youth guilds, 109

Zerikin Zongo, 226–27
see also Malam Isifu Darfi, 98n
Zerikin Zongo ward, 152
Zolberg, A., 11n, 322n